The Great Torah Commentators

by
Avraham Yaakov Finkel

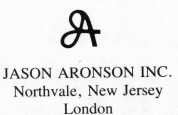

JASON ARONSON INC.
Northvale, New Jersey
London

Library of Congress Cataloging-in-Publication Data

Finkel, Avraham Yaakov.
The great Torah commentators / by Avraham Yaakov Finkel.
p. cm.
Bibliography: p.
Includes index.
ISBN 0'87668'841'5
1. Rabbis—Biography. 2. Scholars, Jewish—Biography. 3. Bible. O.T.—Criticism, interpretation, etc., Jewish—History. 4. Talmud—Criticism, interpretation, etc.—History. 5. Jewish law—History. 6. Musar movement—History. 7. Hasidim—Biography. 8. Philosophers, Jewish—Biography. 9. Cabala—History. I. Title.
BM750.F53 1989
296′.092′2—dc20 89-15168

Manufactured in the United States of America. Jason Aronson Inc. offers books and cassettes. For information and catalog write to Jason Aronson Inc., 230 Livingston Street, Northvale, New Jersey 07647.

This book is dedicated to the memory
of my dear wife Sarah ע״ה
who illuminated our home with the light of Torah.

CONTENTS

ACKNOWLEDGMENT

The ways of God are inscrutable. This book is a case in point. It had its genesis in an act of *chesed*, when, one evening, a stranger stopped his car to offer a ride to my son-in-law Berish Weinberg. It was *Hashgachat Hashem*, Divine Providence, that caused their paths to intersect. The gracious stranger happened to be Arthur Kurzweil, vice-president of Jason Aronson Inc., Publishers; and their ensuing conversation led to my association with Arthur Kurzweil, a man of kindness, resolve, and above all, abiding emunah in Hashem. With keen insight he conceived the idea of this work. His infectious enthusiasm inspired me throughout the phases of its development. I am deeply indebted to him.

My warm thanks to my children, Moshe and Brenda Finkel, Berish and Elisheva Weinberg, Moshe and Judy Klein, Rabbi Chaim and Naomi Finkel, and all my grandchildren, for their loving encouragement and their helpful suggestions.

I am indebted to Muriel Jorgensen and Adelle Krauser of Jason Aronson Publishers, who skillfully edited the manuscript. My thanks also to Nancy Bonaldi, Art Director, for creating the artistic cover design, and to the entire staff of that wonderful organization for their kindness and dedication.

My profound gratitude to my father and mother, who are sources of inspiration to their children, grandchildren, and great-grandchildren. May *Hashem Yisbarach* grant them good health and many happy years together.

INTRODUCTION

One of the greatest wonders of human history is the survival of the Jewish people, the nation of the Torah. Since becoming a nation at Mount Sinai, in the year 2448 of Creation, Israel has maintained its identity, clinging steadfastly to God's word, both in its written and in its oral manifestation. Every Jew is a living link in a mighty unbroken chain reaching back over the millennia to *Mattan Torah,* the Giving of the Torah. Beginning with Moses, God had blessed each generation with spiritual leaders who were giants of learning and wisdom, men of incomparable humility, piety, and purity of soul. These men transmitted the teachings of the Torah to their respective generations, bringing to light new hidden treasures, expounding, codifying God's word, making it accessible to everyone according to his ability to comprehend it. As the Midrash says, "The elders heard the Voice according to their ability, the youths and the young boys according to their ability . . . the suckling babies according to their ability—and even Moses according to his ability."

The books these great sages wrote are in our possession. They are studied eagerly, in the yeshivah, in the synagogue, and in the home. Their words are the subject of animated discussion wherever Torah-observant Jews gather; their ideas pervade our thinking, guide our lives.

Who are these men? When and where did they live and teach? Some of their names have a familiar ring, others may not be on everyone's tongue, while many sages are known only by the titles of their work. It is the purpose of this book to acquaint the reader with a number of the greatest Torah sages of the past 2,000 years. What better way to present them than to let them speak for themselves. Through a sampling of their writings, preceded by biographical sketches, these *gedolim* (luminaries) come to life. We sit at their feet and drink from the fountain of their wisdom. Although their approaches may differ, they have one common goal, *lehagdil Torah ulahadirah*—to make the Torah great and glorious.

It is impossible, within the scope of this volume, to include all the *gedolim* who have enriched our heritage. The selections represent only a few of the great luminaries who developed and shaped Torah knowledge in their respective fields.

The book is divided into seven sections, covering seven areas of research: (1) The Torah commentators, (2) Commentators on Mishnah, Talmud, and Midrash, (3) Halachists, (4) Sages of Mussar (Ethics), (5) Chasidic sages, (6) Philosophers, and (7) Kabbalists. The entries are arranged in chronological order, and an alphabetical index of names and an index of sources have been appended.

When a commentator is mentioned in a chapter other than his own, his name appears in boldfaced letters. When facsimiles of text are used, shaded areas highlight specific commentators' writings.

King David says in Psalm 34:29, *"Ta'amu ure'u,"* which can be translated as "taste it—and see." We can describe the Torah in the loftiest terms, using flowery metaphors and poetic allegories. All these cannot impart any knowledge of its true essence. Only by actually tasting the words of our sages, by biting into them, can we gain an insight into the profound wisdom and beauty of the Torah. The selections that are presented in this book are intended to serve as tidbits to arouse the reader's appetite to study the masters from their sources, thereby finding fulfillment and closeness to God, *"ki heim chayeinu ve'orech yameinu"*—"for they are our life and the length of our days."

With gratitude to HaShem I offer this book with the prayer that it may contribute, in a small way, to a deeper appreciation of the towering greatness of our sages and the timeless legacy contained in their writings.

May their words inspire us to walk in their footsteps and lead us to a stronger commitment to Torah and mitzvot.

I

TORAH

The Torah, the book that is the lifeblood of the Jewish people, contains the essence of God's wisdom. Each letter, each word, each phrase has immeasurable significance. It is our link to the Higher World; it is "longer than the earth and wider than the sea" (Job 11:9). On the surface, the Torah appears deceptively simple—even a young child can understand it. Yet, the foremost sages ponder its meaning, in a never-ending quest for wisdom, discovering enlightening facets and new layers of interpretation.

Traditionally, Torah exegesis has taken a four-pronged approach, known as פרדס, *pardes,* "orchard." The word *pardes* is the acronym formed of the initials of the four methods of exposition:

1. פשט, *peshat.* Searching for the plain, straightforward meaning of the text.
2. רמז, *remez.* Allusion, finding hints or suggestions in the text to unrelated subjects. For example, in the verse "Moses and the Israelites sang this song" (Exodus 15:1), the Hebrew text uses the word *yashir* "*will* sing this song," which prompts the Midrash to comment that this phrase alludes to the resurrection of the dead. (Moses and the Israelites *will* sing this song at that time).
3. דרש, *derash.* Homiletic, metaphoric interpretation; also an interpretation according to the 13 hermeneutical rules by which the Torah is expounded, as enumerated by Rabbi Yishmael in *Sifra.*
4. סוד, *sod.* Mystical interpretation of the text. The prime example of this approach is the Zohar.

Many commentators will adhere to only one approach, whereas others will alternate between two or more approaches. They have given us the key to the *pardes,* the Orchard of Torah, enabling us to partake of its life-giving fruit.

RABBI SHELOMOH YITZCHAKI—RASHI
רבי שלמה יצחקי—רש״י

born: Troyes, France, 1040
died: Troyes, France, 1105
Known as Rashi, the acronym formed of the first letters of his name. Greatest of all the commentators.

Rashi's greatness as a commentator is unparalleled; his words are studied daily by students and scholars, in the yeshivah and in the Jewish home.

He traced his ancestry through the *Tanna'im* (teachers of Mishnah) Rabbi Yochanan HaSandler and Hillel the Elder back to King David. He received his early talmudic training from his father, Rabbi Yitzchak. At a young age he went to Worms, Germany, to broaden his knowledge under Rabbi Yaakov ben Yakar. At age 25 he returned to his native Troyes, as a highly respected and prominent talmudist. Out of great humility he refused to accept a rabbinic post. He wrote his commentaries and was a teacher, earning his livelihood as a wine merchant.

Rashi's commentary on the Torah is included in virtually all editions of the Chumash (Pentateuch). In a clear and concise style he gave both the simple meaning of the text and its homiletic interpretation, based on Talmud and Midrash. He explained the text phrase by phrase, often commenting on grammatical anomalies and translating difficult words into Old French. Besides his Torah commentary, he also wrote a commentary on the Prophets and Writings.[1]

Rashi's work has become a part of Jewish life, the favorite commentary of the common man and scholar alike. A measure of Rashi's greatness is the fact that about 200 books have been written, probing his words.

His commentary to the Talmud (see pages 61–65) is a masterpiece of clarity and brevity. Without it, the Talmud would be a closed book. Rashi gently takes the student by the hand, guiding him through the maze of complex forms of reasoning, obscure concepts, and knotty legal arguments. In clear and simple Hebrew, he clarifies the talmudic text, almost line by line, anticipating the difficulties the student will encounter. It can be said without exaggeration that Rashi is the master commentator and foremost teacher of the Jewish people.

Rabbi Shelomoh Yitzchaki, Rashi.

אונקלוס   ויקרא יט קדושים   258

Rashi's commentary to Leviticus 19:15–16. His commentary is printed in the distinctive Rashi script used in most rabbinical commentaries. From *Mikra'ot Gedolot*. *Mikra'ot Gedolot* ("The Full-Sized Bible") is the most comprehensive edition of the Chumash (Bible), comprised of the main text (in heavy square script) and all the major commentators, who are easily identified by name where their commentaries appear.

SELECTIONS FROM RASHI'S COMMENTARY TO THE TORAH

In the beginning God created heaven and earth.

(Genesis 1:1)

Rashi: *In the beginning*—Rabbi Yitzchak said: Since the Torah was given in order to teach Israel God's laws, it should have begun with: "*This month shall be to you the first of the months*" (Exodus 12:2), for this is the first commandment given to Israel. Why then does it begin with "*Bereishit*," "In the beginning," and the entire story of Creation? The reason is, in order to proclaim God as the Master of the earth: "He declared to His people the power of His works in order to give them the inheritance of the nations" (Psalm 11:6). If the gentile nations say to Israel: You are robbers because you captured the land of the seven (Canaanite) nations, Israel will answer them: The entire universe belongs to God. He created it and He granted it to whomever He saw fit to give it. It was His will to give it to them and it was then His desire to take it from them and turn it over to us.

An eye for an eye, a tooth for a tooth, a hand for a hand, a foot for a foot.

(Exodus 21:24)

Rashi: *An eye for an eye*—If a person blinded someone's eye, he pays him the value of his eye, the equivalent of the decrease in his value if he would be sold as a slave in the market. The same applies to all of them (the loss of a tooth, hand, or foot). But it does not mean taking an actual limb, as our rabbis have explained in the chapter *Hachoveil* (Bava Kama 84).[2]

If a burglar is caught in the act of breaking in, and is struck and he dies, there shall be no bloodguiltiness for him.

(Exodus 22:1)

Rashi: *In the act of breaking in*—This means when he was breaking into the house.[3] *There shall be no bloodguiltiness for him*—This is not considered as a murder; it is as though the thief had been dead from the beginning of his attempted burglary. The Torah is teaching you hereby the rule: "If someone comes with the intention to kill you, be quick and kill him first." And this burglar actually came with the intention of killing you, for he knew most certainly that no one can restrain himself while someone steals his property in front of his eyes, and do nothing. It is clear, therefore, that the thief had in mind that if the owner of the property would stand in his way, he would kill him.

If you follow My laws and you keep My commandments and do them.

(Leviticus 26:3)

Rashi: *If you follow My laws*—You might think that this phrase implies the fulfillment of the commandments; but when the verse continues "and keep My commandments and do them," it is clear that this latter passage refers to the fulfillment of the commandments. How then can I interpret the phrase "If you follow My laws"? It comes to teach you that you are to exert yourself in studying the Torah.[4] *And you keep My commandments*—Work hard at studying the Torah with the intention to take heed and fulfill its laws, as it says, *"And you shall learn them and take heed to do them"* (Deuteronomy 5:1).

Five of you will be able to chase away a hundred, and a hundred of you will defeat ten thousand, and your enemies will fall before your sword.

(Leviticus 26:8)

Rashi: *Five . . . a hundred, and a hundred . . . ten thousand*—But is this the correct proportion? Shouldn't it have stated, *"a hundred of you will defeat two thousand"* (instead of ten thousand)? The explanation is: You cannot compare [the power] of a few who fulfill the commandments of the Torah to the power of the many who fulfill the commandments of the Torah.[5]

God is slow to anger, great in love, and forgiving of sin and rebellion. He will not clear (the guilty), but is mindful of the sins of the fathers for their children, grandchildren, and great grandchildren.

(Numbers 14:18)

Rashi: *God is slow to anger*—with the righteous and the wicked. When Moses went up to heaven he found the Holy One blessed is He sitting and writing, "God is slow to anger." Moses said to Him, "With the righteous?" The Holy One blessed is He replied, "Also with the wicked!" Moses said to him, "Let the wicked perish." God said, "I swear by your life that (the day will come) when you will need this thing." When the Israelites sinned through the golden calf and through the spies, Moses prayed to Him (mentioning the attribute of *erech appayim,* being slow to anger). The Holy One blessed is He said to him, "Did you not say to Me 'with the righteous'?" Moses replied, "But did You not answer me, *'Also with the wicked'?"* (I pray to You), *let the power of God be great to carry out Your word"* (Sanhedrin 111).

He sent emissaries to Balaam son of Beor to Petor, which is by the River, to his native land to tell him the following message: "A people has come out of Egypt, see, they cover the land's surface, and they are now staying over against us."

(Numbers 22:5)

Rashi: *To his native land*—That is, Balak's native land, and he (Balaam) prophesied and said to him, "You are destined to become King." Now, if you will ask, why did God cause His Divine Presence to rest on a wicked heathen (Balaam)? In order that the gentile nations should not be able to argue, "If we had prophets, we would have turned back to the right path." God did give them prophets, but they showed the way to promiscuity; for in the beginning they kept themselves in check with regard to incest, but Balaam gave the advice to offer themselves freely to prostitution.[6]

The following commentaries illustrate Rashi's frequent use of foreign languages and etymology in explaining the text.

Joseph brought his father Jacob and presented him to Pharaoh. Jacob blessed Pharaoh.

(Genesis 47:7)

Rashi: *Jacob blessed Pharaoh*—Vayevarech (in this context) means "greeting," as anyone does who sometimes has an audience with a king (*saluder* in Old French; *saluer*—to salute).[7]

Simeon and Levi are a pair of brothers: instruments of violence are their weapons.

(Genesis 49:5)

Rashi: *Instruments of violence—Mecherotehem* is a term meaning "weapons." The Greek word for sword is μαχαιρα, *machaira.*[8]

The people of Sidon refer to Hermon as Siryon, while the Amorites call it Senir.

(Deuteronomy 3:9)

Rashi: *The Amorites call it Senir—Senir* denotes "snow" in the German language (*Schnee*), as well as in the language of Canaan (i.e., the Slav language, *snih*).

RABBI ABRAHAM IBN EZRA
רבי אברהם אבן עזרא

born: Toledo, Spain, 1089 or 1090
died: location uncertain, 1164[1]
Popularly referred to as Ibn Ezra. Bible commentator, grammarian, philosopher, poet.

Ibn Ezra spent his youth in Cordova, Spain, where he received his Torah education. His entire life was one of poverty and misfortune. Commenting on his tragic life, he once said, "If I were a candle maker, the sun would shine day and night; if I sold shrouds for the dead, no one would die." He established a close friendship with **Rabbi Yehudah Halevi**, the famous poet and philosopher. In 1135 Ibn Ezra was forced to flee to Rome. There he composed his Bible commentary. Later he traveled to Provence, London, back to Provence, and to many other places. Some say that he journeyed to Eretz Yisrael and that he died there.

His Bible commentary, which appears in all editions of *Mikra'ot Gedolot*,[2] is one of the foremost classics of Torah exegesis.

In his commentary Ibn Ezra follows the *peshat*, the interpretation according to the plain meaning, in preference to the aggadic, homiletic, allegoric approach. Many of his comments deal with problems of grammar and syntax. They are written in a style that is extremely terse and often interspersed with obscure allusions. A great number of supercommentaries have been written on Ibn Ezra's work, each attempting to shed light on the many obscure phrases. He fought valiantly for the purity of the Hebrew language and did not hesitate to criticize harshly any infraction of the rules of grammar or style he encountered. His caustic wit is apparent in many sarcastic comments with which he demolishes interpretations he considers incorrect. His commentary is studied by all serious students of Tanach (Bible).

Text of commentary by Rabbi Abraham ibn Ezra. His comments follow the *peshat* approach to exegesis, stressing the simple meaning of the verse, with emphasis on grammatical structure. From *Mikra'ot Gedolot*.

SELECTIONS FROM IBN EZRA'S COMMENTARY

And the children struggled inside her; and she said, "If this is so, why do I live?"

(Genesis 25:22)

Ibn Ezra: *And the children struggled inside her*—Scripture calls them children, because that is what they eventually would become. This is analogous to *"You will remove the clothes of the naked"* (Job 22:6).[3] *She said, if this is so*—she asked women who had given birth whether they had experienced similar symptoms, and they answered that they had not. She then said, *"If this is true, why do I have such an unusual pregnancy?"*[4]

And Joseph's master had him arrested and placed him in the dungeon, the place where the king's prisoners were kept. He remained there in the dungeon.

(Genesis 29:20)

Ibn Ezra: *Beit haso'ar,* dungeon—I do not know if this is a Hebrew or Egyptian term, because it is followed by its definition, by which the verse tells us what it is. This is analogous to *achashteranim,* a Persian word, which the text then explains as *benei haramachim,* (swift steeds) bred of a mare (Esther 8:10).[5]

The elders of Moab and Midian, with magical devices in hand, went to Balaam, and they came to Balaam and spoke to him the words of Balak.

(Numbers 22:7)

Ibn Ezra: *With magical devices in hand*—Rabbi Shmuel Hanagid[6] from Spain renders this phrase *"with fees for magic,"* finding proof for his translation in the word *beyadam, "in their hand,"* but what he says is of no consequence.[7] We must follow the literal sense of the words. Thus, the verse is telling us that Balak sent men to Balaam the magician, men who were versed in the occult,[8] as was he. An additional reason for sending them was so that Balaam would not be able to cause a delay by saying, "I cannot find a propitious day or hour to go and curse them," for these men were his professional equals (and thus he would not to able to deceive them).

If you see among the prisoners a beautiful woman and you desire her, you may take her as a wife.

(Deuteronomy 21:11)

Ibn Ezra: *Beautiful*—in his eyes.[9]

Moses went and spoke these words to all Israel.

(Deuteronomy 31:1)

Ibn Ezra: *Moses went*[10]—He went to each of the tribes to let them know that he was about to die. He did so in order to dispel their fears, and he gave them courage by saying that Joshua "would lead them across, as God had promised." Therefore, it says afterwards (in Deuteronomy 31:7, when Moses addresses Joshua), "You will be the one to make them inherit it (the land)." I think that it was on this occasion that he pronounced the blessings to all the tribes, even though in the Torah these blessings are written two chapters later, (in Deuteronomy 33:1–26).

It is He who sits above the circle of the earth, and its inhabitants are like grasshoppers, Who stretches out the heavens like a curtain and spreads them out like a tent to dwell in.

(Isaiah 40:22)

Ibn Ezra: *Chug, circle*—Compare *mechugah,* compass, the instrument that is used to draw a circle. Here it says that the earth is round[11] and not square, although no verse is needed for the support of this statement, for it is known by convincing proofs. *He who sits above the circle of the earth*—He whose glory fills the entire earth.

Ho, everyone who is thirsty come for water, and he who has no money to buy, come buy and eat; yes, come and buy wine and milk without money and without price.

(Isaiah 55:11)

Ibn Ezra: *Ho, everyone who is thirsty*—With these words God will address those who will then wish to accept the Torah. *And he who has no money to* *buy*—That is, who has no means required for study. *Buy and eat*—The wisdom. Compare "Eat this scroll" (Ezekiel 3:1)—The soul needs wisdom as the body needs food.[12] *Come*—to me. *Buy*—for nothing. *And eat*—without paying. *Wine and milk*—Each serves both as food and drink, as medical authorities agree. Wine and milk are mentioned because the Torah is compared with them.

RABBI DAVID KIMCHI—REDAK
רבי דוד קמחי—רד״ק

born: Narbonne, Provence, France, 1160
died: Narbonne, Provence, France, 1235
Bible commentator and grammarian.
Popularly known as Redak, the initials of his name.

David Kimchi's father, Rabbi Yosef Kimchi, died when David was still a child, and he was raised and educated by his brother Rabbi Moshe Kimchi, himself a great grammarian. Redak's commentary to the Bible covers Genesis, the Prophets, Psalms, Proverbs, and Chronicles. He explains the simple meaning of the verses and the thought connecting them. On occasion he offers midrashic and philosophical explanations, "for lovers of homiletics." A tribute to his greatness as a commentator was a popular play on words with his last name, Kimchi, in an allusion to the Mishnah in *Avot* 3:21, "Without flour (*kemach*—Kimchi) there is no Torah."

Late in life Redak became involved in the controversy surrounding **Rambam**'s (Maimonides') writings. He forcefully sided with Rambam's views and advocated the study of philosophy for anyone whose faith in God was unshakable.

His commentary is printed in most editions of Tanach (Bible). His other works are *Michlol*, on Hebrew grammar,[1] the second part of which is *Sefer Hashorashim*,[2] a dictionary of the Bible used by non-Jewish scholars, such as Reuchlin and Sebastian Münster. He also wrote *Vikuach*,[3] polemics against Christianity.

Text of commentary by Rabbi David Kimchi, Redak. Expounds the *peshat*, plain meaning of the text. Commentary is to Isaiah 5:1. From *Mikra'ot Gedolot*.

SELECTIONS FROM REDAK'S COMMENTARY TO THE TORAH

Noah left the ark along with his sons, his wife, and his sons' wives.

(Genesis 8:18)

Redak: *Noah left*—In relating their departure from the ark, the verse separates the men from the women.[4] A possible reason for this may be that the women were afraid to leave until all the men had left the ark. The women still stood in fear of the Flood, and women are by nature more faint-hearted than men are.

Jacob remained alone. A man wrestled with him until just before daybreak.

(Genesis 32:25)

Redak: *A man*—This was an angel. See also "behold, there stood a man over against him" (Joshua 5:13) and "the man Gabriel" (Daniel 9:21).[5] Whenever an angel speaks or appears in human form to someone, either in a dream-like vision or while that person is wide awake, Scripture describes the angel as "man." God sent this angel to Jacob in order to inspire him not to be frightened by Esau, to assure him that Esau would not be able to defeat him. Just as the angel wrestling with Jacob could not knock him down, so Esau would not be able to vanquish him. *He wrestled with him until daybreak*—As a portent that for Jacob light would follow darkness. Trouble is likened to night and darkness, whereas daybreak symbolizes relief and rescue, which is thus like daylight that follows the dark of night.

Let me sing of my beloved
A song of my beloved concerning his vineyard.
My beloved had a vineyard
On a very fruitful hill
And he dug it and cleared it of stones
And planted it with the choicest vine
And built a tower in the middle of it
And he also hewed a vat in it.
And he hoped that it should bring forth grapes
And it brought forth wild grapes.

(Isaiah 5:1–2)

Redak: *Let me sing*—The prophet uses a parable to describe the relationship between God and Israel, Israel being the vineyard and God its master. The prophet calls God the beloved, based on the passage, "for he has yearned for Me" (Psalm 91:14). *On a very fruitful hill*—As the *Targum* renders it: "on a high hill and on fertile land." The Land of Israel is called *keren*, horn, because it is loftier than all other lands, as the horn is the highest point in an animal's body. The Land of Israel is characterized as "fruitful" because Scripture portrays it as "a land flowing with milk and honey" (Exodus 3:8). *And he dug it*—*vaye'azekeihu*, meaning "*he dug it.*" This is an expression used by the rabbis of the Talmud: *ozeik*, "he digs beneath the olive trees." Or it can be rendered "he built a fence around it." If you want to plant a vineyard, you begin by building a fence to keep out wild animals that might destroy the plants. Then you dig up the earth where you want to plant the vines. Next you clear away the stones, and then you plant the finest vines you can find. All this is stated in the verse. The term *soreik*, "choicest vine," denotes a vine that produces seedless grapes. The meaning of the parable is this: God guarded Israel when He brought them into their Land. The fence alludes to the Clouds of Glory that surrounded them; the stones represent the seven (Canaanite) nations that lived in the Land of Israel. The vine He planted is the Nation of Israel. The true chosen seed of Abraham, Isaac, and Jacob. Israel was expected to produce exquisite fruit.

Homiletically, the word *soreik*, "choicest vine," can be explained by interpreting its numerical value, i.e., 606. Thus, "He planted it with *soreik*" means "He added 606 commandments to the 7 commandments that had been given to the descendants of Noach."[6] *And He built a tower in the middle of it*—If you have a good vineyard, you build a tower in it in order to protect it. So, too, God built a tower, because He promised to watch over Israel. As long as they would listen to His voice, no adversity would befall them.

RABBI MOSHE BEN NACHMAN (NACHMANIDES)— RAMBAN
רבי משה בן נחמן—רמב״ן

born: Gerona, Calabria, Spain, 1195
died: Eretz Yisrael, 1270
Commentator, talmudist, kabbalist.
Popularly known as Ramban, the initials of his name,
and as Nachmanides, "Son of Nachman" in Greek.

Scion of a renowned rabbinical family, a relative of **R. Yonah of Gerona**, Ramban studied under R. Yehudah ben Yakar and R. Nassan ben Meir. His mentors in Kabbalah were R. Ezra and R. Ezriel, both of Gerona. He also studied medicine, which he practiced professionally, languages, and physics. Ramban personifies the best and noblest in Spanish Jewry. His *Milchamot Hashem*, which he wrote in defense of **R. Yitzchak al-Fasi (Rif)**, reflects the greatness of his talmudic scholarship. He also wrote *Torat Haadam*, a compendium of laws of mourning and a number of halachic treatises.

In 1263, King James of Aragon forced Ramban to hold a public religious dispute with the Jewish apostate Pablo Christiani. In the presence of King James and many dignitaries and clerics, Ramban completely demolished his opponent with the logic of his arguments. In admiration, the King rewarded Ramban with a gift of 300 coins. The Dominican priests claimed that their side had won the dispute, whereupon Ramban wrote *Sefer Havikuach*, a detailed account of the questions and his answers. The clerics then charged him with humiliating the Catholic religion, and he was banished from Aragon. Ramban began to write his major work, the commentary on the Torah, in which he offered a penetrating analysis and exegesis of the text, highlighting the moral and ethical lessons to be derived from it. On many occasions he introduced midrashic and kabbalistic expositions, evidence of his surpassing greatness in both the revealed and esoteric aspects of the Torah.

Rabbi Moshe ben Nachman, Ramban.

In 1267, at age 72, Ramban settled in Eretz Yisrael. Finding Jerusalem in utter desolation, in the wake of the Crusaders' excesses, he began to rebuild the devastated Jewish community. His commentary on the Torah is studied widely. It is printed in all editions of *Mikra'ot Gedolot*.[1]

SELECTIONS FROM RAMBAN'S COMMENTARY

I will harden Pharaoh's heart and I will display many miraculous signs and wonders in Egypt.
(Exodus 7:3)

בעל הטורים
רשב"ם
אבן עזרא
רמב"ן
אור החיים
כלי יקר

Text of Ramban's commentary to Leviticus 19:15–16. Analyzes the text, offers ethical and kabbalistic insights. Considered one of the major classic commentaries. From *Mikra'ot Gedolot*.

Ramban: *I will harden Pharaoh's heart*—The Rabbis have discussed the question that everyone asks: "If God hardened his heart, why was Pharaoh guilty of sin?" For this there are two explanations, and both of them are true. One is that Pharaoh, in his wickedness, had, without grounds, committed such great evils against Israel that he deserved to be denied the ways of repentance. It is so indicated in many verses in the Torah and in the Writings. He was judged according to the evil deeds that he had originally committed.

The second explanation is that half of the plagues were brought on him because of his transgressions, for with regard to these it only says: "Pharaoh's heart *remained* hard" and "Pharaoh hardened his heart" (Exodus 7:13,22, Exodus 8:15).[2] Thus Pharaoh refused to let the Children of Israel go for the glory of God. But when the plagues began to overwhelm him and he could no longer endure them, his heart softened and he changed his mind and decided to send them out. He did so because of the impact the plagues were having—but not in order to do the will of his Creator. Then God "*hardened his spirit and made him obstinate*" (Deuteronomy 12:30) so that His name may be declared throughout the earth.

(These words) shall be a sign on your arm and an insignia in the center of your head, because God has brought us out of Egypt with a strong hand.

(Exodus 13:29)

Ramban: *And an insignia in the center of your head*[3]—Through the great, well-known miracles, a person recognizes the hidden miracles that constitute the basis of the entire Torah. For no one can have a part in the Torah of Moses, our teacher, unless he believes that all events and occurrences that happen to us are supernatural and metaphysical phenomena,[4] whether they affect the community or the individual. Now, when a person fulfills the commandments, his reward will be success, and if he violates them, his punishment will be obliteration. All this will come about by decree of the Most High, as I have already mentioned. The hidden miracles will become known to the public when the promises of the Torah will come true with regard to the blessings and the curses, as the verse states, "*All the nations will ask, Why did God do this to the land? They shall answer, It is because they abandoned the covenant of God, the Lord of their fathers*" (Deuteronomy, 29:23–24). Thus it will become known to all nations that their punishment came from God. And of the fulfillment of the commandments it says, "*All the nations of the world will see that God's name is associated with you, and they will be in awe of you*" (Deuteronomy 28:10). I will still explain this, with God's help.

Moses stretched out his hand over the sea and God drove back the sea with a strong east wind all the night, transforming the sea to dry land, and the waters were divided.

(Exodus 15:21)

Ramban: *God drove back the sea with a strong east wind*—It was God's will to divide the sea by a strong drying wind, so that it would appear as if the wind dried the sea. Something similar is written, *"An east wind shall come, the wind of God coming up from the wilderness; and his spring shall become dry, and his fountain shall be dried up . . ."* (Hosea 13:15). Thus He caused the Egyptians to err and then destroyed them, since because of this they thought that perhaps it was the wind that changed the sea into dry land, and that it was not the power of God that did this for the sake of Israel. Although the wind (normally) does not split the sea into parts,[5] they paid no attention even to this and they followed the Israelites into the sea, out of their intense desire to harm them. This is the underlying thought of the verse, *"And I will harden Pharaoh's heart . . . and they will go in after them"* (Exodus 14:4, 17). He hardened their hearts so that each one would say, *"I will pursue my enemies and I will overtake them in the sea"* (Psalm 18:38) and there is no protection from my power. They did not remember now that they themselves had said, *"God is fighting for them against Egypt"* (Exodus 14:25).

You may not eat any (mammal or bird) that has not been properly slaughtered. You may give it to the stranger in your settlements so that he can eat it, since you are a holy nation to God your Lord. Do not cook a kid in its mother's milk.

(Deuteronomy 14:21)

Ramban: *Since you are a holy people to God your Lord*—The meaning of this segment of the verse is linked to the prohibition that follows it, "Do not cook a kid in its mother's milk." Although it is not a repulsive food, He prohibited it because we should be holy through the foods we eat; or in order for us to become holy, in that we do not become a cruel and merciless people by milking the mother and drawing out its milk to cook its kid in it.

And although *any* meat cooked in milk is included in this prohibition (even though it is not cooked in its own mother's milk), nevertheless it is forbidden, because any nursing animal is called "mother" and any suckling offspring is called "kid," and cooking them together involves an element of cruelty in all cases (whether the kid is cooked in its own mother's milk or not).

RABBI BACHYA BEN ASHER—RABBEINU BACHYA
רבי בחיי בן אשר—רבינו בחיי

born: location—? date—1263
died: Saragossa, Spain, 1340
Popularly known as Rabbeinu Bachya or Bachaya.
Torah commentator, kabbalist.

Rabbeinu Bachya, a student of Rabbi Shlomoh ben Aderet (Rashba) (1235–1310), was a rabbinical judge (*dayan*) and preacher in Saragossa, Spain. He wrote a number of books on ethics and Kabbalah, but his most celebrated work was his commentary on the Torah, *Midrash Rabbeinu Bachya*.[1]

In his commentary, the author introduced each weekly portion with a discourse on ethics, based on a verse from Proverbs. He expounded on the Torah according to the four methods of interpretation: *peshat*, the plain, rational meaning; *derash*, midrashic, homiletic exegesis; *remez*, philosophic allusions; and *sod*, kabbalistic interpretation. Throughout the ages, his work has enjoyed widespread acceptance among all Jewish circles.

מדרש
רבינו בחיי
על חמשה חומשי תורה
להרב החכם הכולל, המקובל האלהי, מאור הגולה, גולה ומנורת זהב על ראשו, בחכמת התורה המאירה והמזהירה.
רבינו בחיי ב״ר אשר זצ״ל
למהיה שלתו אלהים, לשאוב מים חיים להשקות ולהחיות נפש הצמאים והרעבים לשמוע את דבר ה׳.
חלק ראשון
בראשית

הוצאת כתר ספרים
ניו יורק, תש״ה

Title page of *Midrash Rabbeinu Bachya*.

SELECTIONS FROM RABBEINU BACHYA'S COMMENTARY

Isaac redug the wells that were dug in the days of his father Abraham and were plugged by the Philistines after Abraham's death. He gave them the same names that his father had given them.
(Genesis 26:18)

Rabbeinu Bachya: *Isaac redug the wells that were dug in the days of his father Abraham and were plugged by the Philistines after Abraham's death*—Allegorically, "*the wells that were dug in the days of Abraham*" may be said to represent the people whom Abraham had converted to believe in one God. Scripture characterizes the opening of hearts to the belief in God as digging. The Philistines who plugged these wells, in their envy, closed the hearts of these newly won converts, causing them to revert to their old pagan ways. In the end, Isaac overcame the Philistines'

64 רבינו בשלח יז בחיי

Rabbi Bachya ben Asher's commentary on the Torah. Explains the text according to *peshat* (its simple meaning), *derash* (the homiletic approach), and *kabbalah;* introduces each approach with *ve'al derech hapeshat, ve'al derech hamidrash, ve'al derech hakabbalah,* as indicated in the text. From a copy of the original standard edition.

nefarious influence. He returned them to the path of true monotheism they had been shown by Abraham. This is expressed in the words, "*Isaac [returned and] redug the wells that were dug in the days of his father Abraham.*"

Jacob lived in Egypt for 17 years. Jacob's days, the days of his life, were 147 years.

(Genesis 47:28)

Rabbeinu Bachya: *Jacob lived in Egypt for 17 years*—This portion is sealed[2] because Jacob wanted to reveal the time of the ultimate redemption, but this knowledge was "sealed" (i.e., concealed) from him. With the words "*I will tell you what will happen at the end of days*" (Genesis 49:1), Jacob referred to the coming of the Messiah at the end of this long *galut* (exile) that we are living in today.

All events that occurred to Jacob, the third of the Patriarchs, are portents of this, our third exile.[3] Now, because Jacob's words allude to the Messianic age, as he says, "*until Shiloh (tranquility) comes*" (Genesis 49:10), this portion was "sealed," indicating that the end he wanted to reveal was sealed to him. The Midrash suggests the following explanation: Yaakov noted that all the letters of the *alef bet* occur in the names of his twelve sons, except for the letters *chet* and *tet*, which combine to form *chet*, "sin." He reasoned, since there is no sin among them, they are worthy to be told the day of the final redemption. Then he observed that there are two more letters that do not appear in their names either, namely, *kuf* and *tzadi*, which together form the word *ketz*, "the end." This led him to the conclusion that his sons did *not* deserve to have the *ketz*, "end," revealed to them. Thus, he did not disclose the future, which is the reason that the portion of *Vayechi* is "sealed."

Speak to the children of Israel and say to them, "When one of you brings an offering to God you shall bring your offering of the mammals, of the cattle, or of the sheep. If the sacrifice is a burnt offering taken from the cattle, it must be an unblemished male. He shall bring it to the door of the Tent of Meeting, that he may be accepted before God."

(Leviticus 1:2–3)

Rabbeinu Bachya: *If the sacrifice is a burnt offering*[4]—The burnt offering is mentioned as the first of all the sacrifices. Why is this so? Interpreting the simple meaning of the text (*peshat*) we can say that the burnt offering represents an atonement for impure and sinful thoughts, whereas the other offerings atone for sinful *deeds*. Since every deed is inspired by a thought that preceded it, it is reasonable that the burnt offering leads the other sacrifices in this chapter.

The Amorites who lived in the highlands came out to confront you and chased you like bees.[5] They struck you down in Seir as far as Chormah.

(Deuteronomy 1:44)

Rabbeinu Bachya: *And chased you like bees*—What is meant by this simile? Bees, by nature, will attack ferociously anyone approaching their beehive, threatening that person's life. But there is more to this simile. A bee will die immediately after delivering its venomous sting. The Torah thus alludes to the fact that, just like bees, the pursuing Amorites were killed.

RABBI OVADIAH SEFORNO
רבי עובדיה ספורנו

born: Cesena, Italy, c. 1470
died: Bologna, Italy, 1550
Popularly known as Seforno.

After receiving a thorough Torah education in Cesena, Rabbi Ovadiah Seforno moved to Rome, where he studied medicine, philosophy, and mathematics. There he taught Torah, wrote many works on Jewish philosophy, and created his renowned commentary on the Torah and on many books of Tanach (Bible).

He gained a reputation as an outstanding talmudist and taught Hebrew to the famous German humanist and scholar Johann Reuchlin. His approach to Torah exegesis is that of *peshat*, interpreting the text according to its simple meaning, clarifying the continuity of the phrases and verses, and often extracting moral and ethical teachings. His commentary is a masterpiece of brevity, clarity, and often lyric phraseology. His profound original insights have been quoted by many later commentators and writers. Truly an immortal work, it is printed in all editions of *Mikra'ot Gedolot* and is available in English translation.[1]

SELECTIONS FROM SEFORNO'S COMMENTARY

God made grow out of the ground every tree that is pleasant to look at and good to eat, and the Tree of Life in the middle of the garden, and the Tree of Knowledge of good and evil.

(Genesis 2:9)

Seforno: *Pleasant to look at*—Gladdening and broadening the heart, preparing it to receive the flow of intelligence, as it says, *And it came to pass when the minstrel played that the hand of God came upon him* (2 Kings 3:15).[2]

אונקלוס ויקרא יט קדושים כ"ף פתוחה ט"ו 258

לֹא־תַעֲשׂוּ עָוֶל בַּמִּשְׁפָּט לֹא־תִשָּׂא פְנֵי־דָל וְלֹא תֶהְדַּר פְּנֵי גָדוֹל בְּצֶדֶק תִּשְׁפֹּט עֲמִיתֶךָ: לֹא־תֵלֵךְ רָכִיל בְּעַמֶּיךָ לֹא תַעֲמֹד עַל־

שפתי חכמים

רש"י

אור החיים

אבי עזר

ספורנו

Text of Torah commentary by Rabbi Ovadiah Seforno to Leviticus 19:15. Follows the *peshat* approach, expounding the straightforward meaning. From *Mikra'ot Gedolot.*

Abram was 99 years old; God appeared to him and said, "I am God Almighty. Walk before Me and be perfect."

(Genesis 17:1)

Seforno: *And be perfect*—Seek to reach the highest degree of perfection attainable by man, namely, knowing Me through knowing My ways and by emulating Me to the degree possible for you; for the actions of every being are a reflection of his essence, as it says, "Allow me to know Your ways, so that I will know You" (Exodus 33:13). Indeed, this is mankind's ultimate perfection and God's purpose in Creation, as it says, "Let us make man with our image and our likeness" (Genesis 1:26).[3]

No woman will suffer miscarriage or remain childless in your land. I will make you live out full lives.

(Exodus 23:26)

Seforno: *I will make you live out full lives*—You will live to the measure of the oil that is in your *lamp of God*[4] (your soul), i.e., the natural powers implanted in you from birth. The opposite of this mostly occurs when man dies from various diseases before his natural powers have run out. These diseases are the result of wrong choices (man made during his lifetime), or due to the stellar constellations (destiny) and the elements.

When a person's number of days are fulfilled, he will in most cases see children born to his children and he will be able to teach them, as it says, *"Make them known to your children"* (Deuteronomy 4:9). Thus, the outlook of the coming generations will be rectified

during the lifetime of their elders, as we are told happened in the case of Levi, Kehat, and Amram.[5]

God brought them out of Egypt; they have the might of a unicorn.

(Numbers 23:22)

Seforno: *They have the might of a unicorn*[6]—The nation (Israel) does not tear its prey to pieces and eat it, but, like a unicorn, rams its opponent with its horns. It was the (Divine) plan to drive out the Canaanites and bring the nation of Israel into the land, without killing its inhabitants, as it says, "You drove out the nations and You planted it[7] (Israel)," for He does not desire the demise of the dead. Likewise, our Sages say, "Joshua sent three epistles (to the seven nations of Canaan): (1) Whoever wishes to evacuate, let him evacuate; (2) Whoever wishes to make peace, let him make peace; (3) Whoever wishes to engage in war, let him fight.[8] The Canaanites, however, defiantly chose to fight a war, so that it became necessary to annihilate them.

Behold, I am placing before you today both a blessing and a curse.

(Deuteronomy 11:26)

Seforno: *Behold*—Look and perceive this, so that you will not steer a middle course in the affairs of your life, as most people do. Because surely, the blessing and the curse I place before you today constitute two extremes. On the one hand, the blessing, which is an overabundance of success—on the other hand the curse, a total lack of all basic needs. Both these are placed before you. The choice is yours.[9]

RABBI MOSHE ALSHICH
רבי משה אלשיך

born: Adrianople, Turkey, 1508
died: Damascus, Syria, 1593
Popularly referred to as Alshich. Commentator, kabbalist.

As a young man Moshe Alshich settled in Safed, where he received *semichah* (ordination) from the illustrious **Rabbi Yosef Karo**. Among his students was **Rabbi Chaim Vital**, the famous kabbalist. In 1587 Rabbi Alshich left Safed in the wake of the great epidemic, moving to Damascus. His important commentary on the Torah, *Torat Moshe*, gained great popularity, and it became known as *Alshich Hakadosh* (the saintly Alshich). He follows the homiletic approach, extracting from the text lessons on ethics, morality, and piety. His lucid style of writing has made the work accessible to a wide circle of readers. Rabbis find it a rich source of material for their sermons. It has seen many editions and is readily available today.

וזאת
התורה אשר שם משה
ספרא רבא דישראל

תורת משה
ספר בראשית

משה שפיר קאמר . גמיר וסביר ודרש דרש משה .
והנה שרף קטפו זהו פרי"ו הנאה לקיים ולדרוש
ולהתיר פה אלמים . פני משה כפני חמה להאיר על הארץ
ולדרים . השלים כל הקרב"נות וסמי"כות הפרשיות
ומקראות ודקדוקי ספורים . וחובר חיבו"ר במקראי קודש
קלים וחמורים . ה"ה ארנא ורבנא הרב האי הגאון הנשר
הגדול מוהר"ר

משה אלשיך

וצוקלה"ה האדיר שבאדירים . צדקת ה' עשה
ומשפטיו עם ישראל שבים ונערים . זכותו יגן
ויעמוד לנו ולצאצאינו ויופיע לדור דורים . אמן :

ווארשא

הוצאות ספרים

כלולת יופי

פובלישינג

שנת תשכ"ו לפ"ס

ווארשא
בבית מסחר הספרים
א) פראנציסקאנער
נומער .1819
ב) נרזיבאוו 4011

ווארשא
בהוצאות הרבני הנגיד
המפורסם מוה'
יהושע גרשון מונק
שנת תרל"ט לפ"ק

Title page of Rabbi Moshe Alshich's Torah commentary. He follows the *derash,* homiletic approach.

SELECTIONS FROM RABBI ALSHICH'S COMMENTARY

These are the chronicles of Noah: Noah was a perfectly righteous man in his generation. Noah walked with God.

(Genesis 6:19)

Alshich: *Noah was a perfectly righteous man in his generation. Noah walked with God*—The gentile nations are identified as *Benei Noah*, descendants of Noah, in contrast to the Jewish people, who trace their origin to Abraham, Isaac, and Jacob. Are we not equally Noah's offspring? Then why are we called children of Abraham, Isaac, and Jacob? Noah, although he was a perfectly righteous man, did not exemplify a Jewish *tzaddik*. He was the epitome of a *tzaddik* of the righteous Gentiles. "*Noah walked with God,*" but not with his fellow men. He was not concerned with the suffering of mankind. His righteousness was focused on himself, for *his* benefit and that of his family. When God commanded him to build

an ark, he obediently built it—board by board, nail by nail—for 120 years. But it never occurred to him to pray to have the decree annulled and to save the world from annihilation.

Abraham's attitude was the exact opposite. He tried to improve mankind. Abraham converted men, while Sarah converted women. He taught the world monotheism, ethics, and morality. And when God announced His intention of wiping out Sodom, Abraham fervently prayed to save these wicked people.

God said to Abraham, "Go away from your land and from your birthplace and from your father's house, to the land that I will show you."
(Genesis 12:1)

Alshich: *Go away from your land, and from your birthplace and from your father's house*—We are struck by the unusual order of progression as it is arranged in this passage. One would say that a person who leaves his country first departs from his father's house, then from his birthplace, and finally, he leaves his homeland. The following, then, should have been the order in which the verse should have listed them: "Go away from your father's house, from your birthplace, and from your homeland." We must understand, however, that Abraham was commanded to take leave of *Ur Kasdim*, not only by physically removing himself, but also in a spiritual sense. He was to distance himself from the society in which he had grown up, to forget completely and erase from his consciousness any trace of his native land, his birthplace, his father's house, and the pagan culture they represented. When it comes to eradicating ingrained impressions and habits, those that were formed in early childhood, in the home environment, are the ones most deeply rooted and the ones that survive the longest. Indeed, the order of priority in the verse is quite appropriate. Abraham would first forget his land, then his birthplace, and only much, much later his father's house, his parents, and his family.

Moses began to plead before God the Lord. He said, "O God, why unleash Your wrath against Your people, whom You brought out of Egypt with great power and a mighty hand?"
(Exodus 32:11)

Alshich: *O God, why unleash Your wrath against Your people, whom You brought out of Egypt*—Moses' plea should be understood as follows: "O God, I pray You, consider from whence they came, what sort of place it was from which You extricated them. It is a place full of the most detestable idolatry and other abomination. If You take that into account, You will conclude that their sin does not exist."[1]

When your brother becomes impoverished and loses his ability to support himself in the community, you must come to his aid. Help him survive, whether he is a proselyte or a native Israelite.
(Leviticus 25:35)

Alshich: *When your brother becomes impoverished*—The preceding segment, dealing with the laws of the Jubilee, is written in the plural. Now that the Torah considers the theme of aiding and supporting the poor, the second person singular is used (*achicha*, "your brother," is addressed to one individual). Often, when people are approached to extend a helping hand to the needy, they will decline, pointing to someone else who is closer to the poor man or is financially better situated to help. To discourage this attitude, the Torah formulates its command to help the needy in the singular. Each person is addressed individually and told, "It is incumbent on *you* to help the poor; don't pass the burden on to someone else."

If the journey is too great for you, so that you are not able to carry it, because the place is too far from you, which the Lord your God has chosen as a site, when the Lord your God has blessed you.
(Deuteronomy 14:24)

Alshich: *So that you are not able to carry it*[2]—If you approach a task with enthusiasm and eagerness, it will never be too difficult for you to accomplish. The same task, done with indifference and a listless attitude, will prove to be an unbearable burden. *If the journey is too great for you*—if you find the journey intolerably long, and *you are not able to carry it*—the burden is too heavy for you to carry, that is a clear indication that *the place is too far from you*; and that God, who is *Hamakom*, the Place of the world,[3] is distant from you.

RABBI YESHAYAH HOROWITZ—THE SHELOH
רבי ישעיה הורויץ—של"ה

born: Prague, Czechoslovakia, 1565
died: Tiberias, Israel, 1630
Popularly known as the Sheloh, an acronym formed of the initials of his work, Shenei Luchot Habberit. *Talmudist, kabbalist, rabbi.*

Yeshayah Horowitz studied in *yeshivot* in Prague, Lublin, and Cracow. He served as rabbi in various cities in Poland and Lithuania, in Frankfort-on-the-Main, Posen, and Metz. In 1615 he returned to Prague to lead the local yeshivah. In 1622 he journeyed to Eretz Yisrael and was chosen as rabbi of Jerusalem, where he composed his major work, *Shenei Luchot Habberit.*[1] It is a compendium of the 613 laws of the Torah. He presents kabbalistic interpretations of the laws, and in a separate section he analyzes the ethical aspects of each mitzvah. The text is interwoven with original homiletic insights and comments. The work became an immediate favorite and has been reprinted many times. It has made a major impact on Jewish thought that has endured until the present. Since it is considered one of our holiest books, it is generally referred to as the *Sheloh Hakadosh*—the holy *Sheloh*—an accolade it shares with only three other works: the *Zohar Hakadosh*, the *Or Hachayim Hakadosh*, and the *Alshich Hakadosh*.

שער האותיות

Page of the Sheloh's commentary. The text discusses kabbalistic interpretations of immersion in a mikveh. From the original standard edition.

SELECTIONS FROM THE SHELOH'S COMMENTARY

And Jacob sent and called Rachel and Leah to the field, to his flock.

(Genesis 31:4)

The Sheloh: *And Jacob sent and called Rachel and Leah to the field, to his flock*—A husband, although he is the head of the household, should not wield his authority or use intimidation on his wife and family. Rather, he should use persuasion and gentle reasoning to induce them to follow his suggestions. This mild and amiable approach was used by Jacob as he spoke to his wives. He had the clearly expressed mandate of God "to return to the land of your fathers" (Genesis 31:3). Yet, broaching the subject of returning, he gradually introduced the idea to Rachel and Leah, reviewing the entire history of his stay with Laban, devoting ten verses to the process (Genesis 31:4–14). All this, in order to make them amenable to his proposed plan.[2]

She quickly emptied her pitcher into the trough and ran again to the well to draw water. She drew water for all his camels.

(Genesis 24:20)

The Sheloh: The haste with which Rivkah acted in fulfilling Eliezer's request manifests her great sensitivity, tact, and intelligence. After Eliezer finished drinking, Rivkah was in a quandary as to what she should do. Should she offer the leftover water to the camels? That would embarrass Eliezer, since it would appear as though she placed him on the same level with the animals. Should she spill the water on the ground? He would be offended to see his leftovers treated as waste. She solved the delicate problem by running toward the drinking trough, making it appear as though in her great haste the pitcher had slipped from her hand, and the water accidentally spilled into the trough. In so doing, she watered the camels, while preserving Eliezer's dignity.

Rescue me, I pray, from the hand of my brother, from the hand of Eisav. For I am afraid of him, for he can come and kill us all, mothers and children alike.

(Genesis 32:12)

The Sheloh: *Rescue me, I pray, from the hand of my brother, from the hand of Eisav*—The Zohar comments on this phrase, that when praying we should clearly define our requests. Yaakov, too, spelled out his wish in detail, saying, "Rescue me from my brother, from Eisav." Don't think, "God knows my innermost thoughts. He will understand what I have in mind." The reason that we must enunciate our prayers is that these are composed of holy letters that ascend upward and that have the power to split the heavens.

The Israelites shall camp with each person near the banner bearing his father's family insignia.

They shall camp at a specified distance around the Communion Tent.

(Numbers 2:2)

The Sheloh: *Each person near the banner bearing his father's family insignia*—The Arizal[3] was wont to say, "Just as there were four banners around which Yisrael was organized on their sojourn in the wilderness, so are there four groupings among the Jewish people, each following differing customs: Sephardic, Ashkenazic, Catalonian,[4] and Italian. Each of these should remain with their 'banner' and maintain their customs. All are expressions of the Word of the Living God."

Balaam said to God's angel, "I have sinned, for I did not know that you were standing on the road before me. If you consider it wrong for me to go, I will go back home."

(Numbers 22:34)

The Sheloh: *"I have sinned, for I did not know*[5]—One may wonder: if Balaam did not know, why is his act considered a sin? This incident teaches us that a person is held liable for failing to be aware of something that he could have known and could have understood. God endowed man with an intellect and the capability of deductive reasoning. He is expected to use his capacity to rationalize. Ignorance is no excuse. Balaam should have concluded that there must be a reason for the donkey's peculiar behavior. The lesson to be derived from this is that we must always be alert and use our intellect to avoid adverse situations.

When you build a new house, you must make a guard-rail around your roof, so that you will not bring blood guilt on your house if someone falls from the roof.

(Deuteronomy 22:8)

Sheloh: *You must build a guard-rail around your roof*—The roof is the highest point of the house. Thus, metaphorically, this verse can be interpreted as a warning to keep one's pride in check. Failure to heed this counsel will lead to "falling from the roof"—his pride will be his downfall. As it is written, "Pride comes before the fall" (Proverbs 16:18).

RABBI SHLOMOH EFRAIM OF LUNTCHITZ— KLI YAKAR

רבי שלמה אפרים מלונטשיץ—כלי יקר

born: Luntchitz, Poland, 1550
died: Prague, Bohemia, 1619
Popularly known as Kli Yakar. Commentator.

Shlomoh Efraim was a disciple of Rabbi Shlomoh Luriah (Maharshal), the famous talmudist and author of *Yam shel Shlomoh*. After leading the yeshivah in Lvov, Rabbi Shlomoh Efraim was appointed rabbi of Prague. A spellbinding orator, he inspired his listeners with fiery sermons, which were published. His most important work is the popular commentary on the Torah, *Kli Yakar*,[1] in which he expounds the text in a homiletic style. It is very readable and has a captivating quality. It is published in many editions of the Chumash.

SELECTIONS FROM KLI YAKAR'S COMMENTARY

By the sweat of your brow you will eat bread until you will return to the ground, for it was from (the ground) that you were taken. You are dust and to dust you shall return.

(Genesis 3:19)

Kli Yakar: *By the sweat of your brow you will eat bread*—This passage supports the opinion of the physicians who say that before sitting down to eat, you should do some physical work to raise your temperature, since that promotes the digestive process. This is in line with the verse, "When you eat the labor of your hands, you are praiseworthy and it is well with you" (Psalm 128:2); also with the verse, "In anguish shall you eat from it all the days of your life," (Genesis 3:17) for *itzavon*, anguish, denotes toil. . . . The phrase *all the days of your life* indicates that you should eat only as much as you need to sustain life, and not indulge in excessive eating.

Text of Kli Yakar commentary on the Torah by Rabbi Shlomoh Efraim Luntchitz. This popular commentary uses the *derash*, homiletic approach to exegesis. From *Mikra'ot Gedolot*.

They will fill your palaces and the houses of your officials and of all Egypt. It will be something that your fathers and your fathers' fathers have never seen since they were in the land.

(Exodus 10:6)

Kli Yakar: *They will fill your palaces and the houses of your officials and of all Egypt*[2]—Without a doubt the king's palace is more impregnable than the houses of the officials, and the houses of the officials are better insulated than those of all Egypt. Then how are we to understand that the locusts would strike the most fortified house first and only after that the unprotected houses?[3] It can only be due to miraculous intervention—as the sin had progressed, so did the punishment. For Pharaoh was the one who initiated the persecution, and subsequently he was emulated by his officials . . . and his people. . . . Perhaps this reverse order is what is meant by the verse, *Never before had there been such a locust plague* (Exodus 10:14)—there may have been such a locust plague before, but never one that spread in this unnatural sequence.

Then you shall count seven complete weeks after the day following the (Passover) festival when you brought the omer as a wave offering, until the day after the seventh week, when there will be a total of 50 days; and you shall present a new meal offering to God.

(Leviticus 23:15–16)

Kli Yakar: *And you shall present a new meal offering to God*[4]—Herein is an allusion to the Giving of the Torah (on Shavuos), for everyone should experience the Torah as something new each day, as though he had received it on Mount Sinai this very day.

The reason why the Torah does not explicitly mention the fact that on Shavuos the Torah was given, I have explained in my treatise *Olelot Efraim:* God did not wish to set aside a particular day for this purpose, because on every day of the year a Jew should feel as though he had received the Torah on Mount Sinai. Indeed, our sages compare the Torah to a mother's breast—Just as a baby always finds new taste in his mother's milk, so does everyone who contemplates the Torah find new insights each day. . . . Thus, to a student of the Torah, every day is *Mattan Torah,* the Giving of the Torah. . . . Therefore, other than in the allusion of the "new meal offering," the day of the Giving of the Torah is not mentioned.

Do not eat it, so that you and your descendants will have a good life, since you will be doing what is morally right in God's eyes.

(Deuteronomy 12:24)

Kli Yakar: *Do not eat it, so that you and your descendants will have a good life*[5]—Why does the verse specifically mention also "your descendants"? The commentaries explain that the consumption of blood predisposes a person to cruelty and awakens in him feelings of ruthlessness. Now, a father's character traits are inherited by his children. Consequently, the verse states, "If you yourself don't eat blood, both you *and* your descendants will have a good life, for no cruel character trait will cling to them."

RABBI CHAIM IBN ATTAR—OR HACHAIM
רבי חיים אבן עטר—אור החיים

born: Salé, Morocco, 1696
died: Jerusalem, Israel, 1743
Reverently known as Or Hachaim. Torah commentator, kabbalist, talmudist.

Rabbi Chaim ibn Attar, the Rabbi of Salé, led a deeply pious life, devoted entirely to the study of Torah and Talmud, fasting and prayer. His saintly way of life gained him the name Or Hachaim Hakadosh, the holy man. In 1740 he moved to Jerusalem, where he established an important yeshivah.

The most famous of Rabbi Chaim's works is *Or Hachaim*, a commentary on the Torah.[1] In this work he employs the four methods of exegesis: *peshat*—explaining the simple meaning; *derash*—homiletic interpretation; *remez*—allusion; and *sod*—the kabbalistic, esoteric approach.

SELECTIONS FROM OR HACHAIM'S COMMENTARY

God called to the man, and He said: "Where are you?"

(Genesis 3:9)

Or Hachaim: *He said to him, "Where are you?"*[2]—This means, "Why do you hide and why don't you show yourself to Me?" (Adam) replied that he was afraid to stand before God, since he had seen himself in his nakedness. The law forbids you to stand naked in the presence of a Torah scroll; then surely this is forbidden in the presence of God, blessed is He.

This is in line with our commentary on verse 7, *their eyes were opened*—they sensed their spiritual decline and their sins. Thus Adam replied that he was ashamed seeing himself in a naked state, devoid of the radiance of sanctity.[3] This interpretation is in agreement with the statement of our sages that "Adam was divested of the garment that the King (God) had draped on him."[4] For

258 ויקרא יט קדושים אונקלוס

לא־תעשו עול במשפט לא־תשא פני־דל ולא תהדר פני גדול בצדק תשפט עמיתך: טז לא־תלך רכיל בעמיך לא תעמד על־

לא תעבדון שקר בדין לא תסב אפי מסכנא ולא תהדר אפי רבא בקושטא תדינה לחברך: טז לא תיכול קורצין בעמך לא תקום

שפתי חכמים

רש"י

אור החיים

ספורנו

אבי עזר

Text of *Or Hachaim*, commentary on the Torah by Rabbi Chaim ibn Attar. Employs all four methods of exegesis.

(Adam) could not have meant that he was literally naked, since he had sewn a garment of fig leaves.

During six days God made the heaven, the earth, the sea, and all that is in them, but He rested on the seventh day. God, therefore, blessed the Shabbat and made it holy.

(Exodus 20:11)

Or Hachaim: *But He rested on the seventh day*—God, in His wisdom, prohibited here the 40 (39) labors that were enumerated by our sages, many of which do not involve any exertion at all, for example, moving an object from a private to a public premise, or vice versa, and many others. Yet the Torah imposes the death penalty for (violating) them. Now, a person might say, "Why should an activity that does not involve any toil carry the death penalty?" The Torah answers him, "For in six days . . . but He rested on the seventh day." If you ponder this you will understand that the matter is not contingent on physical exertion at all. For about God it is written, *He who does not grow tired and does not become exhausted,*[5] and the term *rest* does not apply to Him at all. But the intent of the verse is (to tell us) that the criterion is "creative activity," even an activity that does not demand toil and exertion. Therefore, any activity that is designated *melachah* (labor)— although you do it without exerting any effort—is punishable.

They shall make Me a sanctuary, and I will dwell among them.

(Exodus 25:8)

Or Hachaim: *I will dwell among them*—The verse does not say, *betocho,* "(I will dwell) in *it.*" The phrase *betocham,* "among them," comes to indicate that the place they consecrate as His dwelling place be situated in the *center* of (the encampment) of the children of Israel. Or possibly, another explanation may be that this passage (*I will dwell among them*) was God's reply to Israel's fervent wish. At Mount Sinai, when they (Israel) witnessed God surrounded by divisions of angels, and His Glory in their midst, they felt an intense desire that He might equally reside among them. God, who knows what is in man's heart, answered them, saying "They shall make Me a sanctuary and I will thus dwell among them just as (I dwell among the angels)."

Justice, justice you shall follow, so that you will live and occupy the land that God your Lord is giving you.

(Deuteronomy 16:20)

Or Hachaim: *Justice, justice you shall follow*—The repeated use of "justice" is meant to caution you that in the event that there are in a city two outstanding scholars, as well as two scholars of lesser stature, then a person should not say, "Since the two (lesser) men are qualified to adjudicate and administer justice,[6] I will not burden the eminent scholars with the responsibility of judgeship"; or (he may think) that appointing (the eminent scholars) would involve greater effort and expense. He may, therefore, refrain from appointing the eminent scholars and be content with the second best.

With that in mind, the verse says *Justice, justice you shall follow,* meaning that although you have obtained competent judges, it is your duty to seek out the ones that have superior qualifications.

RABBI ELIYAHU OF VILNA—THE VILNA GAON
רבי אליהו מוילנא—הגר"א

born: Vilna, Lithuania, 1720
died: Vilna, Lithuania, 1797
*Popularly referred to as the Vilna Gaon, the Gra
(initials of Gaon Rabbi Eliyahu), or simply as the
Gaon. Greatest Torah scholar of the past two centuries.*

Even as a child Eliyahu of Vilna amazed the congregation when, at age 7, he delivered a learned discourse
in the Great Synagogue in Vilna. By 10 years of age he
had surpassed all his teachers, and, studying by himself
with total concentration, he acquired knowledge of the
vastness of Torah in both its revealed and mystical
aspects. Every minute of his life was devoted to Torah
study. He never slept more than two hours in a 24-hour
period; he never accepted any rabbinic post or leadership of a yeshivah. He taught a few disciples, selected
from the foremost Torah scholars of his time. The Vilna
Gaon cleared a new path to Talmud study, focusing on
gaining a clear understanding through keen analysis of
the principles and approaches of the early authorities.
His methodology stood in sharp contrast to the *pilpul*
system of the Polish yeshivahs, an intricate system of
creating a complex framework with which a series of
questions would be answered. He toiled hard on
emending the talmudic and midrashic texts. Subse-
quent discoveries of ancient manuscripts confirmed the
soundness of his corrections, which appear in the Vilna
edition of the Talmud (*Haga'ot Hagra*). His works,
which were recorded and published by his disciples,
include *Aderet Eliyahu,*[1] a commentary on the Torah; a
commentary on Ecclesiastes;[2] *Shenot Eliyahu,* a commentary on the Mishnah, Order of *Zeraim;*[3] *Biur
Hagra,* a commentary on the *Shulchan Aruch;*[4] a
commentary on *Sefer Yetzirah,* a kabbalistic work;[5] and
many other works.

His commentary on the Torah is filled with interest-
ing allusions that show the oneness of the Written
Torah and the Oral Law, demonstrating their common

Rabbi Eliyahu of Vilna, the Gra, the Vilna Gaon.

source in Divine revelation. The Vilna Gaon was
revered in Vilna and throughout the world for his
phenomenal knowledge and his saintly character. One
of his most outstanding disciples was **Rabbi Chaim of
Volozhin,** the founder of the yeshivah of Volozhin.
Following the Gaon's approach to learning, this institution spread Torah for more than one hundred years.
Today most yeshivahs follow the study pattern of

A page of *Shulchan Aruch, Orach Chaim,* Laws of Shabbat 299:3, with *Biur HaGra,* commentary by the Vilna Gaon. From the original standard edition.

Volozhin, keeping alive the approach to Torah pioneered by the great Vilna Gaon.

SELECTIONS FROM THE VILNA GAON'S COMMENTARY

Jacob came closer to his father Isaac, and [Isaac] touched him. He said, "The voice is Jacob's voice but the hands are the hands of Esau."

(Genesis 27:22)

The Vilna Gaon: *The voice is Jacob's voice but the hands are the hands of Esau*—The Midrash expounds: "Whenever the voice of Jacob is heard, the hands of Esau are powerless."

At first glance, the text would seem to indicate that the "voice of Jacob" and "the hands of Esau" will prevail simultaneously, contrary to the interpretation of the Midrash. However, upon closer examination, we discover a deeper meaning. In the verse, *kol,* "voice," appears in the abbreviated form, without a *vav.* As such it can also be read as *kal,* "unsteady or timid." Consequently, the verse can be interpreted as follows, in accordance with the Midrash: If the voice of Jacob is *kal,* i.e., wavering and half-hearted, then the hand of Esau will prevail. If, on the other hand, the voice of Jacob is *kol,* in its full form, meaning resolute and vigorous, then the hands of Esau are indeed powerless.

And they embittered their lives with hard labor, in mortar, brick, and all manner of heavy field work. All the labors they made them perform were backbreaking.

(Exodus 1:14)

The Vilna Gaon: *And they embittered their lives*—The cantillation marks on these words allude to the answer to one of the difficult questions regarding the Exodus of the Jewish people from Egypt. Abraham had been told that his children would dwell in exile for 400 years, yet the Torah teaches us that Israel's sojourn in Egypt lasted only 210 years. Our sages explain the discrepancy by telling us that the extreme affliction and bitterness of Egyptian bondage made the 210 years as difficult as 400 years of a more moderate exile.

The cantillation marks are *kadma ve'azla,* which translates "it hurried and went" or "it went before its time." By placing these cantillation marks upon the words "they embittered their lives," the Torah implies that they "went before the time" of the completion of the predestined 400 years of bondage because of their dreadful suffering.

An eye for an eye, a tooth for a tooth, a hand for a hand, a foot for a foot.

(Exodus 21:24)

The Vilna Gaon: *An eye for an eye*—The Talmud in Tractate *Bava Kama* 84a teaches that this passage is not to be applied in its literal sense. Instead, the true meaning of *an eye for an eye* is the right to monetary compensation for the loss of an eye, tooth, or limb. A truly amazing allusion, concealed in the words *ayin tachat ayin,* "an eye for an eye," confirms this legal principle. If we arrange the letters of the Hebrew alphabet, the *alef bet,* in a vertical row, we find that underneath the letters of the word *ayin,* the letters *pei, chaf,* and *samach* appear. These letters can be rearranged to form the word *kesef,* money. The phrase *ayin tachat ayin* can thus be rendered as follows: *ayin,* for an injury to an eye, one must pay *tachat ayin,* that which is *tachat,* "underneath," the letters *ayin,* namely *kesef,* "money."[6]

These shall be your fringes, and when you see them, you shall remember all of God's command-ments so as to keep them. You will then not stray after your heart and eyes, which [in the past] have led you to immorality.

(*Numbers 15:39*)

The Vilna Gaon: *These shall be your fringes*—In the Torah the mitzvah of tzitzit (fringes) follows the paragraph relating the story of the man who violated the Shabbat by gathering sticks. Rabbi Moshe Hadarshan explains this juxtaposition by the fact that both the Shabbat and the mitzvah of tzitzit[7] are equivalent to all the other mitzvot in the Torah.

We can find an astounding allusion establishing an underlying connection between the Shabbat and tzitzit. The Mishnah in *Shabbat* 7:2 enumerates 39 principal works that are prohibited on Shabbat. Similarly, there are a total of 39 coils in the spaces between the five knots of the tzitzit, 7, 8, 11, and 13 coils respectively.

Furthermore, the same Mishnah classifies these 39 works into four categories, analogous to the four groupings of coils on the tzitzit: (1) the category of planting, consisting of eleven labors; (2) the category of weaving, consisting of thirteen labors; (3) the category of processing of hides, consisting of seven labors; and (4) miscellaneous, consisting of eight labors.

Excerpts from *Even Shlomoh,* an anthology of the Vilna Gaon's thoughts.

On learning Torah[8]

You must chew your food well so that your body can benefit from it. The same holds true for Torah study. You must fully "grind and digest" all the details of the holy Torah in order to extract the correct halachah. This is what the sages meant when they said, "If there is no flour, there is no Torah."[9] Being meticulous in your studies helps to improve your character and behavior.

On faith and contentment

It is good to associate with poor and humble people and to live among them. This way you will attain contentment and peace of mind. He who associates with the wealthy, although he may profit greatly, will never be satisfied. He will continually run after more emptiness, as it is written, "No man dies having even half of his desires fulfilled."[10]

RABBI MOSHE SOFER (SCHREIBER)—THE CHATAM SOFER
רבי משה סופר—חת״ם סופר

born: Frankfort-on-the-Main, Germany, 1762
died: Pressburg, Hungary, 1839
Popularly known as the Chatam Sofer, the title of his work. Halachist, commentator.

Rabbi Moshe Sofer was a scion of a distinguished rabbinical family tracing its roots to **Rashi.** At 9 years of age, he entered the yeshivah of the illustrious Rabbi Nassan Adler in Frankfort; he studied also under Rabbi Pinchas Horovitz, author of *Hafla'ah*. In 1798 he was chosen as rabbi in Mattersdorf, Hungary. In 1807 he was appointed rabbi and dean of the yeshivah in Pressburg. Under his inspired leadership the yeshivah enrollment grew to 500 students.

In 1819 the Reform movement originated in Hamburg. Spreading rapidly, it made serious inroads among the observant Jews of Germany and Austro-Hungary. The Chatam Sofer spearheaded the fight against the reformers under the banner of "*chadash assur min haTorah,*" "biblical Law forbids any innovation" (a play on the Torah prohibition of *chadash*, against eating of the new crop before the Omer was offered on the 16th of Nissan). His uncompromising stand stemmed the tide of Reform. As a result, the Chatam Sofer became the most influential *posek* (decider of halachic questions) of his day. His responsa, *Teshuvot Chatam Sofer*,[1] reflect his clear, penetrating thinking. He also wrote *Chatam Sofer*, novellae on the Talmud, and *Torat Moshe*,[2] a commentary on the Torah, in which he explains the text, illuminating it with masterful homiletic insights; it is a widely studied and quoted work to this day.

Rabbi Moshe Sofer, the Chatam Sofer.

SELECTIONS FROM THE CHATAM SOFER'S COMMENTARY

Enoch walked with God, and he was no more, because God had taken him.

(Genesis 5:24)

The Chatam Sofer: *And he was no more, because God had taken him*—Enoch lived an exemplary life, but he lived in isolation. He did not concern himself with his fellow men. In that respect he differed significantly

בעז"ה

ספר

חתם סופר

דרשות

מרבינו משה סופר זצוק"ל.

בעהמ"ח ספר שו"ת חת"ם סופר וחידושי חת"ם על הש"ס ועוד.
נולד בפראנקפורט-א"מ בשבעה לירח תשרי שנת תקכ"ג לפ"ק, ועלה
השמים כ"ה תשרי שנת ת"ר לאלף הששי. ומשה היה רועה עדת
ה' בק"ק דרעזני"ץ, מאטערסדארף, ובק"ק פרעסבורג, ושם חלקת
מחוקק ספון.

החבור הזה בשני כרכים, פולל כשרני מאות דרשות
ואוצר אמרות טהורות למועדים ויתר ימות השנה מכתבי יד
המחבר זצוק"ל שהיו ת"י נכדו הג"מ שלמה אלכסנדרי סופר ז"ל.
[גם נאספו פה, דרשות ומאמרים שנדפסו כבר, בתקונים הרבה].

העתקתים וזכיתי לסדר אותם ולהוציאם לאור, בציונים
מתנ"ך ומחז"ל בפנים הספר וגם הערות בשם .שער יוסף"

אני יוסף נפתלי שטערן

חתן הג"מ שלמה אלכסנדרי סופר ז"ל
בן הגאון מהורש"ם זצוק"ל מקראקא בן רבינו המחבר זצוק"ל.
סערעטה (בוקאווינא, רומאניען)

שנת וקסת הסופר במתניו (תרפ"ט) לפ"ק.

כרך שני:
ניסן-תשרי

בהוצאת המסדר, וניסו מהו"ר בנימין רז"ב סופר נ"י. ובהשתתפות
בית מסחר הספרים אברהם שלעזינגער גראסס-ווארדיין.

יוצא לאור מחדש ע"י
מכון רבינו יוסף נחמי' קורניצר אבדק"ק קראקא זצ"ל
ניו-יארק תשכ"א

Title page of *Chatam Sofer,* Sermons. The word Chatam is an acronym of *Chidushei Torat Moshe,* novellae on the Torah by Moshe.

from Abraham, whose entire being was dedicated to helping others and disseminating the belief in one God.

As a consequence, *ve'einennu,* "(Enoch) *was no more.*" The moment Enoch departed this life, he was forgotten. There was no one to carry on his tradition. By contrast, Abraham, who cared for the welfare of others, will be remembered and lives on for all time.

Laban and Bethuel answered and said, "It is something from God! We cannot say anything to you, bad or good."

(Genesis 24:50)

The Chatam Sofer: *We cannot say anything to you, bad or good*—It is quite understandable that they cannot say anything bad (about Rebecca), but why not something good? We must preface our answer to this question with our commentary on the verse, *I will make a compatible helper for him*[3] (Genesis 2:18). *Ezer kenegdo* literally translates as *"a helper who is his opposite,"* meaning that if the husband, for example, is a lavish spender, it is appropriate that the wife cut expenses and try to make ends meet, so that their capital will not be squandered. Conversely, if the husband is stingy by nature, it is good if his wife gives freely to charitable causes. That is the meaning of *a helper, who is his opposite*—by opposing him, she is actually helping him. By complementing each other, they keep the home on an even keel.

Now, Laban and Bethuel did not know Isaac. They only realized that this match was *something from God.* Being in the dark about Isaac's character and disposition, they were afraid to say something good concerning Rebecca, since perhaps, vis-à-vis Isaac, this may prove to be something bad.

I revealed Myself to Abraham, Isaac, and Jacob as God Almighty and did not allow them to know Me by My name Hashem.

(Exodus 6:3)

The Chatam Sofer: *I revealed Myself to Abraham, Isaac, and Jacob*—**Rashi** expounds this passage, commenting, "I appeared to the *avot,* the patriarchs." Inasmuch as the text enumerates the names of Abraham, Isaac, and Jacob, what novel thought does Rashi impart by saying that these were the patriarchs? The word *avot* can be seen as cognate to the root *avah,* "to desire, to want" (compare to Deuteronomy 2:30). The present passage, according to Rashi, should thus be rendered, "I appeared to those who desired Me." God reveals Himself to those whose hearts yearn for Him. In the same vein, **Ramban** interprets the phrase *I will be Who I will be* as "As you are to Me, so am I to you"—as you perceive Me, so do I make Myself known to you.

Speak to the entire community of Israel and say to them, "You must be holy, since I am your God (and) I am holy."

(Leviticus 19:2)

The Chatam Sofer: *Speak to the entire community of Israel and say to them, "You must be holy"*—The Torah does not demand of us to reach a state of holiness through asceticism and withdrawal into a life of austere monastic isolation. Quite the contrary. The portion of *kedoshim tihyu, you must be holy,* was read before *the entire community of Israel,* as if to say, "Be holy as an involved member of society, surrounded and beloved by your fellowmen."

Designate for yourselves men who are wise, understanding, and known to their tribes.
(Deuteronomy 1:13)

The Chatam Sofer: *Designate for yourselves men* [said as a tongue-in-cheek comment]—There are rabbis whose wives interfere in rabbinical affairs to the point of influencing the rabbi's decisions, so that, in effect, the community is run by the *rebbetzin,* the rabbi's wife.

Our verse addresses this phenomenon when it states, "Designate for yourselves men," meaning "Select the kind of rabbi who will *himself* serve the needs of the community."

(This scroll) must always be with him and he shall read from it all the days of his life. He will then learn to fear the Lord his God and keep every word of the Torah and do these statutes.
(Deuteronomy 17:19)

The Chatam Sofer: *He shall read from it all the days of his life*[4]—A Jewish monarch is to conduct his life in an exemplary fashion, according to the laws of the Torah, so that when he reads the Torah, he shall read from it *all the days of his life,* meaning that his entire life will be reflected in its pages; he will find the Torah to be the story of his life.

RABBI SAMSON RAPHAEL HIRSCH
רבי שמשון רפאל הירש

born: Hamburg, Germany, 1808
died: Frankfort-on-the-Main, Germany, 1888
Rabbi, commentator, historic leader of Orthodox Jewry.

After studying under Rabbi (*Chacham*) Isaac Barnays of Hamburg, Samson Raphael Hirsch went to Mannheim to prepare himself for the rabbinate under the venerable Rabbi Jacob Ettlinger. In 1829 he entered the University of Bonn. One year later, in 1830, he was appointed rabbi of Oldenburg. It was there that he wrote his *Nineteen Letters of Ben Uziel*,[1] in which he addresses the doubts and confusions that perplexed Jewish intellectuals in the wake of the Emancipation. In 1841 he was elected rabbi of the Hannover district, and in 1846 he became rabbi of the prestigious community of Nikolsburg in Moravia and later Land Rabbi of Moravia and Austrian Silesia.

In 1851 Frankfort-on-the-Main's Jewish congregation was entirely in the hands of the reformers. Eleven Orthodox men had withdrawn from the general community and founded the *Israelitische Religionsgesellschaft* (Israelitic Society for Religion). In selfless dedication Rabbi Hirsch gave up his prominent position to serve as rabbi of these eleven men. Under his brilliant leadership the congregation grew into a model Orthodox community of 500 members. From his pulpit and through his writings he led a fierce fight against Reform. From 1866 to 1878 he published his masterwork, *Translation of the Pentateuch and Commentary*.[2] In an elegant, eloquent, poetic style of 19th-century classic German he demonstrates the Divine origin of both the Written and Oral Torah, refutes the hypotheses of Bible Criticism, presents a system of symbolism to explain the reasons for the mitzvot, and offers original psychological and grammatical insights.

Rabbi Samson Raphael Hirsch, by the strength of his character and the power of his word, was instrumental in saving German Orthodoxy and thereby made an impact on Jewish history that endures into the present time and the future.

Rabbi Samson Raphael Hirsch.

SELECTIONS FROM RABBI HIRSCH'S COMMENTARY

These are Ishmael's sons and these are their names, in their courtyards and strongholds, twelve princes in their nations.

(Genesis 25:16)

Rabbi Samson Raphael Hirsch: *Twelve princes in their nations*—The word *nesi'im*, "princes," has the alternate meaning of "clouds."

חמשה
חומשי תורה
חלק ב׳
ספר שמות.
מתורגם ומבואר
מאת
הגאון כמהור״ר שמשון בן כמהור״ר רפאל הירש פ״פ זלה״ה.
היה שומר משמרת הקדש בק״ק עדת ישורון בפ״פ דמי יע״א.
מהדורא ו׳
פראנקפורט דמיין.
פערלאג פאן י׳ קויפפמאנן.
שנת תר״פ לפ״ק.

Title page of Torah commentary by Rabbi Samson Raphael Hirsch, Book of Exodus, sixth edition, 1920.

The term *cloud* accurately describes the concept of prince, national leader, or president. The entire substance of a cloud is derived from the vapors that rise up from the earth. The cloud receives this gift for the purpose of returning it to the earth in the form of blessed, life-giving rain. A *nasi,* "president," like a cloud, derives his power and wealth from the people and is expected to channel bounty back to the people. A nation can count itself fortunate indeed when its leader is a cloud, a *nasi,* who does not seek to increase his own glory but uses his office to bring peace and abundance to the people who gave him power.

These are the chronicles of Jacob; Joseph was 17 years old. As a lad, he would tend the sheep with his brothers, the sons of Bilhah and Zilpah, his father's wives; Joseph brought his father a bad report about them.

(Genesis 37:2)

Rabbi Samson Raphael Hirsch: *Joseph was 17 years old—"Ben"* is an idiomatic expression, denoting age. In its literal translation, "He was a son of 17 years," it conveys a universal truth: We are all sons of the years we have lived. Whether we realize it or not, the years of our lives are our mothers and teachers that shape our character and attitude toward life.

The Nile will swarm with frogs, and when they emerge they will be in your palace, in your bedroom, and even in your bed. They will also be in the homes of your officials and people, even in your ovens and your kneading bowls.

(Exodus 7:28)

Rabbi Samson Raphael Hirsch: *They will be in your palace, in your bedroom, and even in your bed . . . even in your ovens and kneading bowls*[3]—Taking a closer look at the list of areas invaded by the impudent frogs, we find that they represent exactly the basic essentials the Egyptian masters denied their Hebrew slaves.

As slaves, our forefathers possessed no homes, not even bedrooms. They could not enjoy restful sleep, they did not even have bread to eat, a fact we commemorate by our *lechem oni,* the "bread of affliction," our matzah. In all these places, the usually timid frogs jumped about, boldly and noisily, showing the Egyptians what it means to be unable to enjoy your home, your bed, and your bread, in peace.

With that, Moses raised his hand and struck the rock twice with his staff.

(Numbers 20:11)

Rabbi Samson Raphael Hirsch: *And struck the rock twice with his staff*—Against the explicit command of God to speak to the rock, Moses struck it, twice. What could have stirred God's faithful servant to deviate from his mission at this critical moment? After Israel's victory over Amalek, at the outset of the journey through the desert, the staff was deposited in the Holiest of Holies. Now, for the first time after an interim of forty years, Moses is commanded to take the staff in his hand again. As he stood before the assembled nation, the thought must have struck him that forty years ago he had used this same staff to convince the doubters of his divinely ordained mission. Now, forty years later, after countless miracles and revelations, he still needs the staff to gain their confidence; they still challenge his authority. He must have been filled with a sense of bitter disappointment at the apparent failure of his mission. In frustration, he forgot, for a brief moment, God's command to speak gently to the rock. Instead, striking the rock in anger, he hurls recriminations at the people.

God drove them from their land with anger, rage, and great fury, and He exiled them to another land, where they remain even today.
(Deuteronomy 29:27)

Der

Pentateuch.

übersetzt und erläutert

von

Samson Raphael Hirsch,

Rabbiner der Syn.-Gem. „Israelitische Religionsgemeinschaft" zu Frankfurt a. M.

Zweiter Teil: Exodus.

Sechste Auflage.

Frankfurt am Main.

Verlag von J. Kauffmann.

1920.

Title page of Rabbi Hirsch's commentary in German on the Book of Exodus.

שמות כ יתרו 220

20. לא תעשון אתי אלהי כסף ואלהי זהב לא תעשו לכם:

21. מזבח אדמה תעשה־לי וזבחת עליו את־עלתיך ואת־שלמיך את־צאנך ואת־בקרך בכל־המקום אשר אזכיר את־שמי אבוא אליך וברכתיך:

20. gestaltet ihr nichts bei mir; Götter aus Silber und Götter aus Gold sollt ihr euch nicht machen.

21. Einen Altar aus Erde sollst du mir machen und darauf deine Emporopfer und Friedenopfer, dein Schaf und dein Rind opfern; an jedem Orte, wo ich meines Namens gedacht wissen will, werde ich zu dir kommen und dich segnen.

V. 20. לא תעשון אתי, ihr sollt nichts gestalten bei mir! Was ihr, die Menschen, aus euch gestaltet, um euch Übersinnliches zu vergegenwärtigen, das werden immer אלהי כסף וגו', das werden immer Göttergestalten. Die Menschen vergegenwärtigen sich Göttliches in Sinnbildern, — das sollt ihr nicht: לא תעשון כדמות שמשי המשמשין לפני במרום כגון אופנים ושרפים וחיות הקדש ומלאכי השרת — (מכילתא, ר' נתן) שלא תאמר עושה אני כמין דמות ואשתחוה לו; ja selbst bildliche Darstellungen, die ich dir geboten, mußt du auf die Ausführung dieses Gebotes beschränken, nur in meinem Auftrage und nach meinem Auftrage sollst du und darfst du daher Cherubim gestalten, Ich lasse dich dir Menschliches vergegenwärtigen, willkürlich würdest du dir Göttliches vergegenwärtigen, und dein Symbol würde ein Götze שלא האמר הואיל ונתנה תורה רשות לעשות בבית המקדש הריני עושה בבתי כנסיות ובבתי מדרשות ת"ל לא תעשו לכם oder: לפי שהוא אומר ועשית שני כרובים זהב אמר (?) הריני עושה ארבעה ת"ל אלהי כסף וגו' אם הוספת על שנים הרי הם כאלהי זהב (מכילתא), was ihr euch machet, wird immer אלהי כסף, immer ein Gottessymbol sein! Selbst die Tempelräume in ihren architektonischen Dimensionen, die Tempelgeräte in ihren numerischen Konstruktionsverhältnissen dürfen nicht nachgebildet werden: לא יעשה אדם בית תבנית היכל וכו' שולחן כנגד שולחן מנורה כנגד מנורה וכו' (Rosch Hasch. 24 a. b.).

V. 21. Du sollst nicht gestalten, was bei mir, vielmehr lasse ich dich gestalten, was bei dir; nicht Himmlisches zu dir herabzuziehen, sondern alles Irdische zu mir emporzuheben ist deine Aufgabe; und wenn du zu mir hintrittst, hast du dir nicht zu vergegenwärtigen, was du dir im Himmel bei mir vorstellst, sondern wie Ich will, daß sich alles bei dir gestalten soll, die Erde und nicht der Himmel soll dir gegenwärtig sein, wenn du zu mir hintrittst; die durch Menschenthat zu Gott emporzuhebende Erde soll der Altar darstellen, den du mir erbauest. Einen „Erdaltar": unmittelbar von der Erde auf soll er sich erheben שיהא מחובר מארמה (בארמה?) שלא יבננו לא על גבי מחילות ולא על גבי כיפין (Sebachim 58 a.), „nicht auf Höhlen und nicht auf Wölbungen darf er gebaut sein", selbst ein faustgroßer Zwischenraum würde schon den Altar פסול machen, (תוספתא פ"ט אהלות, ר"ש שם, ט"ו) אין מעלין עולות גבוה מן הארץ טפח, der Wanderaltar des Stiftzeltes war selbst ein Erdaufwurf, von einem hohlen Würfel — נבוב לוחות — umkleidet. —

וזבחת עליו, nicht auf ihm, aber mit Hinblick auf ihn, um an ihm und auf ihm die עבודות דם ואיברי', resp. אימורים zu vollziehen, wurde die שחיטה des Opfertiers vollzogen; nicht Vernichtung soll die שחיטה sein, vielmehr in dem Hingeben an die durch den מזבח repräsentierte Hinanhebung alles Irdischen zu Gott ihr positives Ziel und darin so wesentlich ihre Bedeutung finden, daß, wenn im Moment der שחיטה der מזבח im geringsten schadhaft gewesen, alle dort geopferten Opfer פסול geworden, מזבח שנפגם

Page of Exodus 20:21 with German translation and commentary by Rabbi S. R. Hirsch. Rabbi Hirsch uses a classic, highly literate, and at times poetic German to convey his thoughts. From the original German edition.

Rabbi Samson Raphael Hirsch: *And He exiled them*—In the Torah, the letter *lamed,* in the word *vayashlichem,* "*and He exiled them,*" is written larger than the other letters. The outsized *lamed* focuses attention on the message contained in the word *vayashlichem,* "and He exiled them." Wherever Jews are in *galut,* "exile," they were sent there by God as a large *lamed* to serve as a great instrument of "*lamed,*" i.e., teaching,[4] and to disseminate the principles of monotheism, ethics, and morality among the nations of the world.[5]

RABBI MEIR LEIB BEN YECHIEL MICHAEL—MALBIM
רבי מאיר ליב בן יחיאל מיכל—מלבי״ם

born: Volochisk (Volhynia), Poland, 1809
died: Kiev, Russia, 1879
Popularly known as Malbim (the initials of his name).
Commentator, rabbi, orator.

Even as a young boy, Meir Leib was recognized as a genius; people called him the *illui* (genius) from Volhynia. He held a succession of rabbinical posts. In 1839, he was rabbi of Wreschen, followed by a position in Kempen, and in 1858 he became rabbi of Bucharest and chief rabbi of Romania.

He fought resolutely against the encroaching Reform movement, causing ugly disputes in the community. False accusations by the assimilationists led to his imprisonment. He was freed as a result of the intervention of Sir Moses Montefiore on condition that he leave Romania. Persecuted by the assimilationists, he wandered around, accepting rabbinical posts in Leczyca, Kherson, Mohilev, and Koenigsberg.

His monumental commentary on the Bible gained him universal recognition. His commentary on the Torah[1] is a masterpiece of analytical power. His commentaries reflect his principles: (1) in the Torah and Bible there is no repetition of synonymous phrases; (2) every word carries its own specific meaning; (3) there are no redundant or superfluous words; (4) all metaphors are imbued with profound meaning and wisdom; (5) the Written and Oral Law are one inseparable expression of God's will. His original and profound insights make his commentary an immortal work.[2]

Rabbi Meir Leib ben Yechiel Michael, or Malbim.

SELECTIONS FROM MALBIM'S COMMENTARY

If you do good, there will be uplift, but if you do not do good, sin is crouching at the door. It lusts after you, but you can dominate it. Cain spoke to his brother Abel. Then, when they happened to be in the field, Cain rose up against his brother Abel and killed him.

(Genesis 4:7–8)

Malbim: *Cain spoke to his brother Abel*—What did Cain actually say to Abel and why did he kill him; what had he done to him? Cain did not understand what God had told him (in Genesis 4:7). He did not understand that the external, outward man, made up of flesh, sinews, and bones, is not the essential man but only the animal in human form; that the true essence of man is his internal, intellectual aspect that is concealed, yet guides and controls him. He thought that the physical body represents the totality of man. Therefore, he did not know whom God meant when He said that there

ספר
תורת אלהים
עם פירוש
הרב הגאון האמתי המפורסם
רבינו
מאיר ליבוש מלבים
זצללה"ה
הוצאת
תורת ישראל
פובלישינג קא, אינק.
ניו-יורק — התש"י

PUBLISHED BY TORATH ISRAEL PUBLISHING CO., INC., N. Y.

Title page of Chumash with Malbim's commentary.

was sin crouching at his door, wanting to cause him to transgress, but whom he can dominate. He did not know who was meant by this "sin," and since only he and Abel were present then, he thought that God meant that it was Abel who wanted to seduce him into sin and that he, Cain, could overcome him. This is meant by *Cain spoke to his brother Abel*—he said to himself that God had meant Abel. Accordingly, he "*rose up against his brother Abel and killed him*," in keeping with what God had told him, that *you can dominate him*.

Lot looked up and saw that the entire Jordan Plain had plenty of water—this was before God destroyed Sodom and Gomorrah. It was like God's own garden, like the land of Egypt as one comes to Tzoar.

(Genesis 13:10)

Malbim: *It was like God's own garden, like the land of Egypt as one comes to Tzoar*—(In what respect can Sodom be compared to the Garden of Eden and to Egypt?) Today, the Jordan River enters the Dead Sea from the north. But the Dead Sea did not always exist. It was created in the aftermath of the geological upheaval resulting from the cataclysmic destruction of Sodom, when the earth's crust split open, forming a deep fissure, a geological rift. Into this newly formed canyon the waters of the Jordan began to flow, gradually creating the Dead Sea. Before the formation of the Dead Sea, the Jordan had no outlet, so that it periodically overflowed its banks, inundating the entire area of what is now the Dead Sea. As a result, that land produced an abundance of rich crops, much like the Nile Valley, which is irrigated by the overflowing waters of the Nile. The same is said also about the Garden of Eden; "A river flowed out of Eden to water the garden" (Genesis 2:1).

Jacob lived in Egypt for 17 years. Jacob's days, the days of his life, were 147 years.

(Genesis 47:28)

Malbim: *Jacob lived*—A man's final days set the tone for his entire life; and even a person who has lived all his life in misery, if at the end his fortune improves, he will forget his troubles and imagine that his whole life had been filled with contentment. Likewise here, because *Jacob had lived in Egypt for 17 years* in contentment, the years of Jacob were *the days of his life*. It was as though all his years had been years of fulfilled life and success.

Aaron did so, lighting the lamps to illuminate the menorah, as God commanded Moses.

(Numbers 8:3)

Malbim: *Aaron did so*—In the chapter on Creation we read at the end of each paragraph the words *vayehi chen*, "and it was so"—except in the first paragraph, which describes the creation of light, where it says *vayehi or*, "and it was light." Our sages in the Midrash explain this discrepancy by the fact that the light of the first day was put away into a hiding place because God found the world unworthy to be illuminated by the heavenly splendor of this light. God stored it away for the righteous, and instead, a light of lower, physical radiance came into being.[3]

Aaron, by lighting the menorah, returned the glorious primordial light to the world. He thereby reinstated the word *ken*, "so" (that had been replaced by *or*, "light"), for he brought back the light that was originally designed to illuminate the world.

This is the underlying thought of the midrashic comment on the above-mentioned phrase: "This teaches us that Aaron did not change." Now that Aaron had lit the menorah, there was no more need to change from *vayehi chen* to *vayehi or*.

Though I walk in the valley of the shadow of death I fear no evil for You are with me. Your rod and Your staff they comfort me.

(Psalm 23:4)

Malbim: *Your rod and Your staff*—David sees the Shepherd (God) walking beside him to protect him. Metaphorically, he sees the shepherd holding in one hand a small, thin rod with which to guide a straying lamb back to the flock. In the other hand he holds his staff, a tough, heavy stick, to scare away any predator. Accordingly, David says, "When I see both *Your rod and Your staff* I am comforted, for I know that no harm will come to me."

The meaning of the metaphor is that his suffering is for his own good, a means of guiding him back to the right path (represented by the small rod), while at the same time, God is holding His staff to save him from his enemies. It is because of these that he places his trust in God forever.[4]

Text of Malbim's commentary to Genesis 19:4–11. His unique approach demonstrates the unity of the written and oral Torah. From the original standard edition.

RABBI AVRAHAM SHEMUEL BINYAMIN SOFER (SCHREIBER)—THE KTAV SOFER

רבי אברהם שמואל בנימין סופר—כתב סופר

born: Pressburg, Hungary, 1815.
died: Pressburg, Hungary, 1871.
Popularly known as the Ktav Sofer, after the title of his work. Halachist, commentator, rabbinical leader.

Oldest son of **Rabbi Moshe Sofer (the Chatam Sofer)**, the Ktav Sofer succeeded his illustrious father in the rabbinate of Pressburg and as *rosh* (dean) of a yeshivah that had an enrollment of 400 students. Carrying on his father's traditions, he vigorously opposed the Reform movement. In the National Jewish Congress (1868–1869) he spearheaded the struggle for complete separation from the reformers and their adherents. His responsa were published under the title *Teshuvot Ktav Sofer.*[1] The work is testimony to the vastness of his talmudic knowledge. He also wrote a homiletic commentary on the Chumash (Pentateuch) called *Sefer Ktav Sofer,*[2] which won wide acclaim. In spite of his frail health, he led the Pressburg community with a firm yet gentle hand, and he was the recognized leader of Austro-Hungarian Jewry during a very turbulent epoch.

Rabbi Avraham Shemuel Binyamin Sofer, the Ktav Sofer.

SELECTIONS FROM THE KTAV SOFER'S COMMENTARY

Jacob said to his father, "It is I, Esau your firstborn. I have done as you have told me. Rise, if you please, sit up, and eat my game, so that your soul may bless me."

(Genesis 27:19)

The Ktav Sofer: *It is I, Esau your firstborn. I have done as you have told me*—Our Father Jacob certainly did not lie to his father. Yet he did say, *"It is I, Esau your firstborn."* How can this be reconciled? Let us

take a closer look at the name Esau. **Rashi** explains that the name Esau stems from the root *asah*, "to make," "to complete." When Esau was born, everyone called him Esau for they saw that he was born "complete," fully developed, covered with hair. Just as a young goat is born endowed with all the qualities and capabilities of a mature goat, so, too, at Esau's birth he already had reached his final stage of development.

Jacob, on the other hand, would not reach his destiny until he climbed the ladder of Torah and *mitzvot*, culminating in the attainment of spiritual perfection. Upon reaching that stage, he too could rightfully claim

ספר

כתב סופר

על

חמשה חומשי תורה

חברו

גאון ישׂ־אל וקדושו רכבו ופרשו רב רבנים ומבחר הדרשנים רב
פעלים מקבציאל ספרא דישראל בוצינא קדישא רשכבה״ג
כקש״ת מהו״ר אברהם שמואל בנימין סופר זצוק״ל
אב״ד ור״מ בק״ק פרעסבורג יע״א
בעל שו״ת כתב סופר
ממלא מקום אביו רבינו הקדוש בעל התם סופר זצ״קל
משנת ואביטה נפלאות עד גל עיני ואביטה נפלאות.

חלק ראשון

ספר בראשית שמות

Title page of *Ktav Sofer,* commentary on the Torah. The letters appearing after the author's name are an abbreviation of *Zeicher tzaddik vekadosh liverachah,* "May the memory of this righteous and saintly man be a blessing." It is an acronym appended to the names of all departed great rabbis.

to be called "Esau," a complete and accomplished man. Jacob thus spoke the truth when he said "*It is I, Esau,*" meaning "I have achieved perfection." "*I have done as you have told me*"—Jacob implied that by obeying Isaac's will in observing God's laws, he had attained spiritual perfection, becoming, in effect, Esau, "an accomplished man."

But now our soul is dried up, with nothing but the manna to look at.

(Numbers 11:6)

The Ktav Sofer: *But now our soul is dried up, with nothing but the manna to look at*—They complained not about the manna, but rather about the fact that they were being sustained in a miraculous way.

Our sages tell us that a miraculous intervention in a person's life comes at the expense of his merits. The miracle of the daily descent of the manna from heaven would thus diminish their merits for the World to Come; it would reduce their future enjoyment of the spiritual good of eternal life. Accordingly, when they said, "*Our soul is dried up,*" they meant, "We will lose the delight of the soul (in the World to Come) because we are being nourished in a supernatural, miraculous way, by the manna."

On the east bank of the Jordan, in the land of Moab, Moses began to explain this law, saying . . .

(Deuteronomy 1:5)

The Ktav Sofer: *Moses began to explain this law*—Rashi comments on this passage that Moses explained the Torah in the seventy major languages of the world. What is the significance of Moses' explaining the Torah in seventy languages, and why did this take place at this particular moment, before Israel's entrance into the Land? Moses wanted to repudiate the erroneous idea that the Torah laws were designed only for life in the Land of Israel, where the Jewish people live in a homogeneous and isolated community, but that these laws have no validity for Jews living among the gentile nations; decry the fallacy that these Jews must assimilate and adopt the life-style of the surrounding culture. By explaining the Torah in the seventy languages of the world, Moshe conveyed a message contradicting this argument. He implied that, quite to the contrary, the Torah laws are universally binding, not limited by either time or space. They are to be observed regardless of the location or point in history a Jew may find himself.[3]

When God expands your borders as He has promised, and you will say, "I wish to eat meat," because your soul desires to eat meat, you may eat meat as much as your soul desires.

(Deuteronomy 12:20)

The Ktav Sofer: *And you will say, "I wish to eat meat," because your soul desires to eat meat, you may eat as much as your soul desires*—At first glance, the wording of this verse appears redundant. It is quite obvious that if you say, "*I wish to eat meat*," you are motivated by a desire to eat meat. Also, the phrase *as much as your soul desires* seems superfluous.

Closer inspection reveals a deeper meaning of the text. Although the Torah sanctions the consumption of meat, we should eat only such quantities as are required to maintain our health and physical well-being. Each individual must judge his own particular needs. There are people, however, who eat inordinate amounts of meat, not for their health, but in order to satisfy their uncontrollable cravings. They overindulge to the point of damaging their health.

The wording of our verse delicately suggests the proper approach to eating meat: *You will say, "I wish to eat meat," because your soul desires to eat meat.* In other words, if your *soul*, i.e., your intellect, is the source of your appetite, if it is in control and it tells you that meat is good for you in limited quantities, then, *you may eat as much as your soul desires*, but not the huge quantities needed to satisfy your gluttonous bodily appetites.

When you lay siege to a city and wage war against it a long time to capture it, you must not destroy its trees wielding an ax against them, for you may eat of them, but you shall not cut them down; for is the tree of the field man, that it should be besieged by you?

(*Deuteronomy 20:19*)

The Ktav Sofer: *When you lay siege against a city and wage war against it a long time to capture it, you must not destroy its trees*—Figuratively, this passage can be applied to the inner conflict that rages between man's spirit and his *yetzer hara*, his carnal instincts.

Seen in that light, we can interpret the verse as follows: *When you lay siege to a city*—when your spirit engages your physical nature in war. *A long time*—a battle that continues throughout life. *You must not destroy its trees*—do not completely eradicate your physical desires; do not weaken your body by excessive fasting, mortification, and ascetic self-denial. Man is meant to eat and drink in order to serve God better. *For you may eat of them*—and when you enjoy good health you will be able to enjoy the fruits of your mitzvot in this world, while their principal remains intact for you in the World to Come.

RABBI NAFTALI TZVI YEHUDAH BERLIN— THE NETZIV
רבי נפתלי צבי יהודה ברלין—נצי"ב

born: Mir, Poland, 1817
died: Warsaw, Poland, 1893
Popularly known as the Netziv (the initials of his name). Commentator, talmudist, rosh yeshivah.

In 1831 the Netziv married the daughter of Rabbi Yitzchak, son of **Rabbi Chaim of Volozhin**, the founder of the yeshivah of Volozhin. In 1854 he became the *rosh yeshivah* (dean) of that renowned institution. With his preeminence in Torah learning and unparalleled dedication to his students, he transformed the yeshivah into the spiritual center of Russian Jewry. For forty years he headed the yeshivah and introduced a new approach to the study of Talmud that stressed the analysis of the plain meaning in all its ramifications. He attracted over 400 students from far and wide, all outstanding talmudists in their own right, all admiring him for his fatherly love. He firmly opposed the modernization of the yeshivah and the introduction of secular studies demanded by the maskilim (secularists). This ultimately led to the closing of the yeshivah by the Russian government in 1892. The Netziv and his family were exiled. He moved to Minsk and later to Warsaw.

His most popular work is his commentary on the Torah, *Ha'ameik Davar*.[1] His aim is to demonstrate that talmudic exegesis is reflected in the Written Torah in its plain meaning, the *peshat*.

He took a lively interest in the general community and its needs, writing many responsa to questions dealing with all phases of Jewish life, which were collected in his work *Meshiv Davar*.[2]

SELECTIONS FROM THE NETZIV'S COMMENTARY

Not a thread nor a shoelace! I will not take anything that is yours. You should not be able to say, "It was I who made Avram rich."

(*Genesis 4:23*)

Rabbi Naftali Tzvi Yehudah Berlin.

The Netziv: *Not a thread nor a shoelace*—Our sages tell us (*Chullin* 89) that as a reward for saying *not a thread nor a shoelace*, Abraham's descendants merited two mitzvot: the thread of *techelet*[3] of the tzitzit and the straps (laces) of the tefillin. This statement needs clarification. What spiritual concept is implied by the expression *thread and shoelace* to warrant a reward of two great mitzvot? Could it be that Abraham refused to accept any of the spoils of war? Then our sages should have said, "As a reward for saying *I will not take anything that is yours*, his descendants merited two mitzvot. Indeed, the reward *is* for the words *thread* and *shoelace*, for they imply Abraham's greatest achievements, that of sewing together mankind (*Bereishit Rabbah* 39), and that of "mending the tear" that had developed between God and man.

Before Adam's sin, heaven and earth were united. The Shechinah (Divine Presence) dwelled in the higher as well as in the lower spheres. After the sin, the Shechinah withdrew, causing heaven and earth to be

42

שמות כד משפטים   218

הַשָּׁמַיִם לָטֹהַר : יא וְאֶל־אֲצִילֵי בְּנֵי־יִשְׂרָאֵל לֹא
שָׁלַח יָדוֹ וַיֶּחֱזוּ אֶת־הָאֱלֹהִים וַיֹּאכְלוּ וַיִּשְׁתּוּ :
ס יב וַיֹּאמֶר יְהוָה אֶל־מֹשֶׁה עֲלֵה אֵלַי הָהָרָה
וֶהְיֵה־שָׁם וְאֶתְּנָה לְךָ אֶת־לֻחֹת הָאֶבֶן וְהַתּוֹרָה
וְהַמִּצְוָה אֲשֶׁר כָּתַבְתִּי לְהוֹרֹתָם : יג וַיָּקָם מֹשֶׁה
וִיהוֹשֻׁעַ מְשָׁרְתוֹ וַיַּעַל מֹשֶׁה אֶל־הַר הָאֱלֹהִים :
יד וְאֶל־הַזְּקֵנִים אָמַר שְׁבוּ־לָנוּ בָזֶה עַד אֲשֶׁר־נָשׁוּב
אֲלֵיכֶם וְהִנֵּה אַהֲרֹן וְחוּר עִמָּכֶם מִי־בַעַל דְּבָרִים

[Rashi and Ha'ameik Davar commentary blocks in Rashi script appear below the Torah text.]

Text of *Ha'ameik Davar*, "Penetrating the Word," the Netziv's commentary to the Torah, in which he demonstrates that talmudic exegesis is reflected in the written Torah. From the original standard edition.

torn apart. This condition prevailed until Abraham arrived on the scene and reunited heaven and earth, mending the tear, healing the rift, restoring all mankind.

This nation is too powerful for us, so if you would, come and curse this nation for me. Then we may be able to defeat them and drive them from the land. I know that whomever you bless is blessed, and whomever you curse is cursed.

(Numbers 22:6)

The Netziv: *I know that whomever you bless is blessed*—Balaam was a soothsayer who in reality had no power to confer blessings. Being versed in the science of astrology and the occult, he blessed only those persons whose horoscope he knew to hold auspicious portents. When the good omen eventually would be fulfilled, he would attribute the good fortune to his blessing and demand an enormous reward. Balak was well aware of this practice. He so indicates in his message, ". . . for I know that whomever you bless, *mevorach*, was already blessed previously" (was born under a propitious star).

He then declared his parable and said, "Alas! Who can survive God's devastation!"

(Numbers 24:23)

The Netziv: *Alas! Who can survive God's devastation!*—World history records countless wars, many of them wars of conquest, fought for territorial gain. At war's end the victorious side is itself content with slaying or imprisoning the defeated political leaders, while the general population is left unharmed.

In sharp contrast to this stand the wars that are fought for religious or ideological reasons. In the name of religion, every person who did not bow down to the conqueror's deity, every infidel or heretic, was put to death. Those subjects whose racial features did not conform to the victor's standards were exterminated. Genocide is the hallmark of religious and ideological warfare.

When Balaam saw a prophetic vision of the total destruction unleashed by the murderous forces of "religious" wars, he exclaimed, "*Alas! Who can survive the havoc wreaked for the glory of God.*"

You shall take the first of every fruit of the earth produced by the land that the Lord your God is giving you. You must place it in a basket and go to the site that God will choose for His Name to dwell in.

(Deuteronomy 26:1)

The Netziv: *The first of every fruit of the earth produced by the land*[4]—What is the significance of the apparent redundancy in this phrase? Would not *the first of every fruit of the land* or *the first produce of the land* have been sufficient? The word *reishis*, first, actually has two meanings: (1) it denotes *the best quality*,[5] and (2) it signifies *beginning*, preceding all others. In the present verse both meanings coincide. *The first of every fruit of the earth* implies the requirement that only fruit of prime quality be offered as bikkurim (first fruits); *the first . . . produced by the land* indicates that those fruits that were harvested first are the ones to be offered.

RABBI MEIR SIMCHAH HAKOHEN—MESHECH CHOCHMAH, OR SAME'ACH
רבי מאיר שמחה הכהן—משך חכמה, אור שמח

born: near Vilna, Lithuania, 1843
died: Dvinsk, Russia, 1926
Popularly known by the titles of his works, Meshech Chochmah and *Or Same'ach. Talmudist, halachist, and Torah commentator.*

In 1888 Rabbi Meir Simchah Hakohen, or Reb Meir Simchah, as he was affectionately known, was elected to succeed Rabbi Reuven Dinaburg as rabbi of Dvinsk, a post he held until his death in 1926. A charismatic leader of prodigious Torah greatness, he was loved and respected for his kindness and exceptional character. He is the author of *Or Same'ach,* a commentary on *Mishneh Torah* by **Rambam**, and *Meshech Chochmah*, a commentary on the Torah.[1] His works are classics, studied and quoted daily in the yeshivah and the home.

ספר
משך חכמה
באורים ופרושים, רעיונים ודרושים, הערות וחדושים
על
חמשה חומשי תורה
חובר ברצון אבינו שבשמים
מאתי
מאיר שמחה כהן מדווינסק
בעהמ"ח ספר אור שמח על כל חלקי הרמב"ם ז"ל
שנלב"ע ביום ש"ק ד' אלול תרפ"ו תנצב"ה
הובא לדפוס ויצא לאור בהשגחת מרן ר' מנחם מענדל דובער ז"ק שליט"א
הגאב"ד דק"ק ריגא יצ"ו, שנת תרפ"ז לפ"ק.
הוצאת ספרים אשכול
בעיה"ק ירושלים תובב"א

Title page of *Meshech Chochmah,* commentary on the Torah by Rabbi Meir Simchah Hakohen, offering illuminating insights. The title *Meshech Chochmah* is taken from Job 28:18, "The price of wisdom." The word *meshech* is also an acronym of Meir Simchah Kohen.

SELECTIONS FROM MESHECH CHOCHMAH'S COMMENTARY

In the course of time, Cain brought some of his crops as an offering to God. Abel also offered some of the firstborn of his flock, from their fats. God paid heed to Abel and his offering, but to Cain and his offering He paid no heed. Cain became very furious and depressed.
(Genesis 4:3–5)

Meshech Chochmah: *But to Cain and his offering he paid no heed*—Why did God reject Cain's offering while accepting Abel's? The rational explanation is that God desires only an offering that was produced by means of human effort and exertion. In the case of an animal sacrifice, man has invested a great deal of labor in raising the animal. It is for this reason that the Torah forbids an animal to be offered before it is eight days old (Leviticus 22:27). Such an animal was formed by

nature. Man, as yet, has contributed nothing to its existence. The Torah requires a minimum of eight days of human care and nurturing before the animal may be offered on the altar. Analogously, when agricultural products are offered, produce in its natural state, unimproved by human labor, may not be brought on the altar. Thus, grain is not acceptable for a meal offering (*minchah*). Only fine wheat flour or cracked grain may be offered, because its production entails human labor. Also, grapes and olives, fruits as nature produced them, are unsuitable as offerings. Only in the form of wine and oil may they be offered on the altar, for these are the end result of human exertion invested in the processing of grapes and olives. Cain brought *some of his crops* as an offering, in their natural, unimproved state. He had contributed neither care nor labor to their production. Cain did not give anything of himself to God. Therefore, *God paid no heed to Cain and his offering.* Abel, who offered *some of the firstborn of his flock,* had worked hard tending and raising them. *God paid heed to Abel and his offering.*

I will go to Egypt with you, and I will also bring you back again. Joseph will place his hands on your eyes.[2]

(Genesis 46:4)

Meshech Chochmah: *Joseph will place his hands on your eyes*—Homiletically, this phrase can be interpreted as an exhortation to Jacob not to question the Divine command to leave the Land of Israel. Looking from a rational perspective, Jacob could have grounds for doubting the wisdom and purpose of having to go to Egypt and to be brought back again, of leaving the land of his destiny. In this verse God is telling Jacob, "Joseph will place his hands on your eyes," meaning that the amazing story of Joseph's life should teach you to tightly shut your "shortsighted eyes," the eyes that view events from the outlook of logic and reason. Joseph's life should impress upon your mind not to attempt to fathom God's ways, not to judge them with the limited yardstick of the human intellect. Would anyone have believed that Joseph's suffering would culminate in his position of royalty, which enabled him to rescue your entire family and all of Egypt? God's purposes are beyond human understanding; the story of Joseph is the prime example for this.

Do not do unrighteousness in judgment, in measurements of length, weight, or volume.

(Leviticus 19:35)

Meshech Chochmah: Literally translated, this passage reads, *Do not do wrong through justice.* How can you do wrong by acting justly? The verse is to be understood as addressing the following case: If you have a customer who stole from you and refuses to make restitution, or one who owes you money and does not pay his debt, then you may be inclined to obtain that which is rightfully yours by giving him short weight or by falsifying measurements the next time he comes to buy at your store. Don't do that. The Torah decrees, *Do not do wrong through justice . . . in weight*—even though your act constitutes "justice," even though the money you are obtaining in this manner is lawfully yours. Don't use fraudulent means in order to achieve just ends.

Why did you take us out of Egypt and bring us to this terrible place? It is an area where there are no plants, figs, grapes, or pomegranates. There is not even any water to drink.[3]

(Numbers 20:5)

Meshech Chochmah: *There are no plants, figs, grapes, or pomegranates*—Why didn't they also complain of lacking olives and honey-dates?[4] They had no craving for these fruits because they tasted these flavors in their daily portion of the manna. Indeed, the Torah explicitly describes these as the flavors of the manna. *It tasted like a honey wafer* (Exodus 15:31), i.e., dates. *It tasted like an oil wafer* (Numbers 11:8) i.e., olives.

Then you will begin to seek God your Lord, and if you pursue Him with all your heart and soul, you will eventually find Him.

(Deuteronomy 4:29)

Meshech Chochmah: *You will begin to seek . . . you will . . . find Him*—This verse presents a strange dichotomy, in that *uvikashtem—you will begin to seek*—is written in the plural form, whereas *umatzata—you will eventually find Him*—is in the singular. This inconsistency can be explained if we consider that, collectively, the Jewish people may be viewed as one all-encompassing persona, each individual Jew representing one of this persona's organs. This analogy is applicable only if all Jews are united in purpose, all aspiring to the same goal: that of serving the Eternal, living God. For then they are like the radii of a circle, all extending from the same center, all interconnected through that center, the source of their existence—God. At a time when the Jewish people will have abandoned the Torah, as foretold in verse 25 of this chapter, their common allegiance to God is dissolved. As a result, they become separated from one another and lose their sense of unity. Accordingly, in our verse, *uvikashtem*—*you will begin to seek*—is written in the plural, for *many* individuals, all separated from God and from each other, will begin to seek. But *umatzata*—*you will find Him*—is in the singular, for in finding God, they have reestablished their bond with Him and are reunited with their fellow Jews in one indivisible entity.

RABBI YAAKOV KAMENETZKY
הרב יעקב קמנצקי

born: *Kalushkove, Russia, 1890*
died: *Monsey, New York, 1986*
Affectionately known as Reb Yaakov. Talmudist, commentator, rosh yeshivah.

At a young age Reb Yaakov moved to Minsk to study under Rabbi Zimbalist. At age 15 he entered the yeshivah of Slobodka, where he studied for the next 21 years, becoming especially close to **Rabbi Nosson Tzvi Finkel**, the spiritual leader and adviser of that yeshivah. From 1926 to 1937 he served as rabbi in Tzitovyan, near Kelm. In 1937 he arrived in America, where he accepted rabbinical posts in Seattle and Toronto, devoting his considerable energies to raising the standards of Torah learning. His Torah commentary, *Iyunim BaMikra,*[1] attests to his clarity of thought and his mastery of Talmud, the Codes, and their commentaries, which he quoted by heart without error. Many of his comments concern difficulties in grammar and cantillation signs (*neginot*), and he offers highly original insights into the plain meaning of the text. From 1948 to 1968 he led the great yeshivah, Torah Vodaath, in Brooklyn. As a true leader of the Jewish people, he was involved in worldwide activities on behalf of promoting the Torah way of life. Much beloved for the warmth of his personality and his selfless devotion to Torah, he left an indelible imprint on Jewish life in America and throughout the world.

Rabbi Yaakov Kamenetzky.

SELECTIONS FROM RABBI KAMENETZKY'S COMMENTARY

Sarah's life was one hundred and twenty-seven years. These were the years of Sarah's life.
(Genesis 23:1)

Rabbi Yaakov Kamenetzky: *These were the years of Sarah's life*—The phrase appears to be superfluous. To

understand the message contained in these words, let us turn to **Rashi's** comment on Genesis 23:2, where he states that Sarah died of shock when she received the report of Isaac's *akeidah* (the binding; offering of Isaac). We can well imagine that people, attributing her

בעזרת השי"ת

אמת ליעקב

ספר

עיונים במקרא

על התורה

ביאורים ופירושים על פרשיות התורה

נאספו ונערכו לדפוס מתוך כתבי

מרן הגאון הרב יעקב קמנצקי זצוק"ל

מהדורה שניה מורחבת ומתוקנת

עם הרבה הוספות

יצא לאור על ידי בני הגאון המחבר זצוק"ל

נוא יורק תשמ"ו

Title page of *Emet LeYaakov, Iyunim BaMikra,* insights on the weekly portions of the Torah by Rabbi Yaakov Kamenetzky.

death to the *akeidah*, may have said that, were it not for the *akeidah*, Sarah would have lived many years more. Such reasoning leads to grave desecration of God's name, a denial of Divine Justice. It is to counter this argument that the Torah emphasizes *These are the years of Sarah,* meaning that she actually was destined to live this many years. The 127 years were allotted to her at birth. The fatal shock she experienced was only the immediate cause of her death, but did not shorten her life by even one day.

And you must salt every meal offering. Do not leave out the salt of God's covenant from your meal offering. You must also offer salt with all your animal offerings.

(Leviticus 2:13)

Rabbi Yaakov Kamenetzky: *The salt of God's covenant*—Rashi explains that on the second day of Creation, when God divided the waters in order to create the firmament, the water below refused to be separated. It only complied with God's will after being assured by a solemn covenant that it would be offered on the altar in the form of salt, a component of water. It seems strange that the covenant was made with regard to salt and not regarding water itself. After all, with each sacrifice a water libation was also offered. God's covenant regarding the salt was made in order to placate the waters below, as a demonstration that the waters above were not valued more than those below. This idea is palpable in salt. Salt is the residue that remains from the evaporation of sea water. In that process the water vapors rise while the salt sediment remains. By His choice of salt, God indicated His preference for the lowest level of material substance, since even of the waters below He selected the most solid element, the salt. There is a fundamental principle inherent in this. God does not seek spirituality per se in this world. His design for Creation is to bring about the transformation of the lowest elements and cause their elevation to the spiritual, thereby fulfilling their destiny.

The children of Israel shall camp with each person near the banner having his father's family's insignia. They shall camp at a specified distance around the Communion Tent.

(Numbers 2:2)

Rabbi Yaakov Kamenetzky: *The children of Israel shall camp with each person near the banner having his father's family's insignia*—This chapter relates the organization of the camp of Israel into a prescribed formation, grouped according to tribal association. According to Numbers 1:1, the command for this arrangement was given in the second year of the Exodus. The order in which a huge assemblage is traveling is certainly a matter of overriding importance. One may wonder why God did not ordain this plan immediately after Israel's departure from Egypt? Why only in the second year? The answer becomes clear when we realize that structuring a society along tribal groupings brings in its wake division and rivalry. Each tribe tends to promote its own narrow interests, pursues its own ambitions. Instead of national unity, a spirit of factionalism, divisiveness, and intolerance is fostered. The camp of the tribes of Israel had one distinctive feature. Their dwellings, although separated according to tribal affiliation, were all situated around the Mishkan, the Communion Tent. The Mishkan formed the transcending focal point of the nation, uniting the disparate tribes in belief and purpose, precluding any discord between the tribes. Now, according to Exodus 40:17, the Mishkan was erected on the first day of the month of Nissan of the *second* year of the Exodus. The command concerning the order of the camp could only be given after this date.

(The law is) that the man must bring his wife to the priest. When he brings her he must also bring a sacrifice for her consisting of one tenth ephah *of barley meal. He shall not pour oil on it, since it is a jealousy offering. It is a reminder offering to recall sin.*

(Numbers 5:15)

Rabbi Yaakov Kamenetzky: *(The law is) that the man must bring his wife to the priest*—The proceedings described in this chapter are designed to fill a psychological need. Human nature is such that once a husband is obsessed with jealousy and suspicion toward his wife, no force on earth can allay these emotions. According to Torah law, the truth of any claim is established on the testimony of two witnesses. Still, such testimony would not satisfy a jealous husband. Not even a prophet declaring his wife innocent of immoral conduct can quell his misgivings. His doubts can be removed only by one incontrovertible fact—an act of God. Thus, the Torah ordained that God's name be dissolved in the water that the *sotah*, the suspected adulteress, is then made to drink. If she was guilty, "her thigh would rupture, her belly would blow up," and the woman would die. If she remained unharmed, it is as though God Himself attests to her innocence. Clearly, the entire procedure is not a punishment for any wrongdoing. Rather it is designed to ensure that the innocent wife will be fully accepted as pure in her husband's eyes. Then domestic peace will be restored. Our Rabbis summed up this thought (*Chullin* 141a): "The Torah regards the establishment of peace between husband and wife to be of such overriding importance that it mandates that the Name of God that was written in holiness be erased in the water."

II

MISHNAH, TALMUD, AND MIDRASH

The Torah is the soul of the Jewish nation; it is the breath of our life, the blood pulsing through our veins. Its fundamental teachings, firmly anchored in the Written Law, called Torah *shebiktav*, were given to Moshe on Mount Sinai. The rules of interpretation and broader application of these laws were also given by God to Moshe, to be transmitted orally from master to disciple, generation after generation. The Oral Law is called Torah *shebe'al peh*.

The oral transmission continued until the growing might of the Roman Empire, and the resultant tribulations and dispersion of Israel, threatened the survival of the unbroken chain of tradition. Rabbi Yehudah Ha-Nasi, Our Holy Rabbi, yielding to necessity, compiled and wrote down the Oral Law in the book known as the Mishnah. The teachers of the Mishnah are called *Tanna'im*. Its concise form still requires a great deal of exposition and commentary. The teachings and discussions of the Mishnah form the structure on which the Gemara is built. Here the Mishnah is analyzed in minute detail. The teachers of the Gemara, known as the *Amora'im*, search for scriptural sources of the laws and their legal ramifications, and they seek to determine how the laws apply in a variety of situations and cases. Together, the Mishnah and Gemara form the Talmud.

The sages recorded the latent meaning of Torah and Talmud in the books of the Midrash, which concealed profound ethical, philosophical, and mystical truths under a veil of allegorical interpretations and parables.

Although the Oral Law has been written down, it has retained its character of oral tradition, for it is still impossible to fathom the Talmud without the guidance of a teacher who gently and patiently transmits the teachings contained in its pages. Each rabbi and teacher is fulfilling the sacred task of disseminating Torah and keeping alive the flame that was kindled at Sinai. Studying Gemara, we are privileged to listen in on the debates of the *Tanna'im* and *Amora'im*; filled with awe we follow the reasoning of these men of incomparable spiritual greatness and saintliness. No mere words can adequately describe the sublime grandeur of their personalities. The light of their teachings has been a shining beacon during our two thousand years of exile; and today, with renewed vigor, the sound of Gemara reverberates in the voices of tens of thousands of students in yeshivot, *kollelim*, and houses of learning from Jerusalem to Moscow, from New York to Australia.

MISHNAH

The Mishnah is the Oral Law, the explanation of the Written Torah. Both the Written and the Oral Law were given by God to Moses at Mount Sinai in the year 2448 from Creation (1313 B.C.E.). The vast body of the Oral Law was transmitted from teacher to pupil, from generation to generation, as described by **Rambam** in his Introduction to the Mishnah, in an unbroken chain reaching from Moses to Rav Ashi, who "sealed" the Talmud.

The Oral Law had to be transmitted by word of mouth; it was not to be committed to writing. Its sages go by the title of *Tanna* (pl. *Tanna'im*)—Teacher of the Mishnah. However, following the destruction of the Second Temple and the ensuing dispersal of the Jewish people, Rabbi Yehudah HaNasi decided to write down the Mishnah. It was the only way to ensure that Torah and the Jewish nation could survive.

He divided the Mishnah into six orders, which are subdivided into tractates. The Mishnah became the basis for the development of the Gemara, which explains and discusses the subject matter contained in the Mishnah. Thus, the Mishnah and the Gemara are essentially one work—the Talmud—the sine qua non of Judaism.

Indeed, by compiling the Mishnah, Rabbi Yehudah HaNasi saved the Jewish nation at the most critical juncture in its history, ensuring its spiritual survival for all time.

SHISHAH SIDRE MISHNAH— THE SIX ORDERS OF THE MISHNAH
ששה סדרי משנה

1. **זרעים**
   Zera'im—Seeds. Deals with the laws relating to the cultivation of the soil, prefaced by Tractate *Berachot,* which deals with the laws relating to blessings.

2. **מועד**
   Mo'ed—Festivals, seasons. Deals with the laws of Shabbat, Festivals, and Fasts.

3. **נשים**
   Nashim—Women. Deals with the laws regarding family life, marriage, and divorce.

4. **נזיקין**
   Nezikin—Damages. Deals with civil and criminal law and the Sanhedrin.

5. **קדשים**
   Kodashim—Sacred Things. Deals with the laws of the Temple service, sacrifices, dietary laws.

6. **טהרות**
   Taharot—Purity. Deals with laws of ritual cleanness and defilement.

RABBI YEHUDAH HANASI—RABBEINU HAKADOSH, RABBI
רבי יהודה הנשא—רבינו הקדוש, רבי

born:Eretz Yisrael, c. 135 C.E.
died: Eretz Yisrael, c. 200 C.E.
Respectfully referred to as Rabbeinu HaKadosh (our holy Rabbi), or simply as Rabbi. Nasi, *head of the Sanhedrin, compiler of the Mishnah*, Tanna.

Rabbi Yehudah HaNasi was the son of Rabbi Shimon ben Gamliel, whom he succeeded as *nasi* (head of the Sanhedrin). He was a friend of the Roman emperor Marcus Aurelius Antonius, who greatly respected the ideals of Torah and its sages. A brilliant scholar and statesman, Rabbi Yehudah HaNasi established an excellent relationship between the Romans and the Jewish people. He was held in high esteem and was warmly loved by the entire Jewish nation. The Talmud testifies, "From Moses until Rabbi Yehudah HaNasi we do not find Torah and majesty combined in one person" (*Sanhedrin* 36a). The single achievement that earned him the undying gratitude of the Jewish people is his compilation of the Mishnah.[1] (*For excerpts, see pp. 57–60.*)

ר"ע מברטנורה מגילה נקראת פרק א מגילה תוספות יום טוב עט ציונים

למחר. יחל להיות אחר השבת כפרים מקדימין ליום הכניסה. ועיירות גדולות קורין בו ביום. ומוקפות חומה למחר: ג איזו היא עיר גדולה כל שיש בה עשרה בטלנים. פחות מכאן הרי זה כפר. באלו אמרו מקדימין ולא מאחרין. אבל זמן עצי כהנים. ותשעה באב. חגיגה.

שנויי נוסחאות

ראשון לציון

תוספת רעק"א

יכין תפארת ישראל בועז

אור גדול

Page of Mishnah *Megillah* 4:2. On the right of the main text is the commentary of Rabbi Ovadiah of Bartenura; to the left, the commentary Tosefot Yomtov; and on the lower part of the page, the commentary Tiferet Yisrael by Rabbi Yisrael Lipschitz, comprising the sections *Yachin* and *Boaz*. The Mishnah was compiled by Rabbi Yehudah HaNasi. This is from the comprehensive edition named *Tiferet Yisrael, Yachin uBoaz*.

RABBI OVADIAH YAREI OF BARTENURA—RAV
רבי עובדיה ירא מברטנורא—רע״ב

born: Bartinura, Italy, c. 1445–1450
died: Jerusalem, Israel, c. 1500–1510
Popularly known as Rav or Bartenura. Talmudist, commentator on the Mishnah.

Little is known of Rav's early life in Italy. In 1485 he set out for Eretz Yisrael. His journey, which took three years, was interrupted by extended sojourns in Naples, Salerno, and Palermo, where he taught Torah. After further delays in Messina and Egypt, he arrived in Jerusalem. Immediately upon arriving he took the initiative at improving the spiritual life of the Jewish community, which had sunk to a low ebb. After initial failures he succeeded in establishing an important Torah center in the Holy City.

Although little is known of his life, he has gained immortality through his writings, the most important of which is his commentary on the Mishnah. Since the Mishnah is an extremely compact distillation of the massive body of the Oral Law, its meaning is unfathomable without a commentary. In clear and concise language, Rav offers a phrase-by-phrase explanation of the Mishnah, giving the student the gist of the dialogue in the Gemara and the commentaries of **Rashi** and **Rambam.** This makes Rav an indispensable aid in understanding the Mishnah, and as such, his commentary has become an integral part of virtually all Mishnah editions.[1] (*For excerpts, see pp. 57–60.*)

Running commentary to the Mishnah by Rabbi Ovadiah Yarei of Bartenura, Rav. From edition *Tiferet Yisrael, Yachin uBoaz.*

RABBI YOMTOV LIPMANN HELLER—TOSEFOT YOMTOV

רבי יום טוב ליפמן הלר—תוספות י״ט

born: Wallerstein, Bavaria, Germany, 1579
died: Cracow, Poland, 1654
Popularly known as Tosefot Yomtov after the title of his work. Halachist, talmudist.

At the tender age of 18 Yomtov Lipmann Heller was appointed dayan (ecclesiastical judge) in Prague, where he studied under **Rabbi Yehudah Loew,** the famous **Maharal,** and **Rabbi Shlomoh Efraim of Luntchitz.** In 1625 he was chosen to be rabbi of Nikolsburg, and later that year to be rabbi of Vienna. In 1627 he returned to Prague to officiate as its rabbi and *rosh yeshivah*. In the wake of false accusations by his enemies, who denounced him for being disloyal to King Ferdinand II, he was imprisoned and subsequently condemned to death. Upon payment of a huge ransom, his sentence was commuted by the king, provided he leave Prague. He served as rabbi of Nemirov and Ludmir, and in 1644 he was elected to the rabbinate of the prominent community of Cracow, where he also led the yeshivah.

Of the many works he wrote, best known is his commentary on the Mishnah, *Tosefot Yomtov*.[1] It has been incorporated into virtually all editions of the Mishnah, where it appears alongside the basic text. His commentary probes deeply into the opinions of early authorities, such as **Rambam, Ran,** and **Rosh,** and later authorities such as **Bet Yosef** and **Rema,** and others, striving to reconcile contradictions with thoughtful analysis. Among his other works are: *Tuv Taam*, a commentary on **Rabbeinu Bachya,** *Ma'adanei Melech* and *Lechem Chamudot*, commentaries on **Rosh,** and *Megillat Eivah*, an autobiographical work,[2] in which he recounts the tempestuous and tormented story of his life. (*For excerpts, see pp. 57, 59.*)

ר׳ עובדיה מברטנורא   תרומות האשה פרק ח   תוספות יום טוב   לד

Tosefot Yomtov, commentary on the Mishnah by Rabbi Yomtov Lipmann Heller. From edition *Tiferet Yisrael, Yachin uBoaz*.

RABBI YISRAEL LIPSCHITZ—TIFERET YISRAEL
רבי ישראל ליפשיץ

born: location—? date—1782
died: Danzig, Germany, 1860
Known as Tiferet Yisrael—Splendor of Israel—the title
of his work. Talmudist, rabbi.

One of the outstanding rabbis of his generation, Rabbi Yisrael received his early training under his father, Rabbi Gedaliah Lipschitz, rabbi of Hasdeutsch. Rabbi Yisrael served as rabbi in Dessau, Schottland, Weinberg, Lagenfurth, and Danzig, distinguishing himself for his great scholarship, piety, kindheartedness, and benevolence. His magnum opus is *Tiferet Yisrael*—Splendor of Israel—a magnificent commentary on the Mishnah, in which he clarifies all obscure passages in simple, easy-to-understand language. It is composed of two sections: *"Yachin,"* a translation or brief definition of difficult concepts, and *"Boaz,"* a comprehensive analysis of the entire theme. *Tiferet Yisrael* became an instant favorite with the learning public. It has been reprinted many times.

Rabbi Yisrael Lipschitz, Tiferet Yisrael.

SELECTIONS FROM RABBI LIPSCHITZ'S COMMENTARY ON THE MISHNAH

Rabbi Nechuniah ben Hakaneh used to say a prayer as he entered the Bet Hamidrash *(House of Learning) and as he left it—a short prayer. They said to him: What sort of prayer is this? He replied: When I enter I pray that no one shall stumble through me, and when I leave I express thanks for my lot.*

(Mishnah, Berachot 4:2)

Rav: *That no one shall stumble through me*—That I will not render an incorrect halachic decision. My colleagues would then gloat over my error, so that I would be the cause of their punishment.

Tosefot Yomtov: [commenting on Rav's interpretation]—But rendering a wrong decision is in itself no stumbling block to anyone. His colleagues, who are the majority, would outvote him, and the Halachah is always decided according to the majority. The correct Halachah would emerge and no one would be led astray.

Rav and Tiferet Yisrael: *I express thanks for my lot*—that God has set my portion with those who sit in the *Bet Hamidrash* (House of Learning).

We may expound neither on the subject of illicit relationships to a group of three, nor on the account of Creation to a group of two, nor on the account of the Merkavah *to one individual unless*

Tiferet Yisrael, a running commentary on the Mishnah. The shaded section is *Yachin*, giving translations and definitions of difficult terms. The *Boaz* section offers an analysis of the entire topic. From the standard comprehensive edition.

he is wise and understanding through his own knowledge. Whoever speculates on four subjects, it would be better for him had he not come into the world: What is above, what is below, what was before, and what will be after. Similarly, whoever has no regard for the honor of his Maker, it would be better for him if he had not come into the world.

(Mishnah, Chagigah 2:1)

Rav and Tiferet Yisrael: *We may expound neither on the subject of illicit relationships to a group of three*—A teacher may not expound on this subject in the presence of three or more students. Were he to do so, we fear that he would become involved in a discussion with one of the students while the other students talk among themselves. The inattentive students may misunderstand or fail to hear some of the laws expounded by their teacher, with the result that they may permit the forbidden. The danger that students will become engrossed in private discussion to the point of inattentiveness exists particularly regarding this subject, for it involves a matter in which people have powerful urges.

Rav: *Nor on the account of the Creation*—That is, on the subject of what occurred during the Six Days of Creation.

Tiferet Yisrael: This refers to Kabbalah that teaches how our physical world gradually evolved from the realm of the purely spiritual.

Rav: *Nor on the account of the Merkavah* [i.e., the mystical account of the heavenly worlds as it is related in Ezekiel 1 and Isaiah 6]—By pronouncing God's Holy Names, one can gain insight into the functioning of the angels and other Divine Creations as if one had been given Divine Inspiration.

To one individual unless he is wise and understanding through his own knowledge—The secrets of *Merkavah* should not be taught even privately, unless the student is sufficiently wise and understanding to be taught the broad outlines and to understand the rest on his own.

Tiferet Yisrael: *What is above, what is below*—That is, what is above the confines of the finite universe, as by definition the universe must have boundaries.

Rav: *What was before*—before the world was created. *What will be after*—at the end of time. *Whoever has no regard for the honor of his Maker*—one who sins and says, "God is not here; who sees me, and who knows of me?"

If one was sentenced and fled, and then came before the very same court, they do not overturn his sentence. Wherever two stand up and say, "We testify concerning so-and-so that he was sentenced in so-in-so's court, and so-and-so and so-and-so were his witnesses," he is executed. A Sanhedrin *functions both in the Holy Land and outside the Holy Land. A* Sanhedrin *that executes once in a septenary is called a destroyer. Rabbi Elazar ben Azariah says: Once in seventy years. Rabbi Tarfon and Rabbi Akiva say: Had we served on a* Sanhedrin, *no one would ever have been executed. Rabban Shimon ben Gamliel says: They would indeed have increased the number of murderers in Israel.*

(Mishnah, Makkot 1:10)

Tosefot Yomtov: *Before the very same court*—in which he was sentenced. *They do not overturn his sentence*—They do not retry his case, in an attempt to find him innocent, but carry out his execution. *And so-and-so were his witnesses*—They must testify who the witnesses were on whose testimony the defendant was convicted. This must be done so that in the event that they are false, other witnesses may be able to contradict them.

Rav: *A Sanhedrin that executes once in a septenary*—one person in seven years. *Is called a destroyer*—They should have judged slowly and carefully and sought ways of acquitting the defendant.

Rambam: *Rabbi Elazar ben Azariah says, "Once in seventy years"*—The Mishnah's intention is that the judges of a capital case should attempt to find ways of exonerating the defendant. However, should there be no way to do so, they must execute even a thousand on one day.

Rav: *Rabbi Tarfon and Rabbi Akiva say: Had we served on a Sanhedrin, no one would ever have been executed*—Had they lived when the Sanhedrin tried capital cases, they would have examined the witnesses with questions they could not possibly have answered. In murder cases, for example, they would have asked the witnesses if they saw whether the murdered man was healthy or whether he was suffering from an injury that would cause him to die within twelve months. Such a person is considered legally dead, and his murderer would be exempt from execution.

Rabban Shimon ben Gamliel says: They would have indeed increased the number of murderers in Israel—By seeking to acquit the murderers they would not eliminate the murderers, who would then continue to commit more murders.

Tosefot Yomtov: Rabban Shimon ben Gamliel was more concerned with murder than with adultery, because murder is both sinful to God and destructive to people.

If a customer said to a storekeeper, "Give me produce for a dinar," *and he gave it to him; but when* [*the storekeeper*] *said to him, "Give me the* dinar," *he replied, "I gave it to you and you put it into the till,"* the customer (lit. householder) swears.

If he gave him the dinar *and said to him, "Give me the produce," and* [*the storekeeper*] *replied, "I gave it to you and you took it home," the storekeeper swears. Rabbi Yehudah says: Whoever has the produce in his possession has the upper hand.*

(Mishnah, Shevuot 7:6)

Rav: *And he gave it to him*—The Mishnah is referring to a case in which the storekeeper placed the produce in a public domain, so that neither the storekeeper nor the customer has it in his legal possession.

Rav and Tosefot Yomtov quoting Ran: *The customer swears*—The customer takes an oath similar to that of the Torah, which is made while holding a sacred object, and he then receives the produce. Since the storekeeper admits that he sold the produce and demands only the money for it, the customer's claim to the produce is seen as stronger. Therefore, he has the right to swear and keep the produce.

Rav and Tosefot Yomtov: *And he replied, "I gave it to you and you took it home"*—The storekeeper claims that the customer came to him without money and asked for a *dinar*'s worth of produce, promising to return soon with the money. The *dinar* that he just received from him, he claims is payment for that produce, and the produce lying in the public domain is not his, but additional produce the storekeeper brought out to sell. The customer claims that he never took any produce before this, and the *dinar* he now gave him was in payment for the produce lying in the public domain, which he is now buying.

Tosefot Yomtov: *The storekeeper swears*—Since the storekeeper claims that the customer has no connection with this produce at all, and the customer admits that he has not yet purchased it, only that he gave a *dinar* in order to purchase it, the storekeeper's claim has more validity and he is given the option to swear and keep the produce.

Rav: *Rabbi Yehudah says: Whoever has the produce in his possession has the upper hand*—Rabbi Yehudah disagrees with the second ruling and holds that in both cases the customer may swear and take the produce. He reasons that since the produce is outside the store, it is as though it were in the possession of the customer, and therefore he should be given the option to swear and take possession of the produce.

222 הגוזל ומאכיל פרק עשירי בבא קמא

הגוזל ומאכיל את בניו והניח לפניהם פטורין מלשלם ואם היה דבר שיש בו אחריות חייבין לשלם: גמ׳ אמר רב חסדא גזל ולא נתייאשו הבעלים ובא אחר ואכלו ממנו רצה מזה גובה רצה מזה גובה מאי טעמא כל כמה דלא נתייאשו הבעלים ברשותיה דמריה קאי תנן הגוזל ומאכיל את בניו והניח לפניהם פטורין מלשלם תיובתא דרב חסדא אמר לך רב חסדא כי תניא ההיא לאחר יאוש: אם הניח לפניהם פטורין מלשלם: אמר רמי בר חמא זאת אומרת רשות יורש כרשות לוקח דמי רבא אמר רשות יורש לאו כרשות לוקח דמי והכא במאי עסקינן כשאכלום(א) הא מדקתני סיפא אם היה דבר שיש בו אחריות חייבין לשלם מכלל דרישא בגזילה קיימת עסקינן אמר לך רבא הכי קאמר אם הניח להם אביהם אחריות נכסים חייבין לשלם והא מתני ליה רבי לרבי שמעון בריה לא דבר שיש בו אחריות ממש אלא אפילו פרה וחורש בה חמור ומחמר אחריו חייבין להחזיר מפני כבוד אביהן אלא אמר רבא כי שכיבנא ר׳ אושעיא נפיק לוותי דתריצנא מתני׳ כוותיה דתני רבי אושעיא הגוזל ומאכיל את בניו פטורין מלשלם הניח לפניהם גזילה קיימת חייבין אין הגזילה קיימת פטורין הניח להם אביהם אחריות נכסים חייבין לשלם אמר מר אין הגזילה קיימת פטורין נימא תיהוי תיובתא דרב חסדא אמר לך רב חסדא כי תניא ההיא לאחר יאוש אמר מר גזילה קיימת חייבין לשלם נימא תיהוי תיובתא דרמי בר חמא אמר לך רמי בר חמא כי תניא ההיא לפני

Page of the Babylonian Talmud, *Bava Kama,* Chapter 10, folio 111b. The main center portion constitutes the Gemara. It begins with the Mishnah (first three lines of text). The letters *gimel mem* indicate the beginning of the Gemara text that analyzes the Mishnah. Each folio has two sides, *a* and *b*. Rashi's running commentary is located on the center side of the page. Tosafot is on the outside of the page. From the standard Vilna edition, the *Vilna Shas*. (The word *shas* is the abbreviation of *shishah sedarim*, six orders of the Talmud.)

TALMUD

The Talmud, next to the Torah, is the most important book in Judaism. Essentially, it constitutes the explanation of the Mishnah, the Oral Law. But it is much more than that. The scope of the Talmud is as wide and as deep as the sea, to which it has been compared. For three centuries, the teachings of the Written and Oral Torah were studied and analyzed exhaustively, and they were written down in two monumental works, the Jerusalem Talmud and the Babylonian Talmud. When we speak of "learning Gemara," we usually refer to the Babylonian Talmud. The teachers of the Gemara are called *Amora'im* (singular, *Amora*—speaker, lecturer). Whereas the Mishnah is written in Hebrew, the language of the Gemara is Aramaic. Its format may be compared to that of minutes of the discussions of the *Amora'im*, which center on establishing and clarifying the Halachah according to the thirteen hermeneutical rules of textual analysis authorized by the Oral Law, given by God. These discussions are interspersed with sections of Aggadah, which are discourses on ethics, philosophy, family life, history and Torah values. Both the halachic and aggadic sections sparkle with vitality. They offer the profound wisdom of our sages as a guide to our daily life on every level. The Talmud is the lifeblood of our people. It is studied daily by hundreds of thousands of scholars, students, and laymen throughout the world. Since the Gemara is the discussion of the words of the Mishnah, it is structured on the same framework of six orders (*sedarim*) and tractates (*masechtot*).[1]

COMMENTARIES TO THE TALMUD

Many hundreds of commentaries have been written on the Talmud, and even today, new works, novellae, and supercommentaries appear almost every month. Unquestionably, the most significant talmudic commentaries are by **Rashi** and Tosafot. Rashi's is a running commentary, following the talmudic text phrase by phrase. Clearly and concisely he explains each difficult word and phrase, patiently clarifies complex principles and intricate twists of thought, anticipating the student's problems. He is a gentle teacher, leading the pupil along the tortuous path that leads to clear comprehension of the Gemara. Without Rashi, the Talmud would be accessible only to the most eminent scholars. There is a saying that expresses it well: For what purpose has God given man two forefingers?—One finger to point to the Gemara text; the other, to point to Rashi's commentary. Tosafot, meaning "additions" (to Rashi's commentary), is a compendium of expositions on the Talmud, composed by the Tosafists (*Baalei Tosafot*), many of whom were Rashi's disciples or descendants, such as **Rabbeinu Tam** and **Rashbam.** The Tosafists, who lived in Northern France and Western Germany during the twelfth and thirteenth centuries, often disagree with Rashi's interpretations. Focusing on specific themes, Tosafists will compare contradictory statements on the same subject in various parts of the Talmud, and ingeniously reconcile the differences, thereby opening new avenues of understanding to an entire *sugya* (passage dealing with a certain subject). Rashi's commentary is printed on the inside of each folio, while Tosafot can be found on the outside margin of the same page. Together, they surround the talmudic text like a setting into which a precious jewel is mounted.

RABBI YAAKOV BEN MEIR—RABBEINU TAM
רבי יעקב בן מאיר—רבינו תם

born: Ramerupt, France, 1100
died: Troyes, France, 1171
Popularly known as Rabbeinu Tam, after the verse in Genesis 25:27, "Jacob was a tam *(wholesome man), abiding in tents [of the Torah]." Tosafist, halachist, teacher.*

Rabbi Yaakov ben Meir was a grandson of **Rashi.** Like his grandfather, he was a wine merchant. Rabbeinu Tam studied under his father, Rabbi Meir ben Shemuel, and his other brother, Rabbi Shemuel ben Meir, the Rashbam. His yeshivah in Ramerupt attracted the greatest scholars. His discourses served as the basis for Tosafot, the famous commentary on the Talmud. He often disagrees with Rashi's interpretations and opens new vistas with his original, brilliant insights. With sharp-witted genius he analyzes variant versions of talmudic texts, discovering subtle differences that form the basis for a new understanding of the problem at hand. Rabbeinu Tam corresponded with **Rabbi Abraham ibn Ezra**, whom he greatly admired and respected. In 1146, when Crusaders pillaged his home, he was miraculously saved from death. A French nobleman who knew and respected him turned back the bloodthirsty mob by promising them that he would convert the rabbi to Christianity. His name and his writings are familiar to every student of Talmud.

222 הגוזל ומאכיל פרק עשירי בבא קמא

Rabbeinu Tam and the other Tosafists can be found on the outside part of the page. While Rashi explains the running text, Tosafot finds and resolves contradictions and paradoxes between various Gemara texts, often disagreeing with Rashi's interpretations. From the *Vilna Shas* edition of the Talmud.

SELECTIONS FROM TOSAFOT

Example of a dispute between Rashi and Tosafot

A harp was hanging above David's bed. As soon as midnight arrived, a North wind came and blew on it and it played by itself. He arose immediately and studied the Torah till daybreak. After daybreak the wise men of Israel came in to see him and said to him: Our lord, the King, Israel your people need sustenance! He said to them: Let them go out and make a living from each other. They said to him: A handful cannot satisfy a lion, nor can a pit be filled up with its own soil.

(Berachot 36)

Rashi: *A pit cannot be filled up with its own soil*—If you dig a pit, the soil you took out will not fill its cavity. Similarly, we cannot support the poor from our own resources. You must provide other means to give them sustenance.

Tosafot: Rashi explains that if you dig a pit, the soil will not fill its cavity. This interpretation is questionable. The elements in the analogy do not match. King David told them to take from the rich and give to the poor. The analogy would have been correct, if David had told them to take from the poor and give to the poor [the soil that is taken out is the same soil that is replaced into the pit]. Rabbeinu Tam explains it to mean "a well is never filled with the water that flows into it" [water does not fill the well—the rich cannot satisfy the poor]. Ri offers the following explanation: You will never fill a pit by digging in its bottom, moving soil from one place to another. The soil you add here is taken from there. Similarly, the money you take from the rich will be missing from the rich.

Rashi and Tosafot on another Gemara

Mishnah: *The Sages said that no one can fulfill his obligation on the first day of the festival [Sukkot] with someone else's* lulav *[palm branch].*[1]

Gemara: *From what verse do we derive this? From what our Rabbis have taught: "And you shall take" (Leviticus 23:40), [this implies] that each individual shall take with his own hand. "To you" (ibid.) implies that it should be yours, excluding a borrowed or stolen* lulav. *From this verse our sages deduced that no one can fulfill his duty on the first day of Sukkot with someone else's* lulav, *unless the latter gave it to him as a gift. And it once happened that when Rabban Gamliel and Rabbi Yehoshua, Rabbi Elazar ben Azariah and Rabbi Akiva were traveling on a ship, [at Sukkot time]*[2] *and only Rabban Gamliel had a* lulav, *which he had bought for one thousand* zuz; *Rabban Gamliel took it and fulfilled the mitzvah; then he gave it as a gift to Rabbi Yehoshua who took it, fulfilled the mitzvah with it, and gave it as a gift to Rabbi Elazar ben Azariah, who took it, and gave it as a gift to Rabbi Akiva, who took it, fulfilled the mitzvah with it, and then returned it to Rabban Gamliel. Why does he need to mention that he [Rabbi Akiva] returned it? He teaches us something by the way: that a gift made on condition that it be returned is a valid gift. This also follows from what Rava said: [If a man says to someone] "Here is an* etrog *as a gift, on condition that you return it to me, and the latter took it and fulfilled the mitzvah with it, if he returned it, he is regarded as having fulfilled the mitzvah, but if he did not return it, he is regarded as not having fulfilled the mitzvah. For what purpose did he need to mention that [Rabban Gamliel] had bought it for one thousand* zuz? *In order to let you know how precious the mitzvot are to them.*[3]

(Sukkah 41b)

Rashi: *From what verse do we derive this?*—that you cannot fulfill the mitzvah with someone else's *lulav. Why does he need to mention that he [Rabbi Akiva] returned it?*—What lesson can we derive from that fact? *He teaches us*—Although Rabban Gamliel gave the *etrog* to them on the condition that they return it to him, it is, nevertheless, a valid gift. *If he returned it, he has fulfilled the mitzvah*—Because the condition on which the gift was dependent was duly complied with; but if he did not return it, the condition was not carried out, and retroactively, it is a stolen *lulav* [which is invalid].

Tosafot: *If he did not return it, he is considered as not having fulfilled the mitzvah*—Why then did not Rabbi Yehoshua return it, but gave it to Rabbi Elazar ben Azariah, and he did not return it either, but gave it to Rabbi Akiva? The reason is that it was Rabban Gamliel's intent that they all should fulfill the mitzvah and *then* return it.

Example of Tosafot disagreeing with Rashi's interpretation

Rabbi Yehoshua ben Levi says: Women are obligated to read the Megillah,[4] *for they were also included in the miracle [of Purim].*

(Megillah 4a)

Rashi: *For they were also included in the miracle [of Purim]*—That is to say, Haman's decree "to destroy, to slay, and to exterminate all the Jews, young and old, infants and women, etc." applied also to them (the women).

Tosafot: Rashbam [disagreeing with Rashi] explains that women were, in fact, the prime factor in bringing about the miracles: in the case of Purim the rescue was due to Esther's intervention; in the story of Chanukah, deliverance came through Judith; and the miracle of Passover came to pass in the merit of the righteous women of that time. However, this interpretation is problematic, for the following reason: Rabbi Yehoshua ben Levi's statement "for they were also included in the miracle," seems to imply that women played a secondary role.[5] According to Rashbam's interpretation, it should have read, "for they were included . . ." omitting the word "also." The true meaning, it seems to me, is that they (the women) were *also*[6] included in the decree to be killed (by Haman); on Passover they were *also* enslaved by Pharaoh, and in the days of Chanukah the oppression weighed equally hard on them.

Excerpt of a Gemara with Rashi's commentary

A Gentile once appeared before Shammai and said, "I want to be converted to Judaism, but only on the condition that you teach me the entire Torah while I am standing on one foot." Shammai drove him off. The Gentile then went to Hillel, who agreed to convert him and said to him, "That which is hateful to you, do not do to your friend. This is the whole Torah; the rest is commentary. Go and study."

(Shabbat 31a)

Rashi: *That which is hateful to you, do not do to your friend* ["your friend," meaning God. Scripture refers to God as "your friend" in Proverbs 27:10: "Your friend and your father's friend, do not forsake."]—Do not violate God's word, just as you dislike it if someone disregards your wishes. Alternately, we can take "your friend" in its literal sense. Accordingly, you are enjoined not to rob, steal, commit adultery, etc. [not to do anything that is hateful to you]. *The rest*—the other words of the Torah. *Is commentary*—It is an important matter to know the things that are hateful. Go and study, and you will find out.

Excerpt of a Gemara with Rashi and Tosafot

Our rabbis taught that originally the women sat inside the Temple court and the men outside, but some levity took place. It was therefore decreed that the women should sit outside the Temple court and the men within. But levity still arose, so it was ordained that women should sit above [in a balcony] and the men below. . . . It has been taught, Rabbi Yehudah stated: Anyone who has not seen the double colonnade of Alexandria in Egypt has never seen the glory of Israel. It was said that it was like a huge basilica (synagogue), one colonnade within the other, and it sometimes held twice the number of people that went forth from Egypt.[7] There were in it seventy-one cathedras (chairs) of gold, corresponding to the seventy-one members of the Great Sanhedrin, not one of them containing less than twenty-one talents of gold, and a wooden platform in the middle, upon which the attendant of the Synagogue stood with a scarf in his hand. When the time came to answer "Amen," he waved his scarf and all the congregation duly responded.

(Sukkah 51b)

Rashi: *To answer "Amen"*—When the Reader concluded a benediction, not everyone could hear his voice.

Tosafot: *When the time came . . . the congregation duly responded*—Rabbeinu Nissim quotes a conflicting statement in *Berachot 47a:* "The Amen uttered in response should not be orphaned" [i.e., it should not be said by one who has not heard the blessing itself]. In this case [of the Synagogue in Alexandria], where the people did not actually hear the blessing, but merely responded to the waving of the scarf, their Amen would be an "orphaned Amen." Rabbeinu Nissim responds by stating that if by responding "Amen" one wishes to fulfill his obligation of reciting the blessing, then he must hear the blessing from the Reader, and his Amen may not be "orphaned." The Amen response through signaling with a scarf refers to the Reading of the Torah, but not to a blessing with which the Reader fulfills the obligation of the congregation. The latter must be heard before the Amen response can be made.

Excerpts of a Gemara with Rashi and Maharsha

The disciples of Rabbi Yochanan ben Zakkai asked him, "Why does the Torah decree a more severe punishment on a thief (who has to repay twofold, fourfold or fivefold) than a robber (who has to restore what was stolen or repay its value)? He replied, "The robber made the honor of the slave (i.e., man) equal to the honor of his master (i.e., God), but the thief did not make the honor of the slave equal to the honor of the master. He acted as though there were no seeing Eye below and no hearing Ear below."

(Bava Kama 79b)

Rashi: *Decree a more severe punishment*—The thief has to pay twofold, fourfold, or fivefold.[8] *The robber made the honor of the slave equal*—The robber, by doing his guilty act openly, shows that he fears neither man nor God. The thief, on the other hand, who steals secretly, honors the slave (man) more than his Maker, for by stealing secretly he exhibits fear of man, but disregard of God's all-seeing Eye.

Maharsha: *Decree a more severe punishment on a thief*—By stealthily intruding into the victim's home, the thief displays greater fear of worldly justice than of Heavenly justice. By stealing covertly he denies the existence of God and renounces the Principle of Reward and Punishment. The robber does not deny any of these. He has contempt even of the worldly court, which is to him a tangible reality. In his mind he balances the potential profits to be derived from his robbery against the losses he may suffer as a result of worldly and Heavenly justice.

Continuing Bava Kama 79b, the Gemara offers two reasons why "he must repay five oxen for each ox and four sheep for each sheep."

Rabbi Meir said, "Come and see how great is the virtue of work; since by stealing an ox the thief withdrew it from its labor (depriving the owner of its service), he repays fivefold; but in the case of a sheep, where no loss of labor is involved, he repays fourfold." Rabbi Yochanan ben Zakkai said, "Come and see how important is the matter of personal dignity; since the ox walks on his own legs the thief repays fivefold, but since he has to carry the sheep on his shoulders he only repays fourfold."

(Bava Kama 79b)

Rashi: *The sheep he has to carry on his shoulder*—The thief is humiliated thereby; therefore the Torah imposes a lighter sentence on him.

Maharsha: *He withdrew the ox from his labor*—This reason would apply, even if he stole a calf. Although it performs no labor, it has the potential to do so. But according to the second reason of "the loss of personal dignity," the case of stealing a calf presents a problem. Since a young calf has to be carried, why should the thief have to pay fivefold? We can answer by saying that since a calf is classified under the species of ox, which walks on his own legs, the *Tanna* does not wish to make an exception, on the principle of *lo pelug.*[9]

RABBI YAAKOV IBN CHAVIV—EIN YAAKOV
רבי יעקב אבן חביב—עין יעקב

born: Zamora, Spain, c. 1445
died: Saloniki, Greece, 1516
Popularly known as Ein Yaakov (The Well of Jacob), the title of his work. Talmudist.

During the expulsion of Spanish Jewry, Rabbi Yaakov ibn Chaviv fled to Greece, where he spread the knowledge of Torah and wrote his famous work, *Ein Yaakov*. It is a compendium of all the aggadot of the Talmud and includes a commentary based on the classic commentators, such as **Rashi, Tosafot**, and **Ran**. The book is arranged in the order of the tractates of the Talmud, and the author wisely appended an index in which he classifies the aggadot into topics, such as Torah, Prayer, Charity, Justice, Truth, Peace, Repentance, Afterlife, etc. *Ein Yaakov* was first published in Saloniki in 1515. It gained instant popularity, especially among those students for whom the Halachah sections of the Talmud proved too difficult to grasp. *Ein Yaakov* has seen many editions and has remained one of the favorite texts even today. (*For excerpts, see the following pages.*)

ספר
עין יעקב
מאסף
לכל האגדות והמדרשים המפוזרים בשס תלמוד בבלי. ואגדות מתלמוד ירושלמי
עם פירוש רש"י. ותוספות. וחדושי הרמב"ן. הרשב"א. הריטב"א. והר"ן. וחדוש
הכותב ... באור הרב הכותב.
מרנא יעקב בר שלמה ן' חביב זצ"ל
ועליהם נוספו
ארבע עשרה הוספות נכבדות. חדשות ומועילות
עץ יוסף. ענף יוסף. יד יוסף

Title page of *Ein Yaakov* by Rabbi Yaakov ibn Chaviv.

RABBI SHEMUEL ELIEZER EIDELS—MAHARSHA
רבי שמואל אליעזר אידלס—מהרש״א

born: Cracow, Poland, 1555
died: Ostrow, Poland, 1631
Popularly known as Maharsha, the initials of his full title and name. Talmudic commentator, rabbi.

As a young man Maharsha moved to Posen, and in 1605 was chosen as Rabbi of Chelm. In 1614 he accepted the rabbinate of Lublin, and in 1625 the rabbinate of Ostrow, where he established a well-known yeshivah. His massive work, *Chiddushei Halachot*, a commentary on the Talmud, is printed in all editions of the Talmud. With keen and astute insight he expounds the text of the Gemara. The extreme brevity of his style often makes it difficult to follow his reasoning. He habitually closes his remarks with "*vekal lehavin*"—"this is easy to understand [and needs no further elaboration]," while the matter isn't simple at all. In fact, the *Acharonim* (later authorities) spend a great deal of effort analyzing the latent meaning of his comments. He constructs his exposition of the *sugya* (subject matter) on the foundation laid by **Rashi** and **Tosafot**, which makes his work an essential tool in gaining a clear understanding of the Gemara. Alongside *Chiddushei Halachot* we find his *Chiddushei Aggadot*,[1] in which he explains the aggadic segments of the Talmud. Maharsha was greatly respected by his contemporaries, who regarded him as the *gadol hador*—the towering leader of the generation.

SELECTIONS FROM *EIN YAAKOV*, A COMPENDIUM OF THE AGGADAH PORTIONS OF THE TALMUD, WITH COMMENTS BY MAHARSHA

Whoever enjoys this world's pleasures without reciting a blessing is compared to one who steals from God.

(Berachot 35a)

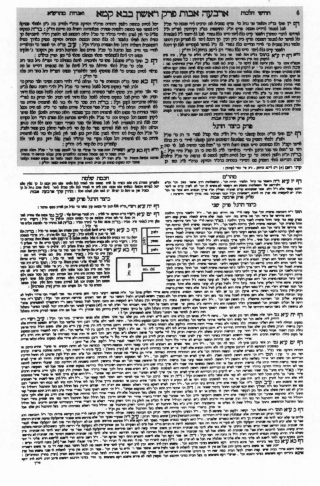

Page of commentary on the Talmud by Maharsha, Rabbi Shemuel Eidels. Printed in all standard editions of the Talmud. For commentaries on halachic sections a larger print is used; for the aggadic sections, a smaller print.

Maharsha: *Steals from God*—For everything belongs to Him.

Rabbi Yehudah said in the name of Rav: Four kinds of people are duty-bound to thank God: those who have returned safely from a sea journey; those who have returned from a desert crossing; those who have recovered from a serious illness; and those who have been released from captivity.[2]

(Berachot 54b)

Maharsha: *Four kinds of people are duty-bound to thank God*—It is to give thanks for the rescue from these four life-threatening hazards that our sages instituted the drinking of the Four Cups at the Seder. At the time of the Exodus our forefathers (1) crossed the Red Sea, (2) safely journeyed through the desert, (3) recovered from the illnesses of Egypt, and (4) were released from Egyptian captivity.

The Emperor [Hadrian] said to Rabbi Yehoshua ben Chananyah, "Why does the food you prepare for Shabbat smell so good?" Rabbi Yehoshua replied, "We have a special spice that we put into it, and its name is Shabbat." "Give me some of it," demanded the Emperor. Rabbi Yehoshua said, "It works for whoever observes the Shabbat, but for those who do not observe the Shabbat, it has no effect."

(Shabbat 119a)

Maharsha: *"We have a special spice"*—The emperor took Rabbi Yehoshua's words to mean that "Shabbat" was a certain savory herb. Rabbi Yehoshua pointed out to him that the "special ingredient" was the spiritual quality of Shabbat.

It is written, "Do not take revenge nor bear a grudge (Leviticus 19:18)." This applies to money or possessions, as we are taught in the following beraita: *How do we distinguish between revenge and bearing a grudge? Revenge is involved when one person asks another, "Lend me your spade," and the other says, "No." The next day, the second man comes to the first and asks to borrow that man's ax. He answers, "I won't lend it to you since you did not lend me your spade." Bearing a grudge is involved when one person asks another, "Lend me your sickle," and the other replies, "No." The following day the second man comes to the first and asks to borrow his spade. He answers, "I will lend it to you, because I am not like you who recently refused to lend me something."*

(Yoma 23a)

Rav said to Rav Shemuel bar Shilat, "Don't accept any pupils until they are six years of age. From six upward take them and fill them with knowledge as you would feed an ox." Rav also said to him, "When you strike a child, use only a shoelace [don't hurt him—Rashi]. If this makes him study, well and good; if not, seat him next to a group of diligent students [this will cause him to pay attention—Rashi].

(Bava Batra 21a)

Maharsha: *Feed him knowledge as you would feed an ox*—Just as you feed an ox in a leisurely fashion, with your hands, so should you teach a child, gently; don't strike or intimidate him. Don't pressure him to study in the way you would force-feed a camel or calves.

If you love your wife as much as you love yourself, and honor her more than yourself; if you lead your sons and daughters on the right path and marry them off while they are still young, this verse applies to you: "And you shall know that there is peace in your tent" (Job 5:24).

(Yevamot 62b)

Maharsha: *If you honor her more than you honor yourself*—By buying her a wardrobe that is more valued and prestigious than your own clothes are. As the saying goes, "Clothes confer respect."

RABBI YESHAYAH HOROWITZ—THE SHELOH
רבי ישעיה הורויץ—של״ה

born: Prague, Czechoslovakia, 1565
died: Tiberias, Israel, 1630
Popularly known as the Sheloh, an acronym formed of the initials of his work, Shenei Luchot Habberit. *Talmudist, kabbalist, rabbi. For his biography, see* *Part II, p. 21.*

SELECTIONS FROM THE SHELOH'S COMMENTARY

They made their lives bitter with hard labor involving mortar and bricks, as well as all kinds of work in the field. All the work they made them do was intended to break them.

(Exodus 1:14)

The Sheloh: *They made their lives bitter*—"Their lives," in a spiritual sense, alludes to God, for He is the life and soul of a Jew. Indeed, God suffered along with the people of Israel.[1] He shared the cup of His children's sorrows, as it says, "I am with him in distress" (Psalm 91:15), and it is also written, "Amid their distress is His distress" (Isaiah 63:9).

I will remember My covenant with Jacob as well as My covenant with Isaac and My covenant with Abraham and I will remember the land.

(Leviticus 26:42)

The Sheloh: *I will remember My covenant with Jacob as well as My covenant with Isaac and My covenant with Abraham and I will remember the land*—This verse forms an integral part of the *tochachah*,[2] the series of terrifying curses that will befall the Jewish people if they do not observe the Torah and mitzvot. It is difficult to understand how this verse, mentioning God's remembrance of the Patriarchs, can be construed as a curse. If we pause to reflect, we realize that this remembrance implies a severe reprimand. Having forefathers of the supreme stature of Abraham, Isaac, and Jacob, and inheriting a holy land like Eretz Yisrael places a heavy responsibility on a Jew's shoulders,

Title page of *Shenei Luchot Habberit* by Rabbi Yeshayah Horowitz, the Sheloh.

making his failings all the more deplorable. The shortcomings of a scion of an aristocratic family who was reared at the royal court are judged more harshly than those of a lowly peasant.

Appoint for yourselves judges and police in all your gates that the Lord your God is giving you, and make sure that they administer honest judgment for the people.

(Deuteronomy 16:18)

The Sheloh: *Appoint for yourselves judges and police in all your gates*—Every person has seven "gates": two ears, two eyes, two nostrils, and his mouth. Through these gates we receive all our impressions and attain our awareness of the outside world, or obtain nourishment from it. Our verse instructs us to "place judges and police at your gates"—be careful that no shameful or immoral perceptions enter through these "gates" of yours, that no forbidden food enter your mouth and no gossip emanate from it. Let your eyes see no evil; let your ears hear no evil.

RABBI AKIVA EIGER
רבי עקיבא איגר

born: Eisenstadt, Austria, 1761
died: Posen, Poland, 1837
Talmudist, great halachic authority.

A descendant of great rabbis, Akiva Eiger distinguished himself for the extraordinary acumen with which he applied himself to his Torah studies. At the age of 13 he wrote a learned book on Tractate *Chullin* and at 15 he was known far and wide as a budding *gaon* (Torah giant). He became the rabbi of Märkisch Friedland, where he made a name for himself for his vast talmudic knowledge and devout piety. His yeshivah attracted hundreds of students, and halachic queries were addressed to him from the far corners of the earth. In 1814 he was elected rabbi of Posen. His forceful leadership, tempered with genuine lovingkindness, made him admired and revered as the outstanding Torah personality of his generation. Among his well-known works are: *Gilyon Hashas, Teshuvot Rabbeinu Akiva Eiger* (Responsa), *Tosefot Rabbi Akiva Eiger* on the Mishnah, and *Chiddushei Rabbi Akiva Eiger* on *Shulchan Aruch*.

Rabbi Akiva Eiger.

SELECTIONS FROM RABBI AKIVA EIGER'S WRITINGS

Excerpt from *Chiddushei Rabbi Akiva Eiger, Bava Metzia* 10b

[*Preface: The Gemara in* Kiddushin *41b derives from Exodus 12:6 the rule that a person can delegate an agent to act on his behalf. Thus, the principal is fully responsible for the acts of his agent. However, this rule does not apply when a person sends an agent to commit a sin. For example, if someone tells his Jewish friend to light a fire on Shabbat, the friend, not the principal, is liable, for we have a rule, "ein shaliach lidevar aveirah"—there is no agent for a sinful act.*]

The Gemara *Bava Metzia* 10b states: Ravina says, "We say there is no agent for a sinful act when the agent is subject to the law prohibiting that act," for we say the agent, instead of heeding the command of his principal, should heed the command of God. Rabbi Akiva Eiger holds that

והגית בו יומם ולילה כי הוא חכמתכם ובינתכם לעיני העמים

תשובות וחדושי

רבינו עקיבא איגר ז"ל

ספר זה כולל תשובות וחדושים מהגאון הנ"ל
אשר אינם נמצאים בשום מקום אחר והם
נדפסו רק פעם אחת מקודם, ומפני שאינם
בנמצא הדפסנוהו עוד הפעם למען הרבצת
תורה בישראל.

הוצאת דעת
שנת תשי"ב

נדפס בבית דפוס של ספראגראף קאמפאני
PRINTED IN THE U.S.A. BY SAPHROGRAPH CO., 194 ELIZABETH ST., NEW YORK 12, N. Y.

Title page of *Teshuvot Rabbeinu Akiva Eiger*, Responsa.

the agent in this case cannot become an agent. He then quotes a differing opinion of the Sma (*Sefer Me'irat Einayim* §182), which suggests that the reason "there is no agent to commit a sinful act" is that the sender thinks that the agent surely will not obey his order. The difference between the two rationales becomes apparent when the agent is a *mumar*, an apostate who abandoned the Jewish religion. In Rabbi Eiger's view the principle would apply, for the *mumar* never became an agent in the first place. According to the Sma's reasoning, the principle does not apply—a *mumar* *does* become an agent to commit a sinful act, because the principal, knowing the *mumar*'s contempt of Judaism, had every reason to think that the *mumar* would obey his order.

Excerpt from *Teshuvot Rabbi Akiva Eiger, Yoreh De'ah*, Responsum 210

The question concerns a patient who died while undergoing surgery. An autopsy on this patient would be useful in teaching improved surgical techniques and reduce the hazards of this operation. Is performing an autopsy forbidden because it constitutes desecration and abuse of the dead, or is it permitted because it can lead to saving lives in time to come?

או"ח רצט הלכות שבת

Page of *Orach Chaim*, Laws of Shabbat 299:3, with commentary Hagaot R'A'K'E, glosses by Rabbi Akiva Eiger.

Responsum: In our case there is no other sick person present whose life could be saved by this autopsy. The motive for performing the autopsy is to obtain knowledge that might be helpful in a similar case in the future. We certainly do not set aside a biblical or even a rabbinical prohibition for a questionable consideration such as this. All hospitals follow the practice of performing autopsies only on cadavers of legally executed criminals or after obtaining prior agreement of the deceased. If, God forbid, we would be lenient in this matter, autopsies would be performed on all corpses, merely for the purpose of studying anatomy, ostensibly so that the knowledge gained thereby will save future lives. There are no valid reasons for permitting it.

RABBI ARYEH LEIB HELLER—KETZOT HACHOSHEN
רבי אריה לייב הלר—קצות החושן

born: Kalish, Poland, 1745
died: Ostrow, Poland, 1813
Known as Ketzot HaChoshen, after the title of his work. Talmudist.

Rabbi Aryeh Leib Heller was the son of Rabbi Yosef of Kalish and grandson of **Rabbi Yomtov Lipmann Heller**, author of *Tosefot Yomtov*. He was one of the foremost talmudic scholars of his age and served as rabbi of Rozantov and Ostrow. In Rozantov, under conditions of extreme poverty, he wrote his celebrated work, *Ketzot HaChoshen*, a commentary on *Shulchan Aruch—Choshen Mishpat*. During the winter months, in his frigid unheated room, the ink in his inkwell would freeze and he would hold it under his pillow to thaw it out. *Ketzot HaChoshen* gained the acclaim of the learning public. Its penetrating analyses of the logical underpinnings of talmudic dicta fascinated rabbis and students alike. He also wrote *Avnei Miluim* on *Shulchan Aruch—Even Ha'ezer*, and *Shev Shemateta* on talmudic topics. Today his books are studied avidly by students of Talmud and Halachah.

Page of *Choshen Mishpat*, Chapter 56, with commentary *Ketzot HaChoshen* by Rabbi Aryeh Leib Heller. The title *Choshen Mishpat* is taken from Exodus 28:15, "breastplate of judgment." It is fitting, since this volume deals with criminal law. The title *Ketzot HaChoshen* is a reference to Exodus 28:26, "the corners of the breastplate." From the original standard edition of *Shulchan Aruch*.

Excerpt from *Ketzot HaChoshen, Choshen Mishpat* 182:1

We have a principle according to which an agent acts as the representative of the person who assigned him, substituting for him in all matters. **Tosefot Rid** (Kiddushin 89) remarks: This being so, an agent should also be empowered to perform a *mitzvah* on someone's behalf. Thus, a person could delegate an agent to sit in the sukkah on his behalf or put on tefillin on his behalf. This is a fallacy. God has commanded us to perform certain mitzvot in person—with our body—mitzvot such as sukkah and tefillin. A Jew cannot exempt himself from these mitzvot by delegating an agent to do them for him, while he does nothing. It seems to me that the underlying principle is this:

An agent can perform an *act* on behalf of someone, but the agent's *body* does not substitute for the *body* of the one who appoints him. Therefore, a person can delegate an agent to slaughter the Passover lamb for him, or marry or divorce his wife by proxy. In these cases the agent's act is tantamount to the principal slaughtering the Passover lamb, marrying or divorcing his wife. By contrast, in the case of tefillin, when the agent puts on the tefillin, it is equivalent to the principal performing the *act* of putting on tefillin, but since the agent's *body* does not replace the principal's *body*, the principal did not put the tefillin on his *own* head; in effect, he placed them on the agent's head. To summarize: In the case of tefillin and sukkah, although the agent's actions are considered the principal's actions, since the agent's body is not the principal's body, the principal did not perform the mitzvah with his body, as required. In the case of the Passover lamb, marriage or divorce, where only the execution of the *act* is required, the agent takes the place of the principal.

RABBI CHAIM YOSEF GOTTLIEB OF STROPKOV—THE STROPKOVER RAV
רבי חיים יוסף גאטליעב

born: Tertzal, near Tokay, Hungary, c. 1790
died: Stropkov, Hungary, 1867
Talmudist, rabbi.

Born into a family of rabbis, Chaim Yosef Gottlieb was a descendant of Rabbi Yoel Gottlieb, rabbi of Galanta, and of the **Sheloh**. Growing up in Kraly, he became an ardent follower of the Kalever Rebbe, a great chasidic leader in Hungary. Studying Torah in the famed yeshivah of the **Chatam Sofer**, he was recognized as an outstanding student. After his marriage in 1813, he settled in Tertzal and dedicated himself to Torah study, developing a close relationship with the town's rabbi, the great scholar Rabbi Yechezkel Paneth, whose students he taught. During this period of studying and teaching he wrote his novellae, most of which were lost, with the exception of one volume, *Tiv Gittin Vekiddushin*, published by his son.[1] The novellae, which give evidence of his brilliant mind, deal with questions relating to the Tractates *Gittin, Kiddushin,* and *Ketubot*, mainly on the laws of marriage, divorce, and related subjects. In 1823 he succeeded Rabbi Paneth as Rabbi of Tertzal, and in 1842 was elected as Rabbi of Stropkov, succeeding the illustrious Rabbi Teitelbaum, author of *Yetev Lev*. Initially, he refused to be recognized as a chasidic rebbe, but upon the urging of the great Rabbi of Sanz, he revealed his eminence in the realm of Chasidut, dispensing advice, blessings, and healing to the thousands who streamed to his door. Large communities vied for the honor to have him serve as their rabbi. He chose to remain in Stropkov, but with the power of his personality he influenced and guided the religious affairs of the entire region. Humility, love of God, and love of His Torah were the hallmarks of his character. After a final visit with the Sanzer Rav, his saintly and fruitful life ended on the 4th day of Adar, 1867.

ספר
טיב גיטין וקידושין
חידושי גפ"ת על סדר נשים
מאת האי סבא קדישא
הרב הגאון הצדיק המפורסם קדוש יאמר לו
מוה"ר חיים יוסף גאטליעב זצללה"ה
אבד"ק טערצאל וסטראפקוב
נדפס פעם א' בשנת תרכ"ח באונגווער
וכעת נדפס פעם שני ע"י נכדי המחבר
בצרוף
תולדותיו מנהגיו ותהלוכותיו
תולדות איש ח"י
נסדרו ע"י נכדו הרב הגאון וכו'
מוה"ר אברהם מאיר איזראעל שליט"א
אבד"ק הוניאד והגליל תצ"ו
ברוקלין תשכ"ג

Title page of *Tiv Gittin VeKiddushin,* by Rabbi Chaim Yosef Gottlieb. Collected discourses and novellae on talmudic themes attesting to the author's wide-ranging knowledge in all areas of Halachah.

The following selection exemplifies the *pilpul* approach to the study of Talmud. It is a lecture on the *sugya* (talmudic discussion) of *chaddash* in *Kiddushin* 37b, delivered by Rabbi Chaim Yosef Gottlieb, Rabbi of Stropkov, published in his work *Tiv Gittin Vekiddushin* (p. 105).

By way of preface, it should be pointed out that the law of chaddash *mentioned in the Torah (Leviticus 23:14) forbids the eating of new grain until after the offering of the Omer on the second day of Passover. Thus, any grain that has not begun to take root before Passover is forbidden until the next Passover (Yoreh De'ah 293:3). Therefore, if wheat is planted in the late spring, after Passover, and harvested in the fall, it may not be eaten until after the next Passover.*

We must also bear in mind that, according to Joshua 5:10, the Children of Israel, upon entering the Promised Land, "kept the Passover on the fourteenth day of the month. . . . And they ate of the produce of the land on the morrow after Passover, unleavened cakes and parched corn, on that day."

We should also be aware of the halachic rule that asei doche lo ta'ase—*a positive commandment overrides a negative commandment. For example, we have a positive commandment to perform the circumcision on the eighth day. There is a negative commandment (prohibition) not to inflict a wound on Shabbat. Now, if the eighth day occurs on Shabbat, the positive commandment of* milah *overrides the prohibition of causing a wound, and the* milah *must be performed on Shabbat.*

The Gemara in *Kiddushin* 37b states: It is written, "They ate of the produce of the land on the morrow of Passover"—that means, they ate it on the day *after* Passover, but not before. On this the Jerusalem Talmud asks: Why could they not have eaten matzot from the new crop on the first day of Passover? Let the positive commandment to eat matzah override the prohibition of *chaddash. Tiv Gittin Vekiddushin* raises a question on the Jerusalem Talmud's question: "As Tosefot states, they ate matzah of the old crop, thereby fulfilling the mitzvah of matzah without violating the prohibition of *chaddash." Tiv Gittin Vekiddushin* cites an objection to the question of the Jerusalem Talmud that was raised by Or Chadash, who asks: The knowledge of *shiurim* [the minimum measurement required for the performance of a mitzvah] was forgotten during the period of mourning for Moses and was rediscovered by Otniel ben Kenaz (the first of the Judges). It follows that in the days of Joshua there still existed the uncertainty whether the required minimum for matzah is "olive size" or "egg size." Now, what were they to do? Should they eat two *kazayit* (olive size) of matzah (of the new crop), then they must be concerned that the actual requirement is only one *kazayit,* so that eating the second *kazayit* constitutes the transgression of *chaddash.* On the other hand, if they ate one *kazayit,* perhaps the requirement calls for two *kazayit,* so that they did not fulfill their obligation, and in this case, too, they violated *chaddash.* He tries to solve the question of the Jerusalem Talmud by quoting a question that was posed by *Mishneh Lemelech:* There is a rule that states that eating forbidden foods in an unusual manner[2] does not constitute a transgression, because it cannot be classified as "eating." Does this rule apply also to the performance of mitzvot? For example, if one eats matzah in an unusual way, has he fulfilled his duty of eating matzah or not? If the answer is yes, then the question of the Jerusalem Talmud, "Why did they not eat chaddash— let the positive command of eating matzah override the negative command of chaddash" is not justified, because they could have fulfilled their obligation by eating matzah in an unusual way and thus not transgress *chaddash.* We must conclude, therefore, that abnormal eating is not considered eating in the case of a positive commandment. According to **Rabbeinu Tam** (in *Tosafot),* they ate one *kazayit* (a quantity the size of an olive) of matzah of the old crop. *Tiv Gittin Vekiddushin* now interprets the question of the Jerusalem Talmud to mean, "Why couldn't they have eaten from the new crop, even two *kazayit,* because the positive commandment of matzah overrides the negative commandment of *chaddash.* If the required minimum for eating matzah is one *kazayit,* they fulfilled the mitzvah, overriding the prohibition, and as for the second *kazayit,* even if it is not required as a mitzvah, they still did not violate the prohibition of *chaddash* because they ate it in an unusual manner.

RABBI CHAIM SOLOVEITCHIK—REB CHAIM BRISKER
רבי חיים סולוייצ׳יק—רבי חיים מבריסק

born: Volozhin, Lithuania, 1853
died: Brisk, Lithuania, 1915
Popularly known as Reb Chaim Brisker, or simply Reb Chaim. Talmudist, rosh yeshivah, *rabbi.*

Rabbi Chaim Soloveitchik's first teacher was his father, the great Rabbi Yosef Dov of Brisk. As a young man he was widely acclaimed as an outstanding Torah scholar with exceptional character traits. In 1880 he was chosen to lead the Yeshivah of Volozhin, a post he occupied for twelve years. It proved to be the golden age of that renowned yeshivah. In his talmudic lectures he introduced a new approach to the study of Talmud and Halachah, based on a penetrating analysis of the topic, searching out the principles on which each law was founded. His novellae are discussed daily in all yeshivahs, as they are a key to the understanding of the most difficult problems. They are especially helpful in reconciling apparently contradictory statements of **Rambam**. In 1892 he succeeded his father as Rabbi of Brisk, Lithuania, where he dedicated his life to his community. With a generosity that was legendary he donated his salary to the poor, extending a helping hand to everyone in need. He was loved and admired by his community and beyond, and until this day the name Reb Chaim evokes reverence and awe in the yeshivah world and among talmudic scholars.

Rabbi Chaim Soloveitchik, the revered Reb Chaim Brisker.

SELECTIONS FROM REB CHAIM'S COMMENTARY

Excerpt from novellae on Jerusalem Talmud, *Berachot* 9:4, The Blessing on Attaching the Mezuzah

A person attaching a mezuzah to the doorpost in someone else's house must recite the blessing. Yet, by his act of attaching the mezuzah he is not fulfilling a mitzvah, because a mitzvah must be performed by the person who has the duty to perform it. The reason that he must say the blessing is that the act of attaching a mezuzah is in itself a "mitzvah act." In that respect it is unlike attaching tzitzit (fringes) to a tallit. Here the attaching does not constitute the mitzvah; rather, it is the *wearing* of a tallit that has tzitzit on its corners that constitutes the mitzvah of tzitzit. Therefore, on fastening the tzitzit, no blessing is said. In the case of mezuzah, it is the *house* that is required to have a mezuzah. Attaching a mezuzah, therefore, constitutes a mitzvah on which a blessing is said.

Excerpt from novellae on Rambam, Laws of Prayer 4:1

Rambam states in the Laws of Prayer 4:1: "Five things are indispensable to prayer, even when its proper time has arrived. . . . [one of them is] concentration of one's thoughts (4:15). What is meant by that? A prayer that is uttered without concentration is no prayer. If one prayed without concentration he should repeat his prayer, concentrating his thoughts. If he is confused and preoccupied, he is forbidden to pray until his mind is composed." The text seems to indicate that concentration is a requirement applying to *all* prayers. This stands in sharp contrast with another statement by Rambam in Chapter 10:1: "He who has prayed without concentration should repeat his prayer with concentration, but if he concentrated his thought while saying the first blessing [of the *Shemoneh Esrei*] he need not repeat it any more." The clear implication is that a lack of concentration constitutes an impediment only with regard to the first blessing [and not with regard to *all* prayers, as is implied by Chapter 4:15]. The two conflicting statements can be reconciled as follows: We can distinguish two kinds of concentration in prayer: one, concentrating on the *meaning* of the words being uttered, and two, concentrating on the fact that while praying, one is standing in the Presence of God, as it is defined in Chapter 4, "removing all extraneous thoughts from one's mind, visualizing himself as standing before the Shechinah (Divine Presence)." This is, in fact, an intrinsic element of prayer. When Rambam rules that without concentration, prayer must be repeated in its entirety, he refers to a lack of awareness that one is standing in the Presence of God. By definition, such prayer cannot qualify as prayer. In Chapter 10:1, however, where he states that as long as one concentrates on the first blessing of the *Shemoneh Esrei* he need not repeat it, he refers to "concentration on the meaning of the words," implying that even though he does not understand the meaning of all the blessings, so long as he understands the first one, it is counted as prayer.

RABBI AVRAHAM YESHAYAHU KARELITZ— THE CHAZON ISH
רבי אברהם ישעיהו קרליץ—חזון איש

born: Kossova, Lithuania, 1879
died: B'nei Brak, Israel, 1954
Known the world over as the Chazon Ish, the title of his work. Talmudist, halachist, outstanding spiritual world leader of Torah Jewry.

One of the preeminent Torah sages of the recent past, the Chazon Ish was the second son of Rabbi Shmaryahu Yosef Karelitz, rabbi of Kossova, author of *Bet Hatalmud*, a commentary on the Mishnah Tractate *Chullin*. He showed early signs of outstanding genius and piety, and at the age of 13 he vowed to devote his entire life to the study of Torah, a vow he kept for the next 62 years. Even as a young man he began to write down his novellae, which he composed in a masterfully clear and literate style. In 1912, the first volume of halachic and talmudic novellae, entitled *Chazon Ish*, was published in Vilna.[1] The work clarifies the law in a straightforward way, avoiding *pilpul*—circuitous reasoning. After World War I he lived in Vilna, and in 1933 he moved to Eretz Yisrael, settling in B'nei Brak, becoming the spiritual focal point of the community. His guidance was sought by Jews of Eretz Yisrael and the entire world. He offered valuable advice, not only on religious matters, but also on personal and business affairs. Even on complex medical questions his insights were unerringly accurate. With his indomitable spirit and phenomenal intellectual prowess he was instrumental in making B'nei Brak a leading center of Torah study, a city that is today teeming with yeshivahs and other Torah institutions, truly a unique, vibrantly alive Torah community. He promoted the observance of *shemittah*, the sabbatical year, whereby the land remains fallow for an entire year (Leviticus 25); he fought against inducting girls into the Israeli army; and with the power of his personality he raised the prestige of Torah and its scholars so that the mere mention of the name Chazon Ish inspires awe throughout the Torah world. Gradually, more volumes of *Chazon Ish* appeared; also a book entitled *Emunah Uvitachon—Faith and Trust*—on themes relating to these concepts. A three-volume biography in Hebrew, *Pe'er Hador*,[2] has been published in which the life and achievements of this towering giant are described in detail.

Rabbi Avraham Yeshayahu Karelitz, the Chazon Ish.

שער החלק הראשון מספר חזון־איש, שהופיע לפני למעלה מיובל שנים

Title page of the first volume of *Chazon Ish* on *Orach Chaim* and *Yoreh De'ah*.

SELECTIONS FROM THE CHAZON ISH'S WRITINGS

Excerpt from *Emunah Uvitachon* 1:8

Imagination is a faculty of the mind that is unrelated to the intellect. It is shallow, not based on reason. It captivates man, prevailing on him not to subject it to intellectual scrutiny. Conversely, the intellect wages an ongoing battle against the imagination. Man's intellect tells him that his imagination is illusory and deceptive. Yet, there are times when man will succumb to the powers of his imagination. Historians base their research on records and documents relating to events in the past. Memoirs and chronicles are the building blocks with which they create the annals of history. They should remember that as a result of man's innate tendency to invent and innovate, historical records are full of lies and distortions. By nature, man does not have an ingrained aversion to falsehood—as a matter of fact, many people have a definite fondness for it. They simply adore fraud and fabrication. It is the historian's task to sift truth from fiction. However, this makes him an easy prey to his own imagination, which may seduce him into making hasty decisions rather than carefully reasoned determinations in weighing the relative merits of the case. His imagination drives him to make instinctive, instantaneous choices as to what is true and what is false.

Excerpt from *Emunah Uvitachon* 12:7.

One of the characteristics of trust in God can be found in the fact that the believer is filled with a spirit of holiness. He is inspired with a sense of inner strength that assures him of the certainty that God will help him. This thought is expressed by King David in Psalm 27:3: "Though an army would besiege me, my heart would not fear; though war would arise against me, in this I trust."

Excerpt from *Chazon Ish*, *Orach Chaim*, Responsum 125—The order in which the chapters of the Torah were given

The details of the order in which the chapters of the Torah were given and the locations and times at which they were given require a great deal of study. It is the subject of much discussion in the Talmud, e.g., in *Gittin* 60a and *Chagigah* 6a. We offer the following analysis of this issue. The Torah states, "He said to Moses, 'Go up to God . . .' (Exodus 24:1). According to **Ramban**, on the 5th of Sivan the Israelites were summoned to listen to God's commandments. Subsequently, upon hearing the shofar (ram's horn) blasts and seeing the mountain smoking, they said, "You [Moses] speak to us and we will listen" (Ramban on Exodus 20:15). Moses then said, "Don't be afraid" (Exodus 20:17). Then they heard the first and second commandment, "I am" and "Don't have any other gods." They heard these from God Himself. The remaining eight of the Ten Commandments they heard as God's Voice but could understand their meaning only through Moses.

That is what is meant by the passage, "Moses spoke and God replied with a Voice" (Exodus 19:19), as explained by **Rashi**. Having received the Ten Commandments, Moses descended from the mountain. At that time the people said to him, "It is true that God our Lord has showed us His glory . . . If we hear the Voice of God our Lord any more, we will die" (Deuteronomy 5:21–22). They thought that they would hear God's Voice enunciating all the mitzvot. To this God replied, "They have spoken well . . ." (Deuteronomy 5:25) for that is what God had originally intended. On that same day Moses returned to the mist, where God said to him, "This is what you must tell the Israelites: 'You have seen that I spoke to you from heaven (Exodus 20:19–20)— "do not allow them to reside in your land" ' " (Exodus 23:33). Thereupon Moses was commanded to write down these words in a book, seal the covenant with the Israelites, and sprinkle the blood on the altar and on the people; he did exactly as he was commanded. On the 6th of Sivan, Moses read the Book of the Covenant to the people and on the 7th of Sivan he built the altar. On that day he returned to the mountain, where he remained for forty days. Our sages tell us that during those forty days he was told all 613 commandments. . . . During his second forty-day sojourn, God repeated the entire Torah to Moses. . . . And in the Plains of Moab he was given the commandments a third time . . . and it was written down "upon the command of God through the hand of Moses."

RABBI AHARON KOTLER—REB AHARON
רבי אהרן קוטלר—רבי אהרן

born: Sislovitch, Russia, 1892
died: New York, New York, 1962
Universally and reverently known as Reb Aharon. Talmudist, rosh yeshivah*, outstanding leader of Orthodox Jewry.*

Rabbi Aharon Kotler.

Even as a young boy, Aharon Kotler had an unquenchable thirst for Torah, and by the age of 6 he had mastered all twenty-four books of the Bible. Before he was 10 years old both his parents had died, and his uncle, Rabbi Yitzchak Pines, a *dayan* (rabbinical judge) in Minsk, took him under his wing. He studied in Minsk together with the young **Rabbi Yaakov Kamenetzky**, before entering the renowned Yeshivah of Slobodka, which was under the leadership of the two illustrious personalities, **Rabbi Nosson Tzvi Finkel** and Rabbi Moshe Mordechai Epstein. When Reb Aharon was 16 years old, the revered **Rabbi Chaim Soloveitchik**, upon meeting him, spoke in glowing terms about the young scholar's brilliance, saying, "Let me assure you, the day will come when the whole world will rest on his shoulders." In 1914, after his marriage to Rebbetzin Channah Perel, daughter of Rabbi Isser Zalman Meltzer—rabbi and *rosh yeshivah* of Slutzk—he became the main lecturer at the yeshivah. He captivated his audiences with his innovative approach to solving talmudic problems. In 1917, in the wake of the Communist Revolution, he fled to Kletzk, Poland, in the company of fifty of his students. There he founded the famous Yeshivah of Kletzk, which attracted students from all of Poland and many other countries because of its high standard of learning. In 1941, Reb Aharon and his family miraculously escaped war-torn Europe. After traversing Siberia and Japan he arrived in the United States, where he immediately devoted all his energies to organizing rescue and relief efforts for European Jewry. As spokesman for *Vaad Hatzalah*, the American rescue organization, he conferred with Secretary Henry Morgenthau and other high officials in the Roosevelt administration about implementing rescue operations. Through his tireless efforts thousands of lives were saved. After the establishment of the State of Israel, he became the driving force behind the creation of *Chinuch Atzmai*, the independent religious school system. As a true leader of the Jewish people he participated actively in all efforts to promote the cause of Torah, fighting fiercely against any innovation or deviation from authentic Halachah. His crowning achievement was the Yeshivah Beth Midrash Govo'ah in Lakewood, New Jersey. With this institution he introduced to America the concept of *Torah lishmah*—Torah study for its own sake, without any ulterior motive. He established a *kollel* where married young scholars pursued their postgraduate studies.

From modest beginnings the yeshivah grew, until, under the leadership of his son Rabbi Yosef Chaim Shneur Kotler, it reached an enrollment of more than 1,000 students. Today, under the leadership of his grandson, Rabbi Aryeh Malkiel Kotler, it has become the foremost academy of its kind in the world. Some of his lectures, responsa, and discourses on Mussar (ethics) have been published under the title of *Mishnat Rabbi Aharon*.[1] Other works are in preparation. With his indomitable spirit he created in America a new climate of respect and admiration for Torah and its scholars. With his yeshivah he set new standards for Torah scholarship that matched those of pre-war European yeshivahs. His piety, humility, and selfless dedication were incomparable. He was truly a *gaon* and *manhig hador*, a Torah giant and leader of the Jewish people.

SELECTIONS FROM REB AHARON'S COMMENTARY

Excerpt from *Mishnat Rabbi Aharon*, Vol. 1— essay entitled "The Torah will not be forgotten"

The prophet Isaiah says: "And I will wait for God, Who hides His face from the house of Jacob, and I will look for Him. Behold, I and the children whom God has given me shall be for signs and for wonders in Israel" (Isaiah 8:17–18). **Rashi** explains that "I and the children" refers to the pupils who are as dear to the prophet as his own children—these pupils will be signs and wonders in Israel, for through them the Torah will live on in Israel. The prophet is saying that the survival of the Torah is one of the miracles of Providence. It is as great a miracle as the survival of Israel among the nations. The events in the history of Israel, a history that is unlike that of any other nation in the world, were predicted in the Torah thousands of years ago, from the first day of Israel's nationhood. In spite of countless revolutionary changes and developments in all phases of existence, the prophecies of the Torah have come true to the letter. The promise of the continuing existence of the Jewish people serves as an everlasting sign of Divine Protection. Included in this promise is also the Divine assurance that "[the Torah] will not be forgotten by their descendants" (Deuteronomy 31:21). Through the Torah, God will reveal Himself in marvelous ways; the Torah will remove its "hidden face," and through the Torah, the Glory of Heaven will be revealed.[2]

Excerpt from *Mishnat Rabbi Aharon*, Vol. 1— essay entitled "Moshe, a man of God"

It is stated in *Bereishit Rabbah* 36:3: "Moses is more beloved than Noah. This is evident from Scripture. At first Noah is described as 'a righteous man' (Genesis 6:9), but in the end he is called 'a man of the soil' (Genesis 9:20). Moshe, on the other hand, at first is called 'an Egyptian' (Exodus 2:19), but ultimately the Torah describes him as 'a man of God' (Deuteronomy 33:1)." It is God's will for man to grow ceaselessly, never to be content with his spiritual achievements, no matter how lofty they may be, but continually to ascend to ever higher levels. Noah is called "a man of the soil" as an admonition for planting a vineyard. Having attained the levels of spiritual elevation and piety as to make him worthy to save the world from extinction, he is chided for taking up the mundane labor of tilling the soil. Moses, by contrast, after performing all the great miracles and ascending to Heaven to receive the Torah from God, never ceased to reach for more exalted spheres. He always viewed himself as standing on the lowest rung of an endless ladder. Spiritual growth is the essence of life. Torah is our life. It is Reality. The reality of this world exists only for the purpose of Torah and the service of God.

Excerpt from *Mishnat Rabbi Aharon*, Vol. 1— essay entitled "The Torah will not be forgotten"

We note that the Torah did not designate any tangible symbols to commemorate the Giving of the Torah at Mount Sinai. Moreover, the Torah does not even mention the fact that Shavuot is the day on which the Torah was given. By contrast, the Torah institutes a great number of rituals to remind us of our redemption from Egypt. On reflection, we can distinguish a distinct difference between the two events. The signs and wonders of the Exodus are miracles that happened *in the past*. We need symbolic reminders to help us relive these glorious events. The idea of the Stand at Sinai, on the other hand, requires no memorial. It is inherent in the Torah itself. The Giving of the Torah is described as "a loud and never-ending voice" (Deuteronomy 5:19), as Onkelos translates it. Indeed, the loud Voice of the Giving of the Torah is manifest in the Torah itself. By being close to Torah sages who engross themselves in the Torah, we earn the reward of having studied Torah, and our life will be filled with the radiance of Torah.

Excerpt from *Mishnat Rabbi Aharon*, Vol. 2—essay entitled "I am my beloved's and my beloved is mine"

It is written: [Before the army went into battle the officers declared] "Is there any man among you who is afraid or fainthearted? Let him go home" (Deuteronomy 20:8). The Gemara in *Sotah* 44a explains that this proclamation is addressed at men who are afraid [to go into war] because of sins they have committed. The Gemara further explains that the reason the Torah also exempts from military service all those who built a house, planted a vineyard, or betrothed a woman, is so as to protect from humiliation those who returned because of sins. Since a great number of soldiers were exempted for the other three reasons, those leaving because of past sins could not be identified. Thus it becomes clear that the Torah permitted only men who were perfectly righteous or had repented of their sins to do the fighting. This teaches us an important lesson in the ways of God. God, Whose Providence guides the world, is not concerned with natural factors. Our conduct in war is dictated by the laws of the Torah. The Torah determines victory and deliverance. The miracles of the Torah, in this case, are plain for everyone to see. The Torah does not mind granting exemptions for even the slightest transgression, even though this will result in a reduction of tens of thousands of fighting men. Add to that the exemptions to all those who built a house, planted a vineyard, or betrothed a woman, granted merely for the purpose of shielding the returnees "for their sins" from humiliation. Shouldn't the Torah be concerned for the enemy gaining the upper hand, God forbid? God, the Giver of the Torah, watches over us. He can send His salvation through the many or by means of a few. As it is written, "God said to Gideon, 'by the three hundred men that lapped will I save you' " (Judges 7:7).

Excerpt from *Mishnat Rabbi Aharon*, Vol. 3—essay entitled "Purim"

It is written in the Torah, "God shall be at war with Amalek for all generations" (Exodus 17:15). This is a war that continues in all generations until the "Restoration of the World," when Amalek will be eliminated. At that time "God will be King over all the world" (Zachariah 12:9). All wars and persecutions against the Jewish people are in essence a form of the war of Amalek, for in reality they are wars against God. They are directed against the Jewish people because it is the nation of God. But Amalek's war can become manifest in another way. When Amalek creates a social climate in which Israel is encouraged to assimilate, that too is a phase of Amalek's war against God—a war that will not end until God's Glory is revealed and evil is destroyed. Whenever the bonds to Torah are weakened, evil is on the rise. Conversely, the stronger the attachment of the Jewish people to the Torah, the more enfeebled is the power of Amalek. "As long as Moses held his hands up, Israel would be winning, but as soon as he let his hands down the battle would go in Amalek's favor" (Exodus 17:11). Moses symbolically represents the people of Israel, and this war is an ongoing war for the supremacy of God's Majesty in the world.

משנת רבי אהרן

ראשית חכמה, שכל טוב, ותוכחת חיים

מאמרים ושיחות מוסר,
חיכם רצוף רוח דעת ויראת ה׳, רוח עצה וגבורה

מאת
רבנו הגדול שר התורה רבן של ישראל
מרן הגאון רבי אהרן קטלר זצוקללה״ה

חלק שני
ימים נוראים

בהוצאת
בית מדרש גבוה לייקוואוד ● מכון ירושלים
ירושלים תשמ״ז

Title page of *Mishnat Rabbi Aharon,* discourses and responsa on talmudic themes.

MIDRASH

Our Midrash literature is a vast treasury of expositions of the Torah text, as well as a rich source of moral and ethical principles. The various midrashim are, in essence, running commentaries on the books of the Bible. Those that interpret and define biblical law are known as midrash halachah, while the midrashim that interpret the text from the ethical point of view are referred to as midrash aggadah. The word midrash derives from *darash*—to seek, to investigate, hence to study (as in *bet midrash*—house of study). Both midrash halachah and midrash aggadah form an integral part of our God-given Oral Torah. The books of midrash halachah, compiled until about 200 C.E. by the *Tanna'im*, the teachers of the Mishnah, are:

1. *Mechilta* of Rabbi Yishmael; *Mechilta* of Rabbi Shimon bar Yochai on Exodus.
2. *Sifra* (also known as *Torat Kohanim*) on Leviticus.
3. *Sifrei Bamidbar, Sifrei Zuta* on Numbers.
4. *Sifrei Devarim* on Deuteronomy.

The most important of the books of midrash aggadah are Genesis *Rabbah*, Leviticus *Rabbah*, Lamentations *Rabbah*, Esther *Rabbah*, and Song of Songs *Rabbah*. These midrashim all consist of a collection of homilies, sayings, and aggadot of the Amora'im (400–640 C.E.) in Aramaic and Hebrew. A very prominent midrashic collection is *Midrash Tanchuma*, by the Babylonian Amora Rabbi Tanchuma bar Abba (fourth century C.E.), a disciple of Rav Huna. The entire collection is aggadic. Of later origin (1200–1300) are the *Yalkutim* (Anthologies), the most prominent of which is *Yalkut Shimoni* on the entire Bible, composed in Germany at the beginning of the thirteenth century. The Midrash teachings are presented in the guise of simple parables, analogies, and anecdotes. The essence of their wisdom is concealed from the casual reader. Their deeper meaning can be understood only when they are studied with a reverential attitude and an awareness that their underlying Divine wisdom is hidden, in the same way as clothes conceal the person wearing them. Only by viewing them from a Torah perspective can we penetrate their outer shell and perceive their radiant core. Throughout the ages, rabbis have used midrashim as texts for their sermons, always discovering new aspects, different nuances, and original interpretations as themes for their messages on Torah, mitzvot, ethics, and morality. They have been a constant source of faith, hope, and solace to the Jewish people.

SELECTIONS FROM VARIOUS MIDRASHIC SOURCES BY MECHILTA, SIFRA, AND SIFREI

God will fight for you, but you must remain silent.
(Exodus 14:14)

Mechilta: *God will fight for you*—Not only at this hour, but until the end of time, against all your enemies.

God said to Moses, "I will come to you in a thick cloud so that all the people will hear when I speak to you. They will then believe in you forever. Moses told God the people's response to that.
(Exodus 19:9)

Mechilta: *So that all the people will hear*—They all proclaimed one thing: "We wish to *see* our King. Hearing His Voice is not the same as seeing Him. "God replied, "Their request is granted, 'for on the third day God will descend on Mount Sinai in the sight of all the people' " (Exodus 19:11).

מדרש נח תנחומא כט

מפניכם, ומקריב אתכם אלי, כדי שתהיו עובדין אותי ביראה, (שם) ועוד אמר רוח הקדש על ידי דוד, עבדו את ה׳ ביראה (תהלים ב יא) : חסלת פרשת נח

פרשת לך לך

[א] ויאמר ה׳ אל אברם לך לך (בראשית יב א). (שנו רבותינו) (א) [ילמדנו רבינו] (ב) מהו לאדם שיקבל עליו מלכות שמים כשהוא מהלך, (ג) רב אידי ורב הונא בשם ר׳ יוסי בר יהודה בשם ר׳ שמואל אמרו אסור לאדם לקבל עליו עול מלכות שמים כשהוא מהלך, (ד) אלא יעמוד על רגליו ויקרא קריאת שמע, וכשיגיע לברוך שם כבוד מלכותו לעולם ועד, יתחיל ואהבת (ה) מיד קורא מהלך ואינו חושש. אתה מוצא מי

הערות ותקונים

Page of *Midrash Tanchuma, Parashat Lech Lecha,* Genesis 12:1. Taken from the edition annotated by Rabbi Shelomoh Buber.

Every person must respect his mother and father, and keep My Shabbat, I am the Lord.

(Leviticus 19:3)

Sifra: What constitutes "respect"? One must not occupy his father's seat. One should neither corroborate nor contradict one's father in his presence. What constitutes "honor"? One must provide them with food and drink and clothing. One should bring them home and take them out.

And Moses sent them, 1,000 men from each tribe as an army, along with Pinchas the son of Elazar the Priest.

(Numbers 31:6)

Sifrei: It tells us that Pinchas was equivalent to all of them. Why did Pinchas go and Elazar not go? Because Pinchas went to take revenge for what was done to Joseph, the father of his mother,[1] as it is stated, "And the Midianites sold him" (Genesis 37:36).

OTHER MIDRASHIC EXAMPLES

Which was created first, heaven or earth?[2]

The School of Shammai said that heaven was created first and then the earth. The School of Hillel said that the earth was created first and then the heaven. Each one gives a reason for his opinion. The School of Shammai compares the matter to a king who made a throne for himself and afterwards a footstool. "Thus said the Holy One, blessed is He, 'The heaven is My throne and the earth My footstool' " (Isaiah 66:1). The School of Hillel compared the matter to a king who erected a palace. He first built the lower stories and then the upper. Rabbi Shimon bar Yochai said, "I am astonished how the fathers of the world, the Schools of Shammai and Hillel, can differ on this point. I declare that both were only constructed like a pot and its lid (at the same time); as it is said, 'When I call them (earth and heaven) they stand up together' " (Isaiah 48:13). Someone asked him, "In that case, why sometimes does Scripture mention earth before heaven and at other times heaven before earth?" He replied, "It comes to teach that they are of equal importance" (Genesis *Rabbah* 1:15).

The creation of woman

God considered from which part of man to create women. He said, "I will not create her from the head that she should not hold up her head too proudly; nor from the eye, that she should not be too curious; nor from the ear, that she should not be an eavesdropper; nor from the mouth, that she should not be too talkative; nor from the heart, that she should not be too jealous; nor from the hand, that she should not be too greedy; nor from the foot, that she should not be wandering about; but from a part of the body which is hidden, that she should be modest" (Genesis *Rabbah* 18:2).

A woman's influence on her husband

The story is told of a pious man who was married to a pious woman. Being childless, they divorced one another. He went and married a wicked woman and she made him wicked. She went and married a wicked man and made him righteous. It follows that all depends on the woman (Genesis *Rabbah* 17:7).

Marriages are made in heaven

A Roman lady asked a Rabbi, "In how many days did the Holy One, Blessed is He, create the universe?" "In six days," he answered. "What has He been doing since then up to the present?" "He has been arranging marriages."[3] "Is that His occupation? I, too, could do it. I possess many male and female slaves, and in a very short time I can pair them together." He said to her, "If it is a simple thing in your eyes, it is as difficult to the Holy One, Blessed is He, as dividing the Red Sea." He then left. What did she do? She summoned a thousand male slaves and a thousand female slaves, set them in rows, and announced who should marry whom. In a single night she arranged marriages for all of them. The next day they appeared before her, one with a cracked forehead, another with an eye knocked out, and another with a broken leg. She asked them, "What is the matter with you?" One female said, "I don't want him." Another male said, "I don't want her." She immediately sent for the Rabbi and said to him, "There is no god like your God, and your Torah is true. What you told me is quite correct" (Genesis *Rabbah* 68:4).

Noah's vineyard

When Noah came to plant a vineyard, Satan appeared before him and asked, "What are you planting?"

"A vineyard."

"What is its nature?"

"Its fruits are sweet, whether fresh or dry, and of them wine is made, which gladdens the heart."

"Come, let us become partners in this vineyard."

"Very well," Noah replied. What did Satan do? He brought a sheep and slaughtered it under the vine; then he brought in succession a lion, a pig, and a monkey, slew each of them, and let their blood drip into the

vineyard and drench the soil. He hinted thereby that before a man drinks wine he is simple like a sheep and quiet like a lamb in front of his shearers. When he has drunk in moderation, he is strong like a lion and declares there is none equal to him in the world. When he has drunk in excess, he becomes like a pig, wallowing in filth. When he is intoxicated, he becomes like a monkey, dancing about, uttering obscenities before all, and ignorant of what he is doing (*Midrash Tanchuma*, *Noach* 13).

Blood, the first of the Ten Plagues

Rabbi Abun Halevi said: The Plague of Blood made Israel rich. How? An Egyptian and an Israelite would live in the same house and their cistern would be filled with water. The Egyptian would come and fill his pitcher from its contents and it would turn to blood, while the Israelite would drink water from it. The Egyptian would say, "Give me a little of the water you are holding in your cup." The Israelite would give it to him, but in the Egyptian's hand the water turned to blood. The Egyptian would say, "Let us both drink together from the same dish." The Israelite would drink water, the Egyptian, blood. But if the Egyptian would buy the water from the Israelite and pay for it, he drank water. That is how the Israelites became rich (*Midrash Tanchuma*, *Va'eira* 14).

How can God, whose Presence fills the universe, choose an earthly House of Worship for Himself?

When the Holy One, Blessed is He, said to Moses, "Make a Tabernacle for Me," Moses was amazed and exclaimed, "The glory of the Holy One, Blessed is He, fills the upper and lower worlds, and He commands me to make a Temple for Him?" Furthermore, he foresaw that Solomon would erect a Temple greater than the Tabernacle and declare before the Holy One, Blessed is He, "But will God really dwell on earth? Behold, heaven and the heaven of heavens cannot contain You; how much less this house that I have built!" Moses then said, "If Solomon, whose Temple is much larger than the Tabernacle says this, how much more must I!" Thereupon he uttered the words, "Whoever sits in the refuge of the Most High, he shall dwell in the shadow of the Almighty"[4] (Psalm 91:1). But the Holy One, Blessed is He, said to Moses, "Not as you think do I think. If I so desire, I make My dwelling place between twenty boards on the north and south and eight boards on the west.[5] Even more than that, I can confine My Shechinah (Divine Presence) within a square cubit" (Exodus *Rabbah* 34:1).

Shabbat

"See that God has given you the Shabbat" (Exodus 16:29). How does "see" fit into this context? Said Rabbi Yosi: See what a pearl I am giving you (*Yalkut Shimoni, Shemot* 16).

Enjoyment of Shabbat

Said Rabbi Berechiah: Shabbat was given to be enjoyed. Said Rabbi Chaggai: Shabbat was given to be used for Torah study. But there is no conflict between their statements. When Rabbi Berechiah sees Shabbat as a day for enjoyment, he has the Torah scholars in mind, who exert themselves on their studies all week long. They may delight in the pleasures of Shabbat. Rabbi Chaggai's statement that Shabbat was meant for Torah study refers to working people, who labor on their job throughout the week. For them Shabbat is the day for Torah study (*Pesikta Rabbah*).

Shabbat candles

If you observe the precept of lighting the Shabbat candles, I will show you the lamps of Zion.[6] For it is said: "And it shall come to pass at that time, that I will search Jerusalem with lamps" (Zephaniah 1:12) (*Yalkut Shimoni, Beha'alotecha*).

Torah means freedom

Said Rabbi Abahu, "The entire forty days Moses spent in heaven he learned the Torah and immediately forgot it. Moses exclaimed, 'Master of the Universe, forty days have gone by and I do not know anything!'" What did God do? When the forty days were completed, He gave him the Torah as a gift, as it is written, *"He gave to Moses . . . two tablets of the Testimony"* (Exodus 31:18). *Two tablets of the Testimony*—Corresponding to heaven and earth, to bride and groom, to the best men and bride's maids, to This World and the World to Come. *They were stone tablets*—In the merit of Jacob, about whom Scripture says, ". . . he became a shepherd, a rock (stone) of Israel" (Genesis 49:24). *The tablets were made by God* (Exodus 32:16)—Every single day a Heavenly Voice emanates from Mount Horeb, proclaiming and saying, "Woe to them, to the people, because of their insult to the Torah! For whoever does not occupy himself with the Torah is called 'rebuked,' as it is said, *'made by God,'* thus they are God's handiwork." *Engraved on the tablets* [*charut*—engraved—can also be read as *cherut*, meaning freedom, signifying that the laws on the tablets mean freedom]—What freedom? Rabbi Yehudah says, "Freedom from the yoke of government," Rabbi Nechemiah says, "Freedom from the Angel of Death," the Rabbis said, "Freedom from affliction" (*Midrash Tanchuma—Ki Tisa* 12).

The tongue is a double-edged sword

Rabbi Shimon ben Gamliel said to Tobi, his slave, "Go to the market and buy for me a good dish." Tobi bought a tongue. Then he said to him, "Now go to the market and buy me a bad dish." Again Tobi bought a tongue. Said Rabbi Shimon ben Gamliel to him, "Why is it that when I told you to buy a good dish, you bought a tongue, and when I told you to buy a bad dish, you also bought a tongue?" Replied Tobi, "A tongue is both good and bad. When it is good, there is nothing better in the world, but when it is bad, there is nothing worse in the world" (Leviticus *Rabbah* 33).

Rabbi[7] prepared a feast for his disciples. He set before them tender and tough tongues. They selected the tender ones, leaving the tough ones. He said to them, "My children, may you be equally gentle in your speech to one another. When you say blessings, your tongue is an instrument of life. When you spread slander, your tongue becomes an instrument of death" (*Yalkut Shimoni*, Psalm 52).

Rabbi Elazar said: Man has 248 parts, some of which stand upright and others which lie flat. The tongue is restrained by two jaws, a steady flow of water passes over it, and it is folded and crumpled. Now consider, how many fires the tongue ignites. How much more harm would it inflict if it would stand upright! (Leviticus *Rabbah* 16).

Honesty

It happened that Pinchas ben Ya'ir was living in one of the cities of the South [of Eretz Yisrael], and some men who visited there left two measures of barley in his possession and forgot about them when they left. He sowed the barley and each year stored the produce. After seven years had elapsed the men returned to that town. He recognized them and told them to receive what belonged to them. It also happened that Shimon ben Shetach bought an ass from an Arab. His disciples found a gem suspended from its neck. They said to him, "It is true of you, 'The blessing of the Lord makes rich' " (Proverbs 10:22). He answered them, "I bought the ass, not the gem. Go, return it to the owner." The Arab exclaimed, "Blessed is the God of Shimon ben Shetach" (Deuteronomy *Rabbah* 3:3).

A man's conduct affects his neighbors

If one man sins, will You be angry with the entire community? (Numbers 16:22). It is like a group of men on board a ship. One of them took a drill and began to bore a hole under him. The other passengers said to him, "What are you doing?" He replied, "What has that to do with you? Am I not making the hole under my seat?" They retorted, "But the water will enter and drown us all!" (Leviticus *Rabbah* 4:6).

Reward for observance of mitzvot

Rabbi Shimon ben Yochai taught: In the case of two mitzvot the Holy One, Blessed is He, has revealed the reward that is granted for the fulfillment of them, one mitzvah being the easiest of all commandments, the other being the most demanding. The easiest is the law of the bird's nest[8]—regarding this mitzvah it says, ". . . you will live long" (Deuteronomy 22:7). The most demanding mitzvah is the commandment to honor one's father and mother, concerning which it says, "You will then live long" (Exodus 20:12). They are thus equal in their reward in this world (Midrash *Tanchuma—Ekev*).

The Ten Commandments

"I am the Lord Your God"—Why are the Ten Commandments not written at the beginning of the Torah? The following analogy will explain it. A man enters a foreign country and announces to the people: "I wish to be your ruler." They will answer him, "What have you done for us that we should choose you as our ruler?" What did the man do? He constructed walls for their cities, installed aqueducts to supply water to their

homes, and led them to victory in their wars. Again he said: "I wish to be your ruler." Now they all exclaimed unanimously, "Yes, yes!" God acted similarly. He led Israel out of Egypt, parted the Red Sea for them, provided them with water from the Well, made a flock of quail descend on the camp, fought for them against Amalek. Then He said to them: "Let Me be your King." They all responded "Yes, yes!" Rabbi said: This teaches you the praiseworthy character of Israel. When they all stood at the foot of Mount Sinai to receive the Torah, they were unanimous in their desire to accept joyfully God's absolute sovereignty (*Mechilta Yitro*).

The synagogue—a miniature Temple

"*I sleep, but my heart is awake*" (Song of Songs 5:2)— The Community of Israel said to the Holy One, Blessed is He, "Master of the Universe, *I sleep*—being deprived of the *Bet Hamikdash* (Temple)—*but my heart is awake*—in the synagogues and the houses of study" (Song of Songs *Rabbah* 5).

A startling statement

Rav was delivering a lecture and noticed that the audience was dozing off. Wishing to rouse them, he said: "There was one woman in Egypt who gave birth to 600,000 babies at one birth." Now there was one student whose name was Rabbi Yishmael ben Rabbi Yosi, who cried out, "Really?" Rav answered, "Yes, the woman was Yocheved, who gave birth to Moses, who was equivalent to the 600,000 men in Israel" (Song of Songs *Rabbah* 1).

Submission to God's will

It happened that while Rabbi Meir was lecturing in the House of Study on the afternoon of Shabbat, his two sons died at home. Their mother laid them on a bed and covered them with a sheet. At the close of Shabbat, Rabbi Meir returned to his house and asked where his children were. His wife said to him, "I want to ask you a question. Some time ago a person came here and entrusted a valuable article in my care. Now he wants it back. Shall I return it to him or not?" He answered, "Surely, a pledge must be returned to its owner!" She then said, "Without asking for your consent I gave it back to him." She thereupon took him by the hand, led him into the upper room, and removed the sheet from the bodies. When he saw them he wept bitterly. She said to her husband, "Did you not tell me that what has been entrusted for safeguarding must be returned on demand? God gave, God has taken away, blessed be the name of God (Job 1:21)" (*Yalkut* Proverbs 964).

The light of God's kingdom

Arise and shine for Your light has come (Isaiah 60:1) —Said Rabbi Yochanan: A parable of a wayfarer walking at twilight. Someone lights a lamp for him, but it is put out. Says the wayfarer: Now I will wait for daybreak. Israel spoke to the Holy One, Blessed is He, in the same manner: We made a Menorah (lamp) for You in the days of Moses (in the Tabernacle); it was extinguished. We made another Menorah in the days of Solomon (in the Temple). It too was extinguished. Now we will wait for Your light, as it is written, "For with You is the fountain of light; in Your light do we see light" (Psalm 36:10) (*Yalkut Shimoni*, Isaiah 60:1).

Mitzvot—our lifeline

So that you may remember and perform all My commandments (Numbers 15:40)—An analogy can be made with a man who fell overboard. The captain, throwing him a lifeline, calls out to him: "Hold on to this rope. Don't let go. If you let it slip from your hands, you'll drown." So does the Holy One, Blessed is He, call out to the people of Israel: "So long as you cling to the mitzvot, this verse will apply to you: 'You who cling to the Lord your God—you are all alive today'" (Deuteronomy 4:4) (*Midrash Tanchuma, Shelach* 31).

All Creation sings God's praises

They say about King David: When he concluded the Book of Psalms, he felt rather proud of himself. He said to the Holy One, Blessed is He, "Master of the Universe, is there any creature in the whole wide world that sings Your praises more than I do?" At that moment there appeared a frog. It said to him: "Don't be too boastful. I offer hymns and praises to God far more than you do" (*Yalkut Shimoni*, Psalm, from *Perek Shirah*).

Material wealth has no lasting value

It may be likened to a fox who found a vineyard fenced around on all sides; but there was just one hole. He wished to enter through it, but was unable to do so. He fasted three days until he became very thin, and then went through the opening. He feasted there and, of course, grew fat again. When he wanted to get out, he was unable to pass through the hole. So he fasted another three days until he had grown thin, and then he went out. When he was outside, he turned back, and looking at it cried, "O vineyard, what use have you been to me and what use are your fruits? All that is inside is beautiful and praiseworthy, but what benefit has one from you? As you enter, so you come out." So, too, is the world. When a person enters it, his hands are clenched, as though to say, "Everything is mine. I will inherit it all." When he departs from the world, his hands are open, as though to say, "I have acquired nothing from the world" (Ecclesiastes *Rabbah* 5:14).

III

HALACHAH

As noted in the sections on Mishnah and Talmud, the Oral Law was transmitted from Sinai and reached us in the form of discussions and debates that clarified and analyzed its parameters and ramifications. Additional rabbinic enactments were instituted to safeguard against transgression of the law of the Torah itself. For example, the Rabbis prohibited the use of certain utensils on the Shabbat (*muktzeh*), lest you use them to perform a labor forbidden by the Torah. This multitude of laws, enactments, and ordinances is scattered throughout the vast sea of the Talmud, often interwoven with lengthy debates on a law's derivation from scriptural verse or with aggadic homilies and stories with deep ethical content. The halachists undertook the monumental task of codifying these laws and offering clear-cut rulings in undecided cases. Since Halachah is a living organism, it provides answers to any given problem or situation that may arise to confront the Jewish community or individual. By applying halachic principles and precedents, rabbis throughout the ages have rendered authoritative *teshuvot* (responsa) to *she'eilot* (halachic questions) that were brought before them regarding all aspects of Jewish life. Indeed, the vast responsa literature provides an accurate reflection of the joys and sorrows that faced Jewish communities at particular junctures in history. Halachah has been the mainstay of Judaism and continues to be the faithful guide that leads Jews on their daily paths through life.

RABBI YITZCHAK AL-FASI—RIF
רבי יצחק אלפסי—רי״ף

born: Kila Chamad, Algeria, 1013
died: Lucena, Spain, 1103
Commonly referred to as Rif, the acronym formed by the letters of his name. Talmudist, codifier.

A student of Rabbi Nissim ben Yaakov and Rabbi Chananel, Rif knew the great Rav Hai Gaon, the last of the Geonim. He settled in Fez, a fact indicated by his name, Rabbi Yitzchak al-Fasi (of Fez). There he headed a large yeshivah. When he was 75 years of age, unknown enemies denounced him to the government and he was forced to flee to Spain. He stayed briefly in Cordova and then settled in Lucena, which had been a bastion of Torah study for more than 200 years. After the death of Rabbi Yitzchak ibn Gias, Rif became his successor as rabbi and head of the yeshivah. Among his disciples are counted Rabbi Yosef ibn Migash and **Rabbi Yehudah Halevi. Rashi** in France and Rif in Spain were acknowledged as the two leading Torah giants of that era. Rif is best remembered for his seminal work, *Sefer Hahalachot*. From the wide-ranging discussions of the *Amora'im* in the Talmud, Rif extracts those segments that have practical application to daily Jewish life. Accordingly, his writings cover only the Orders of *Mo'ed*, dealing with the laws of Shabbat and the Festivals; *Nashim*, dealing with marriage and divorce; *Nezikin*, dealing with torts and damages; and the Tractates *Chullin* (dietary laws) and *Berachot* (blessings). His work presents halachic decisions on all matters affecting a Jew's day-to-day conduct. At the same time, it represents an abridged form of the Talmud, which greatly facilitates the study of the sources of the various laws. Of the aggadic portions of the Talmud, he selected only those that teach ethical conduct and character improvement, omitting aggadot with historical content. Rif's decisions form the basis of **Rambam**'s code, which, in turn, is the work on which **Rabbi Yosef Karo**'s *Shulchan Aruch* is based. Thus, every contemporary decision can be traced directly to Rif's work. Many commentaries were written on *Sefer Hahalachot*, among them, **Ran** and **Rabbeinu Yonah** (on *Berachot*). *Sefer Hahalachot* (Rif) is printed in the Vilna edition of the Talmud, together with a number of commentaries. Rif's work, being the underpinning of every halachic decision, has guided, shaped, and preserved Jewish life for nearly one thousand years. (*For excerpts, see pp. 96–98.*)

Page of Rif's commentary to *Pesachim*, Chapter 1. Rif extracts from the Gemara those segments that are halachically relevant. Surrounding Rif's text is the commentary of Ran. Printed at the end of the standard Vilna edition of the Babylonian Talmud, the *Vilna Shas*.

RABBI NISSIM—RAN
רבי נסים—ר״ן

born: Spain, c. 1290
died: Barcelona, Spain, c. 1375
Popularly known as Ran, the acrostic formed by the initials of his name. Halachist, talmudic commentator.

Ran received his Torah education from his father and at a young age was recognized as the foremost rabbinical authority of his time. In his capacity as rabbi of Barcelona and leading figure in Spanish Jewry, he received thousands of inquiries from France, Italy, North Africa, and even from Safed in Eretz Yisrael. Only 77 of his responsa are extant, and they have been published as *Teshuvot HaRan.*[1] His greatest contribution to Torah scholarship is his commentary on **Rif**'s *Sefer Hahalachot*, which is printed jointly with Rif in the Vilna edition of the Talmud. He clarifies the text, subjecting the opinions of earlier authorities to careful scrutiny. Ran is known to every young yeshivah student for his running commentary on Tractate *Nedarim*, which is printed alongside **Rashi**'s and is indispensable to a clear understanding of this complex Gemara, dealing with vows and oaths. His homiletic work *Derashot HaRan*[2] presents a comprehensive explanation of the tenets of the Jewish faith. Many great thinkers after Ran, such as **Rabbi Yosef Albo** in his *Ikkarim*, built their philosophical systems on the foundation of *Derashot HaRan*. Rabbi Yitzchak Perfet (Rivash), the eminent student of Ran, describes his mentor in the following glowing terms: "No scholar in Israel can compare with him. In his presence they all are like a skin of garlic and a sesame seed."

SELECTIONS FROM THE COMMENTARY OF RIF AND RAN

Excerpt of Rif's commentary from the Gemara in *Shabbat* 23b, in conjunction with the commentary of Ran

The commentary to *Pesachim*, Chapter 1, of Ran, Rabbeinu Nissim, who clarifies and sometimes criticizes Rif. Rif and Ran are printed at the end of the standard Vilna edition of the Babylonian Talmud, the *Vilna Shas*.

Rif: Rava said: It is obvious to me [that if one must choose between] lighting the Chanukah light and the Shabbat candles [Rashi—when Chanukah and Shabbat coincide, and he cannot afford both], the Shabbat candles are preferable because they contribute to the peace in the home. [If he must choose] between the Shabbat candles and wine for *Kiddush* (Sanctification) of Shabbat, the Shabbat candles are preferable because of the peace of the home. Rava asked: What if the choice lies between the Chanukah lights and the *Kiddush* of Shabbat: is the latter more important because it is permanent [coming every week, whereas Chanukah is temporary, coming only once a year]; or perhaps the Chanukah light is preferable because it publicizes the miracle? After asking the question, he himself solved it: The Chanukah light is preferable because it publicizes the miracle.

Ran: *It is obvious to me that* [*if one must choose*] *between the Chanukah lights and the Shabbat candles, the latter are preferable because they contribute to the peace in the home*—If he is poor and cannot afford both, the Shabbat candles are preferable. They create the peaceful atmosphere in the home, because it distresses the family if they are forced to sit in the dark. *If the choice lies between Chanukah lights and Kiddush, the Chanukah lights are preferable, because they publicize the miracle*—You may raise the question: How can the Shabbat lights and the Chanukah lights set aside the Kiddush, which is a biblical command? The answer is that, in fact, the Kiddush is not set aside, because it is possible to recite the Kiddush over bread (see *Pesachim* 106b). Of course, if not for the conflict with the principles of "peace in the home" and "publicizing the miracle," the preferred way is to recite the Kiddush over wine.

Excerpt of Rif's commentary from the Gemara in *Shabbat* 69b, accompanied by the commentary of Ran

Rif: Rav Huna said: If someone is traveling in the desert and does not know when it is Shabbat, he must count six days and observe one. [Rashi—he counts six days from the day that he discovers that he has forgotten when it is Shabbat and he observes the seventh day as Shabbat]. Rava said: Every day he does only work sufficient to stay alive, except on that [seventh] day. And on that [seventh] day, is he to die? He prepared double his needs on the previous day. But perhaps the previous day was Shabbat. [What should he do?]. Every day he does sufficient work to stay alive—even on the seventh day. Then how is that [seventh] day to be recognized? By Kiddush and Havdalah.[3]

Ran: *He counts six days*—from the day that he discovered that he forgot when it is Shabbat. *And he observes*—the seventh day. *And each day he does only work sufficient to stay alive*—but no more, since it may be Shabbat. He may do only the least amount of work needed to sustain life, for this permission is granted only in order to save life. The next question is predicated on this statement: *and on that day is he to die?*—Since on the previous day he only prepared for the bare necessities of that day, if he does not work on the seventh he will die. *But perhaps the previous day was Shabbat?*—Then he would have desecrated the Shabbat unnecessarily, not for the purpose of saving life. *By Kiddush and Havdalah*—just as a reminder, to distinguish one day from the others, so that he will not forget that there is a Shabbat. Now you may ask, let the seventh day be distinguished through his observance of the laws of *techum Shabbat* (Shabbat boundaries),[4] in that he will not walk a greater distance than the *techum* (2,000 cubits). And since this observance does not involve saving life, he might even observe it every day [for every day might be Shabbat]. You might say that *techumin* has not been mentioned, because if he would observe the restrictions of *techum*, he would spend the rest of his life in the desert, desecrate the Shabbat, and die in a wasteland. The actual reason is, however, that the prohibition has not been mentioned because it is a rabbinic ordinance, and this person is, therefore, permitted to walk beyond the Shabbat boundary on the [seventh] day.

Excerpt of Rif's commentary from the Mishnah in *Pesachim* 116b, accompanied by the commentary of Ran

Rif: The matzah (unleavened bread) is [eaten on Passover] because our forefathers were redeemed from Egypt, as it is said, "and they baked unleavened cakes of the dough which they brought forth from Egypt" (Exodus 12:39).

Ran: *The matzah (unleavened bread) is* [*eaten on Passover*] *because our forefathers were redeemed from Egypt—and they could not delay* (Exodus 12:39)—If they could have delayed, they would have allowed the dough to rise. They could have done so without violating any law, because the original Passover that took place in Egypt lasted only for one night and one day (see *Pesachim* 96b). The following day they were permitted to do work and to eat *chametz* (leavened bread). Therefore, if they would have had the time, they would have let their dough rise, as the prohibition of "no leavening shall be seen with you" (Deuteronomy 16:4) did not apply to them. Because they were rushed, they baked it into unleavened bread, and we are commanded to eat matzot in commemoration of that redemption.

Excerpt of Rif's commentary from the Gemara in *Sukkah* 28b, joined by Ran's commentary

Rif: Our Rabbis have taught: All seven days [of Sukkot] you should make the sukkah your permanent dwelling, and your house your temporary dwelling. In what way? If you have beautiful vessels you should bring them into the sukkah; beautiful sofas, you should bring them into the sukkah; you should eat and drink and amuse yourself in the sukkah. From where in the Torah do we know this? Our Rabbis have taught: "During [these] seven days you must live in sukkot" (Leviticus 23:42). *You must live* implies living in the same way you ordinarily live. Therefore they said: All seven days of Sukkot you should make the sukkah your permanent dwelling, and your house your temporary dwelling. . . . You should eat and drink and amuse yourself in the sukkah. You should also study in the sukkah, that is to say, reading,[5] but profound study may be done outside of the sukkah.

Ran: *But profound study may be done outside of the sukkah*—Rashi, agreeing with Rif, explains that profound study that requires great concentration may be done outside the sukkah because [great concentration in a cramped sukkah] causes discomfort, and a person suffering discomfort is exempt from the mitzvah of sukkah. In this case, the fresh air outside the sukkah would relieve his distress and clear his mind.

Excerpt from Rif's commentary on the Gemara *Berachot* 10b, accompanied by the commentary of **Rabbeinu Yonah**.

Rif: Rabbi Yose son of Chaninah said: When praying, one should place his feet in the proper position (Rashi—i.e., close together), as it is written, ". . . and their feet were a straight foot" (Ezekiel 1:7) [Rashi—they appeared as one foot].

Rabbeinu Yonah: *When praying one should place his feet in the proper position*—That is to say, one should place his feet close together, to make them appear as one, as is indicated by the word *"regel"* (foot) [in the singular]. In the Jerusalem Talmud we find a difference of opinion between two *Amora'im*. One says the feet should be positioned as the kohanim's (priests') feet, meaning, the heel of one foot near the toe of the other, simulating the kohanim, who were not permitted to take large steps. They walked, placing heel to toe in compliance with the verse, "Do not climb up to My altar with steps, so that your nakedness not be revealed on it" (Exodus 20:28). The other *Amora* holds that the feet should be placed in the manner of angels, close together, so as to appear as one foot, consistent with the verse, *Their feet were a straight foot*. Our [Babylonian] Talmud sides with the opinion of "in the manner of angels." Therefore, it is required that we place our feet close together to make them appear as one. There are some who follow the custom of spreading their feet at the tips, in keeping with the latter part of the same verse, "and the sole of their feet was like the sole of a calf's foot" (Ezekiel 1:7), but there is no basis for this custom, since the Talmud mentions only placing the feet close together, to make them appear as one.

RABBI MOSHE BEN MAIMON (MAIMONIDES)—RAMBAM
רבי משה בן מיימון—רמב״ם

born: Cordova, Spain, 1135
died: Cairo, Egypt, 1204
Popularly known as Rambam (after the initials of his name) and Maimonides (Greek for "son of Maimon").
Halachist, commentator, philosopher.

In about 1170, Rambam began to write his monumental *Mishneh Torah*, a compendium of all Jewish laws extracted from the Talmud and the works of the Geonim. The work consists of fourteen volumes and is also called *Yad Hachazakah* (the word *yad* in Hebrew is written the same as the number 14, an allusion to the fourteen volumes of his work). For short it is often referred to as *Yad*, or simply the *Rambam*. It was completed in 1180 and written in a lucid and concise mishnaic Hebrew. It was the first comprehensive codification of all Torah laws. It includes both the laws of immediate relevance, such as the laws of Shabbat and family purity, and those pertaining to the Messianic Age, such as laws of the Temple service and sacrifices. Yet, *Mishneh Torah* is not a dry, legalistic book of statutes and ordinances. Its rulings are interspersed with ethical insights and philosophical teachings that infuse it with vitality and spirituality. Vast in scope, it has never been equalled or surpassed by any other work. Rambam has omitted mentioning his sources. This has become the subject of numerous commentaries that attempt to identity the references on which Rambam's rulings are based. Hundreds of thousands of Jews throughout the world daily study one or more chapters of *Mishneh Torah*.[1] (*For additional biographical information, see p. 203.*)

Rabbi Moshe ben Maimon (Maimonides), Rambam.

THE FOURTEEN BOOKS OF *MISHNEH TORAH*

1. *Knowledge*—Sefer Hamada
   ספר המדע
   Basic Principles of the Torah
   Ethical and Moral Conduct
   Study of the Torah
   Idolatry
   Repentance

2. *Love of God*—Sefer Ahavah
ספר אהבה
Recitation of the *Shema*
Prayer
Tefillin, Mezuzah, and Torah Scroll
Blessings
Circumcision

3. *Seasons*—Sefer Zemanim
ספר זמנים
Shabbat
Repose on the Festivals
Matzah
Shofar, Sukkah, Lulav
Sanctification of the New Moon
Fast Days
Reading of the Megillah and Chanukah

4. *Family Life*—Sefer Nashim
ספר נשים
Marriage and Divorce
Levirate Marriage and *Chalitzah*
Virgin
Suspected Adulteress

5. *Holiness*—Sefer Kedushah
ספר קדושה
Forbidden Intercourse
Forbidden Foods
Slaughtering

6. *Utterances*—Sefer Hafla'ah
ספר הפלאה
Oaths
Vows
Naziriteship
Valuations

7. *Seeds*—Sefer Zera'im
ספר זרעים
Mixed seeds
Gifts to the Poor
Tithes
First Fruits
Shemittah and *Yovel*

8. *Service*—Sefer Avodah
ספר עבודה
The Temple
Vessels
Sacrifices
Yom Kippur Service
Trespass

9. *Sacrifices*—Sefer Korbanot
ספר קרבנות
Passover sacrifice
Festival offering
First-born
Errors
Substitute offerings

Title page of *Mishneh Torah*, also called *Yad Hachazakah*, the fourteen-volume compendium of all Torah laws.

10. *Purity*—Sefer Taharah
ספר טהרה
Uncleanness of the dead
Red Heifer
Uncleanness of Leprosy
Uncleanness of Foodstuffs
Mikva'ot—Immersion Pools

11. *Torts*—Sefer Nezikin
ספר נזיקין
Damages
Theft
Robbery and Lost Property
Wounding and Damaging
Murder and Guarding Life

12. *Acquisitions*—Sefer Kinyan
ספר קנין
Sales
Acquisition and Gift
Neighbors
Agents and Partners
Slaves

13. *Judgments*—Sefer Mishpatim
ספר משפטים
Hiring
Borrowing and Deposit
Creditor and Debtor
Pleading
Inheritance

14. *Judges*—Sefer Shofetim
ספר שופטים
Sanhedrin
Witnesses
Rebels
Mourning
Kings and Wars

SELECTIONS FROM RAMBAM'S COMMENTARY

Excerpt from Rambam's *HaMitzvot* (Book of Commandments)[2]

The Groundrules: I shall begin by saying that the sum total of the commandments that God has commanded us, as contained in the Torah, is 613. Of these, 248—corresponding to the number of limbs in the human body—are positive commandments; 365–cor-responding to the number of days in the solar year—are negative commandments. This number, 613, is mentioned in the Talmud at the end of Tractate *Makkot* 23b, where it says, "Six hundred and thirteen mitzvot were given to Moses at Sinai: 365 prohibitions corresponding to the days in the solar year, and 248 injunctions corresponding to the limbs in the human body." Homiletically, the sages have said about the number of positive commandments corresponding to the limbs in the human body, that it is as if each and every limb says to the person, "Perform a mitzvah with me"; and about the number of negative commandments corresponding to the number of days in the solar year, they said, "It is as if each and every day says to the person, 'Do not do a transgression this day.' "

Excerpt from *Mishneh Torah*, Book 2, *Ahavah* (Love of God), Laws of the mezuzah 6:13

A person should be careful in the observance of the mitzvah of the mezuzah, for it is an obligation perpetually binding on everyone. Whenever you enter or leave through a door with a mezuzah on its post, you will be confronted with the declaration of God's unity, and remember His love, and will be aroused from your slumber and your mindless interest in momentary vanities. You will realize that nothing lasts forever except knowledge of the Creator of the world. This awareness will immediately bring you back to your senses so that you will walk in the path of righteousness. Our sages of old said, "He who has tefillin (phylacteries) on his head and arm, tzitzit (fringes) on his garment, and a mezuzah on his door may be presumed not to sin, for he has many who caution him—angels that save him from sin—as it says, "The angel of God encamps around those who fear Him and he releases them" (Psalm 34:8).

Excerpt from *Mishneh Torah*, Book 3, *Zemanim* (Seasons), Laws of Shabbat 30:9

It is an obligation to eat three meals on Shabbat, one in the evening (Friday night), one in the morning, and one in the afternoon. You should be very careful to have no less than these three meals. Even a poor person living on charity should eat three meals on Shabbat. If, however, someone was ill from overeating, or he fasts regularly, he is exempt from having to eat three meals. At each of the three meals you should have wine and two loaves over which to recite the benediction. The same rule applies to festival meals.

186 כסף משנה הפלאה. הלכות ערכין וחרמין פ״ה

פרק חמישי

א המקדיש שדה אחוזתו מצוה עליו לפדותה הוא שהאדון קודם. ואם לא רצה אין כופין אותו. *במה דברים אמורים בזמן שמצות יובל נוהגת שאם יגיע יובל ולא יגאלנה תצא לכהנים כמו שבארנו. אבל בזמן שבטלו היובלות שהרי אינה יוצאת לכהנים אלא סופה להפדות לעולם כופין את האדון לפתוח בה תחלה והיא נפדית בשוייה כשאר ההקדשות. אם נמצא מי שמוסיף עליו וגואל אותה יגאל ואם לאו אומרין לו הגיעתך ויתן מה שאמר ואינו פותח בפחות מארבע פרוטות כדי שיהא החומש שמוסיף פרוטה: ב רצה האדון למכור שדות אחרות משדותיו או ללוות כדי לפדות שדה זו שהקדיש הרשות בידו. בין בזמן שהיובל נוהג בין בזמן שאין היובל נוהג. והוא קודם לכל אדם. וכן אם רצה לגאול חציה גואל. מה שאין כן במוכר להדיוט. זה חומר בהדיוט מבהקדש: ג *המקדיש את ביתו או את בהמה טמאה שלו או שאר ממטלטליו הרי אלו נערכין בשוייהן בין טוב ובין רע. ואם פדה אותן המקדיש או אשתו או יורשו מוסיף חומש. וכופין את הבעלים לפתוח ראשון והדמים לבדק הבית. בין שהיה הבית מבתי ערי חומה בין

השגת הראב״ד

משנה למלך

לחם משנה

מגדל עוז

Page of Rambam, *Mishneh Torah, Sefer Hafla'ah,* Book of Utterances, Laws of Valuations 5:1. From a copy of the standard edition.

Excerpt from *Mishneh Torah*, Book 5, *Kedushah* (Holiness), Laws of *Shechitah* 1:1

It is a positive commandment that anyone who wishes to eat of the meat of a domestic animal, wild beast, or fowl must first perform *shechitah* on it, and only after that may he eat it, as it is said, "You shall slaughter of your cattle and of your small animals" (Deuteronomy 12:21).

Excerpt from *Mishnah Torah*, Book 5, *Kedushah* (Holiness), Laws of *Shechitah* 1:4

This method of slaughtering, which is mentioned in the Torah without definition, must be explained, in order to know on what organ of the animal the *shechitah* must be performed, the parameters of the *shechitah*, with what instrument, when and how it must be performed, what things make it invalid, and who may perform it. All these matters are included in the general Torah commandment, "Then you shall slaughter of your cattle and your small animals . . . in the manner that I have prescribed" (Deuteronomy 12:21), which means that Moses was commanded all these rules orally, as is the case with the rest of the Oral Law.

Excerpt from *Mishneh Torah*, Book 11, *Nezikin* (Torts), 13:1

If, on the road, you encounter a person whose animal is lying under the weight of its burden, you have the obligation to unload the burden from the animal, whether the burden is suited to it or too heavy for it. This is a positive commandment, for it is written, "You must make every effort to help him unload it" (Exodus 23:5).

Excerpt from *Mishneh Torah*, Book 11, *Nezikin* (Torts), 13:2

You may not unload the animal and then leave the other person shaken and upset, and go away; you must help him raise the animal and reload the burden onto it, for it is written, "You must help him pick up the load" (Deuteronomy 22:4), which is an additional positive commandment. If one leaves the other person shaken and upset, and neither unloads nor reloads, he disregards the positive commandment and transgresses a negative commandment, for it is written, "You shall not see your brother's donkey or his ox fallen down by the way" (Deuteronomy 22:4).

Excerpt from *Mishneh Torah*, Book 14, *Shofetim* (Judges), Kings and Wars 12:4

The sages and prophets did not yearn for the days of the Messiah in order that Israel might have dominion over the entire world, or rule over the heathens, or be exalted by the nations, or to eat, drink, and celebrate. Rather, they desired to be free to devote themselves to Torah and its wisdom, with no one to oppress or disturb them, so that they would be worthy of the World to Come.

Excerpt from *Mishneh Torah*, Book 14, *Shofetim* (Judges), Kings and Wars 12:5[3]

In that era there will be neither famine nor war, neither envy nor rivalry. Blessings will be abundant, and all delights will be as commonplace as dust.[4] The sole occupation of the whole world will be to know God.

Therefore, the Jews will be great sages; they will know the things that are hidden and will attain understanding of their Creator, to the utmost capacity of the human intellect, as it says, "The world will be filled with the knowledge of God as the waters fill the sea" (Isaiah 11:9).

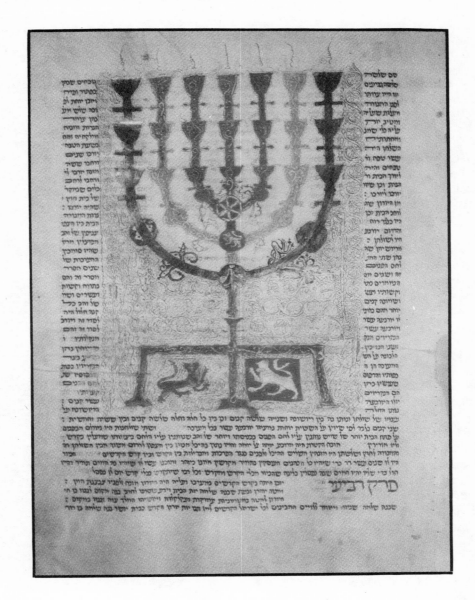

A page from the first known complete copy of a medieval manuscript from the code of Maimonides. From Central Europe, first half of the fourteenth century.

RABBI AVRAHAM BEN DAVID OF POSQUIERES—RAVAD III

רבי אברהם בן דוד מפושקיירש—ראב"ד

born: Narbonne, Provence, France, c. 1120
died: Posquieres, Provence, France, c. 1197
Commonly referred to as Ravad. Talmudist and halachist.

At a young age, Ravad directed a yeshivah in Nimes which, under his leadership, became the foremost learning institution in Provence (in Southern France). Later, he opened an academy at Posquieres and personally paid for the support of his needy students. In spite of his great wealth, he abstained from all luxuries, leading a pious and ascetic life-style. He wrote numerous brilliant treatises on all phases of religious observance. Ravad is best known for his caustic criticism of **Rambam**'s *Mishneh Torah*. He disapproved of the fact that Rambam failed to list the sources on which he based his decisions. Notwithstanding his often biting remarks, Ravad admitted, "Rambam has produced a monumental work in assembling the material from Gemara, *Yerushalmi*, and *Tosefta*" (Laws of *Kilayim* 6:2). For his part, Rambam held Ravad in high esteem, bowing to his criticism. Ravad's critical notes have been incorporated as glosses into the standard text of all full editions of Rambam, as *Hasagot HaRavad* (Ravad's critical notes). From his father-in-law, Ravad II, he received instruction in the teachings of Kabbalah. He reached high spiritual levels of *Ru'ach HaKodesh* (Divine Inspiration) and had the merit of having the Prophet Elijah appear to him. A commentary on the mystical *Sefer Yetzirah*[1] is attributed to him.

186 כסף משנה הפלאה. הלכות ערכין וחרמין פ"ה

פרק חמישי

Page of *Mishneh Torah*, *Sefer Hafla'ah*, Book of Utterances, Laws of Valuations 5:1, with gloss by Ravad. From a copy of the standard edition.

SELECTIONS FROM RAVAD'S COMMENTARY

Excerpt from Rambam's *Mishneh Torah*, Book 14, *Shofetim* (Judges), Kings and Wars 11:3, with commentary by Ravad

One should not presume that the Messianic King must work miracles and wonders, bring about new creations within the world, resurrect the dead, or perform similar deeds. This is not so. [This can be proven by the fact] that Rabbi Akiva, one of the great sages of the

Mishnah, was one of the supporters of King Ben Koziba (Bar Kochba) and would describe him as the Messianic King. He and all the sages of his generation considered him to be the Messianic King until he was killed because of sins. Once he was killed, they realized that he was not [the Messiah]. The sages did not ask him to perform any signs or wonders.

Ravad: [Disagreeing with Rambam's statement that "one should not presume that the Messianic King must work miracles," Ravad] states, "Quite to the contrary, we read in *Sanhedrin* 93b that Ben Koziba declared himself as King Messiah. The sages then tested him to determine if he had the gift of prophecy. When he was unable to demonstrate this power, they had him killed.[2]

Excerpt from Rambam's *Mishneh Torah*, Book 3, *Zemanim* (Seasons), Laws of Lulav 8:5, with commentary by Ravad

If the top of the hadas *(myrtle twig)[3] is broken off, it is valid.*

Ravad: A number of years ago we experienced in our *Bet Midrash* (House of Learning) an appearance of *Ru'ach HaKodesh* (Divine inspiration),[4] from which we learned that such twigs are invalid. As for Rabbi Tarfon's statement that "even if all three twigs are broken, they are valid," he has something else in mind and does not mean that the top was broken.

RABBI ASHER BEN YECHIEL—ROSH
רבי אשר בן יחיאל—רא״ש

born: Germany, c. 1250
died: Toledo, Spain, 1327
*Popularly known as Rosh (*R*abbi* ASH*er). Halachist, talmudist.*

A scion of a rabbinical family and descendant of the illustrious Rabbi Gershon *Me'or Hagolah*, Rosh was the most important disciple of Maharam Rothenburg, whom he succeeded as spiritual leader and halachic authority of German Jewry (in 1293). After the Rindfleisch massacres in 1298, Rosh convened a conference to determine the disposition of the property of victims who had left no heirs. With the worsening situation of German Jewry, Rosh, fearing for his safety, left Germany, arriving in Spain in 1306. There he was welcomed by the great Rashba (Rabbi Shelomo ibn Aderet), Rabbi of Barcelona, with whom he had corresponded while in Germany. Before long he was invited by the community of Toledo to serve as its rabbi. In that capacity he headed the *bet din* (religious court), which was authorized by the Spanish government to enforce its own decrees by imposing judicial punishment—even the death penalty. After Rashba's death, Rosh was recognized as his successor, and thousands of halachic inquiries were directed to him from all parts of the world. His reponsa were published under the title *Teshuvot Harosh*.[1] His yeshivah became the focal point for Torah scholars who came from Spain, France, Germany, Bohemia, and even from far-off Russia. His magnum opus is a monumental halachic code in which he follows the talmudic tractates. His decisions, in which he indicates his sources, are printed in all editions of the Talmud. He also cites the main opinions on each law, showing the process by which the final decision was reached. This work is one of the foundations on which **Rabbi Yosef Karo** based his *Shulchan Aruch*. Rosh's pupils included his own eight sons, the most famous of whom was **Rabbi Yaakov Baal Haturim**, author of the halachic compendium *Arba'ah Turim*.[2] Rosh spread in Spain the teachings of the Tosafists and their approach to interpreting the Talmud, and he wrote a number of talmudic commen-

Text of the halachic code by Rosh, Rabbi Asher ben Yechiel, printed in all standard editions of the Talmud. Rosh decides the halachah, citing his sources. This page is *Bava Kama* 2a. Printed at the end of the standard Vilna edition of the Babylonian Talmud, the *Vilna Shas*.

taries. He is one of the most important halachic authorities in Jewish history.

SELECTIONS FROM ROSH'S WRITINGS

Rosh on *Rosh Hashanah* 4:11

It happened in Mainz [Germany] on Rosh Hashanah 4905/1145 that the *toke'a* (the person sounding the shofar) sounded two times the series of *tekiah-shevarim-teruah-tekiah*[3] sounds, but in the third series, after sounding only two of the three *shevarim* tones, he sounded the *teruah*. Some of the congregants told him to resume from the start, while others told him to sound one short *shevarim* tone and conclude. The *toke'a* thereupon resumed from the start and blew the three prescribed series: *tekiah-shevarim-teruah-tekiah*. When he came to sounding *tekiah-shevarim-tekiah* in the third series, he sounded a *shevarim* of four blasts (instead of three), then concluded with a *tekiah*. He was instructed to begin again, and this time blew correctly three times *tekiah-shevarim-tekiah*. Rabbi Eliyakim ben Yosef angrily told them that, although the *toke'a* showed a lack of proficiency, they should have respected his advanced age and should not have asked him to repeat. His son-in-law, Rabbi Eliezer ben Natan, concurred, adding that the *toke'a*, by unnecessarily repeating the sounds, violated a rabbinic prohibition (of producing sound). By sounding the *teruah* after only two *shevarim* blasts, he did nothing wrong, because both *shevarim* and *teruah* are sounded to comply with the required *teruah*. The reason for sounding both *shevarim* and *teruah* is rooted in our uncertainty as to the actual sound of *teruah*. He should have blown one short *shevarim* blast and followed that with the *teruah*. But if he had completed the *teruah* (after only two *shevarim* blasts), that would constitute an interruption, because the three *shevarim* tones must follow one another. In that case he would have to resume from the start of that series of *tekiah-shevarim-teruah-tekiah*. He did not have to repeat the first two series. Since there was no pause, these have not become invalid.

[Rosh decides]: The *shevarim* must be sounded in one uninterrupted breath. He should have repeated the three *shevarim* sounds and then blown the *teruah*. Even if he sounded the *teruah* [after erroneously sounding only two *shevarim* sounds], he blows three *shevarim* sounds, and the *teruah* he sounded does not constitute an interruption. It happens many times that the *toke'a* is unable to produce the proper sound. He pauses and begins again the *tekiah* or *teruah*. The improper sound

and the pause do not constitute an interruption, because the faulty sound is also part of the process of sounding the shofar. When the *toke'a* sounded four *shevarim* sounds, he did not thereby invalidate the *shevarim*. *Tekiah* and *shevarim* have no prescribed maximum length. Just as we may sound the *teruah* with more than nine tones, so may we make more *shevarim* sounds. If the *toke'a* is unable to continue, his substitute resumes where the first *toke'a* left off. Since he heard the blessings from the first *toke'a*, he need not recite the blessings again. Even if the *toke'a* was unable to sound even one tone, the substitute is exempted from reciting his blessing.

Rosh on *Kesuvot* 1:12

What blessing is recited [at the marriage ceremony]? "Blessed are You . . . Who has sanctified us with His commandments, and has commanded us regarding forbidden unions; Who forbade betrothed women to us and permitted women who are married to us through canopy and consecration." The question is raised: Why don't we say, instead, "Who has commanded us to consecrate a wife." Furthermore, it is asked: Isn't it strange to recite a blessing mentioning something that God has forbidden us? We certainly don't say in a blessing, "Who has forbidden us to eat the limb of a live animal and has permitted us to eat meat from an animal slaughtered by means of *shechitah*"! Furthermore, why mention forbidden unions at a wedding?

[Rosh answers]: This blessing was not ordained for the fulfillment of the commandment of "be fruitful and multiply." This is proven by the fact that this blessing is recited even at the wedding of a couple that is past child-bearing age. . . . This blessing was instituted in order to give praise to God, Who sanctified us with His mitzvot and separated us from the other nations and commanded us to consecrate a woman whom we are permitted to marry and not one who is forbidden to us.

Rosh on *Chullin* 8:26

It is customary [if you don't have a tallit] to wrap yourself in someone else's tallit, even without the owner's knowledge, and to recite the blessing over it. We base this practice on the assumption that "a person derives satisfaction from the fact that someone performs a mitzvah with his property." But if you find the tallit you borrow neatly folded, you must return it neatly folded; otherwise the owner won't take satisfaction in the fact that you performed a mitzvah with it.

RABBI YAAKOV BAAL HATURIM—THE TUR
רבי יעקב בעל הטורים—טור

born: Cologne, Germany, c. 1275
died: Toledo, Spain, 1343
Popularly referred to as the Tur. Halachist, Torah commentator.

Rabbi Yaakov Baal Haturim, the Tur.

Rabbi Yaakov, the third son of **Rosh,** studied under his father and under his older brother, Rabbi Yechiel. On the heels of the Rindfleisch persecutions he and his father fled Germany, arriving in Spain in 1306. After living for a few years with his brother Yechiel in Barcelona, he moved to Toledo, where his father served as rabbi. In 1329 Rabbi Yaakov wrote regarding Germany: "It is forbidden for a person to even traverse a place of mortal danger, let alone to live in the land of blood. . . . Anyone who succeeds in bringing a person out from there (Germany) is considered as having saved a Jewish soul." He lived in dire poverty, but refused to accept a rabbinical post, preferring studying and writing. After his father's death he was appointed as judge in the *bet din* (religious court) in Toledo. Rabbi Yaakov wrote a commentary on the Torah that is an extract of the commentaries of **Rashi, Ramban, Ibn Ezra, Redak,** and others. He prefaced each weekly portion with comments based on *gematrias*[1] and allusions. These prefaces are printed in most editions of the Chumash under the title *Baal Haturim*. His most important work is the *Arba'ah Turim* (Four Rows).[2] It is a summary of all halachot and serves as the basic text for the study of Halachah to this day. It is popularly referred to as the *Tur*. **Rabbi Yosef Karo** wrote his great commentary, *Bet Yosef*, on the *Tur* and patterned his *Shulchan Aruch* on the Tur's system of classifying halachot. Following in his father's footsteps, the Tur quotes all relevant sources and opinions before rendering his decision. Unlike Rosh, who arranged the halachot according to the talmudic tractates, the Tur classified his work by topics, limited to those applicable in the exile period, omitting all laws relating to the Temple service and ritual purity. The *Arba'ah Turim* (Four Rows) are (1) *Orach Chaim* (Path of Life), on daily, Shabbat, and holiday practices; (2) *Yoreh De'ah* (Teacher of Wisdom), on dietary laws, oaths, usury, family purity, *mikveh*, and mourning; (3) *Even Ha'Ezer* (Rock of Assistance), on marriage and divorce; and (4) *Choshen Mishpat* (Breastplate of Judgment), on business, disputes, damages, and torts. Each volume is divided into halachot and paragraphs. This format, coupled with a clear and uncomplicated literary style, makes it easy for the student to find and research a halachah and its derivation.

Title page of *Tur Yoreh De'ah* by Rabbi Yaakov Baal Haturim (part of *Arba'ah Turim*—the *Tur*, a summary of all halachot).

SELECTIONS FROM THE TUR'S WRITINGS

Excerpt from *Tur Orach Chaim*, Laws of Shabbat 242:1

We read in *Shabbat* 118a, "Rabbi Yochanan says, 'He who takes delight in the Shabbat will be granted a heritage that has no limitations.'" But what about the statement of Rabbi Akiva who said, "It is preferable to turn your Shabbat into a weekday rather than being dependent on other people's gifts" (*Shabbat* 118a).

Rabbi Akiva's statement refers to those whose poverty precludes buying special food to enjoy the Shabbat. But if it is at all possible, one should honor the Shabbat according to one's means. I discussed this topic with my honored father of blessed memory (the Rosh) on many occasions. I asked him whether I, in my current situation, owning very little, being needy and dependent on others, should be classified in the category of "one who should turn his Shabbat into a weekday rather than being dependent on other people's gifts." He never gave me an unequivocal response. Subsequently, I found the answer in Rashi's commentary on

Tur Yoreh De'ah, Laws of Forbidden Foods, Chapter 39. To the left of the main text is the commentary B. Y., Bet Yosef, by Rabbi Yosef Karo, who later wrote the *Shulchan Aruch*. From the classic standard edition.

the *Mishnah* in *Pirkei Avot* (5:23): "Yehudah ben Tema said: Be bold as a leopard—to carry out the will of your Father in Heaven." [Rashi comments]: "This Mishnah is preceded (in *Pesachim* 112a) by Rabbi Akiva's statement, 'Turn your Shabbat into a weekday rather than being dependent on people's gifts.'" This juxtaposition teaches us that Rabbi Akiva's statement applies only to people in dire straits, but that everyone else should be as eager as a leopard and an eagle to honor the Shabbat fully. Consequently, one should economize during the week in order to honor the Shabbat. He should not say, "I cannot afford it." On the contrary, the more one spends on the Shabbat, the more will his wealth increase.[3]

Excerpt from *Tur Yoreh De'ah*, Laws of Honoring One's Rabbi and a Torah Sage 244:1

It is written in Leviticus 19:32, "Stand up before a white head and give respect to the old." This is a commandment to rise before any sage, even if he is not an old man, even before a young Torah sage, even if the sage is not one's rabbi. One should also rise before an aged person who has reached the age of seventy years. When should you rise? When he comes to within four cubits of you, until he passes you. You may not look away to avoid having to stand up. It is not becoming for a sage to inconvenience the people by intentionally passing in front of them so as to make them rise. He should choose the most direct route to his destination, but if he makes a detour to avoid passing in front of people, it is considered meritorious. It is a mitzvah to honor non-Jewish aged persons by standing up before them and supporting them with your hand. The seating at a banquet or a wedding feast should be arranged according to age, the most prominent seat to be assigned to the eldest person.

Baal Haturim, a popular commentary on the Torah by Rabbi Yaakov Baal Haturim, which concentrates on finding significant meaning in the numerical value of words. From *Mikra'ot Gedolot*.

RABBI YOSEF KARO—SHULCHAN ARUCH
רבי יוסף קארו—בית יוסף, שולחן ערוך

born: Toledo, Spain, 1488
died: Safed, Eretz Yisrael, 1575
Popularly known as Beit Yosef and Shulchan Aruch, for his major works. Also known as the Mechaber, the author. Talmudist, codifier of Halachah.

In 1492, in the wake of the great expulsion of Spanish Jewry, when Yosef Karo was 4 years old, his family was forced to flee Spain. After protracted wanderings they settled in Constantinople, Turkey. He gained repute as an eminent Torah scholar at an early age, and at age 24, while living in Adrianople, he began writing his famous work, *Beit Yosef*. It is a commentary on *Arba Turim* by **Rabbi Yaakov**, son of **Rosh,** and it took him twenty years to complete. Under the influence of the great kabbalist, Rabbi Shelomoh Molcho, he followed an ascetic life-style of fasting and pious devotion to God. In 1530 he moved to Safed, in Eretz Yisrael, where he was appointed as a member of the Rabbinic Court of Rabbi Yaakov Beirav. He established a yeshivah, counting among his students the great Rabbi Moshe Alshich and the illustrious kabbalist **Rabbi Moshe Cordovero (Remak).** Upon the death of Rabbi Yaakov Beirav, he succeeded him as Chief of the Rabbinic Court in Safed, which served as the main *bet din* (court) for worldwide Jewry. Through his monumental books he became the acknowledged preeminent Torah authority in the world, a reputation that has not waned with the passage of time. In his work *Beit Yosef*, he compiles all the variant views on each halachah and renders a decision as to which opinion is to be the authoritative law. It is printed alongside the text of the *Arba Turim*. Rabbi Yosef Karo follows a cardinal rule in arriving at his decisions. If on a given issue **Rif, Rambam,** and **Rosh** are in agreement, then that matter becomes Halachah (Law). If they disagree, the halachah is decided according to the majority opinion. His rulings reflect his Sephardi[1] background in that they favor Sephardi customs over Ashkenazi[2] practices. After the completion of *Beit Yosef*, Rabbi Yosef

Rabbi Yosef Karo, author of *Shulchan Aruch*, comprehensive and authoritative guide to Jewish life.

Karo wrote the *Shulchan Aruch*.[3] As its title implies, *Shulchan Aruch*—"The Set Table"—presents all Jewish laws and customs relevant to the present time in clear and concise Hebrew, arranged systematically according to topics. This work, consisting of four sections, is the cornerstone of authoritative Halachah to this very day. It is *the* Code of Jewish Law par excellence. Initially, the *Shulchan Aruch* met with resistance on the part of German and Polish rabbinical authorities because its rulings favored Sephardi practices, disregarding Ashkenazi traditions. Foremost among the critics was **Rabbi Moshe Isserles (Rema)** of Cracow, Poland, whose critical comments have been incorporated as glosses into the running text. Among

Rabbi Yosef Karo's other works is *Kesef Mishneh*, a commentary on Rambam.[4] By clearly mentioning the sources on which his decisions are founded, Rabbi Yosef Karo has given Halachah a solid foundation. His work has stood the test of time. Indeed, the *Shulchan Aruch* continues to be the proverbial guide to all facets of Jewish living. (*For excerpts, see p. 115.*)

זה
שולחן המהור
אשר יקרא בשם
ספר
מגיני ארץ
עם
חמשה ועשרים
מפורשים מגדולי הראשונים והאחרונים הנדפסים
על
כל דף במקומו
וכולם מבוארים בשער השני
חלק ראשון
בדפוס והוצאת
מ. פ. פרעסס אינק
ע״י האחים פלאם
נוי יארק
שנת התשכ״ז לפ״ק

Title page of *Shulchan Aruch, Orach Chaim,* with twenty-five commentaries by early and later authorities. This edition is named *Meginei Eretz*, "The Shields of the Earth," a title borrowed from Psalm 47:10.

או״ח רצט הלכות שבת

Page of *Shulchan Aruch, Orach Chaim*, Laws of Shabbat 299:3,4,5, by Rabbi Yosef Karo. From the original standard edition.

THE FOUR SECTIONS OF THE SHULCHAN ARUCH

Orach Chaim
אורח חיים
Daily prayers
Tefillin
Tzitzit
Shema
Berachot (blessings)
Grace after Meals
Shabbat, Festivals, and Fasts

Yoreh De'ah
יורה דעה
Dietary Laws
Shechitah
Salting of Meat
Meat and Dairy
Charity
Circumcision
Torah Scrolls
Mourning

Even Ha'ezer
אבן העזר
Matrimony
Marriage
Divorce
Ketuvot (Marriage Contract)

Choshen Mishpat
חושן משפט
Witnesses
Judges
Loans
Overreaching
Creditor and Debtor
Lost Property
Partnerships and Agents
Sales
Inheritance
Gifts

RABBI DAVID HALEVI—TAZ
רבי דוד הלוי—ט"ז

born: Ludmir, Volhynia, 1586
died: Lemberg, Poland, 1667
Known as Taz, acronym of Turei Zahav, *the title of his major work. Halachist, son-in-law of Rabbi Yoel Sirkes, the rabbi of Brisk and famous author of* Bach (Bayit Chadash), *a commentary on the* Tur.

In 1618, Rabbi David HaLevi became rabbi of Potilitza in Galicia. He later assumed the rabbinate of Posen, where he remained for twenty years. In 1641, he was elected as rabbi of Ostrow, where he founded a renowned yeshivah and wrote his major commentary, *Turei Zahav (Taz) on Shulchan Aruch—Yoreh De'ah.*[1] After a miraculous escape from the murderous Chmielnicki Cossacks, he fled to Lublin and wandered through Germany and Moravia, staying briefly at the home of **Rabbi Shabtai HaKohen (Shach)** in Hollischau. In 1654 he returned to Poland as rabbi of Lemberg. He wrote *Turei Zahav* on all four sections of *Shulchan Aruch*, but the commentary on *Yoreh De'ah* gained the widest acceptance. It is printed alongside the main text, opposite the *Shach*, with whom he often disagrees on halachic points. An indication of the prominence of both commentaries may be seen in the fact that one of the requirements for rabbinic ordination (*semichah*) is a thorough familiarity with *Yoreh De'ah* along with the commentaries of Shach and Taz. (*For an example, see p. 115.*)

Page of *Shulchan Aruch, Yoreh De'ah* 282, 283, Laws of the Torah Scroll, with commentaries by Taz *(Turei Zahav)*, Rabbi David HaLevi; and by Shach *(Siftei Kohen)*, Rabbi Shabtai HaKohen. From the original standard edition.

RABBI SHABTAI HAKOHEN—SHACH
רבי שבתי הכהן—ש״ך

born: Amstibov, Lithuania, 1621
died: Hollischau, Bohemia, 1662
Known as Shach, the initials of his major work (Sifte Kohen) and his name. Halachist.

Shach studied under his father, the rabbi of Amstibov. After his marriage he lived in Vilna, totally immersing himself in Torah studies. In 1648, in the wake of the bloody Chmielnicki pogroms, he was forced to flee to Lublin and from there to Bohemia, where he served in the rabbinate of Dresnitz and Hollischau. He died an untimely death at the age of 41. During his brief life he wrote a number of very important works. He published his famous *Siftei Kohen (Shach),*[1] a commentary on *Shulchan Aruch (Yoreh De'ah* and *Choshen Mishpat* sections).[2] The commentary is printed alongside the main text and is an indispensable tool in the study of *Shulchan Aruch.* He wrote a number of other halachic books and a history of the devastation of Jewish communities during the Chmielnicki massacres.

Rabbi Shabtai HaKohen, Shach.

The following selection typifies a halachic dispute between Taz and Shach on a point of Halachah in Shulchan Aruch—Yoreh De'ah. *It is found in Chapter 89, paragraph 4, and focuses on a gloss by* **Rema.**

If you wish to eat meat after eating cheese, you must remove from the table the rest of the bread you ate with the cheese. It is forbidden to eat cheese on a tablecloth on which you have eaten meat, and it surely is forbidden to cut cheese with a knife used for cutting meat, and even the bread that is eaten with the cheese must not be cut with a knife that has been used to cut meat.

(Yoreh De'ah 89:4)

Rema's gloss: Conversely [it is also forbidden to cut meat with a knife that has been used for cutting cheese]. However, if you stick the knife into hard, compact earth, you are permitted to use it[3] [since the pressure against the compact earth removes any residue that may have been left on the knife].

Taz: The Rema's gloss requiring "sticking the knife into compact earth" refers to the case when you wish to cut cheese with a knife that has been used to cut meat, but cutting the bread with such a knife is permitted after merely wiping it thoroughly.

Shach: The Rema requires sticking the knife into solid earth even if you just want to cut the bread to be eaten with the cheese.

RABBI MOSHE ISSERLES—REMA
רבי משה איסרלש—רמ״א

born: Cracow, Poland, c. 1520
died: Cracow, Poland, 1572
Popularly known as Rema (accent on last syllable), the initials of his name. Halachist, commentator.

Rabbi Moshe Isserles, Rema.

Rema was a scion of a prominent and wealthy family. His father and grandfather were leaders of the Jewish community. The famous Rema Shul, a synagogue in Cracow, built by his father, survived the Holocaust. Even as a young boy he was known as an *illui* (prodigy), and before long his fame spread throughout Europe. As the rabbi of Cracow, he was very active in disseminating Torah knowledge, and he founded a prestigious yeshivah. Rema is one of the first Torah personalities to establish the spiritual predominance of Polish Jewry. It has been said that Rema is the Maimonides of Polish Jewry. He lived in the age of the codification of the Talmud, and he corresponded with **Rabbi Yosef Karo**, author of the *Shulchan Aruch,* the most influential work in that field. Rema was an admirer and, at the same time, a critic of the *Shulchan Aruch,* disapproving of the fact that its rulings are based primarily on decisions of Sephardi authorities, excluding Ashkenazi customs and traditions. He composed glosses on those paragraphs of the *Shulchan Aruch* in which he differs from the author, stating the Halachah as it has been decided by the Ashkenazi authorities, which is binding on Ashkenazi Jews. It should be noted that these halachic differences concern only peripheral matters of custom and tradition. On the fundamental issue of the belief in the supremacy of Torah law and unfaltering commitment to halachic authorities, the two communities stand as one, firmly and inseparably united. Rema named his glosses *Mappah* ("Tablecloth"), as a "cover" for the *Shulchan Aruch* ("the Set Table"). These glosses have been incorporated into the text and are distinguishable in that they are printed in *Rashi* script,[1] as opposed to the bold-faced Hebrew type of the main text. The consolidation of the two works symbolizes the underlying unity of the Sephardi and Ashkenazi communities, whose chief spokesmen were the authors. It is through this unification that the *Shulchan Aruch* became the universally accepted Code of Law for the entire Jewish people. (*For excerpts from Rema's writings, see pp. 119–121.*)

Text of *Shulchan Aruch, Orach Chaim,* Laws of Shabbat 368, with gloss by Rema, written in Rashi script. Each gloss is prefaced by the word *hagah,* gloss. Rema's humility prompted him to state his opinions in the form of glosses to the *Shulchan Aruch,* rather than to write a work of his own about it. From the original standard edition.

Page of *Shulchan Aruch* with an annotation by Rema. He explains here the Ashkenazi usage where it differs from the Sephardi, which had previously been the only usage described in the *Shulchan Aruch.* With the insertion of Rema's glosses, this work achieved universal acceptance.

RABBI YISRAEL MEIR HAKOHEN KAGAN—THE CHAFETZ CHAIM

רבי ישראל מאיר הכהן—חפץ חיים

born: Zhetel, Lithuania, 1839
died: Radin, Lithuania, 1933
Affectionately known as the Chafetz Chaim, the title of one of his books. Halachist, Torah leader of his generation.

Rabbi Yisrael Meir HaKohen Kagan, the Chafetz Chaim.

As a 9-year-old boy, Yisrael Meir HaKohen Kagan entered the great yeshivah in Vilna, where he soon gained a reputation as a genius. He grew not only in wisdom but also in piety. As he matured into manhood, his unselfish devotion to others and uncompromising honesty set an example for his generation and all generations that were to follow. After marrying at 17 years of age, he continued his Torah studies, in spite of extreme poverty, spending every waking moment engrossed in the holy *sefarim* (books). **Rabbi Yisrael Salanter**, the founder of the Mussar movement, said of him, "God has prepared a leader for the next generation." The Chafetz Chaim, who refused to accept a post as rabbi, opened a general store. His wife, insisting that he continue his Torah studies, managed the store. The Chafetz Chaim supervised the absolute accuracy of the weights and measures, the quality of the merchandise, and the fairness of the prices, to make certain that no one was deceived or overcharged in any way. In 1869 he founded the Yeshivah of Radin, which attracted students from all over Europe. His book, *Chafetz Chaim,*[1] made a profound impact on Torah-observant Jewry. It is a compilation of the laws concerning *leshon hara*— spreading gossip and slander—a grave offense that is often ignored. The title *Chafetz Chaim* is based on the verse, "Who is the man who desires life, who loves many days that he may see good? Guard your tongue from evil and your lips from speaking deceit" (Psalm 34:13) (*chafetz chaim* translates as "desires life"). His book *Machaneh Yisrael*[2] offers advice to Jewish soldiers on how to observe Jewish traditions in the army, as well as special prayers to be said before going into battle. A major achievement was his work *Mishnah Berurah,* a comprehensive commentary on the *Orach Chaim* section of the *Shulchan Aruch,* which deals with the general laws of daily conduct, such as prayers, tefillin, blessings, Shabbat, and Festivals. *Mishnah Berurah* explains these laws and their application in present-day situations. In his *Biur Halachah* he offers additional explanations, while *Shaar Hatziun* identifies the sources for his rulings. All these commentaries appear below the text of the *Shulchan Aruch*. *Mishnah Berurah* consists of six volumes and took 25 years to complete.[3] Since its publication, *Mishnah Berurah* has enjoyed extraordinary popularity. It is part of virtually every Jewish home library, its pages

Page of *Shulchan Aruch, Orach Chaim* 386:5, Laws of Shabbat, with commentary *Mishnah Berurah* by the Chafetz Chaim. The Hebrew numbers in the text are reference numbers. From the original standard edition.

consulted daily by scholars, students, and laymen alike. Thanks to the Chafetz Chaim's writings, a growing awareness has emerged of the harmful effects and the seriousness of *leshon hara*. His *Mishnah Berurah* serves as a faithful guide in all situations affecting Jewish daily life. The Chafetz Chaim was a true leader of his people, caring for their needs, bearing the burden of each one of them. A phenomenal scholar, a humble saint, his memory lives on forever.

SELECTIONS FROM THE CHAFETZ CHAIM'S COMMENTARY

Excerpt from *Mishnah Berurah* on *Shulchan Aruch, Orach Chaim* 27:9—Laws of Tefillin

The place for the head-tefillin is from the (33) hairline (34) up to the spot where a child's skull is soft.

Mishnah Berurah: (33) *The hairline*—[Our rabbis received it by tradition] that the words "Between your eyes" (Deuteronomy 7:8) do not mean literally [between the eyes] . . . but where the hair begins to grow. Many people . . . erroneously think that the upper edge of the head-tefillin is placed on the hairline and the tefillin itself lies on the forehead. This is a violation of a biblical prohibition. Torah law requires that the head-tefillin should lie on a place where hair grows, i.e., that the lower edge of the tefillin rests on the hairline. Anyone laying the head-tefillin on his forehead . . . has not fulfilled the mitzvah . . . and the *berachah* (blessing) he said was in vain. (34) *Up to the spot*—the upper edge of the tefillin through which the strap passes should not lie on a place higher than where a child's skull is soft.

Excerpt from *Mishnah Berurah* on *Shulchan Aruch, Orach Chaim* 155:1—Going from the synagogue to the study hall

After praying in the synagogue (1) you should go to the study hall. You should (2) set a certain time for study, and you should not utilize it for any other purpose, even when you expect to make big profits from a transaction.

Gloss by Rema: Even a person who is unable to study Torah should go to the study hall. He will be rewarded for going there. [If he has limited knowledge] he should study a little of the things he knows, and apply these lessons in his daily conduct. This will bring fear of heaven (awe) into his heart.

Mishnah Berurah: (1) *You should go to the study hall*—In the days of the Talmud, when the synagogue was designated for prayer only, and the study hall was set aside for study exclusively, they only prayed in the synagogue. But even in our age, now that we pray in the study hall as well, this rule of studying after prayer applies too. After praying you should join a group of men who are studying Torah, Mishnah, and the like. (2) *Set a certain time for study*—The reason for this is stated in the Gemara, that on Judgment Day a person is asked, "Did you set aside a fixed time for Torah study?"

Excerpt from *Mishnah Berurah* on *Shulchan Aruch, Orach Chaim* 170:13—Conduct during the Meal

When you enter a house (29) you should not say, (30) "Give me to eat" [but you should wait] until they tell you [to eat].

Gloss by Rema: A person should not say to someone, "Come and share a meal with me; I am reciprocating for the meal I enjoyed at your house." The reason is that this is like repaying a debt, and it therefore appears as if the other fellow lent him the food. Consequently, there are grounds for concern that you will give him more food than you took from him, and this involves (31) a consideration of interest. (32) However, you are permitted to say, "Come and share a meal with me and I will have a meal at your house some other time," and then you are permitted to eat even a larger meal at his house.

Mishnah Berurah: (29) *A house*—That is, of a different householder. It is self-understood that the *Shulchan Aruch* is speaking of an instance when the person who enters is not a paying guest. (30) *Give me to eat*—If the food is placed in front of you, there is no longer any need for you to wait until you are told to eat. (31) *A consideration of interest*—What is meant is that it has the appearance of interest, but it is not classed as actual interest halachically, since you did not have this in mind at the outset when you fed him. (32) *However, it is permitted to say*—This is because when you do so, you have no intention whatever of obligating the other fellow to give you a meal in return. You only say this out of courtesy so that he should not refuse your invitation, but should agree to eat with you and not feel uncomfortable about eating your food without paying. The *Taz* is even hesitant about permitting this and is inclined to be stringent; see there.

Excerpt from *Mishnah Berurah* on *Shulchan Aruch, Orach Chaim* 171:1—Halachot that are Relevant to the Meal

A person may do what he needs to do with bread. However, this only applies if the bread will not

become repugnant as a result of what he does with it, (3) but something that will make it repugnant (4) may not be done with it. . . . (9) One may not throw bread, because this constitutes contempt for food. Just as one may not throw bread, one may also not throw other food (10) that will become repugnant through being thrown. However, it is permitted to throw articles of food that will not become repugnant as a result, (11) such as nuts, pomegranates, and quinces.

Mishnah Berurah: (3) *But something that will make it repugnant*—Even in the case of other foods, a use which will make them repugnant is prohibited. (4) *May not*—To do something with food for medicinal purposes is permitted, even if it will become repugnant as a result of what is being done to it. (9) *One may not throw bread*—It is explained by the *Bet Yosef* and other authorities that bread is more important than other food. In the case of bread it is forbidden to throw it even if it will not become repugnant by being thrown, such as when one wishes to throw it on a clean spot, since this is disrespectful to the bread. (10) *That will become repugnant through being thrown*—Such as fully ripened figs, etc., which are soft and get crushed when thrown, and therefore become repugnant. (11) *Such as nuts, etc.*—Which are hard and do not get crushed when thrown. The *Shulchan Aruch* is speaking of a case when one throws the nuts on a clean place, since otherwise it is even forbidden to throw nuts.

Excerpt from *Mishnah Berurah* on *Shulchan Aruch, Orach Chaim* 263:1—Laws of Shabbat

You should take care to prepare beautiful candles [for Shabbat]. Some people especially prepare a light with two wicks (two candles), one for zachor *and one for* shamor.[4]

Rema: One may add to this number, kindling three or four lights. This, in fact, is the custom: a woman who forgets once to kindle [the Shabbat light] kindles (7) three lights the rest of her life.

Mishnah Berurah: (7) *Three lights*—This refers to where she usually kindles two. If originally she was accustomed to kindling three, she must light four the rest of her life. If she forgets many times, she must add one more light each time. All of this is in the way of a penalty, so that in the future she heed scrupulously the honor of Shabbat. Therefore, if she did not kindle lights because of circumstances beyond her control, she need not add to her customary number of lights.

Excerpt from *Mishnah Berurah* on *Shulchan Aruch, Orach Chaim* 274:1—Laws of Shabbat

[On Shabbat] we say the blessing [Hamotzi] over two whole loaves of bread (challot), while holding both loaves in our hands, and we cut the bottom challah-loaf.

Gloss by Rema: [The bottom challah] is cut only on Friday night, but on Shabbat morning or on the eve of a Festival, the top challah is cut. The reason for this is based on Kabbalah.

Excerpt from *Mishnah Berurah* on *Shulchan Aruch, Orach Chaim* 429:1—Laws of Passover

Thirty days before the advent of Passover we [review and] inquire into the laws of Passover.

Gloss by Rema: It is customary [for the community] to buy wheat flour to distribute to the poor. Anyone living in a community for twelve months is required to contribute toward this [fund].

Excerpt from *Mishnah Berurah* on *Shulchan Aruch, Yoreh De'ah* 247:3—Laws of Charity

Whoever has mercy on the poor, the Holy One, Blessed is He, will have mercy on him.

Gloss by Rema: A man should bear in mind that he is continually begging for sustenance from the Holy One, Blessed is He, and just as he prays that God listen to his plea, so should he respond to the supplication of the poor. A man should also consider that the wheel of fortune is ever revolving, and that either he himself, or his son, or his grandson may eventually beg for charity. Let him remember that mercy is shown to him that is merciful to others.

Excerpt from *Mishnah Berurah* on *Shulchan Aruch, Yoreh De'ah* 265:12—Laws of Circumcision

It is customary to make a feast on the day of a circumcision.

Gloss by Rema: It is the custom to invite a minyan (ten adult males) to the meal of a circumcision, which is considered a religious feast. If you are invited to a meal of circumcision and you know that worthy men will be present there, you must attend. It is also the custom to make a feast [at which fruit and drinks are served] on the Friday night following the birth of a male child. This, too, is considered a religious feast.

RABBI YECHEZKEL LANDAU—THE
NODA BIYEHUDAH
רבי יחזקאל לאנדו—נודע ביהודה

born: Opatow, Poland, 1713
died: Prague, Czechoslovakia, 1793
Popularly known as the Noda Biyehudah ("Known in Judah"), the title of his major work. Halachist, rabbi.

Yechezkel Landau was born into a distinguished family that traced its roots to **Rashi.** As a youth he showed precocious knowledge, and at the age of 14 he went to study Torah in Brody, where he was also initiated into the teachings of Kabbalah. At the young age of 20 he was appointed as head of the *bet din* (rabbinical court) in Brody. In 1745 he was elected to the rabbinate of Jampol. His reputation as eminent scholar and peacemaker induced the communal leaders of Prague to offer him the post of rabbi in their prestigious city, so that in 1754 the Noda Biyehudah became the rabbi of Prague and all Bohemia, a post he held for 38 years. With patience and goodhearted cordiality he won the respect and admiration of the entire community. The governmental authorities respected him highly and always acted favorably upon his requests. Under his leadership the Prague yeshivah grew, producing great scholars. He was a staunch opponent of any reform or deviation from traditional Judaism, and he strongly condemned Mendelssohn's German translation of the Torah as a first step toward reform and eventual abandonment of Judaism. History has proven the correctness of his assessment. His best known work is *Noda Biyehudah* ("Known in Judah"),[1] a collection of 860 responsa. It is a guide to halachic problems and is widely consulted by halachic scholars. He also wrote *"Tziyun Lenefesh Chayah,"*[2] notes on the Talmud, and *"Dagul Merevavah."*[3]

Rabbi Yechezkel Landau, the Noda Biyehudah.

Excerpt from *Noda Biyehudah* on *Orach Chaim,* Responsum #3. This is a response to Rabbi Menachem Navari.

You asked whether during the summer months it is preferable to read the morning *Shema* at a later hour, so as to enable the elderly to participate in the services, although the *Shema* would thereby be delayed past the permissible time limit,[4] or pray at the proper hour, early in the morning, which would deter the elderly from praying in the synagogue and force them to pray privately. I am surprised at your question. Can you ask someone to violate a law for someone else to gain merit? Of course not. Those who zealously arise early in the morning are worthy of praise; but those who get up late are in violation of the law. Thus, let the zealous men of your city pray at the proper time; and let the elderly who are too lazy to get up, pray privately, without a minyan.[5] No one should be asked to commit even the slightest sin so that his fellows gain merit by his sin.

Page of *Noda Biyehudah*, Responsa 2, 3, 4, 5, and 6. Responsum #3 is translated in the excerpt included in this book. From a copy of the so-called *Mahadurah Kama*, First Edition, printed in Vilna.

RABBI SHELOMOH GANZFRIED—KITZUR SHULCHAN ARUCH
רבי שלמה גאנצפריד—קיצור שולחן ערוך

born: Ungvar, Hungary, 1804
died: Ungvar, Hungary, 1880
Popularly known as Kitzur Shulchan Aruch, the title of his greatest work. Talmudist, halachist.

Shelomoh Ganzfried's father died while he was still a child, and he received his education from Rabbi Tzvi Hirsch Heller of Ungvar. In 1843 he was elected rabbi of Resevitz, returning to Ungvar in 1850 to serve as its rabbi and as head of the local bet din (rabbinical court). He wrote numerous halachic treatises and books, but the work that gained worldwide renown is the *Kitzur Shulchan Aruch* (*The Abridged Shulchan Aruch*). With consummate skill the author selected from the massive code of the four parts of the *Shulchan Aruch* those laws and customs every Jew should be familiar with. He guides us through all phases of our lives, from the moment we rise in the morning, through our prayers, to the Reading of the Torah, and to the blessings over our food. The book offers a brief outline of forbidden foods, describes the labors that are prohibited on Shabbat, and the laws pertaining to the various Festivals. The *Kitzur Shulchan Aruch* also discusses moral and ethical laws. Chapters concerning charity, honoring one's father and mother, the evils of gossip and deceptive business practices, alternate with laws regarding chastity, marriage, and family purity. Laws concerning a woman at childbirth are followed by precepts of circumcision, rules on visiting the sick, and the laws of interment and mourning. It is written in a concise style. Paragraphs dealing with the minutiae of the law are interspersed with brief homilies to remind the student of the teachings of our sages concerning God's love and compassion and of what our goal in life should be. The *Kitzur Shulchan Aruch* has become the most popular handbook for the Jewish family.[1] The *Kitzur Shulchan Aruch,* through its straightforward simplicity, is the ideal text for anyone seeking practical

קיצור שלחן ערוך

מהגאון מוה״ר שלמה גאנצפריד זצ״ל

עם

לקט בני איש

דברי

משנה ברורה

מהגאון מוה״ר ישראל מאיר הכהן זצ״ל

המתיחסים לקיצור שלחן ערוך

בעריכת

אליקים בן אברהם יצחק ז״ל ושבע שלנגר

נוספו

שיעורי המצוות

מתוך „שיעורין של תורה״ למרן הגרי״י קניבסקי שליט״א

קיצור הלכות תרומות ומעשרות

מהעורך

סדר השביעית

מהחזו״א זצ״ל.

כרך א׳, סימנים א—פ

הוצאת סמינר באר יעקב ע״ש שמואל ופני וולפסון

Title page of the *Kitzur Shulchan Aruch* by Rabbi Shelomoh Ganzfried.

guidance in day-to-day situations affecting the life of a Torah-observant Jew. Of course, for complex *she'eilot* (questions), a qualified halachic authority should be consulted.

SELECTIONS FROM THE WRITINGS OF KITZUR SHULCHAN ARUCH

Excerpt from *Kitzur Shulchan Aruch*, Vol. 1, Rules of Conduct upon Rising in the Morning

"Yehudah ben Tema said, 'Be bold as a leopard, light as an eagle, swift as a deer, and strong as a lion, to do the will of your Father who is in heaven' " (*Avot* 5:23). *Bold as a leopard* means that you should not be ashamed to worship God in the presence of people who ridicule you. *Light as an eagle* refers to our sense of vision, meaning that you should be swift to close your eyes so as not to look at evil, because sight is the beginning of sin; the eye sees, the heart desires, and the limbs—the tools of action—execute the deed. *Swift as a deer* refers to the legs, meaning that our feet should always run to do good deeds. *Strong as a lion* refers to the heart, because the fervor to worship the Creator resides in the heart. It is your duty to invigorate your heart to worship Him and to overcome the evil inclination, just as a heroic warrior makes every effort to subdue his enemy and crush him.[2]

Excerpt from *Kitzur Shulchan Aruch*, Vol. 1, 30:1, Talebearing, Slander, Revenge, and Bearing a Grudge

It is written, "Do not go around as a gossiper among your people" (Leviticus 19:16). What constitutes gossiping? A gossip is a person who goes from one to another, saying, "So and so said this," "I have heard about him this and that." Even if the gossip he spreads is true, and there is no disgrace attached to it, it is, nevertheless, a violation of a Divine Command, and it is a grave sin, which may bring in its wake death to many people. Because of that, this command is followed by "Do no stand still over your neighbor's blood" (Leviticus 19:16). Take, for example, what happened in the case of Doeg the Edomite who told Saul that Achimelech had given to David food and a sword. Although the thing he told was true and was not a discredit to Achimelech, for Achimelech had done

nothing wrong—and even if Saul himself had asked Achimelech, Achimelech would have told Saul what he had done, for he had no intention to sin against Saul by this—nevertheless, the talebearing of Doeg caused the death of many priests.[3] (Based on Rambam, *Hilchot De'ot*, 7:1–2).

Excerpt from *Kitzur Shulchan Aruch*, Vol. 1, 41:1

Before eating real bread, such as that made from the five grains [wheat, barley, oats, rye, spelt], you must recite the blessing *Hamotzi*, and after eating, recite Grace after Meals.

Excerpt from *Kitzur Shulchan Aruch*, Vol. 1, 41:2

Be careful not to interrupt by talking between washing the hands and *Hamotzi*, but you may respond Amen to any blessing you hear. A pause lasting as long as it takes to walk twenty-two cubits [11.88 seconds] or from one house to another, even if it is a short distance, or talking about something not related to the meal, is considered an interruption.

Excerpt from *Kitzur Shulchan Aruch*, Vol. 1, 41:3

As a token of respect of the blessing of *Hamotzi*, you should break off at the choicest part of the bread. The hardest part is considered the choicest, because at that part it begins to bake. . . . It is improper to pause too long between the blessing of *Hamotzi* and the eating of the bread.

Excerpt from *Kitzur Shulchan Aruch*, Vol. 1, 41:4

You should not break off too small a portion of the bread, so that you may not appear miserly, nor should you break off a portion larger than the size of an egg, so that you may not appear gluttonous.

Excerpt from *Kitzur Shulchan Aruch*, Vol. 1, 41:6

It is required to have salt set on the table before breaking bread, and to dip into the salt the piece of bread over which *Hamotzi* is said, because the table represents the altar and the food symbolizes the offerings.

Excerpt from *Kitzur Shulchan Aruch,* Vol. 3, 133:1, The Laws of Yom Kippur

It is forbidden to eat, drink, bathe, anoint, wear shoes, or have marital relations on Yom Kippur. It is also forbidden to do any labor, or to carry anything from one place to another, just as on Shabbat. Since it is necessary to add from the profane to the sacred, all of the above are forbidden on the day before Yom Kippur, a short time before twilight, while it is still day, until the end of Yom Kippur, until a short time after the stars appear.[4]

Excerpt from *Kitzur Shulchan Aruch,* Vol. 3, 133:19, The Laws of Yom Kippur

Boys and girls less than 9 years old should not be permitted to fast, even if they want to fast only part of the day, because it may endanger their health. Children 9 years old and in good health should be trained to fast a little. They should have breakfast a few hours later than usual. Concerning wearing shoes, washing, and anointing, they should be trained even before they are 9 years old.[5]

Excerpt from *Kitzur Shulchan Aruch,* Vol. 4, 184:8, Laws Concerning Physical Injury

If you see that your neighbor is in trouble, Heaven help us, you must come to his rescue, or if you are unable to do so, you must do whatever you can to hire others to save him. If the one who was helped can afford it, he must repay the money that was spent on his behalf. But even if it is known that he cannot afford to repay, you may not keep from helping him, but must save him at your own expense. If you refrain from doing so, you are guilty of violating the prohibition of "Do not stand still over your neighbor's blood" (Leviticus 19:16). Similarly, if you hear wicked people hatching a plot against your fellow man, and you fail to reveal it to him, or if you can satisfy them with money so that they would not carry out their evil plan, and you fail to appease them, you are likewise transgressing the command "Do not stand still over your neighbor's blood." The Mishnah (*Sanhedrin* 37a) tells us, "He who saves one life in Israel is considered as if he had saved the whole world."[6]

Excerpt from *Kitzur Shulchan Aruch,* Vol. 2, 62:1, Laws Concerning Business and Commerce

You should be extremely careful not to deceive your fellow. If anyone deceives his fellow, whether a seller deceives a buyer, or a buyer deceives a seller, he transgresses a negative commandment, for it is said, "When you sell something to your neighbor, or buy from your neighbor, do not deceive one another." (Leviticus 25:14). This is the first question a person is asked when he is brought before the Heavenly Tribunal: "Have you always been honest in your dealings?" (*Shabbat* 31a).[7]

Excerpt from *Kitzur Shulchan Aruch,* Vol. 2, 62:16, Laws Concerning Business and Commerce

A man has the moral obligation to keep his word, even though he gave no deposit as yet, nor did he mark the article, nor was the transaction completed. If the parties agreed on the price, neither the buyer nor the seller may back out. Whoever retracts, whether buyer or seller, is guilty of acting in bad faith, and the spirit of the sages does not look kindly on him. For a Jew should keep his word, as it is written, "The remnant of Israel shall not commit injustice nor speak lies" (Zephaniah 3:13). In addition, a God-fearing man should carry out even his unspoken decisions, that is, if he has decided to sell a certain article at a certain price, and the buyer, not knowing the seller's innermost thoughts, offered him more, he should only accept from him the amount he had originally decided to charge, fulfilling the verse that states, "And speaks the truth within his heart." (Psalm 15:12). The same rule applies to a buyer; if he has decided to buy an article at a certain price, he may not change his mind. This rule applies to all matters in relationships between man and his neighbor; one should fulfill his intentions if he decided to do a certain favor to someone and is able to do it. But regarding his personal needs, if it does not involve the performance of a mitzvah, he need not fulfill even intentions expressed with his lips.[8]

Excerpt from *Kitzur Shulchan Aruch*, Vol. 4, 191:1, Cruelty to Animals

It is forbidden, according to the law of the Torah, to inflict pain on any living creature. On the contrary, it is your duty to relieve the pain of any creature, even if it is ownerless or it belongs to a non-Jew. However, if they cause trouble, or if they are needed for medical research, or for any other human need, it is even permissible to kill them and we disregard their pain. For the Torah has permitted to slaughter them. Therefore, it is permitted to pluck feathers from a living goose, with which to write, if no other feather is available. However, people refrain from doing it because of cruelty.[9]

Excerpt from *Kitzur Shulchan Aruch*, Vol. 4, 192:2, The Sick, the Physician, and the Remedies

Rabbi Pinchas bar Chama preached, "Whoever has a sick person in the house should go to a sage and ask him to plead for mercy on his behalf, as it is written, 'The wrath of a king is as messengers of death, but a wise man will pacify it'" (Proverbs 16:14). It is customary to give charity to the poor on behalf of a sick person, for repentance, prayer, and charity reverse an evil decree. It is also customary to bless the sick person in the synagogue, and if he is seriously ill, he may be blessed even on Shabbat and on a Festival. Sometimes the name of the sick person is changed, for a change of name may also nullify an evil decree.[10]

RABBI MOSHE FEINSTEIN—REB MOSHE
רבי משה פיינשטיין—רבי משה

born: Uzda, near Minsk, Russia, 1895
died: New York, New York, 1986
Affectionately known as Reb Moshe. Talmudist, halachist, preeminent Torah leader of our era.

Born into a family of renowned Torah scholars, son of Rabbi David Feinstein, Rabbi of Starobin, Moshe Feinstein was a child prodigy blessed with a computer-like mind and flawless memory. At the age of 12 he was elected to deliver an original *pilpul* (talmudic discourse) at the dedication ceremonies of the yeshivah in Shklov, where he studied under Rabbi Pesach Pruskin. In 1920, when he was only 25 years old, he accepted a position as rabbi of Luban. He courageously led his community through the bitter years of persecution by the Communists. In 1936 he escaped from Stalinist oppression and arrived in the United States with his family. His fame as an illustrious Torah scholar had preceded him, and almost immediately he was invited to serve as *rosh yeshivah* (dean) of Yeshivah Tiferet Yerushalayim in New York, a position he held for the rest of his life. Under his leadership the yeshivah grew to an enrollment of 500 students. But his primary role was that of *poseik*—decider of halachic questions. Queries from all quarters poured in. He dealt with complex problems from distinguished rabbis, as well as requests for advice from common folk; he felt responsible for all. His responsa have been compiled and published in a six-volume work, entitled *Igrot Moshe* (Correspondence of Moshe).[1] A work of talmudic discourses has been published under the title of *Dibrot Moshe*, and recently, an illuminating commentary on the Chumash has appeared, entitled *Darash Moshe*.[2] His responsa reflect his encyclopedic knowledge, profound understanding, and great sensitivity. His greatness as *poseik hador* (decider of Halachah for his generation) was recognized by all leading authorities of his day. Rabbi S. Finkelman has written a biography, entitled *Reb Moshe*.[3] In 1962, after the death of **Rabbi Aharon Kotler**—the foremost Torah scholar and leader of our generation—the mantle of leadership fell on Reb Moshe's shoulders. With a firm yet gentle hand, he guided and directed all who sought his advice. His faith, piety, unselfishness, love of Israel, humility, and kindness were unparalleled. He was loved like a father by an entire generation.

Rabbi Moshe Feinstein, Reb Moshe.

ספר

אגרות משה

אורח חיים

והם מה שחננו השי"ת להשיב לשואלים אותי מתלמידי וחברי דבר
ה' זו הלכה, וגם מה שבאתי בכתובים לגדולי תורה
להשתעשע בדברי תורה.

מאת

משה פיינשטיין

ר"מ מתיבתא תפארת ירושלים בנוא יארק
ומלפנים אבד"ק ליובאן, פלך מינסק

בן אאמו"ר הצדיק חסיד ועניו מרן ר' דוד זצ"ל
שהיה אבד"ק אוזדא וסטראבין ברוסיא

נוא יארק
שנת תשי"ט לפ"ק

Title page of *Igrot Moshe*, the monumental collection of responsa by Rabbi Moshe Feinstein. A nine-volume work dealing with all phases of Jewish life.

SELECTIONS FROM REB MOSHE'S WRITINGS

Excerpt from *Igrot Moshe, Yoreh De'ah* 109, re: A Convert Who Returned to Torah Observance

Responsum: Your question concerns a woman who converted to Judaism before a *bet din* (religious court) and subsequently was married in Montreal, but since her husband did not observe Torah, she did not observe Torah either. Two years ago, the husband became a *baal teshuvah* (returnee to Torah observance), and she too began to observe Torah law scrupulously. They were thoroughly interviewed by two outstanding young Torah scholars, who made the determination that she believes in God and His Torah, observes all mitzvot, and pledges to keep all mitzvot in the future. Since there exists an uncertainty as to whether her conversion was valid, it is an important mitzvah that she undergo *tevilah* (immersion in a kosher *mikveh*) once again. . . . The boys, in view of the uncertainty surrounding their mother's conversion, should also undergo *tevilah*. This will merit them greatly, inasmuch as they now are being raised in the spirit of Torah. The little girl should wait two years before she too undergoes *tevilah*. It should be understood, that since there exists the possibility that the conversion was valid, the law does not require *hatafat dam berit* (a symbolic circumcision that is achieved by drawing a drop of blood). The *tevilah* for the boys is sufficient in this case.

Excerpt from *Igrot Moshe, Yoreh De'ah* 140, re: Donating Organs for Medical Research

Responsum [Addressed to Rabbi Moshe Sherer, President of Agudath Israel of America]: Concerning the question you have been asked by the Office of the President of the United States regarding the use of organs that were bequeathed by a deceased person for the benefit of medical research: I respond briefly, according to Torah law, which our rabbis received from their respective teachers, in an unbroken chain of tradition, reaching to Moses our Teacher, through whom we received the Torah on Sinai. No person in the world has the right to will that anything be done with his remains or with any part or organ of his body, not even for purposes of medical research. All the more must it be said that his children or relatives are not empowered to do this . . . It is their duty to inter him as soon as possible, on the day of his demise, without effecting any alteration on his body. It is forbidden to perform an autopsy on a body or to make even one incision. The deceased must be buried unblemished, as he was at the instant death occurred.

Excerpt from *Igrot Moshe,* re: The Feminist Movement

Responsum: You wish me to express my opinion on the question of women who in their zeal to fight for equal rights for women want to introduce these ideas into the laws of the Torah; who wish to pray wearing a tallit, and the like. At the outset, it should be stated that one of the fundamental principles of our pure faith is that the entire Torah, both its written and oral components, were given by the Holy One, blessed is He, Himself, on Mount Sinai, through our Teacher Moses. It is impossible to change even one iota in it, so as to make it either more lenient or more rigorous. . . . The responsibility for raising children has been placed on the women. This is their supreme task for God and His Torah . . . which is the reason that they (women) were relieved of the responsibility of studying Torah and fulfilling those commands that are dependent on a fixed time. It should be recognized that this does not imply that women are regarded as subordinate to men. In regard to *kedushah*—sanctity—they are equal to men. All verses in the Torah relating to sanctity were addressed to men and women alike, beginning with the opening statement that led to the Acceptance of the Torah, "You shall be My special treasure among all nations. . . . You will be a kingdom of priests and a holy nation to Me" (Exodus 19:5–6), which was directed at "the House of Jacob"—meaning the women. It is exactly for this reason that women, when reciting a blessing, formulate the *berachah*, "*asher kiddeshanu bemitzvotav . . .*"—Who has sanctified us with His commandments—even when they are performing a mitzvah to which they are not obligated by the Torah. Bear in mind, our history records many women who were prophets, who thereby were subject to all the laws that govern male prophets. Scripture and the writings of our sages abound with sayings and aphorisms praising women for their superiority to men in wisdom, understanding, and character traits. Explain these facts again and again when you are confronted with pressure of this nature. Be firm and resolute in your stand, which represents Torah law, in your opposition to those misguided women who persist in their foolish notions. Do not permit the slightest deviation from the holy customs of Israel.

Excerpt from *Igrot Moshe, Orach Chaim* 126, *re:* Reading the Megillah through a Microphone

Responsum: Concerning your query in which you state that on Purim, the synagogue in the girls' school you are leading is very crowded. Without a microphone, the girls are unable to hear the reading of the Megillah. You ask whether a microphone may be used, since this constitutes an emergency. It is my opinion that it should not be used. It is preferable that the girls pray the *Maariv* prayer in the synagogue. Then they wait with the reading of the Megillah until the dining room is cleaned. The Megillah should then be read as in previous years, in the synagogue and in the dining room; and there should be a minyan of men (a quorum of ten) in both places. This is better than introducing something new. Women are equally obligated to hear the Megillah as men are. Therefore, it should be read in two places, even if they have to wait while the dining

room is readied; and then the Megillah should be read in both places simultaneously.

Excerpt from *Igrot Moshe, Yoreh De'ah* 35, re: Smoking Marijuana

Responsum: Regarding the matter that a few students of the yeshivah have begun to smoke marijuana. It is clear that this is forbidden, based on several fundamental tenets of the Torah:

1. The user destroys his body and his mind; he is unable to think clearly; it interferes with his Torah studies, his prayers, and the performance of his mitzvot—if these are performed without awareness they are void.
2. Its use stimulates a strong dependence, more powerful than the desire for food and drink, which are basic necessities; it is the grave transgression referred to in the chapter of the "rebellious son" (Deuteronomy 21:18).
3. Ultimately, his addiction will cause him to commit robbery.
4. By hurting his parents he violates the commandment to honor his father and his mother.
5. He transgresses the Torah decree of "You must be holy" (Leviticus 19:2).
6. In summary, it is self-evident and certain that this is one of the gravest sins. No effort must be spared to eradicate this foulness from the midst of the Jewish people, and from yeshivah students in particular.

Excerpt from *Igrot Moshe, Orach Chaim* 49, *re:* Translating the Blessing of *Hamotzi*

Responsum: With regard to your query as to whether it is permissible to repeat the blessing of *Hamotzi* in English before partaking of the bread: If one said the entire *berachah* (blessing) in English, he has fulfilled his obligation, but if he then repeats it in Hebrew, this *berachah* is in vain, for blessings may be recited in any language (**Rambam**, *Berachot* 1:6). If he says the *berachah* first in Hebrew and then repeats it in English, then perhaps the *berachah* in English is not in vain, because he does not actually enunciate the Divine Name. . . . But the translation after saying *Hamotzi* constitutes a prohibited interruption. . . . Therefore, it is forbidden to say the blessing and to translate it before eating the bread. One should eat the bread immediately after saying the *berachah* and then translate the blessing into English.

IV

MUSSAR

The Mussar movement that had its roots in the 19th century must be seen as an effort to redirect Torah thinking to the original sources. It sees the Torah essentially as a system of character refinement that embraces all of man and life. Each Torah law is designed to bring about human perfection. With the passage of time Torah literature had become progressively more restricted in scope and was confined largely to the fields of law and commandment. The element of human perfection was placed in the background. Students of Talmud devoted themselves exclusively to understanding the intricacies of talmudic debate, completely overlooking the most crucial aspect of Torah which deals with ethical and spiritual perfection. Confronted with this one-sided approach to Torah study, Mussar sought to broaden the scope of Torah research to include all the commandments, whether they involved action or thought, the heart or the mind. Just as a Jew refrains from desecrating the Shabbat, or eating non-kosher food, so must he avoid anger, evil gossip, giving insult, robbery, or cheating. Mussar sages speak out against performing mitzvot routinely, half-heartedly, and with indifference. They call for clear understanding, deeper feeling, *hitpa'lut*,—involvement of our entire being in all our actions. Mussar recognizes that the main obstacle to achieving human perfection is man's selfish nature, his urge to seek his own gain and self-satisfaction. In Job's words, "Man is born a wild ass's colt" (Job 11:12). Man is admonished to scrutinize the motives that prompt every action, to search his heart and analyze his thoughts relentlessly. His tools are the *sifrei mussar*—the Mussar writings. Through them he will learn the truth about himself and find the road to self-improvement. The Mussar movement saved Lithuanian (nonchasidic) Jewry from the onslaughts of assimilation and Reform. It proved to be the powerful antidote against the blandishments of their seductive, spurious siren song. It struck roots in all parts of the world, traversing the oceans to Israel and the United States, where it continues to exercise a powerful influence on Jewish thought and deed.

RABBI MOSHE CHAIM LUZZATTO— MESILLAT YESHARIM

רבי משה חיים לוצטו—מסילת ישרים

born: Padua, Italy, 1707
died: Acco, Eretz Yisrael, 1747
Popularly known as the Mesillat Yesharim, the title of his work. Ethicist, kabbalist, poet.

From early youth Moshe Chaim Luzzatto was educated in both religious and secular studies. A child prodigy and accomplished linguist, he mastered Hebrew, Italian, Aramaic, Latin, Greek, and French. A distinguished poet and ardent student of Kabbalah, he could faultlessly cite all the works of the **Ari** at the age of 14. He led an extremely ascetic and pious life. With three likeminded friends he studied mysticism and ways to self-improvement and achieving perfection. His saintly way of life gave rise to suspicion and strong opposition. His detractors, led by Rabbi Moshe Chagiz, forced him to emigrate. He moved to Amsterdam, where his Torah lectures attracted a large number of students. There he wrote his most important work, *Mesillat Yesharim.*[1] It is a guide to perfection. It is considered the foremost text on Mussar and has been an inspiration to thousands. With deep wisdom the author probes every aspect of the human personality and its weaknesses, offering advice on ways to overcome them. Luzzatto also authored more than forty other books on ethics, philosophy, poetry, and Kabbalah. In 1743 Rabbi Moshe Chaim Luzzatto moved to Eretz Yisrael, where in 1747 he and his family fell victim to an epidemic in Acco.

ספר
מסלת ישרים
כולל ענני מוסר ויראת ה׳
מאת רבנו משה חיים לוצאטו זצוק״ל
נצרף
מפתח הענינים העקריים שבספר ומאמרי חז״ל
המובאים בו. לפי דפוס ראשון של שנת ת״ק לפ״ק.

מוספים לספר:

א) ספר דרך עץ חיים
לרבנו משה חיים לוצאטו זצ״ל

ב) אגרת הרמב״ן
לרבנו משה בר נחמן זצ״ל

ג) אגרת המוסר
לרבנו ישראל ליפקין מסלנט זצ״ל

ד) אגרת הגר״א
לרבנו אליהו מוילנא זצ״ל

הוצאת ספרים אשכול עיה״ק ירושלים ת״ו
שנת ה׳תשכ״ד לפ״ג

Title page of *Mesillat Yesharim,* foremost work on Mussar by Rabbi Moshe Chaim Luzzatto.

SELECTIONS FROM REB MOSHE CHAIM LUZZATTO'S WRITINGS

Excerpt from *Mesillat Yesharim*[2]

The foundation of saintliness and the root of perfection in the service of God lies in man's coming to a clear understanding and recognizing as a truth the nature of his duty in the world and the goals toward which he should set his sights in all of his life's endeavors . . . . When you look further into the matter, you will see that only attachment to God constitutes true perfection, as King David said: "But as for me, the nearness of God is my good" (Psalm 73:28) and "One thing I asked of God, that will I seek: that I dwell in the house of God all the days of my life" (Psalm 27:4). For only this is the true good, and anything else that people consider good is nothing but futility and hollow emptiness. For a man to attain this good, he ought to begin by working hard, exerting himself in an effort to acquire it. In other words, he should make a diligent effort to cling to God by means of actions that bring about this result. These actions are the mitzvot.

Excerpt from introduction to *Mesillat Yesharim*

Rabbi Pinchas ben Yair says:
"Torah leads to watchfulness,
Watchfulness leads to alertness,
Alertness leads to cleanliness,
Cleanliness leads to abstinence,
Abstinence leads to purity,
Purity leads to saintliness,
Saintliness leads to humility,
Humility leads to fear of sin,
Fear of sin leads to holiness,
Holiness leads to the Holy Spirit,
and the Holy Spirit leads to the Revival of the Dead."
(*Avodah Zarah 20b*)

It is on the basis of this *Baraita* that I have undertaken to write this book, in order to teach myself and to remind others of the conditions for perfect service of God according to their levels. Of each I shall explain its nature, its subdivisions or details, the manner you can acquire it, the things that stand in its way, and how to protect yourself from them.

Excerpt from *Mesillat Yesharim*, Chap. 3, Having Faith in Our Sages

To what can we compare this? To a maze, an entertainment designed for kings. . . . Anyone walking along the paths has no way of knowing whether he is on the right path or on a false one, for they are all alike, and to the eye there is no difference between them. . . . The one who is standing in the tower can see all the paths and he can distinguish between the true and the false, and so he can direct the walkers as to which way to go. Whoever is willing to believe him will reach his destination, but someone who does not want to

listen to him, but would rather follow his own judgment, will certainly stay lost and will never reach it. The same is true in our case. A person who has not yet gained control of his *yetzer* (inclination, natural instincts) is as if he is walking along the paths without being able to distinguish between them. Those who have mastered their *yetzer* are like those who have already reached the tower . . . and can see all the paths clearly in front of them. They can offer advice to those who are willing to listen, and it is them we must trust.[3]

Excerpt from *Mesillat Yesharim*, Chap. 11, On the Particulars of the Trait of Cleanliness

To summarize; if someone is hired by his neighbor to do any kind of work, all of his hours are sold to his employer for the day . . . as our sages said, "Hiring yourself out is equivalent to selling yourself for the day" (*Bava Metzia* 56b). Any time he uses for his personal benefit in whatever manner is all-out theft; and if his employer does not forgive him, he is not forgiven. As our teachers have stated, "The Day of Atonement does not atone for a person's sin against his neighbor until he appeases him" (*Yoma* 85b). What is more, even if he performs a mitzvah during his working hours, it is not considered a righteous deed but a transgression. A transgression cannot be a mitzvah . . . as our sages have said, "If someone steals a measure of wheat, grinds it, bakes it, and recites a blessing over it, it is not a blessing but an insult (*Bava Kama* 94a), as it is written ". . . and the thief who blesses, insults God" (Psalm 10:3). This is in line with what our sages say concerning a stolen *lulav*:[4] "Stealing an object is stealing, and stealing time is stealing (*Yerushalmi, Sukkah* 3:1).

Excerpt from *Mesillat Yesharim*, Chap. 5, On Obstacles to Watchfulness

For the evil inclination has a powerful hold on a person, and unbeknownst to him, it grows stronger and eventually comes to dominate him. Now, a man can use all schemes imaginable. If he does not take the remedy that was created for him, namely the Torah, as I have written, he will neither recognize nor feel the worsening of his illness until he dies and his soul is lost. To what can this be likened? To the case of a sick man who consulted a doctor. The doctor correctly diagnosed his sickness and prescribed a medicine for it. This man, although unfamiliar with medical science, discards the drug and takes instead whatever medicine he happens to think of. Is there any doubt that he will die? The same is true in our case. No one understands the disease of the evil inclination and what it is capable of doing except the Creator who brought it into being. And He Himself cautioned us that the only antidote to it is Torah. Who, then, can cast it aside and take something else and expect to live?

RABBI CHAIM OF VOLOZHIN—REB CHAIM VOLOZHINER
רבי חיים מוולאז׳ין

born: Volozhin, near Vilna, Lithuania, 1749
died: Volozhin, near Vilna, Lithuania, 1821
Popularly known as Reb Chaim Volozhiner. Talmudist, ethicist.

One of the most prominent disciples of the **Vilna Gaon**, Reb Chaim Volozhiner established the Yeshivah of Volozhin. It endured for more than 100 years, becoming the mother of all Lithuanian yeshivahs. He continued to teach the Vilna Gaon's study method of penetrating analysis of the talmudic text, seeking to elicit the intent and meaning of the writings of the *Rishonim*—the Early Commentators. This approach was followed by all the great Lithuanian yeshivahs, such as those of Slobodka, Mir, Kelm, Kletzk, and Telz. His major work is *Nefesh Hachaim*.[1] It reflects the saintly purity of his character, his greatness in Torah, and his profound wisdom. Its purpose is "to implant the fear of God, Torah, and pure worship into the hearts of the upright who are seeking the ways of God." He also wrote a commentary on Tractate *Avot*, entitled *Ru'ach Chaim*, and a collection of responsa under the title *Nishmat Chaim*. *Nefesh Hachaim* became the most widely studied text in the Mussar yeshivahs and has been reprinted many times. The ever-increasing number of great yeshivahs in America, England, and Israel are carrying on the tradition of Volozhin. They are a living testimonial to its illustrious founder, Reb Chaim Volozhiner.

יראת ה
לחיים
קונטרסים מכתבי קודש של הגאון אמתי המפורסם בתורתו וצדקתו
ומעשיו המכריזים עליו · פאר הדור ומופתו · חסיד ועניו · כקש״ת מו׳
חיים נ״ע ראב״ד ור״מ דקק וולאזין · אשר יקרא כחתימתו בכתיבתו׳
בשם
נפש החיים
וכמאמרם ז״ל בירושלמי דשקלים דף ו׳ תני רשב״ג אין עושין נפשות לצדיקים
שדבריהם הן זכרונן וזכר צדיק לברכה
שנגהי
שנת תשי״ד לפ״ק

Title page of *Nefesh Hachaim* by Rabbi Chaim Volozhiner. A very rare edition, published in 1944 in Shanghai under Japanese occupation, by the students of the Mirrer Yeshivah who had miraculously escaped the fires of the Holocaust.

SELECTIONS FROM REB CHAIM VOLOZHINER'S WRITINGS

Excerpt from *Nefesh Hachaim* 1:5

"Do not come any closer," said [God]. "Take your shoes off your feet. The place upon which you are standing is holy ground."

(Exodus 3:5)

The human body is, in a figurative sense, like a shoe to the soul. Just as the shoe clothes only the lowest part of the body, so is the body a garment for only the lowest aspect of man's soul. Man's essence is anchored above in the root of his upper, transcendent soul, and passes through myriads of worlds until its lower end enters man's body. This lower end remains connected to its heavenly source by means of a "spiritual rope." Each of man's actions in this world exercises an influence on his heavenly source, just like a rope that, when shaken on one end, produces movement on the other end. Predicated on this thought, the underlying meaning of the phrase "Take your shoes off your feet" is thus: "Divest yourself of your physical body."[2]

Excerpt from *Nefesh Hachaim* 4:26

Rava saw Rav Hamenuna prolonging his prayers. He said: "They forsake eternal life and occupy themselves with temporal life."

(Shabbat 10a)

Torah study lies at the core of the existence of the universe. The preservation of the world depends on it. We are therefore duty bound to ponder over it and engross ourselves in it constantly. We thereby uphold and ensure the continued existence of the world. If, God forbid, there would arrive an instant at which no one in the entire world would be studying Torah, the entire universe would instantly revert to nothingness, God forbid. This is not so with the fulfillment of mitzvot, not even the mitzvah of prayer. If, for a moment, all Israel would fail to pray to God, this would not cause the world to end. The Torah is therefore described as "eternal life," whereas prayer is characterized as "temporal life." . . . in Halachah: "A synagogue may be converted into a house of study" (*Megillah* 27a).

Excerpt from *Nefesh Hachaim* 4:86

The law of Your mouth is better to me than thousands of gold and silver.

(Psalm 119:72)

I am glad and I rejoice in my labor of studying the holy Torah when I realize that it is the Teaching of Your Mouth. [This may be taken quite literally, in the sense that] I am aware that each word of the Torah that I am probing at any given moment is simultaneously emanating from Your Holy Mouth. When a person is engaged in Torah study in the physical world,

his identical words are being uttered by God's Holy Mouth along with him. We find proof of this in Tractate *Gittin* 6b.[3]

Excerpt from *Ru'ach Chaim* 4:41

The Holy One, Blessed is He, causes His Shechinah (Divine Presence) to rest only on one who is strong, wealthy, wise, and humble.

(Nedarim 38a)

One may ask a serious question here. Why does God not cause His Shechinah to descend on a person who, even before birth, was destined to be poor and infirm? If he lives a decent life and performs good deeds, why does God not allow His spirit to rest on him? We must understand that the overriding quality required for a man to be worthy of the Divine Presence is the trait of humility, as stated in *Avodah Zarah* 20b, "Humility leads to fear of sin, fear of sin leads to holiness, holiness leads to the Holy Spirit. . . ." Now, a man who has no qualities at all cannot be considered a modest person, even if he humbles himself—for he has nothing to be proud of. On the other hand, a person endowed with many admirable attributes, who nevertheless is not aware of his merits but is meek and unpretentious—that person can be characterized as humble. A man in whom all the world's good qualities converge, who still maintains perfect humility, is the most humble of all. The three values mentioned in the present quotation—power, wealth, and wisdom—represent the sum total of mankind's aspirations. If a man, having attained all of these, still remains truly modest, he is indeed humble and worthy of receiving the Shechinah.[4]

Excerpt from *Ru'ach Chaim, Avot* 4:9

. . . trouble and sorrow I would find; then I would invoke the Name of God . . .

(Psalm 116:3–4)

I consider the fact that trouble and sorrow engulf me to be a fortuitous find. For whatever the Merciful One does is for the good. He surely placed me in this predicament in order that I "invoke the Name of God," proclaiming His Majesty.

RABBI YISRAEL LIPKIN OF SALANT—REB YISRAEL SALANTER

רבי ישראל ליבקין מסאלאנט—רבי ישראל מסאלאנט

born: Zager, near Kovno, Lithuania, 1809
died: Koenigsberg, East Prussia, Germany, 1883
Popularly known as Reb Yisrael Salanter. Founder of the Mussar Movement. Talmudist, rosh yeshivah *(dean).*

Yisrael Lipkin's father, Rabbi Zev Wolf Lipkin, a descendant of the **Vilna Gaon**, served as rabbi in Telshe, Lithuania. Reb Yisrael's primary mentor was the saintly Reb Zundel of Salant, who introduced him to the study of the Mussar classics. Mussar is an incisive approach to self-analysis and introspection, with the aim of improving personal character traits and devotion to God. Reb Yisrael Salanter was a master in all areas of Torah. He would go into seclusion to concentrate on Mussar thoughts and ways of self-improvement. A compilation of his thoughts, letters, essays, and sermons was published under the title *Or Yisrael*[1], by his foremost student, Rabbi Yitzchak Blazer of Petersburg. Recognizing the danger to Torah inherent in the emerging Haskalah (enlightenment) movement, he came out of seclusion, and in masterful oratory warned of the peril it represented. In 1840 he became *rosh yeshivah* (dean) of the Rameillas Yeshivah in Vilna. He opened a yeshivah in Kovno, attracting the greatest young scholars of that day. He involved himself with the plight of Russian Jewry and traveled throughout Europe seeking to bring back the lost Jewish youth to Torah observance. In 1860 Reb Yisrael Salanter moved to Memel, Germany, where he opened a study hall and in 1877 established a *kollel* (yeshivah for advanced Torah scholars). The alumni of this *kollel* subsequently established yeshivahs and *kollelim* throughout Europe. The seeds planted by this Torah giant are bearing fruit today in yeshivahs and *kollelim* that span the globe. His message of Mussar and Torah lives on in the present generation.

עזרי מעם ה׳ ספר עשה שמים וארץ
אור ישראל
כולל קבוצת מכתבים ומאמרים שונים להלהיב הלבבות
ליראת ה׳ ולימוד היראה והמוסר כתובים בכתי״ק כ״ק
אדמו״ר הרב הגאון הגדול רשכבה״ג החסיד והעניו אור
עולם המפורסם בכל קצוי ארץ מרנא ורבנא ישראל
ליבקין מסאלאנט זצוקללה״ה.
ונלוו להם מאמר על דבר לימ׳ היראה והמוסר יכונה בשם
שערי אור. קצות דרכי אדמו״ר והילוכו בקדושה בשם
נתיבות אור. מאמרים שונים ביראת ה׳ ודרכי התשובה
יכונה בשם כוכבי אור.
כל אלה חוברו יחדיו מאתי תלמידו
יצחק בהרב מוהר״ש בלאזער מלפנים רב בעיר המלוכה
פעטערבורג.
ווילנא
שנת תר״ם לפ״ק

Title page of *Or Yisrael,* a compilation of thoughts, letters, and essays of Rabbi Yisrael Salanter.

SELECTIONS FROM REB YISRAEL SALANTER'S COMMENTARY

Chanoch walked with God, and he was no more, because God had taken him.

(Genesis 5:24)

Rabbi Yisrael Salanter: *Chanoch walked with God*—Our Rabbis in *Midrash Talpiot* tell us, "Chanoch [2] was a shoemaker, and with every single stitch that he made he achieved mystical unions with his Creator." This midrash cannot possibly mean that while he was sitting and stitching shoes for his customers, he was concentrating on mystical concepts. This would be forbidden by Torah law. How could he divert his attention to other matters while engaged in work he had been hired to do by others? No, the mystical unions were actually the attention he devoted to each and every stitch, making sure that it would be good and strong and that the pair of shoes he was making would be a good pair, giving comfort and pleasure to whomever would wear it.

The Israelites saw the great power that God had unleashed against Egypt, and the people feared God and they believed in God and in His servant Moses.

(Exodus 14:31)

Rabbi Yisrael Salanter: *The people feared God and they believed in God*—To fear God is the first prerequisite to achieving perfection. Laws of ethics that regulate man's conduct toward his fellowman will not be observed if they are predicated solely on humanitarian principles. If ethical laws are not based on faith in the Creator and a pure fear of God, they have no binding force. All intellectual postulates, all humanitarian principles will melt into oblivion as soon as they are confronted with the touchstone of reality; they shatter into a thousand pieces against the hard rock of selfishness and sensual lust. The fear of God is the only power strong enough to restrain man, potent enough to curb his natural drives and instincts. But there is also this to consider. Faith itself springs primarily from fear of God. Without *yir'ah* (fear of God), *emunah* (faith in God) will not endure. This is the intent of the present verse: *The people feared God and they believed in God*—Fear of God precedes faith. Without a firm foundation of *yir'ah* the true faith can easily be distorted and falsified to suit anyone's liking, adopting new and alien forms. The fear of God serves as the conscience that guides the *emunah* (faith) along the path of authentic and unadulterated Judaism. [3]

If a person has a blotch, discoloration, or spot on the skin of his body [combining to] form a leprous mark on his skin, he shall be brought to Aaron the priest or to one of his sons the priests.

(Leviticus 13:2)

Rabbi Yisrael Salanter: *If a person has . . . on the skin of his body . . . a leprous mark*—In the preceding weekly portion, *parashat Shemini*, the Torah enumerates the various species of animals and birds that are permitted and forbidden to be eaten. Immediately following that chapter, the Torah sets forth the laws of *nega'im* (plagues, diseases). Our sages tell us that these sicknesses come as a penalty for the sin of *leshon hara*, slander, gossip, talebearing. People are more scrupulous not to eat forbidden foods than they are not to "devour" another human being by destroying his reputation through slander. The juxtaposition of these chapters teaches us that "consuming" your fellowman by means of *leshon hara* (gossip, slander) is no less sinful than is eating pork. [4]

Moses was very humble, more so than any other man on the face of the earth.

(Numbers 12:3)

Rabbi Yisrael Salanter: *Moses was very humble, more so than any other man on the face of the earth*—These words were not said in the closing days of Moses' life, before his demise. They were not written in the final pages of the Torah. Quite the contrary. This passage is describing Moses at the height of his active life; we find it in the center of the Torah. The underlying message is that Moses remained Moses. He did not change. The fact that God said about him, "Moses was very humble, more so than any other man on the face of the earth," did not affect him in the least. Not even the faintest trace of pride or conceit penetrated his thoughts. Such modesty represents the loftiest stage of humility,[5] a stage that has never been attained by any other man on the face of the earth.

Realize it today and ponder it in your heart: God is the Lord in heaven above and on the earth below—there is no other.

(Deuteronomy 4:39)

Rabbi Yisrael Salanter: *Realize it today and ponder it in your heart. Realize it today*—intellectually; grasp it and become aware of it rationally. But knowledge of God is but a first step; by itself it is not sufficient. *Ponder it in your heart*—The knowledge of God must penetrate our heart and soul so that it becomes the force governing our actions. The level of our moral and ethical progress must keep pace with our intellectual achievements. There is as wide a gap between total ignorance and recognizing God on an intellectual level as that which exists between intellectual recognition of God and "God penetrating your heart," God becoming the dominant force in your life.[6]

Excerpt from *Or Yisrael*

It is a well-known fact that the Creator constantly observes every person's ever so minute action or thought. Each of man's actions evokes a commensurate response from God—the more you direct your thoughts and actions to God, the more He will watch over you. This idea is expressed in the midrash on the verse, "God is your shade" (Psalm 121:5). The shade responds to all your actions; show it one finger, and the shade will show you one finger, too. Hold out your full hand to it, and the shade will show you a full hand in return. God is like the shade. In the same manner that you approach Him, so will He reveal Himself to you and respond to you.

Rabbi Yisrael Salanter enumerated the following thirteen character traits that each person should develop and perfect within himself.

1. אמת   -*Emet*—Truth. Always be truthful.

2. זריזות -*Zerizut*—Alertness, quickness.

3. חריצות -*Charitzut*—Diligence.

4. כבוד   -*Kavod*—Respect. Treat everyone with respect.

5. מנוחה -*Menuchah*—Tranquility. Develop inner serenity.

6. נחת   -*Nachat*—Gentleness, quietness. Speak in a soft voice.

7. נקיון -*Nikayon*—Cleanliness.

8. סבלנות -*Savlanut*—Patience.

9. סדר   -*Seder*—Orderliness. Conduct your affairs in an orderly fashion.

10. ענוה   -*Anavah*—Humility.

11. צדק   -*Tzedek*—Righteousness. Be just in all your dealings. Be willing to yield even when the law does not require you to do so.

12. קמוץ   -*Kimutz*—Thrift.

13. שתיקה -*Shetikah*—Silence. Think before you speak.

Excerpt from *Shaarei Or*, an essay on Mussar (Torah ethics) by Rabbi Yitzchak Blazer,[7] a disciple of Rabbi Yisrael Salanter

The study of Mussar is the remedy for the ills of the soul. Before he will see the need for taking this medicine, a person must recognize that his soul is in a very unhealthy state. This realization will induce him to seek relief for his disease of the spirit, which he will find in doing God's will and serving Him wholeheartedly. All this requires a great deal of self-analysis. Without Mussar to show the way, there can be no introspection and self-appraisal. Without studying Mussar, what would arouse you to seek a therapy for the affliction of your soul? The therapy of Mussar tastes bitter at first, but in the end it is sweet. When you accustom yourself to studying Mussar books, you realize that worldly pleasure is nothing but vanity. You understand that it is futile to close your eyes to the fact that life comes to an inevitable close, that Judgment Day is at hand. Mussar opens your eyes to distinguish between good and evil, to see what lies ahead, to prevent the coming of Perdition. Mussar makes you rejoice in your lot and causes you to "exult with trembling."[8]

RABBI SIMCHAH ZISSEL OF KELM— THE *ALTER* OF KELM

רבי שמחה זיסל מקלם

born: Kelm, Lithuania, 1824
died: Kelm, Lithuania, 1898
Affectionately referred to as the Alter *of Kelm. Ethicist, talmudist.*

A descendant of the illustrious **Maharal of Prague**, Simchah Zissel became an outstanding disciple of **Rabbi Yisrael Salanter**, founder of the Mussar movement. With total dedication he acquired a broad and profound knowledge of the Talmud and the Codes. He was universally admired for his keen insight and his devout piety. He inspired thousands to follow the teachings of Mussar ethics. He founded a yeshivah in Kelm that gained great fame for its high scholastic standards and dedication to Mussar. His collected writings were published under the title *Chochmah Umussar*.[1] They reflect his distinctive Mussar doctrine, which is based on a deep understanding of human psychology. He considers the intellect to be the dominant factor in the human personality and the instrument with which man can subdue his natural inclinations. Since his essays were written to his advanced students who were acquainted with his ideas, he often alludes to major themes with brief references, discernible to his students but obscure to the uninitiated. Many of his disciples became prominent Torah personalities in their own right, such as **Rabbi Nosson Tzvi Finkel of Slobodka**, Rabbi Moshe Mordechai Epstein of Slobodka, Rabbi Isser Zalman Meltzer of Slutzk, **Rabbi Yosef Hurwitz of Novardok**, and many others.

ספר
חכמה ומוסר
ספר שלם בתורת היראה והמוסר, כלליה ופרטיה.
מגלה עמוקות בכוחות הנפש, הכרת עצמו, דרכי המדות
ותקונן בהלכתא גבירתא ע״פ התורה.
מלמד להועיל להבין דברי חז״ל וצורת התורה לאמתה
באור חכמה ומוסר יתלכדו יחדיו ולא יתפרדו.
מאמרים חוצבים להבות אש ביסודות הדת והאמונה,
מלהיבים הלבבות ללמוד היראה והמוסר.
מעשה ידי האדם הגדול בענקים אשר דלה דלה והשקה מתורת רבו
הגאון רשכבה״ג קדוש **ישראל מסלנט** זצוקללה״ה
והעמיד תורה ויראה בישראל
רב רבנן ומאור הגולה רב האי גאון סבא קדישא מקלם
מרנא ורבנא ר׳ **שמחה זיסל זיו** זצוקללה״ה
— ערוכים בכתב יד קדשו —
הותחל בהוצאה להאיר לדורות ע״י עטרת ראשנו אור עולם אאמו״ר
הגה״ח מרן ר׳ **ירוחם הלוי ליוואוויץ** זצוקללה״ה
תם ונשלם
ש׳ ל׳ ב׳ ע׳
ירושלים עיה״ק, תשכ״ד

Title page of *Chochmah Umussar,* a profound work on Mussar by Rabbi Simchah Zissel of Kelm.

SELECTIONS FROM RABBI SIMCHAH ZISSEL'S COMMENTARY

God said, "Let us make man with Our image and likeness. Let him dominate the fish of the sea, the birds of the sky, the livestock animals, and all the earth—and every land animal that walks the earth."

(Genesis 1:26)

Rabbi Simchah Zissel of Kelm: *Let us make man with Our image and likeness*—**Rashi** explains the meaning of "in Our image and likeness" as having the ability to understand and conceive. Thinking is a process that is unique to mankind, distinguishing man from all other living creatures. Reasoning power is the very essence of man; it constitutes the "image of God" intrinsic to him. The intellect opens man's eyes and leads him on the path of understanding and insight. By means of his intellect he acquires wisdom and knowledge. A failure to think leads to man's downfall; without a probing, searching, contemplating mind there can be no hope for man.[2]

Excerpt from *Chochmah Umussar*, "On the Bond between Wisdom and Mussar"

If you give it some thought, you will conclude from the simple narrative of the Written and the Oral Torah that Mussar ethics is the foundation of wisdom. In its opening paragraphs, the Torah relates the story of Adam's sin in eating from the fruit of the Tree of Knowledge. Now, isn't it puzzling that the Torah reveals this sin? In an analogous case (Joshua 7[3]), God's reaction to sin is quite the opposite: God refuses to divulge the identity of the sinner, Achan, saying to Joshua, "Do you take Me for an informer?" (*Sanhedrin* 11a). Adam, created by the Hands of God, was the Perfect Man. By publicizing Adam's sin, the Torah teaches us the lesson that even the most sublimely endowed man is fallible and can stumble and fall, just as the lowliest person can; that regardless of status, everyone must be extremely careful not to lapse into sin. That is the message of Mussar. . . . By overcoming his physical nature, man transcends the level of angels, who are not physical in nature. In that Adam failed, and therein lay his sin. And so it becomes clear from the very beginning of the Torah that the study of Mussar is essential.

In the middle of the night he got up and took his two wives and his two handmaids and his eleven sons and sent them across the Yabbok River shallows.

(Genesis 32:23)

Rabbi Simchah Zissel of Kelm: *And his eleven sons*—Rashi wonders, "Where was Dinah?" and he answers, "Jacob had placed her in a chest, locking it securely, so that Esau would not cast lustful glances at her." Rashi continues, "Jacob was punished for keeping her out of his brother's reach; she might have changed him into a decent man. His punishment was that Dinah fell into the hands of Shechem." Rashi's comment needs clarification. What constituted Jacob's sin? After all, he acted as a father should, consistent with the rabbinical dictum, "Giving your daughter in marriage to an ignoramus is equivalent to placing her tied hand and foot before a hungry lion." Jacob's sin manifested itself in the way in which he approached this delicate problem—in the lack of sensitivity he exhibited. Simply hiding Dinah from Esau's view would have been sufficient. In locking the chest, he went too far.[4]

When the Israelites camp, each individual shall be in his own camp, each one designated by the banner for his division.

(Numbers 1:52)

Rabbi Simchah Zissel of Kelm: *Each individual shall be in his own camp, each one designated by the banner for his division*—Order and self-discipline are vital elements in the attainment of perfection.[5] If you are careless and untidy in the way you lead your personal life, your mind and your thinking are equally muddled and disorganized. You are incapable of accomplishing any creative work. . . . The entire Torah is built on order and precision: a split second separates Shabbat from the weekdays; a hair-breadth separates a *shechitah*[6] that is kosher from a nonkosher one. . . . Levites are forbidden to perform priestly service; *kohanim* (priests) may not perform the service assigned to Levites, "each performing *his* service, carrying *his* load" (Numbers 4:19).

RABBI YOSEF YOZEL HURWITZ OF NOVARDOK—THE *ALTER* OF NOVARDOK

רבי יוסף יוזל הורביץ מנאווארדאק—הסבא מנאווארדאק

born: Plungian, Lithuania, 1848
died: Kiev, Russia, 1920
Popularly known as the Alter *of Novardok. Ethicist,* rosh yeshivah.

Yosef Yozel Hurwitz's father, the rabbi and dean of the yeshivah, was his first teacher. A brilliant student, he gave regular talmudic lectures in the yeshivah at the age of 16. After his marriage, he successfully conducted his mother-in-law's drygoods business. Upon meeting **Rabbi Yisrael Salanter**, the founder of the Mussar movement, he was profoundly moved. His life changed drastically, and at age 25 he abandoned his business pursuits and moved to Kovno to study Torah, devoting himself to Talmud and Mussar (ethics) for eighteen hours a day. He often retreated into solitude to meditate and concentrate on self-analysis and self-improvement. His life changed tragically when his wife died in childbirth and he was left to care for their small children. Upon the advice of **Reb Simchah Zissel of Kelm**, he now devoted his life to propagating Torah. With great courage and energy he founded a yeshivah in Novardok, in 1896, which quickly grew into an entire network of yeshivahs called Bet Yosef, attracting large numbers of students. These yeshivahs followed the *Alter* of Novardok's brand of Mussar, which stressed the importance of communal work, breaking one's ingrained habits and character traits, and above all, an uncompromising search for the truth. His thoughts on Mussar are collected in his book, *Madregat Ha'adam*. His ideals live on in the Novardok yeshivahs in America, Eretz Yisrael, France, and other countries, where the name *Bet Yosef* is perpetuated.

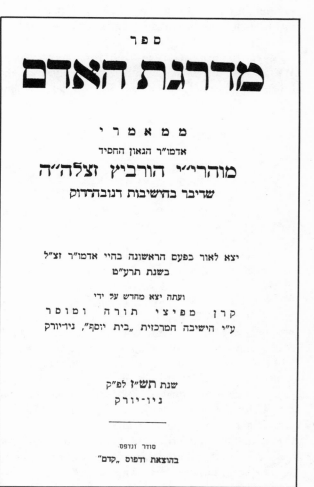

ספר

מדרגת האדם

ממאמרי

אדמו"ר הגאון החסיד

מוהרי"י הורביץ זצלה"ה

שדיבר בהישיבות דנובהרדוק

יצא לאור בפעם הראשונה בחיי אדמו"ר זצ"ל

בשנת תרע"ט

ועתה יצא מחדש על ידי

קרן מפיצי תורה ומוסר

ע"י הישיבה המרכזית „בית יוסף", ניו־יורק

שנת תש"ז לפ"ק

ניו־יורק

סודר ונדפס

בהוצאת ודפוס „קדם"

Title page of *Madregat Ha'adam*, lectures on Mussar themes by Rabbi Yosef Yozel Hurwitz, the *Alter* of Novardok.

SELECTIONS FROM RABBI YOSEF HURWITZ'S WRITINGS

Excerpt from *Madregat Ha'adam*, Chapter *Mezakeh et Harabbim*, Bringing Others Closer to God

The Midrash relates, "Elkanah (the Prophet Samuel's father) would take his wife, children, sisters, and all his relatives along on the Festival pilgrimage to the House of God. On their way they would make camp in the square of every town they passed so that all the townspeople would notice and ask, "Where are you going?" "To the House of God in Shiloh," they would answer, "for from there go forth Torah and mitzvot. Why don't you come with us?" The eyes of the townspeople would immediately fill with tears as they said, "Yes, we will go with you!" The first year five more families went; the next year, ten, until finally everyone went. Then God said to Elkanah, "You have tipped Israel's scales to the side of merit. You have educated them in the performance of mitzvot, and the people have gained merit because of you. Therefore, I will bring forth from you a son who will tip Israel's scales to the side of merit and educate them in mitzvot." Thus, the Prophet Samuel was born as a reward to Elkanah. (*Yalkut,*[1] I Samuel). Lofty ideals often become a reality through the initiative of a lone individual. As this Midrash tells it, the mitzvah of the Festival pilgrimage had been all but forgotten until Elkanah was observed plodding along on his journey to Shiloh. Gradually, step by step, through persistence, patience, and kindness, the mitzvah was brought back to life until it was practiced universally by all Jews. We all know how difficult it is to get a single person to do something—especially if it requires effort or expense, or a change in personal habits—not to mention exercising an influence on an entire nation! Here one man accomplished the impossible and thereby brought joy to God and to man. How did Elkanah do it? Simply by setting himself as a living example of dedication, sincerity, and unselfishness. These qualities drew people like a magnet, to learn about the mitzvah. Elkanah is an everlasting example of how a pure and faithful person can go up to the House of God and bring all of Jewry along with him.

Excerpts from *Madregat Ha'adam*

A person who refuses to work for the community because he is too burdened with other things will find that he is always too burdened.

If a person would work as hard for the benefit of the community as he works for the benefit of a single member of his family, he could establish a hundred yeshivahs.

Even in searching out the bad character traits within him, a person may mislead himself, for the *yetzer hara* (evil inclination) joins the search and steers him away from the areas that really need searching. This is like the case of the government agent sent to inspect a house that was under suspicion of harboring an illegal distillery. With a broad smile the owner greeted the agent and showed him through the house. The owner was extremely helpful, bending to look here, stretching to look there. Impressed by the man's helpfulness, the agent followed him faithfully. When they reached the place where the illegal operations were being carried out, the owner gently steered the agent aside, saying, "Here there is nothing to look for." In such a search, not only will the character traits remain soiled, but the person will even fool himself into thinking he has actually repented of his sins.

The advantage of *teshuvah* (repentance) over all other ventures is that even losses are converted into profits.

Excerpt from *Madregat Ha'adam*, Chapter *Mezakeh et Harabbim*, Working for the Good of the Community

The Talmud in *Bava Metzia* 88b relates, "What did Rabbi Chiyah do? He went and sowed flax, made nets from the flax cords, trapped deer whose flesh he gave to orphans, and prepared scrolls from their skins, on which he wrote the Five Books of Moses. Then he went to a town that had no teachers and taught the Five Books to five children and the Six Orders of the Talmud to six children, and he instructed them to teach each other the Chumash and the Mishnah, and thus he preserved the Torah from being forgotten in Israel! This is what Rabbi meant when he said, 'How great are the works of Chiyah.'" We can also serve the community by emulating Rabbi Chiyah's method of "students teaching other students." On that principle, schools and study groups can be established in cities, towns, and villages. In so doing, the entire young generation can be mobilized under the banner of Torah and *Yir'ah* (Fear of God). This is a duty that is incumbent on each individual. Each person can promote the advancement of Torah in his own way. One may be capable of giving lessons, another can organize rallies, a third may be in charge of the technical details, while a fourth travels around to register new students. Whoever can lend a helping hand to strengthening Torah, step forward! Don't shirk your responsibility, don't look for the easy way out! Be stout and stalwart! Go full speed ahead, wandering from town to town, founding new yeshivahs. Who will be held responsible for the low state of Torah? Precisely those faithful Jews who had it within their power to raise it, trusting in God to answer their prayers. The responsibility rests squarely on your shoulders!

RABBI NOSSON TZVI FINKEL OF SLOBODKA—
THE *ALTER* OF SLOBODKA

רבי נתן צבי פינקל מסלאבאדקא—הסבא מסלאבאדקא

born: Rasein, Lithuania, 1849
died: Hebron, Israel, 1927
Popularly known as the Alter *of Slobodka. Ethicist,*
talmudist.

A devoted disciple of **Rabbi Simchah Zissel of Kelm,** Rabbi Nosson Tzvi Finkel devoted his life to the dissemination of Torah and Mussar. In 1884 he founded a yeshivah in Slobodka, a suburb of Kovno, where for almost half a century he taught Torah and Mussar to thousands of students. A man of legendary humility, he was the embodiment of *chesed*—lovingkindness—and self-sacrifice in the service of others. His writings, lectures, and sermons were published by his students under the title *Or Hatzafun.*[1] His work mirrors his novel approach to Mussar. Rather than concentrating on man's fallen state as a means of subduing his evil instincts, the *Alter* chose to highlight the sublime greatness of the human soul. The awareness of having been created by God and having been endowed with a pure soul infuses man with the ambition to attain perfection. Under his inspired leadership, the Slobodka Yeshivah grew to be the predominant yeshivah in the Torah world. His best students were chosen to establish new yeshivahs in other towns so that there emerged a large network of high-caliber yeshivahs throughout Lithuania, Poland, and Russia. In 1925 the *Alter* of Slobodka emigrated to Eretz Yisrael, where he opened the famous Hebron Yeshivah. His influence is manifested today in the evergrowing number of yeshivahs that are the spiritual offspring of the Slobodka Yeshivah.

Rabbi Nosson Tzvi Finkel, the *Alter* of Slobodka.

SELECTIONS FROM RABBI NOSSON TZVI FINKEL'S WRITINGS

Abraham came forward and said, "Will You actually wipe out the righteous with the wicked?"
(Genesis 18:23)

Rabbi Nosson Tzvi Finkel of Slobodka: *Abraham came forward and said, "Will You actually wipe out the righteous with the wicked?"*—This dialogue, in which Abraham implores God to spare the people of Sodom, is mystifying. Abraham and Sodom are diametrically opposed: Abraham—the epitome of kindness; Sodom—the personification of wickedness and corruption, the antithesis of Abraham's way of life. It would stand to reason that the impending destruction of Sodom would be a source of joy to Abraham. Yet, he does not rejoice. Instead, he fervently prays to have the decree annulled. What motivated Abraham? Taking delight in the downfall of Sodom would in itself be a manifestation of a Sodomite character trait, whereas it was Abraham's mission in life to eradicate every trace of wickedness. He prayed for the people of Sodom because it was his desire that *sin*—not *the sinners*—be eliminated from the face of the earth. This corresponds with the talmudic interpretation of Psalm 104:35, which our sages render homiletically, "Let sins cease to be perpetrated on the earth, then the wicked will be no more—for everyone will be righteous" (*Berachot* 10a).

Jacob awoke from his sleep. "God is truly in this place," he said, "but I did not know it."
(Genesis 28:16)

Rabbi Nosson Tzvi Finkel of Slobodka: *"God is truly in this place," he said, "but I did not know it"*—**Rashi** remarks that by saying "but I did not know it," Jacob implied, "Had I known it, I would not have slept in a holy place such as this." Jacob blamed himself for acting improperly by sleeping at this sacred site. He reproached himself, even though it was through this sleep that he experienced the gift of great spiritual elevation and prophecy. There is a lesson in this for all of us. We must never violate the rules of common decency, even if by disregarding them we would attain the loftiest spiritual heights.[2]

If you follow My laws and are careful to keep My commandments, I will provide you with rain at the right time so that the land will bear its crops and the trees of the field will provide fruit.
(Leviticus 26:4)

Rabbi Nosson Tzvi Finkel of Slobodka: *If you follow My laws . . . I will provide you with rain at the right time*—Rainfall is the spark that triggers the growth of crops, in keeping with the Divinely ordained natural laws of germination and botany, as stated in the present verse, "I will provide you with rain . . . so that the land will bear its crops." By the same token, it is a natural law, a process of cause and effect, that "if you follow My laws . . . then I will provide you with rain."

Excerpt from a discourse in *Or Hatzafun*

People think that the creation of the world means that something was created from nothing, *ex nihilo*—that this world has some substance to it. In reality this is not so. In all of creation there is nothing we can grasp and identify as the ultimate matter, for as minute as the object may be it can always be broken down into even smaller particles, infinitely smaller than specks of dust, that cannot be discerned even with a powerful microscope. To put it plainly, we never see matter in its physical form, but rather, the spiritual force that binds it together. We are thus witnesses to the exact opposite: nothing from something—everything is transcendental and spiritual. This being so, why does the world not abound with spirituality? Clearly, because man has the unique ability to transform the spiritual into the physical. Man tends to concretize everything and not to see clearly. Man must therefore strive to imitate his Maker, for only in that way will his materialism be refined somewhat, and his eyes truly opened to perceive only spirituality in all of creation.

RABBI ELIYAHU LAPIAN
רבי אליהו לאפיין

born: Greyva, Poland, 1876
died: Kfar Chasidim, Israel, 1970
Ethicist, talmudist.

After having studied Talmud at the yeshivah in Lomza under Rabbi Eliezer Shulevitz, Eliyahu Lapian proceeded to Kelm, which stood under the leadership of the aged **Rabbi Simchah Zissel of Kelm.** Rabbi Eliyahu Lapian founded a yeshivah in Kelm and, with brilliant oratory, captivated the entire community, leading them in the struggle against the emerging secularist and socialist trends. In 1928 he moved to London, where he promoted the study of Torah and Mussar. In 1950 he settled in Eretz Yisrael and became the *mashgiach* (spiritual adviser and supervisor) of the Yeshivah of Kfar Chasidim. Although he was of advanced age, his lectures and fiery Mussar sermons attracted large audiences and had a profound impact on the Torah world. His thoughts and discourses were compiled by his students and were published under the title, *Lev Eliyahu*.[1] It is a work steeped in Mussar ideology, presented in a lucid and uncomplicated style. The anecdotes recorded in the segment of Rabbi Eliyahu's biography, some of which have miraculous undertones, reveal the saintly personality of this illustrious Torah giant.

Rabbi Eliyahu Lapian.

SELECTIONS FROM RABBI ELIYAHU LAPIAN'S WRITINGS

Excerpt from *Lev Eliyahu,* Chapter *Shevive Lev* 174

Our sages compare the evil inclination to a fly. What similarity is there between the two? A fly will flit away from a clean environment to swoop down on a spot filled with grime and filth. The evil inclination does the same. When it finds in a person a stain of sin, that is the place to which it will choose to attach itself.[2]

Excerpt from *Lev Eliyahu,* Chapter *Shevive Lev* 53

In the Torah, in the chapter of the *sotah,* the suspected adulteress, we read, "If the woman is pure and has not been defiled to her husband, she will remain unharmed and will become pregnant" (Numbers 5:28). Our sages comment, "If she was barren until now she will conceive." So says Rabbi Yishmael. Rabbi Akiva says, "She will have a much better pregnancy than previ-

ספר
לב אליהו
מערכי לב, חכמה ומוסר
יסודות וביאורים נפלאים בתורה

מאת
רבנו הגה״צ סבא קדישא
מרן אליהו לאפיאן זצוק״ל
שהרביץ תורה בישראל כשבעים שנה ובאחרונה מנהל רוחני
בישיבת כנסת חזקיהו כפר חסידים
נקלטו מפיו בסרטי הקלטה, ונעתקו ללשון הקודש

יוצא לאור ע״י
הועד להוצאת כתבי מרן ז״ל

מהדורה שניה

פעיה״ק ירושלים תובב״א
שנת תשל״ב

Title page of *Lev Eliyahu*, a collection of discourses on Mussar by Rabbi Eliyahu Lapian.

ously" (*Berachot* 31). At any rate, both agree that she profited from the experience. Now, if we reflect on this, the question arises, "Why does she deserve a reward? We have here a woman whose husband warned her not to be alone with a certain man. Paying no attention to his warning, she secluded herself with this man—an adulterer. Although she did not commit the adulterous act itself, she certainly behaved in a licentious manner. Why, then, does an immodest woman, as she is, deserve a reward? For a correct understanding we must view this woman's actions from a different perspective and will thereby learn a fundamental prin-

ciple. By hiding out with this man in defiance of her husband's warning, she acted indecently. We must conclude that she was compelled by an uncontrollable erotic drive. This being so, why did she not commit the sinful act itself? There can be only one explanation. That in the final moment she overcame her passion "and remained pure"! It is for subduing her *yetzer,* her inclination, that she merited a heavenly reward.[3]

Excerpt from *Lev Eliyahu,* Chapter *Shevive Lev* 22

Jacob worked seven years for Rachel. But it seemed like no more than a few days because he loved her so much.

(Genesis 29:20)

Rabbi Eliyahu Lapian: *But it seemed like no more than a few days because he loved her so much*—This appears paradoxical. When you love something and are looking forward to obtaining it, then each day spent waiting seems like a year. Yet our verse states the exact opposite. People have a habit of distorting the truth by using inaccurate terminology. For example, they will say about someone, "This man loves fish." But what does he do to the fish he loves so much? He cuts it up, boils it or fries it, and eats it. That man does not love fish—he loves himself! But when the Torah describes a person as "one who loves," that person truly loves his fellowman for the good qualities he has; he loves him without a trace of self-interest. Such unselfish love gives him the ability to turn years into days. Our verse clearly confirms this. "It seemed like no more than a few days because he loved *her* so much—*her,* not himself.

Excerpt from *Lev Eliyahu,* Chapter *Shevive Lev* 63

Rambam states that the urge to commit adultery can gain control only in a heart devoid of wisdom. Note that he does not say, "In a *head* devoid of wisdom." He emphasizes the heart, in order to teach us this important lesson: A man may be the greatest philosopher, an intellectual giant. Still, if his knowledge is only in his head, if he has not absorbed it into his heart, experienced it emotionally, assimilated it into his personality, then he will succumb to the passion for committing adultery.

RABBI ELIYAHU ELIEZER DESSLER
הרב אליהו אליעזר דסלר

born: Libau, Lithuania, 1892
died: B'nei Brak, Israel, 1953
Rosh yeshivah, *eminent Mussar teacher, educator.*

Rabbi Eliyahu Eliezer Dessler's father was a disciple of **Rabbi Simchah Zissel of Kelm,** *the* disciple of **Rabbi Yisrael Salanter** (the founder of the Mussar movement). Studying for eighteen years at the yeshivah in Kelm, he gained mastery in Talmud and Mussar. In 1927 Rabbi Dessler settled in London, where he became a rabbi of congregations, gathering a private circle of students whom he molded in Talmud and Mussar. In 1941 he became the director of the *kollel* (postgraduate school for advanced talmudic studies) in Gateshead, England. In 1948 he accepted an offer to become the *mashgiach* (spiritual guide) of the Ponevezh Yeshivah in B'nei Brak, Israel. His profound lectures on Jewish life and thought were published under the title *Michtav MeEliyahu,*[1] dealing with subjects of paramount importance, such as Nature and Miracles, Trust in God and Human Endeavor, and Free Will and Determinism. His work reflects his attempt to create a synthesis between Chasidism and Mussar. It is a classic of modern Torah thought. *Michtav MeEliyahu* has had remarkable success and can be found in most Torah home libraries. The work has influenced the thinking of Jews throughout the world, contributing greatly to the esteem and admiration accorded the *kollel* fellow and postgraduate talmudic studies in general.

SELECTIONS FROM RABBI ELIYAHU DESSLER'S COMMENTARY

Excerpt from *Michtav MeEliyahu,* Vol. 2

And God saw that the light was good and God divided between the light and the darkness.
(Genesis 1:4)

Rabbi Eliyahu Eliezer Dessler.

Rabbi Eliyahu Eliezer Dessler: *And God saw that the light was good*—Our sages infer from this verse that God saw that the ethereal light of Creation was too precious to be exploited by the wicked. He therefore stored it away for the future to be enjoyed by the righteous (**Rashi**, Genesis 1:4). This raises the question, Why did God create this light in the first place, if He was only going to store it away? The underlying principle is that once a light of such supernal quality has existed in the world, the path to reaching it has been cleared. Traveling this path means returning to a preexisting, albeit latent, condition.[2] In a similar vein, we find that a fetus, in the moments prior to birth, is shown the vast expanse of the universe and is taught all the wisdom contained in the Torah. The instant he is born he forgets it all. Here, too, the purpose for

ספר
מכתב מאליהו
כרך ראשון
מאת
רבנו הגה"צ מרן אליהו אליעזר דסלר זצ"ל

מבחר מתוך כתביו בתורת המוסר וההשקפה

בעריכת:
אריה כרמל
אלטר האלפרן

יצא לאור על ידי חבר תלמידיו
לראשונה ליומא דהילולא קמא דמרן זצ"ל כ"ה טבת תשט"ו
וכעת יר"ל מהדורה חמישית
בני-ברק תשכ"ה

Title page of *Michtav MeEliyahu*, perspectives on Mussar ideology by Rabbi Eliyahu Eliezer Dessler.

imparting this soon-to-be-forgotten knowledge is to pave the way for him to return to this level of understanding by his own initiative and effort.

Excerpt from *Michtav MeEliyahu*, Vol. 2

God saw all that He had made and behold, it was very good.

(Genesis 1:31)

Rabbi Eliyahu Eliezer Dessler: *And behold it was very good*. The Midrash expounds: *Very good*—This is a reference to the evil inclination.[3] This apparent paradox requires clarification. The destiny of all Creation hinges on the evil inclination. We must realize that the sole purpose of Creation is to bring about the sanctification of God's Name by means of man's free choice. Without the option of following his evil inclination, man has no freedom of choice. By resisting his evil inclination and attempting to do God's will, man is sanctifying God's Name. But even if he succumbed to *yetzer's*[4] temptation, even if he chose to do evil, the ultimate outcome would still be a *kiddush HaShem* (sanctification of God's Name). For he will suffer God's retribution and people will learn from it to shun the evil that is inherent in sin. God's justice will thereby be revealed to the world. Consequently, God's greatness will be publicly proclaimed in either case: by virtue of the free choice of the righteous man or by the retribution incurred by the evil doer.

Excerpt from *Michtav MeEliyahu*, Vol. 1, On Love between the Sexes

The love that exists between man and wife is a remarkable phenomenon in human psychology. At first glance, we might think that this love has no actual content. Perhaps it is part of the Divine master plan to ensure the continued existence of the human race, just as hunger is given us to maintain the body. But this seems most unlikely. After all, to achieve this end the biological drive and the yearning for children would be sufficient. Then, why the need for this additional emotional bond? I have heard it said that this love stems from gratitude. Husband and wife are grateful to each other because they help each other to fulfill their natural desires. But this idea is wrong. There are plenty of ungrateful people in the world, but we do not find that they are lacking in husband-wife affection. Rather we must say that this love arises between husband and wife because they complement each other. This fact is the result of the nature with which God has endowed them. Alone, every person is defective and unable to carry out his function, as our rabbis say: "He who has no wife is not a complete human being" (*Bereishit Rabbah* 17). Together, they complement each other, and by giving each other this completeness they grow to love each other, on the principle we have already explained: "The one who gives, loves." Of course, their love will make them want to go on giving and bestowing joy and pleasure on one another.

Excerpt from *Michtav MeEliyahu*, Vol. 1

This, then, is the deeper meaning of the blessing we find in the *Shema*, "And you will eat[5] and be satisfied" (Deuteronomy 11:15).There is no one in existence who is truly satisfied with worldly goods. One who pursues the pleasures of this world never attains them to the fullest. He is always hungry for more. Only a person who sets spiritual happiness as his goal, who sees all worldly matters only as a means to that end, who in truth and with eagerness desires nothing but the service of God, that person is the one who is satisfied with God's bounty, in this world, too. He is filled with happiness—all the time.

Excerpt from *Michtav MeEliyahu,* Vol. 3, On Laboring for Torah

The Talmud teaches us, "Praiseworthy is he who enters this place (the World to Come), retaining his studies in his hand" (*Pesachim* 50a). Note, it does not say, "retaining his studies in his *head,*" but "in his *hand,*" implying that he enters the World to Come with the learning he acquired through toil and determination. This teaches us that in the World to Come the yardstick used to measure a person's Torah learning is not his intellectual prowess, but the exertion he expended in gaining it. . . . Consequently, an intelligent, sharp-witted fellow who with faultless memory has amassed an encyclopedic amount of Torah knowledge will be considered an ignoramus in the World To Come! Conversely, a dull-witted person, with a weak memory and minimal intellectual achievement, who exerted himself, straining every nerve to learn Torah, enjoys great prominence in the World to Come. He earned his preeminence because that which he achieved by his toil is all his own. That is really what is meant by the Talmudic statement (referring to the World to Come): "I found it to be an upside-down world—the high-placed ones were inferior and the inferior ones were on top." The upshot is that a bright fellow who does not study intensely will be a dullard in the World to Come. The ambitious, hardworking student will be the brilliant one there, as a reward for his diligence.

RABBI CHAIM LEIB SHMULEVITZ
רבי חיים ליב שמואלביץ

born: Stutchin, Poland, 1901
died: Jerusalem, Israel, 1979
Rosh yeshivah *of the Yeshivah of Mir.*

Rav Chaim was the son of Rabbi Refael Alter, dean of the yeshivah in Stutchin, son-in-law of the **Alter of Novardok,** one of the preeminent leaders of the Mussar movement. Young Chaim was orphaned at age 16, when both his parents died within six months of each other. Having received his early Torah instruction from his father, he continued to study diligently, acquiring mastery of the entire Talmud and its main commentaries. In 1921, when Rav Chaim was only 19 years old, Rabbi Shimon Shkop, the famous dean of the yeshivah of Grodno, recognizing his genius, chose him for Talmud lecturer at his yeshivah. His fame as a favorite educator spread rapidly, and in 1925 he received a call to join the staff of the Yeshivah of Mir, which stood under the leadership of Rabbi Eliezer Yehudah Finkel, known as Reb Leizer Yudel. Rav Chaim inspired his students with his lucid analyses and novel approaches to complex talmudic problems, and he honed their character with his soul-stirring Mussar discourses, stressing the importance of self-control, orderliness, and organization in daily conduct and in the thinking process. In 1930 Rav Chaim married Reb Leizer Yudel's only daughter and continued studying with awesome intensity. His lectures contained flashes of genius and amazed his audience. In 1939, with the outbreak of World War II, the yeshivah escaped from the advancing Soviet Army by fleeing to Vilna in Lithuania, which had not been invaded yet. From there the yeshivah made a miraculous escape to Japan, traveling via Moscow, across Siberia via Vladivostok to Kobe, Japan, finally settling in Shanghai, where they resumed their studies with greater fervor than ever before. Reb Leizer Yudel, having emigrated to Eretz Yisrael, had handed the reins of the yeshivah to his son-in-law Rav Chaim, who tended and nurtured its 400 students during its stormy years of lonely exile in

Rabbi Chaim Leib Shmulevitz.

far-off Shanghai, lifting their spirits with words of Torah and Mussar. After World War II, the main body of the yeshivah emigrated to the United States, where eventually, under the leadership of Rabbi Avraham Kalmanowitz, a flourishing yeshivah was established

ספר

שיחות מוסר

מאת

אדוננו מורנו ורבנו

הגאון החסיד

מרן רבי חיים ליב שמואלביץ זצוקללה"ה

ראש ישיבת מיר

דרך חיים תוכחות מוסר

שלימד לרבים בישיבה הק'

פה עיה"ק ירושלים תובב"א

בשנים תשל"א-תשל"ג

שנת תש"מ

Title page of *Sichot Mussar* by Rabbi Chaim Leib Shmulevitz.

in Brooklyn. Rav Chaim moved to Eretz Yisrael, where, after Reb Leizer Yudel's passing, he became the spiritual head of the yeshivah, which grew into a world-renowned talmudic academy, attracting students from all parts of the world. In his Mussar discourses he stressed the appreciation of man's greatness—believing that being mindful of one's greatness deters one from committing a sin. A compilation of his discourses on Mussar was published as *Sichot Mussar*.[1] A biography entitled *The Rosh Yeshivah,* by Rabbi Reuven Grossman, was translated into English.[2] Through exhausting toil, indomitable will power, and an unquenchable thirst for Torah, Rav Chaim became the beloved *rosh yeshivah* of his students and one of the foremost Torah leaders of our age.

SELECTIONS FROM RABBI SHMULEVITZ'S WRITINGS

Excerpt from *Sichot Mussar* I:20, Faith

It is written, "But the seventh year is a sabbath of sabbaths for the land. It is God's sabbath, during which you may not plant your fields nor prune your vineyards" (Leviticus 25:4). The *Yalkut*[3] comments on this verse: "Bless God, you His angels, you who are mighty in strength, who fulfill His word, listening to the voice of His word" (Psalm 103:20). Says Rabbi Yitzchak Nafcha, "This verse speaks of those who observe the Sabbatical Year. As a rule, people perform a mitzvah for a day, for a week, even for a month. But a whole year! And this farmer watches his field in desolation, his vineyard a wasteland, and he says nothing. Isn't that the epitome of heroism!"[4] Man can overcome his natural inclination for a day or two; by making a serious effort he might subdue it even for an entire week or month. But resisting it for a full year—watching his land lying fallow, the fruits of his hard labor ownerless, for anyone to take, standing impassively, day after day, week after week, without a word of protest—takes superhuman strength. Any resolution we make, any good intentions we have, are bound to erode gradually. The people who observe the Sabbatical Year are nothing short of angels. As the verse states, "His angels, You who are mighty in strength, who fulfilled His word." The inner strength exhibited by the observers of the Sabbatical Year is superhuman, placing them in the category of "angels of God."

Excerpt from *Sichot Mussar* I:27, Reflections on the Portion of Balak

By giving us a description of Balaam, the Torah shows us a man whose personality represents a complete contradiction. He is a man inspired by two opposite drives, by forces that are poles apart. Such was Balaam's character. On the one hand he recognized God as the Supreme Being. In his own words, "[I] know the Highest One's will" (Numbers 24:16). According to our sages, he even reached the level of prophecy attained by Moses. Yet, at the same time, he was a man who breached all restraints of morality, a man who sank to the depths of depravity and bestiality (*Avodah Zarah* 4b). In the story of Balaam, the Torah teaches us that opposite character traits can reside in the heart of one and the same man. This is a fundamental lesson of Mussar. Along similar lines, we can explain a paradox in the following statement by our sages: "At the time of the Crossing of the Red Sea, a slave girl saw visions greater than those beheld by the prophet Ezekiel." In spite of that, she remained a slave girl, as frivolous and inane as she had been before. Seeing heavenly visions did not effect any change in her personality. She retained her "slave girl" outlook on life. Not so Ezekiel. He became a prophet through self-improvement, laboring long years at eradicating all traces of evil from his heart. Although his prophetic visions could not match those of the slave girl, still he became a prophet of God. And so it was with Balaam. The level of greatness he reached was handed to him, without any toil or exertion on his part. Therefore, in spite of his lofty spiritual perceptions, he remained the same corrupt individual he had been before.

Excerpt from *Sichot Mussar* I:30, Interruptions and Distractions

In the chapter delineating the duties of the monarch we read, "He must write a copy of this Torah scroll . . . and it must always be with him and he shall read from it all the days of his life. He will learn to be in awe of God his Lord" (Deuteronomy 17:18–19). This Scripture means that he must literally carry the Torah scroll with him continually, without cease. **Mesillat Yesharim** infers from this verse that mental distraction is the most damaging factor in man's attempt at acquiring awe of God. Herein lies the root of our tragedy—the reason that we seem to be unable to attain true greatness—and I mean even those of us who are studying Torah full time. Distraction is what stands in our way. After each interruption we must begin all over again. The result is that we do not make any progress. You can compare it to someone trying to boil some water. If he continually removes the kettle from the flame before the water has come to a boil, replacing it only after it has cooled off, he will never get boiled water, even if he replaces it a thousand times. The kettle must remain on the flame without interruption until the water is boiling.[5] Before Moses' death, God showed him all the regions of the Land of Israel, "the land of Gilead as far as Dan, all of Naphtali, the land of Ephraim and Menasseh, the land of Judah . . . the Negev, the flat plain" (Deuteronomy 34:1–3). Thereafter, God said to him, "This is the land" (Deuteronomy 34:4), meaning that God showed him once again one overview of the entire land. Seeing Eretz

Yisrael in its entirety is different than seeing each part separately.[6]

Excerpt from *Sichot Mussar* II:6, Peace

The Torah relates that Rachel, upon giving birth to Joseph, jubilantly exclaimed, "God has taken away my humiliation" (Genesis 30:23). Rashi, quoting the Midrash, explains the source of her humiliation: "As long as a woman is childless she has no one on whom she can place the blame for her blunders. Once she has a son, the blame will fall on him. [Now her husband, instead of blaming her, will say,] "Who broke this vessel? I imagine your son must have done it." "Who ate these figs? Your son probably ate them." Now isn't this astonishing! Could this be a true reflection of Rachel's feelings toward Jacob her husband, who sacrificed fourteen years of his life laboring for the right to marry her? Would Jacob really mind if she broke a cup or ate some fruit? What's more, she said these words on the day she gave birth to her first-born son, after having been childless for many years. To her, becoming a mother was akin to rising from the dead, as she herself said previously, "Give me children, or else I'll die" (Genesis 30:1). Now, on this momentous day, all Rachel can think of is the seemingly trivial detail that from now on she will have someone on whom to blame her missteps! To us it may seem trivial, but to our holy Fathers and Mothers it was a matter of primary importance. They understood the paramount significance of peace. To Rachel, the birth of a son represented the removal of a potential source of friction between herself and her husband, be it ever so small. The elimination of even an indiscernibly slight potential crack in their union, the attainment of perfect domestic peace, evoked Rachel's sublime expression of joy.

Excerpt from *Sichot Mussar* III:9, "We Will Do and Obey"

The Midrash says, "When God gave the Torah to Israel, birds did not chirp, oxen did not moo, angels did not fly, seraphim did not intone 'Holy,' the sea ceased to surge, people did not speak, the world stood in deep silence as the Voice rang forth, 'I am the Lord your God' " (Exodus 20:2). He silenced the entire world so that all creatures would know that there is nothing besides Him (Song of Songs *Rabbah*, Yitro). The commandment "I am your God" is interconnected with

"There is nothing besides Him" (Deuteronomy 4:35).If the Oneness of God is to become manifest in the world, it is imperative that all voices of nature be stilled. Even seraphim proclaiming "Holy" would flaw the truth of "there is nothing besides Him" (Deuteronomy 4:35). God, therefore, silenced the entire world, rendering it void and empty, as though devoid of living creatures—and God's glory alone illuminated the universe. The question may be asked, if God gave the Torah, it follows that there were recipients whose existence was not nullified. How then, could these recipients hear the words, "There is nothing besides Him," when they themselves were existing, thinking, perceiving beings?

The answer can be found in the mystery of "Na'aseh venishma"—"we will do and obey" (Exodus 24:7). They accepted the Torah as quintessential servants; as servants whose will is completely subordinate to the will of their Master, the Master of the universe. Thus, with their very being they proclaimed, "There is nothing besides Him." If, at the Giving of the Torah, they would have had even the slightest inkling of "self," this notion would have precluded "I am the Lord your God." Only by subjugating themselves to God's will, in effect negating themselves by declaring, "We will do and obey," did they remove all barriers to "there is nothing besides Him."

V

CHASIDISM

Chasidism is a movement of spiritual revival. Its message added life and meaning to the observance of Torah and mitzvot, but it did not create anything new. The core of its thought is rooted in the mystic writings of the Zohar and other kabbalistic works, whose hidden facets of beauty and harmony it brought to the surface. Chasidism places the focus on enthusiasm in Jewish living. Prayer, the bridge leading from the mundane to the sublime, must be uttered with *kavanah*, fervor, and emotion. When praying, a Jew should be overcome with a yearning to be united with God, with a feeling of total self-negation. "Serve God with gladness" (Psalm 100:2) is one of the pillars of chasidic thought. Whatever a Jew does should be done with *simchah*, joy. Sadness and despair lead to sin; joy is the source of holiness. Mitzvot are to be performed in a happy mood—the Master of the universe delights in the happiness of His people. Sing, dance, be joyous; banish grief and worry from your heart. Share your joy with others. Joy leads to love, brotherhood, and unity. By living in harmony on earth, we establish harmony with our Father in Heaven. Chasidism eliminates the gap that separates the rich from the poor, the learned from the unlearned. Together they sing and dance, striving to come closer to God.

The central figure in Chasidism is the personality of the truly righteous rebbe, the *tzaddik yesod olam*—the righteous one, the foundation of the world. Consumed by a feverish longing for God, his soul yearns to be reunited with its Creator. The rebbe is the chasid's ideal, his guide in both spiritual matters and family and business affairs. His love and compassion comfort him; his Torah thoughts inspire him.

No analysis can do justice to the marvelous phenomenon of Chasidism. It can be dissected, its various elements scrutinized, but no true picture will emerge unless the depth of its emotion, its joy, and its enthusiasm are experienced. With God's blessing, in the aftermath of World War II, Chasidism has seen a strong rebirth, rising from the ashes of the murderous Nazi pyre. In Israel, the United States, and other parts of the world, Chasidism is a growing force, gaining new adherents daily. The Rebbes of Lubavitch, Belz, Ger, Satmar, Vizhnitz, Bobov, Munkacz, Skver, and many others have established dynamic communities, with burgeoning yeshivahs and other institutions that infuse the entire spectrum of Jewish life in the world with a new spirit of enthusiasm and hope for the future.

An anthology of chasidic thoughts, entitled *Netivot Bemachashevet HaChasidut*, by Rabbi Moshe Shelomoh Kasher (Jerusalem, 1975), offers chasidic perspectives on a wide range of topics, citing sources. It provides a wellspring of illuminating insight into the world of Chasidism.

RABBI ISRAEL BEN ELIEZER—THE BAAL SHEM TOV, BESHT
רבי ישראל בן אליעזר—בעל שם טוב, בעש"ט

born: Okop, Podolia, South Poland, 1700
died: Medzibosh, South Poland, 1760
Known as the Baal Shem Tov—Master of the Good
Name. Often referred to by the initials Besht. *Founder*
of Chasidism.

In his twenties, Israel ben Eliezer went into retreat in the Carpathian Mountains to immerse himself in prayer, study, and contemplation. On his 36th birthday he revealed himself as a spiritual leader. Many people were drawn to him by his charismatic personality and the miracles he performed. He loved his fellow Jews, gave much charity, and helped ransom prisoners and captives. Among the main elements of the Baal Shem Tov's teachings are: A Jew should live his life in joyous ecstasy with God. He should strive to attain *devekut*, a state of attachment to God; as he states, "Faith is the attachment of the soul to God." A Jew feels God's nearness even in his mundane life: in his business, in his eating and drinking. God is reached through joyful prayer rather than through fasting, mortification, and preoccupation with sin. God delights in the happiness of His people; therefore, it is important to dance, sing, and be jubilant. His message was eagerly received by the thousands of hard-working, simple Jews of Southern Poland. The chasidic movement spread rapidly through all the regions of Eastern Europe. It inspired and gave new hope to the impoverished, persecuted, and humiliated Jewish population. Chasidism became a vibrant force in Judaism and flourishes today in the burgeoning chasidic centers in Israel, America, and Europe. The Baal Shem Tov did not put his teachings into writing; he did not even permit others to do so. Twenty years after his death, his disciple, Rabbi Jacob Joseph, published the sermons and comments he had heard from his master, under the title *Toledot Yaakov Yosef.*[1]

Rabbi Israel ben Eliezer, the Baal Shem Tov.

SELECTIONS FROM THE TEACHINGS OF THE BAAL SHEM TOV

God said to Abraham, after Lot left him, "Raise your eyes and look from the place where you are now standing, to the north, to the south, to the east, and to the west."

(Genesis 13:14)

Baal Shem Tov: *And look from the place where you are now standing*—Man follows his thoughts.[2] Wherever his thoughts are focused, that's where he is. He may be standing in the synagogue, praying, but if his mind wanders off to the ends of the world in pursuit of his business, then he is in fact in his business and not in the synagogue. This concept is indicated in this verse. *And look*—Concentrate your thoughts on the spiritual and the holy, *befitting the place where you are now standing.* Don't let your mind be distracted; don't let your thoughts drift to other things and places.

He then took (Abraham) outside and said, "Look at the sky and count the stars. See if you can count them." (God) then said to him, "That is how (numerous) your descendants will be."

(Genesis 15:5)

Baal Shem Tov: *Look at the sky and count the stars*—To the human eye, the stars appear as miniscule sparks of light, while in reality they are heavenly bodies of immense proportions. The same holds true for the Jewish people. In this world they appear as lowly and contemptible creatures, but in heaven they are mighty and exalted, since all creation is dependent on them.[3]

But your heart may then grow haughty and you may forget your God, the One who has brought you out of the land of Egypt out of the house of slavery.

(Deuteronomy 8:14)

Baal Shem Tov: *But your heart may then grow haughty*—Why is it that nowhere in the Torah is it written that being humble constitutes a mitzvah (commandment)? If there would be a commandment to be humble, there would be people who would fulfill this mitzvah in all its ramifications. They would then proudly announce that in addition to all their other admirable qualities, they now have acquired also the praiseworthy character trait of modesty.

SELECTIONS FROM *NETIVOT BEMACHASHEVET HACHASIDUT*

Baal Shem Tov: *The Shemoneh Esrei* prayer[4] opens with the following words: Blessed are You, Lord, our God, and the God of our forefathers, God of Abraham, God of Isaac, and God of Jacob. Why don't we simply say: God of Abraham, Isaac, and Jacob. Why do we instead associate God's name with *each* of the Patriarchs? Each of the three Patriarchs arrived at the recognition of God through his own efforts, through an approach uniquely his own. Each of the Patriarchs had a way of serving God that was original.[5]

Cast me not off into the time of old age; when my strength fails forsake me not.

(Psalm 71:10)

Baal Shem Tov: *Cast me not off into the time of old age*—This verse is strange indeed, for don't we also need God's help when we are still young? The answer is this: A person sometimes becomes passionately excited about a cause, such as Torah study or prayer; but his enthusiasm doesn't last. Before long his fervor cools and the mitzvah that moments ago stirred him to ecstasy now appears to him as a timeworn and antiquated ritual. This is what the Psalmist has in mind with this verse: Don't cast out our enthusiasm. Don't cool our fervor, making our mitzvot appear to us as obsolete and old-fashioned routines. Keep our enthusiasm alive and burning, so that the mitzvot will always remain fresh and young in our eyes (*Sifte Tzaddikim, Hakolel*, p. 69).[6]

One day the Baal Shem Tov tarried a long time over his *Minchah* prayer. When asked for the reason, he explained that he knew of a *baal teshuvah* (a returnee to Torah observance) who had previously broken every law of the Torah. He had repented and was at that moment praying the *Minchah* prayer from the depth of his heart. His prayer was breaking through all Heavenly Gates. The Baal Shem Tov was striving to have his own prayer included with that of the *baal teshuvah*[7] (*Yechi Reuven, Chagigah* 22b).

Turn from evil and do good, seek peace and pursue it.

(Psalm 34:15)

Baal Shem Tov: *Turn from evil and do good*—Transform the evil within you into good (*Porat Yosef*, p. 244).

The Mishnah in *Avot* 4:1 states, *"Who is strong? He who subdues his natural inclination."*

Baal Shem Tov: It is necessary to subdue the evil inclination and transform it into good, from bitterness to sweetness, from darkness to light. If you fail to do that, but instead drive off the evil inclination, it will just come back to haunt you and you will spend all your life struggling with it. But if you deal with it wisely, it will never come back[8] (*Ramatayim Tzofim*).

And it cast down the truth to the ground.
(Daniel 8:12)

Baal Shem Tov: You cannot help but wonder. Truth, this exquisite jewel, the seal of the Almighty, is wallowing in dirt. Why is there no one to pick it up? You see, you cannot pick up this jewel unless you first bend down. And no one is willing to bow his head.

RABBI LEVI YITZCHAK OF BERDITCHEV—THE BERDITCHEVER
רבי לוי יצחק מברדיצ׳ב

born: Hoshakov, Galicia (Poland), 1740
died: Berditchev, Poland, 1810
Popularly known as the Berditchever. Foremost chasidic leader, commentator.

Rabbi Levi Yitzchak was a student of the Maggid of Mezritch and Rabbi Shmuel of Nikolsburg. He served as rabbi in the communities of Britchvahl, Zelichov, and Berditchev. He is known for his work *Kedushat Levi*, a commentary on Torah, *Pirke Avot*, and Mishnah. His chasidim were inspired by the burning enthusiasm with which he performed the mitzvot, which was unparalleled. His dedication to Torah and mitzvot was matched by his *ahavat Yisrael*—his all-embracing love for the people of Israel. He would plead with God for their deliverance, accusing God, as it were, of being too harsh on His children: "Though they may have sinned, compared to the other nations, Israel is a paragon of virtue." The Berditchever is the legendary advocate of the Jewish people. Many anecdotes surrounding his life have become proverbial classics.

SELECTIONS FROM THE BERDITCHEVER'S COMMENTARY

Abraham was old, well advanced in years, and God had blessed Abraham with everything.
(Genesis 24:1)

Rabbi Levi Yitzchak of Berditchev: *And God had blessed Abraham with everything*—A true tzaddik prays not only for himself; he prays for the welfare of his entire community. He is not satisfied when only he himself is blessed. If his community is not blessed also, the tzaddik's happiness is incomplete, and his life is unfulfilled. And so, when God wants to bless a tzaddik,

ספר
קדושת לוי
על התורה
אשר השאיר אחריו ברכה כבוד אדוננו מורינו ורבינו גאון עוזנו, ה"ה הרב הגאון האמתי איש אלהים רשכב"ג המפורסם בכל קצוי ארץ, כבוד שמו קדוש מוהר"ר לוי יצחק זצלה"ה, שהיה אב"ד ור"מ דק"ק בארדיטשוב יע"א ודק"ק זעליחאוו והגלילות, אשר חיבר על חמשה חומשי תורה. גם כמה ליקוטים על פסוקים ומאמרות ומדרשים אשר צלל לעומק העיון במעין החכמה מילין דמיטמרין אתגליין ליה, זכותו יגן עלינו אמן
בהוצאת ועד הדפסה „מפיצי אור"
אצל
ישיבת חכמי לובלין
שנגהאי
(מדינת כינה)
שנת תשו' לפ"ק

Title page of *Kedushat Levi*, by Rabbi Levi Yitzchak of Berditchev. Rare copy, published in Shanghai in 1946 by the students of the Yeshiva of Lublin who had escaped the Nazi onslaught and continued their studies under the Japanese occupation of China.

he blesses his entire community. That is the meaning of the statement, "God blessed Abraham with every thing." The blessing became a true blessing by the fact that everyone else was blessed also. Therein lies, in fact, the main idea of Abraham's blessing.[1]

The number of Jacob's descendants was seventy persons; and Joseph was in Egypt [already].
(Exodus 1:5)

Rabbi Levi Yitzchak of Berditchev: *And Joseph was in Egypt*—Even though Pharaoh had given Joseph the Egyptian name of Tzaphnat Paane'ach,[2] he kept his Hebrew name. Even in Egypt he remained Joseph.

God said, "I have indeed seen the suffering of My people in Egypt. I have heard how they cry out because of what their slave-drivers do, and I am aware of their pain."
(Exodus 3:7)

Rabbi Levi Yitzchak of Berditchev: *I have indeed seen* [The Hebrew idiom for "I have indeed seen" is *ra'oh ra'iti*—literally "seen, I have seen." The commentary addresses the question for the reason of the repetitive *ra'oh ra'iti*—seen, I have seen.]—The Midrash states, "God said to Moses, you are seeing only one vision, but I see two visions (hence, *seen, I have seen*). You view the people of Israel as they are coming to Mount Sinai to receive the Torah. I see them as receiving My Torah—*ra'oh*, see,—but also *ra'iti*—I have seen—I see them as worshipping the Golden Calf." Now the question arises. Why indeed did Moses, the greatest of all prophets, see only one vision, that of Israel receiving the Torah. Why did he fail to see their downfall at the Golden Calf? Were his prophetic powers impaired somehow? Most emphatically not! A prophet who sees Israel's shortcomings is no tzaddik and no prophet. Moses, the faithful shepherd, saw only the good in Israel, the receiving of the Torah. He did not see the making of the Golden Calf.[3]

As soon as I came to Pharaoh to speak in Your name he made things worse for these people. You have done nothing to help Your people.
(Exodus 5:23)

Rabbi Levi Yitzchak of Berditchev: *As soon as I came to Pharaoh to speak in Your name, he made*

things worse for us—Far be it from us to say Moses, the greatest of all prophets, spoke rebelliously against God! Moses intended this statement to serve as a pattern to be used by all future defenders of the Jewish people in pleading Israel's cause before God. Moses' words are to be interpreted as follows: "As soon as I came to Pharaoh to speak in Your name, he made things worse for these people." The root cause of all forms of anti-Semitism is that "I came to speak to Pharaoh in Your name"—that we propagate Your name, that we proclaim the truth of the Torah in the world. It is for *Your* sake that we suffer; it is for *Your* sake that everyone hates us; every day we sacrifice our lives for *You*. Therefore, You *must* save us from our enemies.[4]

And Aaron did so, lighting the lamps to illuminate the menorah, as God commanded Moses.
(Numbers 8:3)

Rabbi Levi Yitzchak of Berditchev: *And Aaron did so*—**Rashi** comments on this passage, "This comes to tell us the praise of Aaron that he did not deviate from the command he was given." Any other person charged with a task as sublimely sacred as lighting the holy menorah, for sheer ecstasy would have lost his composure completely. His heart aflutter, his hands trembling, he would have spilled the oil and dropped the wicks. It was to Aaron's everlasting credit that, in spite of his inner agitation, he performed his task with the utmost precision, exactly as he was told. It takes a superhuman measure of self-control to achieve this.

Today you have declared allegiance to God, making Him your God, and pledging to walk in His paths, keep His decrees, commandments, and laws, and to obey His voice. God has similarly declared allegiance to You today, making you His special nation, as He promised you, and to keep all His commandments.
(Deuteronomy 26:17–18)

Rabbi Levi Yitzchak of Berditchev: *Today you have declared allegiance to God, making Him your God . . . and . . . to keep . . . His commandments* (Deuteronomy 26:17). *God has similarly declared allegiance to you today, making you His special nation . . . and to keep all His commandments* (Deuteronomy 26:18).

Why the repetitive use of the phrase "to keep His commandments"? Verse 18, the second of the two verses, refers to God. If we may say so, it is God who promises to keep and uphold all "*His mitzvot*" toward the "*am segulah*," His "special nation." God pledges to pay Israel's wages, their reward for observing the Torah and doing good deeds, by showering on them the blessings of "children, health, and sustenance."

RABBI SHNEUR ZALMAN OF LIADI—THE BAAL HATANYA
רבי שניאור זלמן מלאדי—בעל התניא

born: Liazna, Russia, 1747
died: near Kursk, Russia, 1812
Popularly known as the Baal HaTanya, author of Tanya, his major work. Founder of Chabad movement in Chasidism.

Rabbi Shneur Zalman was a disciple of the Maggid of Mezritch. The Maggid, who was the most prominent student of the **Baal Shem Tov**, transmitted to Rabbi Shneur Zalman the teachings of Kabbalah, particularly those of the **Ari** (**Rabbi Yitzchak Luria**). Over a twelve-year period, the Maggid revealed to him the world of *nistar* (mysticism). Rabbi Shneur Zalman became the leader of the Chasidim of White Russia and introduced a new ideology that sought to create a synthesis between Chasidism and Torah scholarship and to unite the mystical and revealed aspects of Torah. His philosophy is contained in his work, *Likutei Amarim*, popularly referred to as *Tanya*,[1] its opening word. He delves into the concepts of Unity of God, *Tzimtzum* (the contraction of the Infinite in order to create the "space" for the existence of the universe), Divine emanations, the creative process that continues at every moment, and many other profound themes. An equally important work is his *Shulchan Aruch Harav*,[2] a Code of Jewish Law, that is highly respected and consulted by chasidic and nonchasidic scholars alike. The new branch of Chasidism became known as *Chabad*, which is an acronym of *Chochmah* (wisdom), *Binah* (insight), *Da'at* (knowledge). It is also referred to as Lubavitcher Chasidism and today is a mighty movement, extending into virtually all parts of the world.

SELECTIONS FROM THE BAAL HATANYA'S WRITINGS

Excerpt from *Likutei Amarim (Tanya)* 48

Rabbi Shneur Zalman of Liadi, the Baal HaTanya, founder of *Chabad* Chasidut.

ספרי אוצר החסידים ליובאוויטש

לקוטי אמרים

- תניא -

אוצר החסידים

Title page of *Likutei Amarim (Tanya)*.

In every generation and on each and every day one must look upon himself as if he personally had come out of Egypt on that very day. This refers to the Divine soul coming out of the prison that is the human body. This is accomplished by studying the Torah, performing the mitzvot in general, and in particular through the acceptance of God's absolute sovereignty by reciting the *Shema*. By saying the words "the Lord our God, the Lord is One," one accepts upon himself His absolute Oneness. . . . Abraham attained this recognition through his deeds and his saintly way of life, ascending gradually to ever higher levels, as it says, "Abram continued on his way, moving steadily" (Genesis 12:9). We, however, received it as a legacy and a gift, in that God gave us His Torah, which encompasses His Will and His Wisdom, which are bound up in perfect union with His Essence. It is as if He gave Himself to us, if one may say so. This is the deeper meaning of the words, "And You gave us the Lord our God with love" (from the Festival prayer) and "for with the light of Your countenance You gave us the Lord our God" (daily prayer). Thus there is nothing to prevent our soul from clinging to His Unity and His Light, except our will. If, God forbid, a person does not wish to attach himself to Him . . . as soon as he willingly accepts His sovereignty by reciting "The Lord our God, the Lord is One," his soul is included in God's Oneness. This is the concept of "Going out of Egypt" and this is the reason that the paragraph of "Going out of Egypt" has been made part of the *Shema*.

Excerpt from *Likutei Amarim* (*Tanya*), *Shaar Hayichud Veha'emunah 1*

It is written, "Forever, O God, Your word stands firm in the heavens" (Psalm 119:89). The Baal Shem Tov, of blessed memory, has explained that "Your word" that You uttered, "Let there be a firmament in the midst of the waters" (Genesis 1:6), these very words and letters stand firmly forever within the firmament of heaven and are forever clothed within all the heavens to give them life, as it is written, "The word of our God shall stand firm forever" (Isaiah 40:8) and "His words live and stand firm forever" (morning prayer). For if the letters were to depart even for an instant, God forbid, and return to their source, all the heavens would become naught and absolute nothingness, and it would be as though they had never existed at all, exactly as before the utterance, "Let there be a firmament." And so it is with all created things in all the upper and lower worlds, and even in this physical world. . . . If the letters of the Ten Utterances by which the earth was created during the Six Days of Creation were to depart from it but for an instant, God forbid, it would revert to naught and absolute nothingness, exactly as before the Six Days of Creation.

Excerpt from *Likutei Amarim* (*Tanya*), *Chinuch Katan*—The Education of the Child

Concerning the love of God it is written at the end of the portion *Ekev*, "which I command you to *do* it, to love God" (Deuteronomy 11:22). It is necessary to understand how an expression of doing can be applied to love, which is in the heart. The explanation is that there are two kinds of love of God. One is the natural yearning of the soul to its Creator. . . . Those who merit this state are called tzaddikim. . . . Yet, not everyone is privileged to attain this state. . . . The second is a love that every man can attain when he engages in profound contemplation in the depth of his heart on matters that arouse the love of God, which is in the heart of every Jew. Be it in a general way, that He is our very life, and just as one loves his soul and his life, so he will love God in his true soul and actual life . . . or in a particular way, when he will understand and comprehend the greatness of the King of kings, the Holy One, Blessed is He, to the extent that his intellect can grasp and even beyond. . . . Then,

"as in water, face reflects face" (Proverbs 27:19), love will be aroused in everyone who contemplates and meditates on this matter in the depth of his heart—to love God with an intense love and cleave unto Him, heart and soul. . . .[3]

RABBI SIMCHAH BUNAM OF PSHIS'CHA—
REBBE REB BUNAM
רבי שמחה בונם מפשיסחא—רבי רב בונם

born: Wodzislaw, Poland, 1762
died: Pshis'cha, Poland, 1827
Popularly known as the Rebbe Reb Bunam. Prominent chasidic leader.

As a young man, Simchah Bunam studied in the yeshivahs of Mattersdorf and Nikolsburg under the guidance of Rabbi Mordechai Banet, an outstanding talmudist. He became a follower of the *Chozeh* (Seer) of Lublin and of the *Yid Hakadosh* (the Holy Jew) of Pshis'cha, whose most trusted disciple he became, succeeding him as Rebbe of Pshis'cha. His teachings have been published by several of his disciples under the title of *Kol Simchah*.[1] His writings and homilies express the new approach to Chasidism he taught, which placed great emphasis on introspection, self-examination, and intensive Torah study. His most famous disciple was **Rabbi Menachem Mendel of Kotzk**.

Rabbi Simchah Bunam of Pshis'cha.

SELECTIONS FROM THE TEACHINGS OF RABBI SIMCHAH BUNAM

The eyes of both of them were opened and they realized that they were naked. They sewed together fig leaves and made themselves loincloths.
(Genesis 3:7)

Rabbi Simchah Bunam of Pshis'cha: *The eyes of both of them were opened*—This phraseology is somewhat awkward. We would have expected to read, "Their eyes were opened." The significance of the wording "the eyes of both of them" is that before partaking of the Tree of Knowledge, Adam and Eve's personalities were fused into a perfect union of total identity of purpose and thought. After eating the forbidden fruit,

their eyes were opened and they realized that they were two separate individuals, each with his own distinct personality and self-interest. *The eyes of both of them*, of two persons, each viewing the world from his own perspective.

No one in this house has more power than I have. He has not kept back anything at all from me, except you—his wife. How could I do such a great wrong? I would be committing a sin before God.
(Genesis 39:9)

ספר
קול שמחה
השלם והמתוקן
חדושי תורה מאת אדמו"ר הרב הגדול האור הבהיר
המאיר ומזהיר עיני חכמים בעבודה. חכם הרזים
איש האלהים בוצינא קדישא מפורסם מאד בישראל
בשם הרבי ר' שמחה בונם מפרשיסחא זי"ע.
אשר העתיקו מפיו תלמידיו צדיקי הדור. גם מעט
מחדושי פלפולו העתקנו.

הובא לדפוס פעם ראשונה בשנת תרי"ט לפ"ק בעיר ברעסלא
ע"י נכדי רבינו זצ"ל ולא הי' נאמר בו כלל כי טוב
מרוב השיבושים שעלו בו עד אין מספר. ועתה נדפס בתכלית
השלמות ובהגהה מדויקת עד מאד כמבואר מעל"ד בהקדמה.
ובכמה הוספות למעליותא.
ע"י הרב ר' אהרן וואלדען נ"י מווארשא

Produced By Books Export Enterprises Ltd
For: LYON PRESS INC.
Brooklyn, N.Y.

Title page of *Kol Simchah,* Rabbi Simchah Bunam's Torah thoughts collected and published by his followers.

Rabbi Simchah Bunam of Pshis'cha: *How could I do such a great wrong? I would be committing a sin before God*—Why did Joseph say, "I would be committing a sin"? [He should have said, "*We* would be committing a sin,"] for she also would be a participant in the sin. Joseph did not want to be associated with Potiphar's wife in any way, shape, or form. The use of the pronoun "we" would have verbally united him with her. Joseph could not bear even the thought of verbally being associated with her *(Kol Simchah)*.[2]

Justice, justice shall you pursue, that you may live and inherit the land which the Lord your God gives you.

(*Deuteronomy 16:20*)

Rabbi Simchah Bunam of Pshis'cha: *Justice, justice shall you pursue*—What is the meaning of the seemingly redundant use of the word "justice"? The verse means to teach us that the method by which you pursue justice must itself be just and truthful. Pursue justice *with* justice. Don't use falsehood and deception in order to achieve justice.[3]

You called in trouble and I rescued you, I answered you in the secret place of thunder, I tested you at the waters of Merivah.

(*Psalm 81:8*)

Rabbi Simchah Bunam of Pshis'cha: *I answered you in the hidden place of thunder*—I answer you when the thunder[4] is concealed.

On repentance[5]

Rabbi Simchah Bunam said this about *teshuvah* (repentance): At first glance it may appear that *teshuvah* is a very easy thing to do, for it can be accomplished merely by thinking certain thoughts. Still, you should be aware that *teshuvah* involves a total disintegration of the soul and the heart. It is just like falling from a roof and shattering every bone in your body (*Ramatayim Tzofim*).

On insincere seclusion

Someone told Rabbi Simchah Bunam about a pious man living in seclusion. He replied, "Many a hermit goes into retreat in the wilderness but peeks through the bushes to see whether there is anyone admiring him from afar."[6]

RABBI NACHMAN OF BRATZLAV
רבי נחמן מברסלב

born: Mizhbozh, Podolia, 1772
died: Uman, Podolia, 1811
Great chasidic leader.

A great-grandson of the **Baal Shem Tov**, Rabbi Nachman was one of the early leaders of the chasidic movement. Even as a young boy he amazed his townspeople with his dedication to Torah and his keen intellect. After his marriage, at age 13, he settled in Midvidovka near Kiev, where he withdrew from the world, living like a hermit, absorbed in meditation and self-purification through fasting and mortification. Living an ascetic life of self-denial, he would spend many days in the surrounding forests seeking communion with God. By divesting himself of the corporeal, he experienced the ecstatic, pure spiritual joy of sensing God's nearness. Word of his saintly way of life spread rapidly, and people from all over the region began to converge on his modest home to be inspired by him. Before long he became the rebbe of thousands of dedicated chasidim. In 1798 he left for Eretz Yisrael but stayed for only a short time. After a harrowing return trip he settled in Bratzlav, in 1802, where his Chasidut began to flourish, drawing thousands of followers from near and far. That same year, after falling ill with tuberculosis, he moved to Uman. On the last Rosh Hashanah of his life, even though he was bleeding internally, he delivered a Torah discourse to thousands of chasidim. Before his death he instructed his followers to burn most of his manuscripts. In spite of that, fifty-two books written by Rabbi Nachman were printed by his closest disciple, Rabbi Nathan Sternberg. Among these were *Likutei Moharan* and *Sipurei Ma'asiyot*, the latter a collection of stories and parables with inspirational messages. Rabbi Nachman died without appointing a successor. Nevertheless, Bratzlav Chasidut continued to grow. Today there are Bratzlav chasidic centers in America and Israel. Rabbi Nachman's books are printed in large quantities and distributed at nominal cost or free of charge throughout the world. Annually, thousands of chasidim travel to Uman to pray at the tomb of Rabbi Nachman. Since they have no living rebbe, the Bratzlav chasidim sometimes good-naturedly are referred to as "the *toite*

ספר

ליקוטי מוהר"ן

הנכבד והנורא. מי כמוהו מורה. הפלא בקדושה ובטהרה. מפי קדש קדשים. נבון לחש וחכם חרשים. ה"ה כבוד אדונינו מורינו ורבינו. הרב המאור הגאון הקדוש האמיתי. נחל נובע מקור חכמה. אור ישראל וקדושו. המפורסם בכל קצוי ארץ ואיים רחוקים. שמו קודש. מורינו ורבינו הרב רבי נחמן זצוקל"ה מק' ברסלב . ...

הובא לדפוס ע"י הרה"ח

ר' פסח ב"ר יוסף הכהן קורנדרקסלר וזוגתו דבורה פייגא ומשפחתו נ"י

לע"נ בנם האברך ר' נחמן ז"ל

נלב"ע בדמי ימיו בן ד"ל שנים בירושלים

ז' טבת תשמ"ז

ת.נ.צ.ב.ה.

בני ברק תשמ"ח

Title page of *Likutei Moharan*, by Rabbi Nachman of Bratzlav. Most important of Rabbi Nachman's writings.

(dead)" chasidim. But although Rabbi Nachman is not among the living, his movement of Bratzlav Chasidut is very much alive.

SELECTIONS FROM RABBI NACHMAN OF BRATZLAV'S WRITINGS

Excerpt from *Likutei Moharan* 59

And also the Strength of Israel will not lie.
(I Samuel 15:29)

[The "Strength of Israel" refers to God.] We all know that strength and truth usually do not go together. We see very often that those in power use strength to suppress the truth. The victor is blind to the truth, even when it stares him in the eye. But God is not like man. God, although He is the Almighty and the All Powerful One, adheres to the truth. Even in victory He will not deviate from His Principles. That is what is meant by the verse, "The Strength of Israel (God) will not lie."

Excerpt from *Likutei Moharan* 112

For one little sensation of pleasure that lasts only fifteen minutes, a person may lose life in this world and in the World to Come.

Excerpt from *Likutei Moharan* 196

"When you pray, do not make your prayer a set routine but pray with mercy and supplication.
(Mishnah Avot 2:18)

The word *keva*, generally translated as "set routine," can be seen as derived from the verb *kava*, to rob, as in Proverbs 22:23, "He will rob those who robbed them" (*Vekava et kove' eihem nefesh*). What does the Mishnah mean by "do not make your prayer a robbery"? The Mishnah teaches you that you should not pray too insistently. In other words, it is forbidden to demand from God that He fulfill your request. That would be tantamount to taking something by force, akin to robbery. Rather, pray to God, beg of Him, beseech Him. If He grants your wish, fine; but if He does not, so be it. That is the intent of our Mishnah, "Do not make your prayer a robbery." When you ask God for success in business, for children, or have any other request, don't insist stubbornly that He fulfill your

prayer. Instead, pray in a spirit of meekness and submissiveness.

Excerpt from *Likutei Moharan* 202

". . . Even today, if we but heed His call."
(Psalm 95:7)

Remember this important rule. When serving God, concentrate your thoughts only on the present. Do the same when it comes to your physical needs and your livelihood—don't worry about tomorrow. When you worship God, think of nothing but "today," the "now." A person may be discouraged from embarking upon a life of serving God, in the belief that such a life would be too heavy a burden. Let him think in terms of serving God for one day only. That would present no difficulty at all. You should also remember not to procrastinate, thinking that tomorrow you'll begin to pray with the proper concentration. Remember, the present is all you have in this world. Tomorrow is a new world altogether. That's why the verse emphasizes, "Today, if we but heed His call."

Sayings from Rabbi Nachman of Bratzlav[1]

I beg of you, don't give up hope! There is no such thing as hopelessness (*Likutei Moharan Tanina* 75). It's a great mitzvah to be always happy—*Mitzvah gedolah li'yot besimchah tamid* (*Likutei Moharan Tanina* 24).

Solitude is the very highest level you can reach (*Likutei Moharan Tanina* 25). If you believe that lives can be destroyed, you must also believe that lives can be repaired (*Likutei Moharan Tanina* 112). Everything will turn out well (*Sichot Haran*). Remember that in life, man must walk a very narrow bridge. The main thing is not to be afraid of anything (*Likutei Moharan Tanina* 48).

Excerpt from *Erech Apayim*, Be Slow to Anger

You may ask, why did God arrange the world in a way that makes it so difficult for me to earn my livelihood, that requires me to work so hard, day after day? It is important that you realize that this stems from God's abundant love for you. He yearns to hear your voice as you pray, speaking to Him, as a child asking his father, "Please, Father, give me food and clothing." Let me assure you that all the myriads of worlds in God's possession to Him cannot equal in value the one moment when a Jewish soul, clothed in a garment of flesh, tormented with hardship, pain, and confusion, stands before Him and asks, "Father, please grant me, and the souls who are dependent on me, our sustenance." Our sages say in *Sifre Beha'alotecha*, "Why didn't the manna descend just once a year [why did it fall each day]? In order that the Children of Israel turn their hearts toward their Father in Heaven." If a Jew had a family of five children, he would wonder anxiously, "What if tomorrow there will be no manna; we'll all starve from hunger. Please God, let the manna come down." Thus, they would all pray to God. Whatever God causes to happen, especially with regard to one's livelihood, happens for the purpose of drawing him closer to God. Because man receives his livelihood not in a straightforward, easy manner, but by means of an intricate web of causes and effects, he clearly recognizes the greatness of God, the One who makes it all happen.

Excerpt from *Erech Apayim*, Be Slow to Anger

A great deal of patience is required in raising children, especially adolescents, because there is widespread atheism and immorality in the world today. It is very easy for youngsters to be caught in the web of the secularists and evil-doers. Let this be a strong warning to parents who are fortunate enough to have children growing up in the right direction, and these children associate with chasidic friends or enter a Lithuanian yeshivah.[2] The father may come from a different background or follow different customs and will therefore scold and admonish his son for deviating from the ways of his parents, who are not chasidim or do not follow Lithuanian customs. Such reprimands lead to needless heartache and will bring rancor and quarreling in their wake between father and son—and all for nothing, with constant arguments, yelling, screaming, and the father threatening, "If I catch you again with those chasidim/Lithuanians, you'll regret it!" The father is distressed and complains about his misfortune. And it is all foolishness and shortsightedness, making a mountain out of a molehill. Why doesn't the father reflect for a moment on what he would do if, God forbid, his son would abandon Judaism, eat nonkosher food, desecrate the *Shabbos*, etc., and come home wearing long hair, looking like a demon, may God have mercy. And what would he do if his son would leave home altogether, marry a non-Jewish girl, and he

would never see him again? Unfortunately, things like that are happening very frequently, even in very Orthodox homes. Now that your son has been inspired with a spirit of purity and associates with a group of God-fearing friends, or has entered a yeshivah that does not reflect your views exactly, should that be a reason for turning your home literally into hell, fighting and bickering with your son, venting your rage on him, even striking him, all because he refuses to join the particular chasidic group you belong to, or to enroll in a Lithuanian yeshivah? Instead, you should be jumping for joy every day, giving thanks to God, that no matter what group he has joined, your son is a faithful, God-fearing, kosher Jew. . . . Leave your son alone; let him go to whatever place he chooses. Don't stand in his way. . . . All this surely holds true if a man has the great merit of having a son who chose to join the Bratzlaver chasidim, who are truly righteous men.

Excerpt from *Erech Apayim*, Be Slow to Anger

It is an important mitzvah to bring back to Judaism people who are far removed from Torah. But a great deal of patience is required, the patience of a Hillel who suffered greatly from the foolish questions he was asked by people who wanted to convert to Judaism. If you know in your heart that you have no patience, you are forbidden to approach these people, for you'll be held accountable if they are deterred or discouraged. The patience and tolerance that are needed are based on the notion that you should always give the other fellow the benefit of the doubt, thinking that even the most corrupt person might still do *teshuvah* and return to God, Whose mercy is infinite. You should never give up, for even from the depth of the abyss one can return to God. We read in *Yoma* 86a, "Repentance is so great, it reaches the Heavenly Throne," and in *Midrash Rabbah Parashat Bo* we read, "The Holy One, Blessed is He, does not reject anyone. He is ready to receive everyone. The Gates are always open. Whoever wants to enter is welcome." . . . When you approach people in an attempt to bring them back to Torah, your sole aim should be to reveal to them the truth and bring them close to God. Don't seek any personal glory. If your sole intent is to bring them closer to God, you will be successful and no harm will come to you. Consider yourself as nonexistent; even when you speak to others, consider yourself as merely an instrument, a conduit for revealing God's existence. . . . Be very patient with them. It is forbidden to rebuff them, God forbid, for

God loves them very much. As the Midrash says, "God bestows honor on anyone who repents of a sin, calling him His beloved" (*Shocher Tov Tehillim* 18).

Excerpt from *Erech Apayim*, Be Slow to Anger

Some people are obsessed with the notion that it is their mission to change the world. To them it appears as though their cause represents the ultimate truth and that the whole world had better recognize that. Any dissenter deserves to be harmed. In their mind it is a great mitzvah to humiliate him publicly and to persecute him without mercy. Strife and discord are the tools of Satan. Through them he perverts the truth, changing vices into virtues, turning outright sins into mitzvot. Wherever hatred and conflict prevail, Satan is very much at home. There it is easy for him to don the mantle of righteousness and mitzvot. He seduces a person into thinking that he is performing a good deed by tormenting his fellow Jew for following this or that custom or not sharing his beliefs or not belonging to his group. Of course, nobody is perfect. We all have flaws, and it is our task in life to improve ourselves. But we must never look at the dark side of a Jew; we should search for the good in him. For we can find much good in every Jew, as our sages put it, "Even the ignorant among Israel have as many mitzvot to their credit as a pomegranate has pits" (*Berachot* 57a). Therefore, always look for the good in people . . . and before you set out to reform others or harass and ridicule them, look carefully into your own heart and make sure that you are not being tempted by Satan into turning lies and sins into mitzvot.

RABBI YITZCHAK KALISH OF VORKI—
THE VORKER REBBE
רבי יצחק קליש מוורקי

born: Poland, 1779
died: Poland, 1848
Popularly known as the Vorker Rebbe. Outstanding chasidic leader and communal worker.

Originally a student of the *Yid Hakadosh* (the Holy Jew) of Pshis'cha, Rabbi Yitzchak became one of the three closest disciples of the **Kotzker Rebbe**, the other two being **Rabbi Yitzchak Meir of Ger** and Rabbi Chanoch of Alexander. Rabbi Yitzchak, the Vorker Rebbe, was a man of surpassing nobility and deep wisdom. Most of all, his heart overflowed with *ahavat Yisrael,* a burning love of the Jewish people. His commentaries on the Torah, which are scattered throughout a number of works, radiate the warmth of his great soul, his piety, and his vast knowledge. As the accepted leader of all groupings of Polish Orthodox Jewry, he was involved in all communal affairs, and in 1846 met with Sir Moses Montefiore of England to ask him to intercede with the czarist government for the annulment of an antireligious decree. The Vorker Rebbe is one of the most genuinely loved figures in the world of chasidim.

Rabbi Yitzchak Kalish of Vorki.

SELECTIONS FROM THE VORKER REBBE'S WRITINGS

God heard the boy weeping. God's angel called Hagar from heaven and said to her, "What's the matter, Hagar? Don't be afraid. God has heard the boy's voice where he is."

(Genesis 21:7)

Rabbi Yitzchak Kalish of Vorki: *God heard the boy weeping*[1]—But it doesn't say that the boy made even the slightest sound! The truth is, there is weeping that is voiceless. It is the kind of weeping that pierces

heaven, and only God, Who knows what is in a man's heart, hears it. [The Vorker Rebbe was wont to say: You can tell an exalted person by three things: he weeps without making a sound, he dances without moving, and he bows down with his head held high.[2]]

Jacob awoke from his sleep. "God is truly in this place," he said, "but I did not know it."

(Genesis 28:16)

Rabbi Yitzchak Kalish of Vorki: *Jacob awoke from his sleep*—When you say, "The tailor or the shoemaker

174

is asleep," you wouldn't really be telling the truth. When they are sleeping they are not plying their trade; thus they cannot be called tailor or shoemaker. But when you say, "The Rebbe is asleep," you are indeed stating the truth, for a Rebbe is a Rebbe, even while he is asleep.[3]

These are the chronicles of Jacob: Joseph was seventeen years old. As a lad he would tend the sheep with his brothers, the sons of Bilhah and Zilpah, his father's wives. Joseph brought his father a bad report about them.
(Genesis 37:2)

Rabbi Yitzchak Kalish of Vorki: *Joseph brought his father a bad report about them.*—How could *Yosef Hatzaddik,* the righteous Joseph, be guilty of tale-bearing and slander? A father who has one son with exceptional character traits will compare his other, less perfect sons to the outstanding one. Next to this paragon of virtue, the other sons will appear as moral failures. Although they may be upright and honest, their father will take them to task for not behaving in as saintly a manner as their brother does. The verse tells us that Joseph, by being his perfect self, placed his brothers in a bad light. This was the "bad report" he brought to his father. In spite of his superior character traits, Joseph was punished with the misfortune that happened to him, for he should have concealed his piety so that no one, not even his father, would notice it.[4]

Joseph sent them portions from his table, giving Benjamin five times as much as the rest. They drank and became intoxicated with him.
(Genesis 43:3–4)

Rabbi Yitzchak Kalish of Vorki: *They drank and became intoxicated with him*—It is inconceivable that the sons of Jacob would get drunk. They were intoxicated—thrilled and exhilarated—with the feeling of brotherhood and cordiality toward their benefactor. The present verse clearly indicates that this was so. "They drank and became intoxicated *with him,*" not with the wine. The drinking sparked such feelings of friendship and rejoicing that they became drunk with love.[5]

Do not take revenge nor bear a grudge against the children of your people. You must love your neighbor as you love yourself; I am the Lord.
(Leviticus 19:18)

Rabbi Yitzchak Kalish of Vorki: *You must love your neighbor as you love yourself*—Included under the general heading of "love your neighbor" is the mitzvah of *hachnasat orechim* (offering hospitality to guests). **Rashi** teaches (Genesis 18:3) that this is so exalted a mitzvah that Abraham took leave of the Divine Presence in order to care for his guests. Why is it that this important mitzvah is mentioned in the Torah only tangentially, by implication, as a subparagraph of "love your neighbor," whereas the mitzvah "Do not muzzle an ox when it is treading grain" (Deuteronomy 25:4) rates an entire verse? If *hachnasat orechim* (offering hospitality) would be listed separately, as an explicit commandment, people would welcome a guest as a mitzvah object; they would recite a blessing over him and detain him in their home, even if this would inconvenience the traveler who wished to leave in order to reach his destination. Thus, the Torah classifies *hachnasat orechim* under "love your neighbor" to tell you that if the wayfarer is pressed for time and cannot stay, you should not detain him. If he wishes to remain, then by all means, show him your hospitality.[6]

Pinchas, the son of Elazar, the son of Aaron the priest, has turned away My wrath from the children of Israel, in that he was very zealous for My sake around them, so that I did not consume the children of Israel in My jealousy.
(Numbers 25:11)

Rabbi Yitzchak Kalish of Vorki: *In that he was very zealous for My sake among them*—What thought is imparted by the apparently superfluous word *betocham* ("among them")? Although Pinchas, in zealously taking up God's cause, acted in an aggressive and hostile manner when he killed Zimri, the prince of the tribe of Simon,[7] he did not isolate himself from the Jewish people; neither was he treated as an outsider by them. On the contrary, the verse attests that he remained *betocham,* "among them," associating with them on cordial and loving terms.

They left Kivrot Hataavah and camped in Chatzerot.

(Numbers 33:17)

Rabbi Yitzchak Kalish of Vorki: *They left Kivrot Hataavah and camped in Chatzerot*—The literal meaning of *taavah* is "lust, craving"; "*chatzerot*" translates "courtyard, corridor." The juxtaposition of "lustful cravings" and "corridor" suggests a helpful strategy for controlling your passions: Consider the world as a *chatzer*, a corridor, through which we pass on our life's journey to the World to Come. That will quell your *taavah*, your appetite for hedonistic pleasures.

Selflessness[8]

The Vorker Rebbe asked, "What kind of person is most suited to helping others?" He answered, "Someone who is completely self-effacing, who is like sugar, which dissolves in water, losing its identity, and in the process sweetening it" (*Ohalei Tzadikim*).

The alef bet (alphabet)

Once the Vorker Rebbe was asked, "What is the reason the *Ashamnu* prayer—the Confession of Sins—is arranged according to the *alef bet*?" The Rebbe replied: "Otherwise we would not know when to stop striking our chest. For there is no end to our sins, and our guilt feelings are boundless; but the *alef bet* comes to an end."

The innkeeper

The Vorker Rebbe once was heard to praise an innkeeper who was very accommodating and attentive to all his guests' wishes. "Look, how this man exerts himself," he said, "in fulfilling the commandment to be hospitable." "But he gets paid for it," someone objected. "The money he takes," the Rebbe retorted, "is just to enable him to fulfill the mitzvah."

RABBI MENACHEM MENDEL OF KOTZK—THE KOTZKER REBBE
רבי מנחם מענדל מקאצק

born: Goray, near Lublin, Poland, 1787
died: Kotzk, Poland, 1859
Popularly known as the Kotzker Rebbe. Famous chasidic rebbe.

Menachem Mendel's father, Leibush Morgenstern, gave him a disciplined talmudic education. He became a follower of the *Chozeh* (Seer) of Lublin, and later of the *Yid Hakadosh* (the Holy Jew), and after that of **Rabbi Simchah Bunam of Pshis'cha**. He was a giant of the spirit. His writings and commentaries are collected in *Ohel Torah* and *Emet Ve'Emunah*.[1] He continued and intensified Rabbi Simchah Bunam's new direction of turning inward and of intensified Torah study to the point of going into seclusion for long periods of time. He sought to infuse the movement with new spiritual life and strength, decried routine prayer and false piety, and valued the absolute objective truth above all else. In brief comments, searing like blinding flashes of lightning, he forces the Jew to confront his shortcomings, makes him face the truth, removes the mask of hypocrisy, and thus brings him closer to God. The echo of his thunderous words is heard wherever Torah is studied.

אמת ואמונה
דברי תורה
מרבנו הקדוש, מרנא ורבנא
מנחם מנדיל זצהל"ה מקאצק

עם הרבה מאמרים חדשים
וצוואת ומכתבים מכבוד קדושת אדמו"ר מגור זצלה"ה

מלוקט מפי סופרים וספרים עם תכן הענינים ונדפס מחדש בתל-אביב, א"י, שנת תשל"א בהוצאת "אהבת הקדמונים", ברוקלין נויארק למען טהרת המשפחה ועזרת תורה בארץ ישראל.

נדפס באופסט ברודי את כץ
תל־אביב, רח' יצחק שדה 34, טל. 38441.
Printed in Israel — נדפס בישראל

Title page of *Emet Ve'Emunah*, commentaries by the Kotzker Rebbe, Rabbi Menachem Mendel of Kotzk, compiled and published by his followers.

SELECTIONS FROM THE KOTZKER REBBE'S COMMENTARY

In addition to what your brothers shall share, I am giving you Shechem, which I took from the Amorite with my sword and my bow.
(*Genesis 48:22*)

Rabbi Menachem Mendel of Kotzk: *With my sword and my bow*—**Rashi** interprets "*with my sword and my bow*" in a metaphoric sense, meaning "with my prayer and my supplication." In what way can prayer be likened to a bow? We all know that the closer you pull the string of a bow toward you, the farther the arrow will fly. So it is with prayer. The more you concentrate, the more fervently and passionately you pray, the more power your prayer has to penetrate the Gates of Heaven and reach the Throne of Glory.[2]

Therefore, say to the Children of Israel, "I am the Lord. I will take you away from your forced labor in Egypt and free you from their slavery. I will liberate you with a demonstration of My power and with great acts of judgment."

(Exodus 6:6)

Rabbi Menachem Mendel of Kotzk: *"I will take you away from your forced labor in Egypt"*—The first step to freedom is to rise up against slavery. As long as the people of Israel are resigned to being slaves, as long as they are reconciled to being oppressed, they cannot be redeemed. In the above passage, Moses announces to Israel that God will remove from their heart the *sivlot*[3] of Egypt, their sense of submission to their condition of servitude, so that they won't be able to put up with it any longer. He will infuse them with a spirit of defiance, the mental attitude needed before the Divine liberation can sprout.

Command Aaron and his sons, saying, "This is the law of the burnt offering. The burnt offering shall remain on the altar's hearth all night until the morning so that the altar's fire can be ignited with it."

(Leviticus 6:2)

Rabbi Menachem Mendel of Kotzk: *On the altar's hearth*—The word *mokedah* (hearth or fireplace) is written in the Torah with a letter *mem* that is smaller than the other letters. Therein lies an allusion to the thought that if a person has a burning enthusiasm for Torah and serving God, this ecstasy should not be displayed openly, for all to see. Rather, it should remain concealed in the inner recesses of the heart, hidden in the depth of the soul.

Aaron did so: he lighted the lamps so as to illuminate the menorah as God commanded Moses.

(Numbers 8:3)

Rabbi Menachem Mendel of Kotzk: *Aaron did so*—Rashi comments on this phrase: This teaches us that Aaron did not change. The message contained in this statement is that throughout his performance of the entire holy service in the Tabernacle, Aaron did not exhibit any outward change; he did not betray the intense fervor and emotional exultation he experienced as he was standing before the Divine Presence. His feelings remained locked and concealed in his heart. True *deveikut* (attachment to God) is not visible to the outside world. Indeed, Aaron did not change, externally.[4]

The officers shall then continue speaking to the people and say, "Is there any man among you who is afraid or faint-hearted? Let him go home rather than have his cowardice demoralize his brethren."

(Deuteronomy 20:8)

Rabbi Menachem Mendel of Kotzk: *Is there any man among you who is afraid or faint-hearted?*—Rashi explains that this passage is addressed at those who are fearful because of past sins. Now, since no one is free of sin, everyone would go home, and who would be left to do the fighting? The men who are sent home for being fearful because of past sins are in fact virtuous people. Their only fault is that they are obsessed with guilt feelings over a sin they committed long ago. Their constant self-reproach makes them despondent, gloomy, and morose. A dispirited person has no place in a Jewish army.[5]

No division[6]

The Kotzker Rebbe insisted that his chasidim not wear scarves while praying. Said he, "So that there should be no division between the mind and the heart."

Why write a book

The chasidim once asked the Rebbe of Kotzk why he didn't write a book. After a brief pause he replied, "Let's assume I did write a book. Who would buy it? Our own people would buy it. Now, when do our people have time to read a book? After all, all week long they are busy earning their livelihood. On *Shabbos* they have time to read a book. And when on *Shabbos*? In the morning you go to the *mikveh* to immerse yourself; then it is time to learn and pray. After that comes the *Shabbos* meal. Ah, but after the *Shabbos* meal, then there is time to read a book. So he stretches out on the couch, picks up the book, opens it. And because he has had a good meal, he feels drowsy and dozes off, and the book drops to the floor. Now, I ask you, Why should I write a book?"

God's dwelling place

Once, the Kotzker surprised a group of learned guests by asking them, "Where does God dwell?" They were amused. "What kind of question is that! The whole world is filled with His glory!" But he answered his own question, saying, "God dwells wherever people allow him to come in."

Truth

Even the slightest crease in your forehead must not be dishonest (*Shaare Torah*).

RABBI YISRAEL OF RIZHIN—THE RIZHINER
רבי ישראל מרוזין

born: Pogrobisht, Ukraine, 1797
died: Sadagora, Galicia, 1850
Revered chasidic leader. Popularly known as the Rizhiner.

A scion of the Sadagora dynasty, great-grandson of the Maggid of Mezritch, the Rizhiner conducted his "court" with great pomp and ceremony, maintaining it with all the trappings of royalty, thereby attracting thousands of loyal chasidim. The czarist government, accusing him of seditious activities, imprisoned him in Kiev for two years. After his release he fled to Galicia, Poland, settling in Sadagora, where he resumed his chasidic leadership, drawing tens of thousands of devoted followers. The outward show of opulence was designed to raise the standards of Torah and Chasidut. On his deathbed he testified, "I assure you that I did not derive any enjoyment at all from this world." The Rizhiner's commentaries were recorded and anthologized under the titles *Irin Kaddishin*,[1] *Kenesset Yisrael*,[2] and *Pe'er Layesharim*.[3] Selections of these works were published as *Nachalat Yisrael*.[4] His comments, which are interspersed with profound kabbalistic insights, bring to life the lofty personality of a principal chasidic leader.

SELECTIONS FROM RABBI YISRAEL'S COMMENTARY

He took the book of the covenant and read it out aloud to the people. They replied, "We will do and hear all that God has declared."

(Exodus 24:7)

Rabbi Yisrael of Rizhin: *We will do and hear all that God has declared*[5]—This passage gives rise to the question, How can anyone do something before he has heard the command of what he is to do? It should have

ספר
נחלת ישראל

אמרי קדוש ישראל, אשר יצאו מפה קדוש ממלל רברבן,
ה"ה כ"ק אדונינו מורינו ורבינו, אספקלריא
המאירה, בוצינא דנהורא, צים"ע, נזר
ישראל ותפארתו, מרנא
ורבנא קה"ק וכו'

מו"ה ישראל מרוזין זצוקללה"ה
זי"ע ועכי"א

נערך ונסדר עם המראה מקומות ע"י
שואל אלכסנדר ביסטריצקי

יצא לאור ע"י
ה"מרכז להוצאת ספרי חסידות מבית רוזין"

ניו יארק, ה'תשי"א

Title page of *Nachalat Yisrael,* Torah insights by Rabbi Yisrael of Rizhin. The abbreviation appearing underneath his name is the acronym of *Zechuto yagein aleinu ve'al kol Yisrael, amen,* May his merit protect us and all Israel, amen.

180

stated, "We will hear and do" rather than "do and hear." If you want to do something, it is obvious that you don't have to instruct your hand as to what action it is to take. Your head and mind encompass all the parts of your body, and if your head and mind decide on a certain action, your hand instinctively senses this and needs no conscious directive. Similarly, at the time of the Giving of the Torah, God was the head of the people of Israel. Now, when God wanted Israel to accept the Torah, they instinctively sensed this. They did not have to be told. They responded in a reflex action, without hesitation, "We will do."

Speak to the Children of Israel and say to them: When one of you brings an offering to God, you shall bring your offering of the mammals, from the sheep and from the cattle.

(Leviticus 1:2)

Rabbi Yisrael of Rizhin: *When one of you brings an offering to God*—Bringing an offering to God means offering yourself to God. Fasting is also a form of offering, for you diminish and weaken yourself physically; you are in effect offering your flesh and blood. However, in a spiritual sense, Torah study and prayer are also considered an offering, because by means of these you offer your whole personality to God and elevate the entire universe to greater closeness to the Creator.[6]

This is the law of the burnt offering, the meal offering, the sin offering, the guilt offering, and the peace offering which God gave to Moses at Sinai.

(Leviticus 7:37)

Rabbi Yisrael of Rizhin: *This is the law*—This is the nature of the Torah: Whoever studies it for its own sake, in order to know and keep its laws, to him the verse applies: "For the ways of the Lord are right; the righteous walk in them" (Hosea 14:10). But those who study the Torah for extraneous reasons, to them the second clause of the verse in Hosea applies: "but transgressors stumble over them." The same principle

is expressed in the present verse. To those who approach Torah study in a spirit of reverence, it is the *"law of the burnt offering and the meal offering,"* but to the others it is *"the sin offering and the guilt offering."*[7]

This is not true of My servant Moshe, who is a trusted servant throughout My house.

(Numbers 12:7)

Rabbi Yisrael of Rizhin: *Who is a trusted servant throughout My house*—The tzaddik, the outstanding spiritual leader, being the counterpart of *Moshe Rabbeinu* (our Teacher Moses), acts as the conduit for the abundance God showers on His people. In the physical world, care must be taken that a water pipe not become clogged by the impurities contained in the water that flows through it. The same holds true in the spiritual world. The tzaddik, being the channel for material abundance, must be on guard not to derive any benefit from that abundance. He is involved daily with mundane, corporeal matters, but he may never personally be affected by them. This thought is expressed by the term *ne'eman,* "trusted servant." A wealthy man will entrust all his possessions to a faithful servant in the knowledge that the servant will not misappropriate even the smallest coin. The tzaddik, following in Moses' footsteps, may also be called *ne'eman,* "faithful servant," for he deals with a multitude of worldly affairs, yet he himself does not derive any enjoyment from them, nor is he touched by them in the least.[8]

[God] does not look at wrongdoing in Jacob and He sees no vice in Israel. God his Lord is with him and he has the King's friendship.

(Numbers 23:21)

Rabbi Yisrael of Rizhin: *He does not look at wrongdoing in Jacob. . . . God his Lord is with him*—Even when a Jew is steeped in sin, even when he sinks to the depths of the abyss, there still flickers in him a Divine spark; a gleam of repentance still glows in his heart. Yes, even when he sins, "God his Lord is with him."[9]

RABBI YITZCHAK MEIR ALTER OF GER—CHIDDUSHEI HARYM

רבי יצחק מאיר אלטר מגור—חידושי הרי"ם

born: Mognuszew, near Radom, Poland, 1799
died: Ger, Poland, 1866
Popularly known as Chiddushei Harym (Novellae of RYM), the initials of Rabbi Yitzchak Meir. Great chasidic leader, talmudist, halachist.

Chiddushei Harym's family can be traced back to the renowned Rabbi Meir of Rothenburg (b. 1215), one of the last Tosafists. As a young man, his prodigious talmudic prowess became known throughout Poland. He studied under the Maggid of Mezritch, later becoming a chasid of **Rabbi Simchah Bunam of Pshis'cha** and **Rabbi Menachem Mendel of Kotzk,** whose most eminent pupil he was. In 1859 he was elected Gerrer Rebbe over tens of thousands of devoted chasidim. Following the Kotzker methodology, he stressed the primary importance of Torah scholarship. His phenomenal talmudic genius speaks to us from every page of his books: *Chiddushei Harym on Shulchan Aruch,*[1] *Chiddushei Harym on Tractate Chullin,*[2] *Teshuvot Harym,*[3] and *Chiddushei Harym on Torah and the Festivals.*[4] Testimony to his greatness is the fact that his books are studied in all yeshivahs, chasidic and "Lithuanian" (nonchasidic) alike.[5]

ספר

חידושי הרי"מ

על התורה, מועדים וליקוטים

אוסף דברי תורה ומאמרים

מאת כבוד קדושת אדוננו מורנו ורבנו, רשכבה"ג,
שר התורה, צדיק יסוד עולם, איש אלקים קדוש

מרן יצחק מאיר זצוקללה"ה מגור

לוקט וסודר ע"י נכדו
הרה"ח ר' יהודה לייב לוין ז"ל

מהדורה חדשה, מתוקנת ומורחבת

הוצאת
מוסד הרי"ם לוין
ירושלים – תשמ"ז

Title page of *Chiddushei Harym,* novellae on Torah and the Festivals, by Rabbi Yitzchak Meir Alter of Ger.

SELECTIONS FROM CHIDDUSHEI HARYM'S COMMENTARY

People did not see each other and no one rose from his place for three days. The Israelites, however, had light in the places where they lived.
(Exodus 10:23)

Chiddushei Harym: *People did not see each other and no one rose from his place*[6]—Darkness is most palpable when a man doesn't want to see his brother's misfortune and lend him a helping hand. Now, when a person is indifferent to his neighbor's plight, the result is that he becomes spiritually paralyzed, as the verse indicates, "No one rose from his place," an allusion to spiritual stagnation.

And the stork, the heron after its kind, the hoopoe, and the bat.

(*Leviticus 11:19*)

Chiddushei Harym: *And the stork*[9]—The Talmud (*Chullin* 63) remarks on this verse that "the stork, *chasidah*, is identical with the bird named *dayah*. Why, then, is it called *chasidah*? Because it does favors (*chesed*) for its friends."[10] Now, since the stork has such benevolent qualities, why is it counted among the unclean birds? The answer can be found in the fact that "it does favors for its friends," implying that it does favors *only* for its friends but not for others. Benevolence must be extended to all creatures, without qualifications or restrictions. Limiting favors to friends only is a manifestation of callousness, a mark of uncleanness.

Moses stood up at the camp's entrance and announced, Whoever is for God, join me! All the Levites gathered around him.

(*Exodus 32:26*)

Chiddushei Harym: *All the Levites gathered around him*—There were, in fact, many more who did not worship the Golden Calf. We know this because only 3,000 people were killed (Exodus 32:28). But there were many who did not have the courage to challenge the worshippers of the Golden Calf. They preferred to stay on the sidelines and avoid getting involved in a dispute. The Levites were the only ones who stood up in defense of the glory of God, taking up the sword to champion His honor. This prompts God to state, "And the Levites shall be Mine" (Numbers 3:11).[8]

Our cattle also shall go with us, there shall not be a hoof left behind, for we must take from it to serve God our Lord. And we will not know with what to serve God, until we come there.

(*Exodus 10:26*)

Chiddushei Harym: *And we will not know with what to serve God until we come there*—We cannot gauge the true value of our service to God until we reach "*there*," the higher world, the World to Come. Only then will we learn whether our Divine worship was pleasing to God.[7]

On the east bank of the Jordan, in the land of Moab, Moses began explaining this law, saying;

(*Deuteronomy 1:5*)

Chiddushei Harym: *Moses began explaining this law*—**Rashi** comments that Moses explained the Torah in seventy languages.[11] Why was it necessary to explain it in seventy languages? Inherent in the spiritual makeup of each nation there is a certain force that opposes the Torah. It was Moses' intent to prepare Israel for the coming exile, so that they would be able to observe the Torah wherever they would find themselves. By explaining the Torah in the seventy languages of the seventy nations of the world, he instilled them with the strength to overcome the anti-Torah force innate in each nation.

RABBI SHLOMOH HAKOHEN RABINOWITZ OF RADOMSK—TIFERET SHLOMOH
רבי שלמה הכהן רבינויץ מרדמסק—תפרת שלמה

born: Wlosziva, Poland, 1803
died: Radomsk, Poland, 1866
Popularly known as Tiferet Shlomoh, after the title of his work. Prominent chasidic rebbe.

Rabbi Shlomoh HaKohen was a disciple of two chasidic luminaries: Rabbi Meir of Apta and Rabbi Yehoshua of Pshedburz. In 1834 he was chosen as Radomsker Rebbe, and with his charismatic personality he attracted many thousands of chasidim. His work, *Tiferet Shlomoh*,[1] is a commentary on the Torah and the festivals. The Radomsker Rebbe's mastery of Torah, both in its revealed and mystical aspects, and his saintlike piety speak from every page of this work. It contains a wealth of astounding allusions, often based on kabbalistic themes, teaching lessons of righteousness, humility, and the importance of Torah study. The Radomsker Rebbe was known for the inspiring way he led his chasidim in prayer. With his lyrical, resonant voice he moved the worshippers' souls, lifting them to the heights of spiritual ecstasy. He was a tzaddik in the true sense of the word.

ספר
תפארת שלמה
על התורה
זה ספר כתבי קודש דברי תורה אשר יצא מפי אותו הצדיק איש חי ורב פעלים. חכם הרזים המאיר לארץ ולדרים דולה מבארות עמוקים. דברים נחמדים שבעתים מזוקקים. מפז ומפנינים יקרים. שפתי כהן ישמרו דעת ותוקים ישרים. על סדר פרשיות התורה תביאים וכתובים וליקוטים מש״ס המה מסודרים. כולו ממתקים ומחמדים. ותוכם רצוף רזים צפון לישרים. שמו נודע בשערים. כבוד אדמו״ר הרב הגאון חסידא ופרישא זצ״ע ע״ה פ״ה נ״י אספקלריא המאירה פאר הדור מו״ה שלמה בהרב המופלג החסיד מו״ה דוב צבי הכהן זלה״ה אבדק״ק ראדאמסק. שלמה שמו ושלימה משנתו. לזכר עולם יהיה צדקתו. מהרה ישמע קול מבשר טוב לשארית בנ״י חבל נחלתו. הכהן יעמוד לאורים ויחיש לנו קץ פדותו.
ברוקלין, ניו יארק
שנת תשל״ו לפ״ק

Title page of *Tiferet Shlomoh* by Rabbi Shlomoh HaKohen Rabinowitz of Radomsk.

SELECTIONS FROM TIFERET SHLOMOH'S COMMENTARY

When he finished speaking with Abraham, God left him. Abraham returned to his place.

(Genesis 18:33)

Tiferet Shlomoh: *Abraham returned to his place*[2]—The phrase "*returned to his place*" can be interpreted as "resumed what he had been doing," in other words, Abraham persisted in praying for his fellowmen. Although God had left him, indicating that his prayers were not accepted, Abraham carried on, pleading and imploring God not to destroy the cities. In so doing, Abraham set an example for us never to despair. Even when it appears that our prayers are of no avail, we should not abandon hope for God's mercy, but continue praying to Him.

And now, don't be sad or feel guilty because you sold me. Look, God has sent me ahead of you to save lives.

(Genesis 45:5)

Tiferet Shlomoh: *And now, don't be sad or feel guilty because you sold me*[3]—Implicit in the word *ve'ata* (and now) is the idea of *teshuvah* (repentance). What connection is there between *"now"* and *teshuvah*? The *baal teshuvah* (returnee to Torah observance) turns over a new leaf. He says to himself, *"teshuvah* has wiped my slate clean; from *now* on, a new life begins. The past is forgiven; only the present, the *'now'* matters." When Joseph said, *"And now don't be sad,"* he implied, "You should do *teshuvah* for the injustice you committed against me by selling me into slavery. But let that not be a source of sadness. *Teshuvah* must not be done in a sorrowful and grieving state of mind. Remember, *teshuvah* is a Torah command, and every mitzvah must be performed joyfully, as it is written, "Serve the Lord with gladness" (Psalm 100:2). Therefore, *"and now,"* when you do *teshuvah*, "don't be sad"—don't dwell on the failings of the past. Look at the present, the *"ve'ata,"* and be joyful.

Aaron lifted his hands toward the people and blessed them, and he came down from offering the sin offering and the burnt offering and the peace offering.

(Leviticus 9:22)

Tiferet Shlomoh: *He blessed them, and he came down from offering the sin offering*—When a person is inspired to offer prayers to God, his *yetzer hara* (evil inclination) tries to cool his fervor by telling him, "How dare you approach God, you who are burdened with sin." This argument is patently invalid.[4] The truth is that God hears everyone's prayer and has compassion for all his creatures. This idea finds expression in Psalm 34:15, *"Turn from evil and do good"*—when you are engaged in doing good deeds, remove evil from your heart—put your wicked deeds out of your mind and forget them. The above-mentioned phrase also implies this thought. *He blessed them and came down from . . . the sin offering*—when Aaron blessed the people of Israel, he banished all negative thoughts of their sin from his mind.

Along with the cities that you shall give to the Levites shall be the six cities of refuge, which you shall provide as places to which a murderer can flee. Besides these (six) you shall provide an additional forty-two cities.

(Numbers 35:6)

Tiferet Shlomoh: *The six cities of refuge . . . an additional 42 cities*[5]—The six cities of refuge allude to the six words in the verse *"Shema Yisrael, Hashem Elokeinu Hashem Echad,"* "Hear, O Israel, the Lord our God, the Lord is One" (Deuteronomy 5:22). These words do indeed provide a spiritual refuge for a Jew's troubled soul. The additional forty-two cities suggest the forty-two words that make up *"Ve'ahavta,"* the first paragraph of the *Shema*, through which a Jew submits his entire being to God's will.

Moses went and spoke the following words to all Israel.

(Deuteronomy 31:1)

Tiferet Shlomoh: *Moses went and spoke the following words to all Israel*[6]—The commentators are mystified by the words "Moses went." Where did he go? For what purpose? The Torah does not provide an answer. We can interpret the verse as follows: *Moses went*—to *Gan Eden* (the Hereafter), but even though he departed this life and is no longer with us, *he spoke the following words to all Israel*—he is still speaking his words of Torah wisdom to the Jewish people. Throughout the ages, whenever Torah is being studied, the sound of Moses' voice is heard reverberating in the yeshivahs and houses of learning. He continues to speak to us from the pages of the Chumash, the Talmud, the commentaries—through the mouths of the myriads of students of the Torah, both young and old.

RABBI CHAIM HALBERSTAM OF SANZ—
THE DIVREI CHAIM
רבי חיים הלברשטם מצאנז—דברי חיים

born: Tarnogrod, Poland, 1793
died: Sanz, Poland, 1876
Popularly known as the Divrei Chaim, the title of his work. Talmudist, halachist, famous chasidic leader.

Born into a family of great Torah scholars, Rabbi Chaim Halberstam was a descendant of the Chacham Tzvi and the kabbalist, Rabbi Chaim Sender of Brody. He studied Talmud under the Divrei Shemuel of Phemishl, and his mentor in Chasidut was the well-known tzaddik Rabbi Naftali of Ropshitz. Rabbi Chaim's fame as eminent halachist and kabbalist spread rapidly, and halachic queries were addressed to him from the far corners of the earth. His work, *Divrei Chaim*,[1] a collection of responsa and Torah insights, attests to his analytical prowess and his formidable erudition. As one of the most prominent chasidic leaders of his age, he served as rabbi of Sanz for forty-six years, dispensing help and advice to thousands of faithful chasidim. He devoted all his energies to improving the welfare of the Jews of Sanz and to raising the standards of Torah study and observance. He was wont to say: "When I was young I thought I could change the world, but I soon realized that I'd better just concentrate on the Jews of Sanz. When I failed in that, I took it upon myself to improve the conduct of my family. I gave up on that too, and I'm trying to improve myself, but even in that I have failed." He was truly a saintly person. His prayers, which he uttered with total self-abnegation and intense fervor, pierced all heavens. Many of his descendants were outstanding chasidic leaders of the Sanz dynasty. The Bobover Rav, the illustrious leader of the Bobover chasidim today, is a direct descendant of the Divrei Chaim and carries on the glorious Sanzer tradition.

Rabbi Chaim Halberstam of Sanz, the Divrei Chaim.

SELECTIONS FROM THE DIVREI CHAIM'S COMMENTARY

Excerpt from *Divrei Chaim, Parashat Chayei Sarah*

Abraham was old, well advanced in years, and God had blessed Abraham with everything.

(Genesis 24:1)

Since this is the first time old age is mentioned in the Torah, the Gemara in *Bava Metzia* 87 comments that until Abraham appeared on the scene, old age did not exist. This seems to contradict the fact that the earlier generations lived to a much older age than Abraham did. We must look at this Gemara from a different perspective. We all know that, in the Higher World, days in which there is no spiritual growth do not count. They are nonexistent. Before Abraham's time the world existed in a spiritual vacuum. Most people frittered away their lives in idle pursuits. Time had no meaning; their days did not count in the Higher World. Even though some of them lived well over 800 years, they had no old age in this world, either. Abraham, by teaching mankind to believe in God, restored spirituality to the world. He made the days and years count in the Higher World. Thus, he introduced the concept of old age into this world as well.

Excerpt from *Divrei Chaim, Parashat Yitro*

God said to Moses, "Go to the people and sanctify them today and tomorrow. Let them immerse their clothing."

(Exodus 19:10)

The phrase *sanctify them today and tomorrow* appears somewhat awkward. It would have been more simple to say "sanctify them for two days." The phraseology can be explained if we bear in mind that God gave this command in preparation for the Giving of the Torah. At that time the Israelites yearned with all their heart for the Divine Revelation, proclaiming, as the Midrash relates, "We want to see our King." It was God's wish to capture this moment of utter selfless devotion and make it last forever. That is the intent of this verse. Moses is to sanctify them, to elevate them spiritually to the level of holiness appropriate to receiving the Torah, *and tomorrow* meaning metaphorically, "in the distant future"—that this lofty spirit of self-denial may endure forever.

Excerpt from *Divrei Chaim, Parashat Emor*

When you sacrifice a thanksgiving offering to God, do so of your own free will.

(Leviticus 22:29)

A thanksgiving sacrifice is brought by a person who has been spared from a life-threatening situation. It surely would be preferable if, instead of performing a miracle to save his life, God, in His goodness, would have let him stay at home, safe and contented. Even though he would not thank God with a tangible sacrifice, he would willingly and wholeheartedly offer his thanks to Him for the privilege of being alive and well. This is what this verse means to convey. When you sacrifice a thanksgiving offering to God, let it be of your own free will. Let it not be an obligatory sacrifice that you must bring to give thanks for a miracle that happened to you whereby your life was saved. Rather, may you be well and in good health and let your thanksgiving offering be a voluntary expression of gratitude to God for all the good He has bestowed on you.

Excerpt from *Divrei Chaim*, Responsa, *Yoreh De'ah* 58

In the matter of a man who does everything with his left hand, except handling a spoon and writing, which he does with his right hand. The man is a scribe by profession. He states that, as a child, his father forcibly trained him to use his right hand. *Responsum:* You are uncertain as to whether you should dismiss this scribe in compliance with the ruling of the *Peri Megadim* Par. 32:5, who states that a scribe like this should not be hired. I wish to state that in my opinion there is no objection whatsoever to retaining this scribe in his position. [There follows a lengthy dissertation in which the Divrei Chaim explains his decision and the halachic sources on which it is based.]

RABBI YEHUDAH ARYEH LEIB ALTER OF GER—SEFAT EMET

רבי יהודא אריה ליב אלטר—שפת אמת

born: Warsaw, Poland, 1847
died: Ger, Poland, 1905
Popularly known as Sefat Emet ("Language of Truth"), the title of his work. Outstanding chasidic leader, talmudist.

Because his father, Rabbi Avraham Mordechai, died when Yehudah Aryeh Leib was only 8 years old, he was raised by his grandfather, **Rabbi Yitzchak Meir, Chiddushei Harym,** the first Gerrer Rebbe. He immersed himself in the study of Talmud, Tanach, the Zohar, and Chasidism, becoming a *gaon* (preeminent authority) both in *niglah* and *nistar,* the revealed and mystical aspects of Torah. In 1870 he reluctantly agreed to becoming the second Gerrer Rebbe. His monumental work, *Sefat Emet al Hatorah,*[1] is a commentary on the Torah in five volumes. His comments stress the moral and ethical lessons to be derived from the text, offering many kabbalistic allusions. The author's vast knowledge, profound wisdom, and total dedication to God and Torah are reflected in all his writings. *Sefat Emet* on Tractate *Kodashim* is studied avidly by the entire spectrum of Torah scholars, ranging from chasidic to "Lithuanian." The Sefat Emet was succeeded by his son, Rabbi Avraham Mordechai Alter, the Imrei Emet, under whose leadership Gerrer Chasidut grew to embrace more than 100,000 chasidim, most of whom were annihilated by the Nazis. The Imrei Emet escaped miraculously. From the ashes of the Holocaust he rebuilt an ever-growing vibrant Gerrer movement, centered around the splendid Yeshivah Sefat Emet in Jerusalem, currently under the leadership of the Gerrer Rebbe, Rabbi Bunam Alter, and his brother, the *rosh yeshivah* Rabbi Pinchas Menachem Alter. Today, Gerrer Chasidut spans the globe, making Ger once again a mighty force for Torah-observant Judaism.

ספר

שפת אמת

חלק חמישי

מאת

כבוד קדושת אדונינו מורינו ורבינו הדוש ישראל ותפארתו רשכבה"ג מרי יהודא ארי' ליב זצוקלה"ה מגור יע"א. אשר השאיר אחריו ברכה כתוב בעצם כתב ידו הקדושה. וזה יצא ראשונה חידושי תורה על כל שבתות השנה והמועדים.

הוצאה חדשה על ידי

נכדי השפת אמת בירושלם

ירושלים

Title page of *Sefat Emet,* novellae on the weekly Torah portions by Rabbi Yehudah Aryeh Leib Alter of Ger. The abbreviation appearing before his name is the acronym of *Rabban shel kol benei hagolah,* Teacher of all the children of the Diaspora, a title reserved for an illustrious sage.

SELECTIONS FROM SEFAT EMET'S COMMENTARY

It was the end of days and Cain brought some of his crops as an offering. And Abel, he also brought some of the first-born of his flock, from their fattest ones. God paid heed to Abel and his offering.

(Genesis 4:3–4)

Sefat Emet: *And Abel, he also brought*—The syntax appears somewhat awkward. The verse could have simply read, "And Abel brought . . ." What is the significance of the words "he also brought"? Abel brought *"also himself"* as an offering. He sacrificed his *ani*, his "self," his ego. It was for this reason that God paid heed to Abel and his offering.[2]

And when all the land of Egypt also began to feel the famine, the people cried out to Pharaoh for bread. Pharaoh said to all the Egyptians: "Go to Joseph. Do whatever he says."

(Genesis 41:55)

Sefat Emet: *Do whatever he says*—**Rashi** remarks that Joseph told them to circumcise themselves. Now you may ask, what prompted Joseph to demand their circumcision? Joseph was so scrupulously careful in the observance of the mitzvah of *brit milah* that because of this he is called *"tzaddik yesod olam"*—a tzaddik on whom the entire world rests—the quintessential tzaddik.[3] As such, he simply abhorred an uncircumcised person. Nevertheless, as our sages tell us, the fact that he conferred the seal of the holy covenant on the Egyptians was deemed a sin on his part. For a Jew must be forbearing, even with those who are diametrically opposed to his views.

This month shall be the head month to you. It shall be the first month of the year.

(Exodus 12:2)

Sefat Emet: *This month shall be the head month to you*[4]—The Jewish people maintains the lunar calendar, which measures the year by the revolutions of the moon. By contrast, the non-Jewish world, using the solar calendar, measures the year according to the sun. Therein is reflected the difference between Israel and the gentile nations. The non-Jewish nations endure only as long as the sun of fortune shines brightly on them. When their sun begins to set and their good fortune turns, they fade from the pages of history. Israel, on the other hand, continues to illuminate the world even during periods of darkness and oppression, like the moon that lights up the world during the darkest night.

Love the Lord your God with all your heart, with all your soul, and with all your might.

(Deuteronomy 6:5)

Sefat Emet: *Love the Lord your God*—The command to love God is difficult to understand. Since love is a feeling, an emotion that is beyond man's control, how can he be commanded to love God? How can feelings be dictated? What should he do if he simply does not feel any love? This question may be answered by pointing out that the very fact that the Torah gives the commandment of *ve'ahavta* ("you shall love") indicates that inherently man has an innate love of God. This love is in a dormant state in the inner recesses of his soul, and must be aroused and actualized. It is this process of awakening that constitutes the mitzvah of "Love the Lord your God," which means, in effect, to do all you can to awaken your latent love of God.

And when they had eaten them up, there was no way of telling that they had eaten them. The cows looked just as bad as they had at first. Then I woke up.

(Genesis 41:21)

Sefat Emet: *And when they had eaten them up, there was no way of telling that they had eaten them*— How can evil exist in a world created by God, the Beneficent One? It can exist, because entrapped deep inside the force of evil there is a spark of goodness. This spark is the source of life of the evil tendency. Although this spark cannot be discerned at all—*there was no way of telling that they had eaten them*—nevertheless, *they had eaten them*—it is present inside of evil. Now, it is the specific mission of the Jew to free the entrapped holy sparks from the grip of the forces of evil by means of Torah study and prayer. Once the holy sparks are released, evil, having lost its life-giving core, will cease to exist.[5]

RABBI YOEL TEITELBAUM OF SATMAR—THE SATMAR RAV
רבי יואל טייטעלבום מסאטמאר

born: Sighet, Hungary, 1887
died: New York, New York, 1979
Popularly known as the Satmar Rav. Talmudist, chasidic leader.

Rabbi Yoel of Satmar was born into a famous rabbinic family, descendants of **Maharsha** and **Rema.** His father, Rabbi Yomtov Lipa Teitelbaum, author of *Kedushat Yomtov,* served as rabbi in Sighet. Rabbi Yoel showed early signs of extraordinary scholarly brilliance and piety, as he immersed himself in talmudic research and the great books on Mussar (ethics), such as *Chovot Halevavot* by **Rabbi Bachya ibn Pakudah,** which he studied daily. He was a follower of the great chasidic rebbe of Shinowa, under whose tutelage he deepened his knowledge of the revealed and hidden aspects of Torah. At age 17 he was appointed rabbi of Muzsa in Czechoslovakia, and after serving as rabbi of Orshowa and Kroli he became the rabbi of Satmar. He held this post until 1944, when, at the height of the Nazi deportations and killings of Hungarian Jewry, he was miraculously rescued. He was one of the 1,684 Hungarian Jews on the famed "Kastner train," which was taken via Bergen-Belsen to Switzerland, as a result of Rabbi Michael Ber Weissmandl's negotiations with Eichmann. In 1946 the Satmar Rav arrived in the United States, where he zealously labored at rebuilding Torah and Chasidut. With his charismatic personality and oratorical talents, he attracted thousands of followers and built a vibrant chasidic community in the Williamsburgh section of Brooklyn.[1] He distinguished himself by his intellectual prowess, great piety, and the strength of his character. He became known for his uncompromising stand against even the slightest deviation from tradition, and he fervently believed that a Jewish state will be established only upon the coming of the Messiah. Thus he fiercely opposed Zionism or any group participating in the Israeli government. His halachic novellae, responsa, sermons, and essays have been collected under the titles *Vayoel Moshe* and *Divrei Yoel.* They give evidence of his profound erudition and defiant spirit in defense of his convictions.

Rabbi Yoel Teitelbaum, the Satmar Rav.

SELECTIONS FROM THE SATMAR RAV'S COMMENTARY

Excerpt from *Divrei Yoel,* Essay on "The Three Vows"

I cited the opinion of **Ravad** in **Rambam's** *Commentary on the Mishnah* to the effect that even after the

זה השער לה׳ צדיקים יבואו בו

בעזהי״ת

ספר

דברי יואל

על התורה

חידושים יקרים ונעימים בדרך פרד״ס

מאת כ״ק אדמו״ר הגה״ק רשכבה״ג

מרן מהר״י ט״ב שליט״א

האבדק״ק סאטמאר והגלילות יצ״ו

חלק שלישי

שמות—בשלח

יצא לאור ע״י

אפרים יוסף דוב אשכנזי

בהוצאת בית מסחר והוצאת ספרים „ירושלים״

ברוקלין שנת תשל״ד לפ״ק

Title page of *Divrei Yoel* by the Satmar Rav, discourses on the weekly Torah portion. The abbreviation comprising the name of the author reads: "Our rabbi, Rabbi Yoel; the letters tet-bet stand for Teitelbaum, and the abbreviation *shlita* stands for *shyichyeh le'orech yamim tovim,* 'may he live to a ripe and good old age.'"

coming of the Messiah, the Jewish people will not return to Eretz Yisrael before they repent. Rambam does not delve into the details of what will occur after the coming of the Messiah, because it is impossible to know these things. But one thing is clear: the return to Eretz Yisrael is contingent on repentance. Now, any intelligent person can readily recognize the terrible misfortune that has befallen us, in that a group of nonbelievers and atheists, Heaven help us, established independence and a government before the appointed time . . . and even if all the ministers of the Knesset were righteous and holy men, it still would be a sin. It is a dreadful and appalling thing to seize redemption and governmental control in advance of the appointed time.

Excerpt from *Divrei Yoel, Beha'alotecha*

Regarding any issue, we must pause to think and be concerned from the very beginning whether it will lead to harmful results. This is true especially regarding issues that are of fundamental importance to the preservation of our beliefs. In such cases, particular caution and vigilance must be applied from the very outset, even before any concrete steps have been taken. This is exactly the method by which corruptive new ideologies are introduced into the hearts of the Jewish people by the various political parties. Initially, they deviate from the Torah on minor and insignificant points, with the excuse that they wish to attract secular Jews. This requires that they make small concessions in order to be able to relate to them. From the start we must be strongly on guard against them, and not stray from the right path even in small nuances. It all depends on the initial steps. . . .

Excerpt from *Divrei Yoel, Vayishlach*

Everyone knows that my life was saved through great miracles, with God's help. Without a doubt, I am not worthy of the many miracles God performed on my behalf. I conclude that the purpose of my rescue was that "now I have become two camps" (Genesis 32:11). Indeed, I was saved only for the purpose of establishing all these Torah institutions. It is written, "Let us rejoice and be glad in Your salvation." Now, who would not rejoice in that great Salvation? Why mention it at all? The answer is that on that day there will be many who wish to rejoice but will be unable to do so because of shame over their deeds that will then be revealed. With that in mind, we pray to God that we may make the proper preparations, so that we will be able to rejoice when salvation comes. And when the Righteous Messiah comes we will merit greeting him with gladness and rejoicing.

Excerpt from *Divrei Yoel, Vayishlach*

And Jacob remained alone.

(Genesis 32:25)

[By dividing this phrase it can be explained homiletically.] *And Jacob remained alone*—How can Jacob remain alive? How can the ideals of Jacob survive? The answer can be found in the word "alone." Only when Jacob isolates himself, does not permit any mingling with Esau and Laban, has no attachment or affinity with them whatsoever, can he endure. Jacob followed this road of isolationism and thereby overpowered the forces of Esau and Laban, so that they could have no effect on him or his way of life. Correspondingly, in the end of days, the world will recognize God as the One and only God, and the verse "on that day God *alone* will be exalted" (Isaiah 2:17) will be fulfilled. On that day "the world will be filled with the knowledge of God" (Isaiah 11:9), and all mankind will recognize that there is none beside Him.

VI
PHILOSOPHY

Since the Torah, Talmud, and Midrash embrace the totality of Jewish knowledge and thinking, initially philosophy was not a separate branch of study. However, with the passage of time, as alien philosophic trends began to make inroads into Jewish life, the need arose to refute fallacious theories and to postulate in clearly defined terms the Torah *Weltanschauung*. Jewish thinkers, in response to the challenges presented by Karaite, Aristotelian, Christian, Moslem, and other doctrines, formulated the fundamental tenets of Judaism, presenting the authentic Torah way of thinking on such issues as God's unity, Divine omniscience, reward and punishment, miracles, the immortality of the soul, the "Days of the Messiah," and the resuscitation of the dead. In an age when the Jewish people was exposed to the missionary efforts of other religions, there existed an urgent need to spell out unequivocally the basic doctrines of Judaism. In so doing, the rabbis safeguarded the Jewish credo against all attempts at watering it down or surreptitiously contaminating it with false ideologies.

RABBI SAADYAH GAON
רבינו סעדיה גאון

born: Al Fayyum, Egypt, 882
died: Sura, Babylonia, 942
Universal leader of Jewry, religious philosopher.

Receiving his early education in Egypt, Saadyah Gaon rapidly rose to outstanding scholarship. At age 29 he published his *Sefer Ha'egron* on Hebrew grammar and style. The Karaites, a sect that misinterpreted the Torah and denied the Divine origin of the Oral Law, had gained adherents in Egypt. Rabbi Saadyah published several polemics disproving their fallacious theories. At the age of 46 he was appointed to the high office of *Gaon* of the Great Torah Academy of Sura, Babylonia, a position previously held by the greatest scholars of Jewry. He wrote more than twenty-four works, including a number of compositions of liturgical poetry. His most famous work is *Ha'emunot Vehade'ot*[1] (Faith and Belief), the first major work on Jewish philosophy, written in Arabic and translated into Hebrew by Rabbi Yehudah ibn Tibbon. Rabbi Saadyah's purpose was to counteract the influence of the Greek philosophers by exposing the falsehood of their ideas. He demonstrates that the teachings of the Torah will stand the test of logical inquiry. He offers unassailable proofs that the universe was created *ex nihilo*—out of nothing, that the Creator is One, that man has a soul, that the Torah was given to the Jewish people by God at Mount Sinai, and that man has the freedom to choose between good and evil and receives reward or retribution accordingly. The work was the forerunner of all later philosophical books and has remained popular to this day. **Rambam** summed up Rabbi Saadyah's life: "Were it not for Saadyah, the Torah would almost have disappeared from among Israel."[2]

ספר

האמונות והדעות

והוא כולל עשרה מאמרים, מדבר מעניני האמונות האמתיות, והדעות הישרות, שיבור לו האדם, ע"פ התורה והחכמה והמוסר. ונכפלו עוד אמונות כוזבות ודעות נפסדות, והסתירה עליהם, ותשובות על שאלות המינים והכופרים.

חברו בלשון ערב

הגאון רבינו סעדיה ז"ל הפיומי,

ראש ישיבה במתא מחסיא,

והעתיקו

ר' יהודה ן' תיבון דיין מרמון ספרד ללשון הקדש.

נדפס מחדש כמו שנדפס בקושטנטינא בסדר יותר נאה עם מראה מקומות הפסוקים המובאים בתנ"ך.

על הוצאות

ירוחם פישל

לייפציג
תרי"ט

ועתה נדפס מחדש עם תיקונים ע"י:

הוצאת אום ניו יורק
שנת תש"ז לפ"ק

Title page of *Ha'emunot Vehade'ot* by Rabbi Saadyah Gaon.

SELECTIONS FROM RABBI SAADYAH GAON'S COMMENTARY

Excerpt from *Ha'emunot Vehade'ot*, Chap. 9, Reward and Punishment in the World to Come

We find that Isaac offered himself willingly to be sacrificed, in order to follow God's decree. Now, if he would have believed that good deeds are rewarded only in this world, what recompense would he expect to accrue to him after his death? . . . Similarly, Chananiah, Mishael, and Azariah threw themselves into the fiery furnace so as not to worship the idol. They wanted to pay homage to no one but God. If they would have believed that reward is given only in this world, what could they have hoped for after having died in the flames? Daniel, too, chose death in the lion's den for worshiping the Almighty. If reward is paid only in this world, what would be left of him after the lions ate him? All the foregoing proves that the prophets were unanimous in their view that reward is not received in this world but only in the World to Come.

Excerpt from *Ha'emunot Vehade'ot*, 8:3

I must mention the computation of the time of the end of the Exile. Concerning this matter God showed His prophet Daniel three angels, one standing above the waters of the River *Chidekel* (Tigris), the other two standing on either bank. The two angels asked the one standing above the water, "How long shall it be until the coming of the Redemption?" and he replied, raising his hands to heaven, swearing—even though he had not been asked to swear about the time of the final Redemption—"that it shall be for a time, times, and a half" (Daniel 12:7) . . . but Daniel did not know the meaning of "a time, times, and a half." He asked the angel standing above the water about this, as it says, "And I heard it, but I did not understand. Then I said, 'My lord, what shall be the final end of these things?' " (Daniel 12:8). The angel told him why these things are "shut up and sealed till the end of time." It was done to keep it a secret from fools and boors. When they would know how long the Exile was to endure, they would not accept any admonishment. They do not look forward to the everlasting bliss of the World to Come since they care only about worldly pleasures. They do not have the aspirations of the wise men who long for the rewards of everlasting life.[3]

RABBI BACHYAH IBN PAKUDAH—CHOVOT HALEVAVOT
רבי בחיי אבן פקודה—חובות הלבבות

Saragossa, Spain, early 11th century
Popularly known as Chovot Halevavot, after the title of his work. Ethicist, philosopher.

Very little is known of Rabbi Bachyah's personal life. He was a dayan (ecclesiastical judge) in his home town, presumably Saragossa. In 1040 he wrote his sublime classic, *Chovot Halevavot* ("Duties of the Heart"), a work that has been described as perhaps the noblest work of post-talmudic literature on Jewish ethics. He wrote it in Arabic, the familiar vernacular of Jews in the lands of Islam, including Spain and Portugal.[1] Rabbi Bachyah argues that the Torah's ethical teachings are of primary importance: Mitzvot that are performed primarily "with the limbs" also require participation of the heart. The book is divided into ten sections, called Gates *(She'arim)*. *Chovot Halevavot* is an expression of unshakable faith in God's goodness. It exhorts a Jew to trust in God rather than in his own intellect and ability, to be concerned with the needs of the soul rather than the needs of the body. It became the textbook of the Mussar movement, founded by **Rabbi Yisrael Salanter**, and is today widely studied by Jews all over the world.

The Ten Gates (She'arim) of *Chovot Halevavot* ("Duties of the Heart")

1. **שער היחוד**
   Shaar Hayichud—Gate of Unity.
   A discourse offering proofs of God's existence, based on rationalistic investigation, leading into a discussion of the theme of God's oneness.

2. **שער הבחירה**
   Shaar Habechirah—Gate of Recognition.
   The recognition of God's wisdom, power, and goodness as it is evident in the universe.

ספר
חובת הלבבות
מהרב הגדול החסיד
רבינו בחיי דיין ספרדי בר יוסף זצ"ל
חברו בלשון ערבי והעתיקו לעברי
החכם רבי יהודה אבן תבון ספרד זצ"ל
עם פירוש מספיק — ועם ביאור חדש נפלא
נקרא בשם — נקרא בשם
מרפא לנפש — פת לחם
CHOWAS HALWUWOS
LEMBERG DRUCK A. J. MADFES.
1874.

Title page of *Chovot Halevavot,* by Rabbi Bachya ibn Pakudah.

3. **שער עבודת אלהים**
Shaar Avodat Elohim—Gate of the Service of God.
The duty to serve God.

4. **שער הבטחון**
Shaar Habitachon—Gate of Faith.
The meaning of trusting in God.

5. **שער יחוד המעשה**
Shaar Yichud Hama'aseh—Gate of Dedication of Purpose.
The need for humility before God.

6. **שער הכניעה**
Shaar Hakeniah—Gate of Humility.

7. **שער התשובה**
Shaar Hateshuvah—Gate of Repentance.

8. **שער חשבון הנפש**
Shaar Cheshbon Hanefesh—Gate of Self-Communion.
Self-examination and meditation.

9. **שער הפרישות**
Shaar Haperishut—Gate of Self-Denial.

10. **שער אהבת ה׳**
Shaar Ahavat Hashem—Gate to Love of God.
The end goal of conviction of God's existence.

SELECTIONS FROM RABBI BACHYAH'S WRITINGS

Excerpt from *Chovot Halevavot*, Gate of Unity, Chap. 6

There are people who say that the world came into existence by chance, without a Creator who caused and formed it. I wonder, how can a normal rational person entertain such an idea. . . . We all know that things that take place without plan or purpose do not show any evidence of wisdom or power. Don't you realize that if someone would accidentally spill ink on a blank piece of paper, it would be impossible that proper writing or legible lines would result, as though they were written with a pen? If someone brought us a page with meaningful writing that could only have been written with a pen and said that the ink had spilled on the paper

and these written characters had come into being by themselves, we would immediately accuse him of falsehood, for we are certain that this could not have happened without a thinking person's intent. Since this appears to us an impossibility in the case of standard characters, how can anyone assert that something far more delicate in its art and whose fashioning is infinitely beyond our comprehension could have happened without purpose, wisdom, and power of a wise and mighty Maker.

Excerpt from *Chovot Halevavot*, Gate of Unity, Chap. 7

The second argument for the unity of God is based on the wisdom that is evident in every part of the universe in its celestial reaches or on earth, in its mineral, vegetable, and animal kingdoms. If we reflect on it we will be convinced that the entire universe is the design of one Designer, the work of one Creator. For we find that with all the differences in its structure and basic elements, it shows a similarity in its end products, a uniformity in parts.[2] The marks of Divine wisdom evident in the smallest as well as in the largest creatures testify that they all have one wise Creator. . . . The wisdom evident in the creation of the huge elephant is not more marvelous than that shown in the creation of the tiny ant. On the contrary, the smaller the creature, the more it manifests the Creator's wisdom and power . . . . This proves that all things are the design of one Designer and Creator. . . . If the universe had more than one Creator, the creative wisdom would exhibit different forms in the different parts of the world in their entirety and in their components.[3]

Excerpt from *Chovot Halevavot*, Gate of Recognition, Chap. 6

Imagine that your condition here on earth is like that of a child born in a prison belonging to a king. The king took pity on him and commanded that he should be provided with everything good for him and that all his personal needs should be filled until he grew up and attained mature intelligence. The boy knew nothing except the prison and what was in it. A royal officer visited the boy regularly, bringing him all he needed—light, food, drink, and clothing—and informed him that he was a servant of the king and that the prison and all it contained, as well as the food he brought him, belonged to the king. He was, therefore, obligated to

thank and praise the king. The boy replied, "I praise the owner of this prison who has accepted me as his servant, bestowed all his bounties on me, and paid special attention to me." Said the officer, "Don't speak like this—it is sinful. The royal kingdom does not consist of only this prison. The territory he rules is infinitely larger than its limited space. Neither are you his only servant; his subjects are countless. And all the favors and benevolence you have received are insignificant compared to those he has bestowed on others."
. . . The lad now obtained some understanding . . . of what the king was. . . . Reverence for the king penetrated his heart. . . . Reflect, brother, on this parable . . . think of the Creator as He is, and His goodness and lovingkindness with which He has favored you will be more appreciated by you.

Excerpt from *Chovot Halevavot*, Gate of Humility, Chap. 6

A pious man, we are told, passed by the carcass of a dog that gave out an offensive odor. His disciples said to him, "How repulsive does this carcass smell!" He said to them, "How white are its teeth." The disciples then regretted the derogatory comment they had made about it. If it is reprehensible to make a derogatory remark about a dead dog, then surely it is blameworthy to do so about a living human being. And just as it is good to praise a dog's carcass for the whiteness of its teeth, surely it is a duty to praise an intelligent and understanding human being. It was, in fact, the intent of the pious man to exhort his students not to accustom themselves to speak evil, so that this should become natural to them. They should become accustomed to speaking good of others, and this should become their natural habit.

RABBI YEHUDAH HALEVI
רבי יהודה הלוי

born: Toledo, Spain, c. 1080
died: Eretz Yisrael, c. 1145
Philosopher, poet.

Rabbi Yehudah Halevi studied under the great **Rabbi Yitzchak al-Fasi (Rif)** and his disciple, Rabbi Yosef ibn Migash, who was the mentor of **Maimonides**. In addition to being an accomplished talmudic scholar, Rabbi Yehudah wrote masterful lyric poetry, in Hebrew and in Arabic. His odes to Zion are liturgical gems that bespeak his undying love for the Land of Israel. He earned his livelihood as a physician. His closest friend was **Rabbi Abraham ibn Ezra**, who often quotes him in his commentary to the Torah.

According to legend, Rabbi Yehudah Halevi reached Jerusalem after a long and arduous journey. Overcome by emotion at seeing the sacred place of his longings, he fell to the ground, only to be brutally trampled to death by an Arab horseman.

Rabbi Yehudah Halevi's greatest achievement is *The Kuzari*, a work of philosophy, written in 1140 in Arabic[1] and translated into Hebrew by Rabbi Yehudah ibn Tibbon.[2] The framework of the book is the conversion to Judaism of the pagan king of the Khazars, a Central Asian empire. Searching for the true religion, the king questions a Christian scholar, a Moslem scholar, and a Jewish scholar. *The Kuzari* is structured on the Jew's dialogue with the Khazar king, in which he expounds on the philosophical fundamentals of Judaism and analyzes a multitude of other facets, from music to the location of the international dateline, from a discussion of the oral tradition to the theme of reward and punishment.

Yehudah Halevi's principal belief is God's revelation through history, in contrast to the belief of **Rabbi Saadyah Gaon**, in which creation *ex nihilo* is the fundamental tenet of Judaism. Yehudah Halevi rises to poetic heights in his description of the Jewish people as the heart of all nations and the Land of Israel as the land superior to any other land. The book has been a major influence on Jewish thought and has inspired successive generations with a burning love for Torah and

ספר
הכוזרי
מיוחס להחכם החבר ר' יצחק הסנגרי ז"ל.
עם שני באורים, נעימים וטובים:
האחד והשני
קול יהודה. אוצר נחמד.
ועוד כמה הוספות טובות ומועילות המבוארות
בשער השני.
בחמשה חלקים.
ווילנא
בדפוס ר' א"צ ראזענקראנץ ז"ל, ור' מ"מ שריפטזעטצער.
שנת תרע"ד לפ"ק
יצא לאור בהוצאת בית מסחר הספרים
של ר' יצחק פונק בווילנא.

Title page of *The Kuzari,* by Rabbi Yehuda Halevi. A momentous work on Jewish philosophy, written in the form of a dialogue between the Kuzari, the non-Jewish ruler of the Khazar tribe, and a rabbi. *Amar haKuzari,* the Kuzari says; *Amar hechaver,* the rabbi responds.

16 ספר מאמר שני הכוזרי

ג אמר הכוזרי איך תעשה במדות שהם יותר גשמיות, כמו רואה ושומע ומדבר וכותב על הלוחות ויורד על הר סיני ושמח במעשיו ומתעצב אל לבו :

ד אמר החבר הלא דמיתיו לך בשופט צדק שאין חטא במדותיו ויוצא מדיניו הצלחת עם וכבודם, ויקרא אותבם ושמח בהם, ונוזר על אחרים בהריסת בתיהם

אוצר נחמד — קול יהודה

A page of text from *The Kuzari*. From the original Vilna edition with two commentaries, *Kol Yehudah* and *Otzar Nechmad*.

Eretz Yisrael. It radiates warmth as it addresses particularly those who have fallen under the spell of alien cultures. It is not surprising that *The Kuzari* has found wide acceptance among modern Jews.

SELECTIONS FROM RABBI YEHUDAH HALEVI'S WRITINGS

Excerpt from *The Kuzari* 2:42, The Relationship of God to Israel

The effect of Divine Influence is felt in the world through its effect on the Jewish people. It could be said that the relationship of the Divine Influence to the Jewish people and of the Jewish people to the world is the same as that of the human body to the heart. Just as the body receives its life and strength from the heart, so, too, does the entire world receive Divine Influence through the Jewish people. For this reason it is said, "Only you have I known of all the families on the earth; therefore I will punish you" (Amos 3:2). This verse refers to their iniquities and describes their vulnerability to punishment. . . . Just as the heart is essentially pure and even-tempered, making it suitable for the living soul of man attached to it, so too is Jewry essentially and organically fit for the Divine Influence to be attached to it. Similarly, as the heart is affected by illnesses generated by other organs, such as those caused by the uncontrolled desires of the liver, stomach, and procreative organs, so too is Jewry vulnerable to the social and moral diseases generated by the nations of the world to whom it is exposed. . . . Do not wonder therefore that the nations will say in time to come, "He [Israel] has borne griefs influenced by us and has suffered sorrows we have caused" (Isaiah 53:4). This is why Jewry suffers exile and oppression while the rest of the world enjoys tranquility.[3]

Excerpt from *The Kuzari* 2:64–65, Music

Such was the prominence of music in our nation that it was assigned exclusively to the aristocracy, the Levites,[4] who played various instruments and sang in the Holy Temple at every important function. The Levites were fully supported by the tithes contributed by the Jewish people so that they had no need to seek a livelihood. Their sole occupation was the study and performance of music. Music is a highly esteemed art among men, so long as it is not abused and degraded by uncultured people, and so long as it is preserved by those of noble and pure spirit. The first to establish the concept and art of music among Jewry were King David and the prophet Samuel. There is no doubt that music reached its perfection in the Holy Temple, where it inspired man and elevated his soul to so high a level that it changed his very nature. It is impossible that it should attain a similar level today. It has declined because it has become the occupation of inferior people. It has degenerated from its former greatness, as we too have come down from our former prominence.

Excerpt from *The Kuzari* 4:22–23, The Prominence of the Jewish People

God has a secret and wise design for keeping us in exile for so long. This plan can be compared to the process of disintegration that a seed undergoes when it falls into the ground. To the human eye, the seed is transformed into earth and water as it rots, and no trace is left of the seed itself. The truth, however, is that through Divine wisdom the seed dominates and influences the earth and the water, absorbing them and causing their transformation into its own substance. . . . After it takes root, the seed gradually expels its outer husks and other extraneous elements until the true essence of the original seed begins to appear. In time the seed will have the ability to develop into fruit that duplicates the fruit from which it originally sprang. Similarly, even though it appears that other faiths reject the Torah of Moses, they are in effect transformed by it and are influenced by its authentic truths. These various faiths merely serve to introduce and prepare the way for the long-expected Messiah, who is [in terms of our metaphor] the seed and the essence of the fruit. Ultimately, if they acknowledge him, they will become his fruit and there will be only one tree. Then they will revere the source they formerly despised, as Isaiah long ago observed, "Behold, My servant will prosper" (Isaiah 52:13).[5]

Excerpt from *The Kuzari* 5:12, Immortality of the Soul

One of the proofs that the soul is distinct from and independent of the body is that one's physical capacities are weakened through strain. The eye is damaged by overexposure to the sun and the ear is damaged by overloud sounds, while the rational soul becomes ever stronger and more retentive as a result of the intellectual challenges presented by difficult problems or situations. Another example is that old age weakens the body but not the soul. The influence of the soul is stronger after one's fiftieth year, while the body is on the decline. The activity or functions of the body are limited, while the ability of the rational soul is unlimited. Similarly, while the visible forms of geometry, arithmetic, and logic are limited, their concepts or theories are unlimited.

Excerpt from *The Kuzari* 5:22, Living in the Land of Israel

What benefit is there today in living in the Holy Land, since the Divine Presence is absent from it? With a pure heart and mind, and with a strong desire, one can be near God in any place. Why should we risk danger on land and sea and among strange peoples to go and live there? We realize that the "visible" Divine Presence has disappeared, because it is revealed only to a prophet, or to a community that has found favor in the eyes of God, and only in a specially designated place. For this we pray when saying, "Let our eyes behold the return of God to Zion" (Isaiah 52:8) and "May our eyes behold Your return to Zion" (daily *Shemoneh Esreih* prayer). However, the invisible, spiritual Shechinah (Divine Presence) is to be found with every Jew who lives righteously and is pure of heart and mind before the God of Israel. Because it is saturated with sanctity, the Holy Land motivates a person who lives there to be pure in heart and upright in deeds, and he is, therefore, more apt to find the invisible Divine Presence. . . . Man's love and yearning for the Holy Land help speed the fulfillment and realization of the awaited promise, as it is said, "You will rise and have compassion on Zion when its time to be favored will come, when the appointed time will come; when Your servants will take pleasure in her stones and bestow their favor on her dust" (Psalm 102:14–15). This means that Jerusalem will be rebuilt only when Jewry yearns for it to the extent that even its stones and dust are precious to us.

RABBI MOSHE BEN MAIMON (MAIMONIDES)— RAMBAM
רבי משה בן מיימן—רמב״ם

born: Cordova, Spain, 1135
died: Cairo, Egypt, 1204
Popularly known as Rambam (after the initials of his name) and Maimonides (Greek for "son of Maimon"). Halachist, commentator, philosopher.

Rambam received his first Torah instruction from his father, a noted scholar who traced his ancestry back to **Rabbi Yehudah HaNasi**, compiler of the Mishnah, and King David. When he was thirteen, Cordova was conquered by the invading Almohads, a fanatical Moslem sect. The family was forced to flee, wandering from place to place for twelve years, ultimately settling in Fez, Morocco. In 1165 Rambam settled in Cairo, where he found asylum and religious freedom. At age 23 Rambam began writing his commentary on the Mishnah, Peirush Hamishnayot, in Arabic.[1] It is appended to the Vilna edition of the Talmud. The work analyzes each mishnah and provides an introduction clarifying fundamental tenets of Judaism. Rambam's philosophical treatise in the introduction to the tractate *Berachot* is known as *Shemonah Perakim* (Eight Chapters). It deals with the diseases and cures of man's soul, prophecy, reward and punishment, free will, and the rule of the "golden mean." In his commentary on *Sanhedrin* 10:1, he enunciates the thirteen principles of the Jewish faith. When his brother David, who supported the entire family, perished at sea, Rambam began to study medicine and became a physician of note. He was appointed as doctor to the court of Sultan Saladin. He used his influence to help his fellow Jews. In about 1170, Rambam began to write his monumental *Mishneh Torah*,[2] a compendium of all Jewish laws extracted from the Talmud and the works of the *Gaonim*. The work consists of fourteen volumes and is also called *Yad Hachazakah*.[3] For short, it is often called *Yad*, or simply the *Rambam*. It was completed in 1180 and was written in a lucid and concise mishnaic

ספר
מורה נבוכים
להרב האלהי רבינו משה בן מיימון הספרדי ז״ל.
בהעתקת
הרב ר׳ שמואל אבן תיבון ז״ל.
עם שלשה פירושים יקרים הנודעים ומפורסמים לתהלה.
ה״ה
אפודי, שם טוב, ן׳ קרשקש.
והרביעי הכי נכבד הנוסף כעת, להשר וגדול בישורון רבינו
דון יצחק אברבנאל ז״ל.
עוד נקבצו באו בו
א) כוונת כל פרק מפרקי המורה על דעת החכם ר׳ יהודה ברבי שלמה אלחריזי ז״ל.
ב) פירוש מלות הזרות לרבי שמואל אבן תיבון ז״ל, מוגה ומתוקן.
ג) כל פסוקי תורה נביאים וכתובים אשר באו זכרם בספר המורה, נסדרו כסדרן בציון החלק והפרק שהובאו בהמורה.
חלק ראשון
הוגה בעיון נמרץ ובהשגחה רבה ע״פ ספרים מדויקים.
תוצאת בית מסחר הספרים של ר׳ יצחק פונק בווילנא.
ווילנא
בדפוס ראזענקראנץ ושריפטזעצער.
שנת תרעד לפ״ק

Title page of *Moreh Nevuchim*, "Guide of the Perplexed," by Rambam, his answer to Aristotelian philosophy. Commentaries by Efudi, Shem Tov, Ibn Crescas, and Don Yitzchak Abarbanel.

מורה נבוכים חלק ראשון פרק נג

שם טוב

אפודי

אברבנאל

קרשקש

A page of text from *Moreh Nevuchim*, "Guide of the Perplexed." From the standard Vilna edition.

Hebrew. It was the first comprehensive codification of all Torah laws. *Mishneh Torah* immediately gained immense popularity. It became the most authoritative text on *Halachah*, and over 325 commentaries were written on it. Over the centuries, no novella was written, no talmudic discourse was given without discussion of the relevant rulings in *Mishneh Torah*. Rambam's *Sefer Hamitzvot*, written in Arabic, enumerates and elucidates the 613 precepts of the Torah. In 1185 Rambam wrote a major philosophical treatise, *Moreh Nevuchim* ("Guide of the Perplexed"), written in Arabic and translated by Shmuel ibn Tibbon.[4] It addresses the persons who were baffled by seeming contradictions between the teachings of the Torah and Aristotelian philosophy. Rambam demonstrates that there is no conflict between the two if the fundamentals of both are properly understood and interpreted. The book gave rise to bitter controversy. Rabbi Shlomoh of Montpelier in Provence was joined by many other scholars in his opposition to the study of philosophy in general and *Moreh Nevuchim* in particular. Despite the acrimonious discord, Rambam has remained the undisputed Torah authority. His supremacy as a scholar is best expressed in the famous dictum, inscribed on his tomb, "From Moshe (Moses) till Moshe (Rambam), no one arose like Moshe." *(Other biographical data is on p. 99.)*

SELECTIONS FROM RAMBAM'S WRITING

Excerpt from *Shemonah Perakim*, constituting the introduction to his Commentary on Tractate *Avot* (Ethics of the Fathers), Chap. 4—Concerning the Cure of the Diseases of the Soul

Good deeds are those that are balanced, forming the mean between two extremes that are equally bad—the too much and the too little. . . . Thus, generosity is the mean between stinginess and extravagance; courage, the mean between recklessness and cowardice . . . . The medium course is the one that is truly praiseworthy. It is the one to which everyone should strive, always carefully weighing his actions so that they are balanced. . . . The perfect Torah that leads us to perfection recommends none of these things (such as the practice of mortification, excessive fasting, going into seclusion, etc.). On the contrary, the Torah's intent is that man follow the path of moderation, in accordance with the dictates of nature, eating, drinking, having marital relations, all in moderation, and living among people in uprightness and honesty, but not dwelling in the wilderness or in the mountains, or wearing a hairshirt or afflicting the body. The Torah even warns us against such practices.[5]

The Thirteen Principles of Faith from the prayerbook, based on Maimonides' formulation in his *Commentary on the Mishnah, Sanhedrin* 10:1:

1. I believe with perfect faith that the Creator, Blessed is His Name, creates and guides all creatures, and that He alone made, makes, and will make everything.
2. I believe with perfect faith that the Creator, Blessed is His Name, is One and there is no oneness like His in any way, and that He alone

is our God, Who was, Who is, and Who always will be.

3. I believe with perfect faith that the Creator, Blessed is His Name, has no body, that no physical attributes apply to Him, and that nothing can be compared to Him at all.

4. I believe with perfect faith that the Creator, Blessed is His Name, is first and last.

5. I believe with perfect faith that it is only proper to pray to God. One may not pray to anyone or anything else.

6. I believe with perfect faith that all the words of the prophets are true.

7. I believe with perfect faith that the prophecy of Moses our Teacher, peace be upon him, is true, and that he was the father of the prophets—both before and after him.

8. I believe with perfect faith that the entire Torah that we now have is that which was given to Moses our Teacher, peace be upon him.

9. I believe with perfect faith that this Torah will not be changed, and that there will never be another Torah from the Creator, Blessed is His Name.

10. I believe with perfect faith that the Creator, Blessed is His Name, knows all the deeds and thoughts of man, as it is said, "He molds all their hearts together, He comprehends all their deeds" (Psalm 33:15).

11. I believe with perfect faith that the Creator, Blessed is His Name, rewards with good those who observe His commandments, and punishes those who violate His commandments.

12. I believe with perfect faith in the coming of the Messiah, and though he may tarry, nevertheless I await his coming every day.

13. I believe with perfect faith that the dead will come back to life whenever the Creator, Blessed is His Name, wills it.

Excerpt from Commentary on the *Mishnah Sanhedrin* 10:1, The Eighth Principle of Faith

Every word of the Torah is full of wisdom and wonders for one who understands it. It is beyond human comprehension, wider than the earth, broader than the sea. All we must do is follow in the footsteps of David, the anointed of the God of Jacob, who prayed, "Open my eyes that I may behold the wonders of Your Torah (Psalm 119:18). The traditional commentary of the

Torah is also the Word of God. The sukkah we build today, or the *lulav*, shofar, tzitzit, and tefillin we use have the same forms as the ones God showed to Moses, which he faithfully transmitted to us. This fundamental principle is taught by the verse, "This shall demonstrate to you that God sent me to do all these things and that I did not do it on my own accord" (Numbers 16:28).[6]

Excerpt from *Moreh Nevuchim*, Part 2, Chap. 13

The entire universe, that is to say, everything other than God Himself, was created out of absolute nothingness. God alone existed. There was nothing else, neither an angel nor a sphere nor anything within the sphere. He then created everything that exists from absolute nothingness. It was His will and desire. Time itself is also among the things created by God. Time is dependent on motion, and for motion to exist there must be things that move. And all things were created and came into being after not having existed. . . . Without a doubt, time is an accident,[7] one of the created accidents, such as blackness and whiteness. And although it is not a quality, it is an accident flowing from motion, as is clear to anyone who understands the discourse of Aristotle explaining the nature of time and the true reality of its existence.

Excerpt from *Moreh Nevuchim*, Part 3, Chap. 24

Now concerning the story of Abraham at the akeidah—the binding of Isaac—it contains two important principles of the Torah. One of these principles is the limit of love for God and to what degree we must fear Him. For in this story [Abraham] was ordered to do something that cannot be compared with either sacrifice of property or with sacrifice of life. Indeed, it is beyond anything that could ever happen in the world, a thing that no one could imagine that human nature was capable of. Here is a childless man, longing to have a son; he is a wealthy and respected man, wishing that his offspring should become a nation. When this man, after having lost hope, has a son, how great will be his affection and love for him! However, because of his fear of God and because of his love to fulfill His command on this beloved child, he gives up all his hopes for him and agrees to slaughter him after a journey of three days. . . . For Abraham our Father did not hasten to slaughter Isaac because he was afraid that God would kill him or make him poor, but only in order to make it known to mankind to what extent man should love and fear God and not, as we have explained in several passages, for any hope of reward or fear of punishment. . . .

The second principle is to let us know that the prophets believed as true that which came to them from God in prophetic revelation. One should not think that what they heard or what appeared to them in a parable was not true or subject to doubt, just because the revelation came to them in a dream or a vision, as we have explained, and by means of imaginary faculty. The Torah wants to let us know that all that is seen by a prophet in a prophetic vision is, in the opinion of the prophet, the absolute truth; that the prophet has no doubt whatsoever concerning it; that it has, in his opinion, the same validity as all existing things that are perceived through the senses or the intellect. A proof of this is the fact that Abraham agreed to slaughter "his son, his only son, whom he loved" (Genesis 22:2) as he had been commanded, even though this command came in a dream or a vision. For if the prophets had any doubts concerning a prophetic dream or vision, they would not have agreed to do something that was against their nature, and [Abraham] would not have consented to perform such a momentous act if there had been any doubt about it.

Excerpt from *Moreh Nevuchim*, Part 3, Chap. 51

Know that all the practices of worship, such as reading the Torah, prayer, and the performance of the other commandments have as their only purpose to train you to occupy yourself with God's commandments and to turn away from worldly concerns. . . . But if you pray by merely moving your lips while facing the wall and your thoughts are on your business, or if you read the Torah with your tongue but your mind is on the house you are building and you do not consider what you are reading; and likewise, all the commandments you only perform with your limbs, as if you were digging a hole in the ground or chopping trees in the forest, without reflecting on the meaning of your action or on Him who commanded you or on His purpose, do not think that you have achieved your goal. Rather, you are much like those of whom it is said, "You are near in their mouth but far from their reins" (Jeremiah 12:2). . . . The first thing you should do is that when you recite the *Shema* and pray, you should empty your mind of everything. You should not be content with concentrating on the first verse of the *Shema* and saying the first blessing [of the *Shemoneh Esrei*].

Excerpt from *Iggeret Teiman*, Rambam's famous letter to the Jews of Yemen who were suffering religious persecution. His words of encouragement inspired them to remain true to their faith.

Remember, my brethren, this great, incomparable, and unique historical event[8] is proved by the best evidence. For never before or since has an entire nation witnessed a revelation from God or beheld His glory. The purposes of [the revelation] were to strengthen us in our faith so that nothing could change it and to reach a level of certitude that would sustain us in these trying times of fierce persecution and absolute tyranny, as it is written, "For God has come to test you" (Exodus 20:17). The Torah means that God revealed Himself to you thus in order to give you strength to withstand all future trials. Now, do not stumble nor err, be firm in your religion, and persevere in your faith and its duties.

RABBI YONAH OF GERONA—RABBEINU YONAH
רבינו יונה גירונדי

born: Gerona, Spain, c. 1180
died: Toledo, Spain, 1263
Popularly known as Rabbeinu Yonah.
Ethicist, author of Shaarei Teshuvah.

A relative of **Ramban** and disciple of Rabbi Shlomoh of Montpelier, Rabbi Yonah was actively involved in the controversy surrounding **Rambam**'s philosophical work, *Moreh Nevuchim*. He later regretted his antagonism, publicly declared that he had been wrong, and vowed to travel to Tiberias to Rambam's grave to beg his forgiveness. He wrote a number of halachic commentaries and novellae, a commentary on Tractate *Avot*,[1] and *Sefer Hayir'ah*.[2] He is best known for his work *Shaarei Teshuvah*, a famous classic of Mussar literature.[3] The author offers a system for self-improvement derived from biblical and talmudic sources. It forms the basis of all later works on Mussar ethics. Rabbeinu Yonah set out on his pilgrimage to Tiberias but was detained in Barcelona and Toledo, where he was asked to raise the standards of Torah study and give talmudic discourses. Most prominent among his students was Rabbi Shlomoh ben Aderet, author of *Rashba*, a penetrating commentary on the Talmud.

ספר
שערי תשובה
לרבינו יונה ז"ל
עם
ביאור
זה השער
מהדורה שניה מתוקנת
שנת התש"ל בני ברק

Title page of *Shaarei Teshuvah* by Rabbi Yonah of Gerona.

SELECTIONS FROM RABBEINU YONAH'S COMMENTARY

Excerpt from *Shaarei Teshuvah*, Gate 1, The Eighth Principle: Humility in Actions

Speak in a gentle tone of voice, as it says, "A soft answer turns away anger" (Proverbs 15:1). *Speak in a low voice*—it is the mark of humility, as it says, ". . . and your speech shall be low out of the dust" (Isaiah 29:4). The opposite is said concerning the arrogant rich man—". . . but the rich man answers with impudence" (Proverbs 11:23). *Don't concern yourself with elegant clothes and jewelry*, as it says, "Now take off your jewelry" (Exodus 33:5). It is written about Ahab, ". . . he fasted and lay in sackcloth and walked softly" (I Kings 21:27). God said

about this, "Do you see how Ahab humbles himself before me?" (I Kings 21:27). Now, about the idea of "walking softly." This is the exact opposite of the way in which royalty conducts itself. When a king goes about, he is accompanied by a great deal of pomp and fanfare. *Always keep your eyes downcast*, as it says, "He saves those whose eyes are downcast" (Job 22:29). The [aforementioned outward] signs of humility: a gentle tone of voice, soft speech, and downcast eyes serve to remind you to humble yourself inwardly, in your heart.

Excerpt from *Shaarei Teshuvah*, Gate 2:25

Our rabbis said (*Avot* 3:1): Consider three things and you will not come into the grip of sin: Know whence you came—from a putrid drop; where you are going—to a place of dust, worms, and maggots; and before Whom you will give justification and reckoning—before the King Who reigns over kings, the Holy One, Blessed is He. This can be explained as follows: Reflection on one's origins will induce humility and an aversion to pride. Man's contemplation of his mortal nature will help him recognize the futility of worldly goods and pleasures, that these should be placed in the service of God. The constant awareness of the Day of Judgment will inspire man with the true fear of God.

Excerpt from *Sefer Hayir'ah*

Every morning, as you wake up, you should be filled with a sense of trepidation and overwhelming awe, realizing God's kindness and grace, which He bestowed on you in returning your soul to you. You will then be inspired to praise and love the Creator for giving you renewed strength. Don't remain in bed as lazy people do, but arise swiftly and eagerly, without delay. Now, if you are overcome by an urge to laziness, say to yourself: If a creditor or a client were waiting for me, I would get up immediately, out of respect for that person or because of the anticipated profit. Or imagine there were a fire raging in your neighborhood, or the

king called for your services—you certainly would get up instantly. Then surely you must jump out of bed full of energy when you are about to serve the King of kings, the Holy One, Blessed is He. . . . When you get dressed you don the small tallit (fringed garment) underneath your shirt. The tzitzit (fringes) must always be worn because the mitzvah of tzitzit was given in order to remind a person not to stray after his heart's desires and the cravings of his eyes, for these lead to sin.[4]

Excerpt from commentary on Tractate *Avot*

He said to them[5]: Go out and see which is the proper path a man should follow. Rabbi Eliezer said: A good eye. Rabbi Yehoshua said: A good friend. Rabbi Yose said: A good neighbor. Rabbi Shimon said: One who considers the consequences of an action. Rabbi Eleazar said: A good heart.

(Mishnah Avot 2:13)

Rabbeinu Yonah: *Which is the proper path a man should follow*—meaning, which quality in particular should you try to master. His [Rabbi Yochanan's] premise is that you should select one particular character trait in which to attain perfection. It is better to reach excellence in one single trait than to aspire to many good qualities, failing to master any of them. Perfection in one trait is conducive to acquiring all other good traits. *Rabbi Eliezer said: A good eye*—meaning generosity. Generosity is an excellent and commendable trait . . . that will bring about perfection in all other qualities. *Rabbi Yehoshua said: A good friend*—meaning, it is *you* who should be a good friend to whomever you choose as a friend. Train yourself in being charming and likable. The result will be that everyone will cherish you. *Rabbi Yose said: A good neighbor*—meaning, it is *you* who should be a good neighbor. Once you are a trusted friend to five or eight people, it is only a small step to loving all mankind and finding happiness in developing all good character traits.

RABBI YOSEF ALBO—THE BAAL HA'IKKARIM
רבי יוסף אלבו—בעל העקרים

born: Spain, c. 1380
died: Spain, c. 1440
Popularly referred to as the Baal Ha'ikkarim (author of Sefer Ha'ikkarim*).*
Religious philosopher.

Rabbi Yosef Albo studied under Rabbi Chasdai Crescas and in 1403 served as rabbi in Daroka, a Saragossa district. In 1414 he was one of the main participants in the religious debate in Tartosa, where he courageously defended the Talmud against the vicious attacks by the apostate Joshua Halurki. An expert on philosophy, medicine, and mathematics, he is best known for his famous *Sefer Ha'ikkarim* (Book of Principles),[1] a treatise on the principles of the Jewish faith. He condenses all principles of Judaism to three *ikkarim* (basic ideas). All other principles are derivatives of these three fundamentals. He identifies these secondary principles as "roots." A third category, "branches," are beliefs that are not absolutely binding. The work aims at giving the Torah a philosophical framework, emphasizing the fact that nothing in Judaism contradicts the intellect and logic. Written in a clear style, *Ha'ikkarim* became a favorite to a wide spectrum of readers whose Jewish faith was bolstered by it against the onslaughts of the Church's polemics.

ספר
העקרים
שחבר החכם השלם איש האלהי מרנא ורבנא
כש״ת יוסף אלבו זצ״ל
עם באור טוב ויפה אף נעים, בלשון צח ורחב. חברו האלוף התורני מוהר״ר גדליה בן הח״ר שלמה יצ״ו, וקרא אותו בשם שרשים. ועוד הוסיף בו נופך משלו, קצת ענפים נושאים פרי טוב, מיוסדים על אדני פז בדברים נכבדים ויקרים, במקראי קודש ובמדרשי חז״ל השייכים לענייני הספר, וקרא אותו בשם ענפים. גם הוסיף בו מראה מקום על הפסוקים והמדרשים הבאים בזה הספר. ובהיות שעתה נשלם כל חלקי האילן, והם עקרים שרשים וענפים, ועלין שהן המראה מקומות, על כן קרא הספר הזה בכלל בשם:
עץ שתול
על שם הכתוב והיה כעץ שתול על פלגי מים וגו׳:
ווארשא
בדפוס ר׳ יצחק גאלדמאן נ״י
רוח דעת ויראת ה׳ לפ״ק.
צולם ונדפס מחדש
בעיה״ק ירושלים

Title page of *Sefer Ha'ikkarim* by Rabbi Yosef Albo.

SELECTIONS FROM RABBI YOSEF ALBO'S WRITINGS

Excerpt from *Sefer Ha'ikkarim* 1:110

The Divine faith is based on three fundamental principles: (1) the existence of God, (2) the Divine origin of the Torah, and (3) Divine reward and retribution. There can be no doubt that these three beliefs are required basic conditions of faith in God. The omission of even one of them voids the entire religious belief. If we do not believe in the existence of a God as the source of religion, religion loses its Divine character. Even if we do believe in the existence of God, but do not believe that the Torah is Divine in origin, we negate faith in

God. [And even if we do believe in the existence of God and the Divine origin of the Torah] but do not believe that God rewards and punishes, both physically in this world and spiritually in the World to Come, what would be the purpose of faith in God? If its only purpose were to establish guidelines for social and political interaction, then manmade rules of ethics and etiquette would suffice to accomplish this end. It is clear beyond a doubt that Divinely ordained religion is designed to raise man to a degree of perfection that manmade rules cannot attain—perfection that results from spiritual elevation.

Excerpt from *Sefer Ha'ikkarim* 3:13

It would be appropriate at this time to reflect if the one Divinely ordained religion could, with the passage of time, be transferred to another nation or whether its eternal characteristic precludes this. It is impossible to say that the Divinely ordained religion can ever change, because of He who gave it and because of the nature of the religion itself. It cannot be said that God wants something at one time and at another time wants the opposite. He cannot desire that which is right one time and that which is wrong another time. Why then should God exchange His Divine religion for another? As for the receiver of this religion . . . it cannot be asserted that just as a boy undergoes physical changes as he grows into manhood and from manhood into old age, so do religious principles change as time goes by. . . . The wisdom inherent in religion is not subject to temporal change. Thus, there can be no change in the religion of God, neither on the part of the religion itself nor on the part of the Giver or the receiver.[2]

VII

KABBALAH

Mysticism is generally defined as a profound yearning to come close to God. Kabbalah is much more than that. Kabbalah, meaning "something handed down by tradition," embraces the revealed teachings regarding the mysteries of God and angels and the relationship between the Divine and the life of man and Creation. These are concepts that are beyond the grasp of the human intellect, abstractions our mind cannot comprehend. Kabbalah uses anthropomorphic images, expressing Divine attributes and actions in human terms: God has to make "room" for the world, His Presence "reaches" the world through a series of ten "vessels" or emanations; Kabbalah speaks of God's "Throne," His "Crown," His "Chariot" . . . all symbols for profound metaphysical ideas. The essence of Kabbalah remains shrouded under a cloak of mystery and is accessible to only very few people of great piety and pure spirit. The excerpts we present were chosen because their superficial meaning can be understood; their deeper significance, however, cannot be fathomed.

RABBI SHIMON BEN YOCHAI
רבי שמעון בן יוחאי

Lived in Eretz Yisrael, 2nd century C.E.
Tanna, *author of the Holy Zohar.*

Rabbi Shimon Ben Yochai, the saintly *Tanna* of the mishnaic period, was a disciple of Rabbi Akiva, who was put to death by the Romans for studying Torah. Rabbi Shimon ben Yochai, who attacked the Romans for their cruelty, was himself condemned to death. Together with his son Elazar, he went into hiding in a cave in the mountains near Peki'in in the Galilee, where he stayed for 13 years. The Talmud in *Shabbat* 33b relates that a miracle occurred and a carob tree and a well of water were created for him, to provide him with food and water. During his 13 years in seclusion, Rabbi Shimon ben Yochai wrote the holy Zohar, which forms the basis of Kabbalah. The word *Kabbalah* is a noun meaning "receiving" or "transmission." It is the transmission of this branch of knowledge from the kabbalist sages of one generation to those of the succeeding generation. Kabbalah is sometimes called *Torat CHeN,* CHeN being the acronym of *Chochmah Nisteret* (Hidden Knowledge). Scholars of Kabbalah are referred to as *Yode'ei CHeN* (enlightened in CHeN).

The *Sefer HaZohar* (Book of Splendor) deals with the mystical aspects of the Torah and delves into the hidden depths contained in its holy words and letters. Only men of great piety and holiness are capable of penetrating its mysteries concerning God, Creation, Man, Israel, the Divine Light and its emanations, and many other esoteric themes. This great body of mystical knowledge was given orally by God to the Jewish people on Mount Sinai. With the passage of Israel's tragic history, these teachings were lost to most people, until Rabbi Shimon ben Yochai recorded them in the Zohar. According to the **Ari**, he was granted permission to write the Zohar because, more than any one of his predecessors, he had the ability to clothe and protect its mystical teachings. The Zohar has enriched Jewish spiritual life immeasurably. In the words of **Rabbi Moshe Chaim Luzzatto**, "After the 13 years he spent

ספר הזהר
על חמשה חומשי תורה
מהתנא האלקי
רבי שמעון בן יוחאי ז"ל
עם הפירוש
דרך אמת
ועם הביאורים הנפלאים
הסולם
מבאר ומתרגם כל דברי הזהר במלואם, החל מענינים הפשוטים עד המקומות הסתומים ביותר, ואינו מניח אף מלה אחת בלי פירוש. ומלבד אותם המקומות שבספר הזהר, העוסקים בחכמת הקבלה, הרי הוא ביאור שוה לכל נפש.
מראות הסולם
הוא מלוי אל ביאור הסולם:
אותם המקומות, שצריכים לאריכות יתירה, הוקבע מקומם במראות הסולם.
מסורת הזהר
מראה מקומות לענין המדובר, שנמצא בג' חלקי הזהר, תקוני זהר, זהר חדש ותקונים חדשים.
חלופי גרסאות
מביא כל השינויים שבאו בדפוסים הקודמים משנת שי"ח עד הנה.
לוח השואת הדפים
משוה הדפים בתקוני זהר, זהר חדש ותק"ח של דפוסים שונים, להדפים שב„מסורת הזהר" (נמצא בחלק א')
כדי להקל על המעיין להבין הביאורים במקומות
שעוסקים בחכמת הקבלה, הוספנו בחלק א' הספר
פתיחה לחכמת הקבלה
חלק ז
פרשיות: שמות — בשלח
כל אלו הם ממחבר הספרים המפורסמים „פנים מסבירות" ו„פנים מאירות" על עץ חיים מהאריז"ל „תלמוד עשר ספירות" ט"ז חלקים, „בית שער לכונות" וספר „האילן הקדוש"
הגה"ק מרן הרב יהודה ליב הלוי אשלג זצוק"ל
שנת תשל"ה לפ"ק

Title page of the Zohar, Book of Splendor, a kabbalistic interpretation of the Torah, written by Rabbi Shimon ben Yochai.

טו משפטים

ז) ינקי מגו תוקפא דאמהון. וקב"ה חמי, דאי יתקיימון בעלמא, יבאשון ריחיהון, ויחמצון כחומץ דא. לקיט לון זעירין, ל בעוד דיהבי ריחא.

מג) מה עביד. שביק לון לאתעשקא בידא מ דההיא נ אמה, ודא ס איהי לילית דכיון *) ע דאתייהיבו ברשותה, פ חדאת בההוא ינוקא, צ ועשיקת ליה, ואפיקת ליה מעלמא, ק כד איהו יניק בתוקפא דאמיה.

מד) ואי תימא, ר אינון נשמתין דיעבדון טב לעלמא. לאו הכי. דכתיב אם רעה בעיני אדניה, ש דיחמיץ ההוא גברא בה לבתר יומין, ת אי אתקיים בה. דא אתעשקת, ואחרא לא אתעשקת. ועל אלין כתיב, ל) ואראה את כל העשוקים וגו' והיינו אם רעה בעיני אדניה.

מה) אשר לא יעדה, לא באלף כתיב. אי תימא, דהא בההוא סטרא אחרא, אזמין לה קב"ה מיומא דהות. לא. והשתא בגלגולי טיקלא, לו יעדה בוא"ו. מה דלא הות מקדמת דנא.

מו) והפדה, מאי והפדה. פריק לה קב"ה א השתא, דסלקא ריחא, עד לא תחמיץ, ב וסליק לה לרומי מרומים, במתיבתא דיליה, ואי תימא כיון דאתעשקת מההוא סטרא אחרא, יהיב לה, כמה דאמרו לחסידי שאר עמין, ג ולאינון ד ממזרי ת"ח. אתא קרא ואוכח, לעם נכרי לא ימשול למכרה ודאי, בבגדו בה, דעשיק לה בעשיקו דגלגולא דטיקלא, אלא לישראל ודאי, ולא לאחרא. וכד נפקת מן טיקלא, לא תצא כצאת העבדים, אלא מתעטרא בעטרהא בארמא על רישיה.

מסרת הזהר

ל) (קהלת ד) ח"ב קיא. קיב: קיג. : ח"ג רג. רלד.

דרך אמת ז) קטנים הצריכים עדיין לאמותיהם.

חלופי גרסאות

ל בעי. מ דהאי. נ אימא. ס ל"ג איהי. ע דאתייהיבת. פ אחרא. צ עשוק ול"ג ועשיקת ליה. ק ל"ג כד איהו. ר ל"ג אינון ; דאינון. ש דיוזמון ההוא גבר. ת ואי. א דהשתא. ב וסלקא. ג ולממזרי ול"ג ולאינון ול"ג ת"ח. ד ת"ח ממזרי ; ל"ג ממזרי.

מאמר הסולם הסבא

יבאישו ריחם ויחמצו כחומץ הזה. ע"כ לוקטם כשהם קטנים בעוד שנותנים ריח טוב.

מג) **מה עביד לון** וכו': מה עושה להם הקב"ה, עוזב אותם להתעשק ביד אמה ההיא, חו היא לילית, וכיון שניתנו ברשותה, שמחה בילד ההוא, ועושקת אותו, ומוציאו אותו מן העולם בעוד שהוא יונק מתוקפה של אמו.

מד) **ואי תימא אינון** וכו': ואם תאמר, שאלו הנשמות יעשו טוב בעולם, אינו כן, שכתוב, אם רעה בעיני אדניה, כי איש הזה יוחמץ בה לאחר זמן, אם יתקיים בה. נשמה זו נעשקת, ואחרת אינה נעשקת, ועל אלו כתוב, ואראה את כל העשוקים וגו'. והיינו אם רעה בעיני אדניה.

מה) **אשר לא יעדה**: לא כתוב עם א'. אם תאמר שבצד האחר ההוא נתן אותה הקב"ה מיום שהיתה. לא. כי עתה בגלגולי המאזנים לו יעדה, לו עם ו', מה שלא היה מקודם לכן.

מו) **והפדה, מאי והפדה** וכו': כתוב והפדה, מהו והפדה. ומשיב, פודה אותה הקב"ה עתה, בעוד שמעלית ריח טוב, מטרם שתחמץ, ומעלה אותה לגבהי מרומים אל הישיבה שלו. ואם תאמר, כיון שנעשקה בידי צד האחר ההוא, נותן אותה, כמו שאמרו, (לעיל אות ל"א) לחסידי שאר העמים ולממזרים תלמידי חכמים בא הכתוב, ומוכיח, לעם נכרי לא ימשול למכרה ודאי, בבגדו בה, שעשק אותה בעושק גלגול המאזנים, אלא יתן אותה ודאי לישראל ולא לאחר. וכשיוצאת מן המאזנים, לא תצא כצאת העבדים אלא מתעטרית בעטרה ברמה על ראשה.

557 (דפו"י דף צ"ו ע"א *) דף צ"ו ע"ב)

ואי

A page of text from the Zohar. The commentary *HaSulam* was written by Rabbi Yehudah Leib Ashlag. The text is Exodus 21:8; the discourse is called *Ma'amar Hasaba* and deals with reincarnation and transmigration of the soul.

in the cave, the Gates of Wisdom were opened for him, in order to provide light for all Israel, until the end of time."[1] After being hidden for many years, a Zohar manuscript was discovered and copied by the Kabbalist and traveling scribe, Rabbi Moshe de Leon (Spain, 1250–1305). The first editions of the Zohar appeared in Mantua and Cremona, Italy, in 1558–1560. Later editions were published in Lublin (1623) and Sulzbach (1684). It has been printed more than 65 times, mostly in Poland and Russia. The very obscure Aramaic of the Zohar has been explained and translated into Hebrew by Rabbi Yehudah Leib Ashlag.[2] Special mention should be made of two sections of the Zohar, the *Idra Rabba* in the portion of *Naso* and the *Idra Zuta* in the portion of *Ha'azinu*. These sections are expositions on the nature of the emanations. They are incomparable gems of holiness and purity.

The Ten Sefirot, the spheres or vessels through which the Light of the Creator is emanated to man (in descending order):

כתר עליון	Keter Elyon	Supreme Crown
חכמה	Chochmah	Wisdom of God
בינה	Binah	Intelligence of God
גדולה־חסד	Gedulah or Chesed	Greatness or Love, Mercy of God
גבורה־דין	Gevurah or Din	Power or Judgment of God
תפארת־רחמים	Tiferet or Rachamim	Beauty or Compassion of God
נצח	Netzach	Lasting Endurance of God
הוד	Hod	Majesty of God
יסוד	Yesod	Foundation of all active forces in God
מלכות	Malchut	Kingdom of God

The Five Levels of the Soul (in ascending order):

נפש	Nefesh	Lowest of the five levels of the soul
רוח	Ru'ach	Second level
נשמה	Neshamah	Third level
חיה	Chayah	Fourth level
יחידה	Yechidah	Highest level of the soul. Total union with the Light of God. A level unattainable until the coming of the Messiah.

SELECTIONS FROM RABBI SHIMON BEN YOCHAI'S WRITINGS

Excerpt from Zohar, *Bereishit*

Rabbi Yitzchak said: The Holy One, Blessed is He, showed Adam the image of all generations to come, all the wise men of the world, and all the kings that were to rule over Israel. When he beheld the life of David, his birth and his death, he said, "Let me add a number of my years to his life." Thereupon, seventy years were subtracted from Adam's life and added to David's. It was for this reason that David sang praises, saying, "For You have gladdened me, God, with Your deeds, at the works of Your hands I sing a glad song" (Psalm 92:5). [David means to say] "Who is the source of my gladness?—It is Adam, who is the work of Your hands."

Excerpt from Zohar, *Pinchas*

David, as he was walking along the banks of the river, recited the following verse: "Surely I have stilled and quieted my soul, like a weaned child with his mother; my soul is with me like a weaned child" (Psalm 131:2). Then he said, "Master of the Universe, is there another person in the entire world who thanks and exalts his Creator as I do?" Just then a frog appeared. It said, "David, don't be haughty. I am superior to you. I sacrificed my life for God's Holy Name, as it says, "The Nile will swarm with frogs"[3] (Exodus 7:28).

What's more, I praise my Creator incessantly, day and night." At that moment David said, "Lord, my heart is not haughty, nor are my eyes lofty" (Psalm 131:1).

Excerpt from Zohar, *Bereishit* 335

When Noach was born, he was given his name, because Noach suggests consolation (Noach and *nechamah*—consolation—are etymologically related). It was hoped that God would send His consolation. But the Holy One, Blessed is He, did otherwise. He brought the Flood upon them, since he had hoped that they would repent. By inverting the letters of Noach, the word *chen*—graciousness—is obtained, as is indicated by the verse, "Noach found *chen*—favor, graciousness—in the eyes of God" (Genesis 6:8). Rabbi Yosi comments, "*Chen* is synonymous with Noach, because their letters are identical. The names of the righteous produce good things for them, but the names of the wicked beget evil for them. The inversion of the letters of Noach's name produced *chen*, a beneficial result. But with Er, Judah's first-born son, the inversion resulted in *ra*—evil—as it is written, "Judah's first-born Er was evil in God's eyes . . ." (Genesis 38:7).

Excerpt from Zohar, *Lech Lecha* 125

Rabbi Yitzchak opened his discourse, saying, "A righteous man will flourish like a date palm, like a cedar in Lebanon he will grow" (Psalm 92:13). [He asked], Why is the righteous man likened to a date palm? [He answered]: When a date palm is cut down, it takes seventy years for it to grow back. The same holds true for a righteous man. When the world has lost a tzaddik, seventy years will pass before another tzaddik will appear to take his place. The seventy years are the seven *sefirot*[4] of *Chochmah* (Wisdom), *Gevurah* (Power), *Tiferet* (Beauty), *Netzach* (Victory), *Hod* (Glory), *Yesod* (Foundation), and *Malchut* (Kingdom), each of which consists of "ten." Since perfection is achieved only in *Malchut*, the seventh *sefirah*, the required time is seventy years.

Excerpt from Zohar, *Chayei Sarah* 121

How fortunate are *ba'alei teshuvah* (returnees to Torah observance)! In one day, in one hour, in one instant they become close to the Holy One, Blessed is He, something not even a perfect tzaddik can achieve. Only after many years does he reach the nearness of God. Abraham did not reach this lofty stage until he was very old. Similarly, about David it is written, "Now King David was old, well advanced in years . . ." (I Kings 1:1). But a *ba'al teshuvah* can enter immediately and attach himself to the Holy One, Blessed is He.

Excerpt from Zohar, *Chayei Sarah* 122

Rabbi Yosi said: We have learned that in a place where *ba'alei teshuvah* are standing, not even a perfect tzaddik is permitted to stand. *Ba'alei teshuvah* are closer to the King than anyone else. They pray with more sincere concentration and intense fervor to draw the flow of Abundance from above, thereby drawing nearer to the King.

Excerpt from Zohar, *Chayei Sarah* 119

Abraham drew near to the Holy One, Blessed is He. He yearned for this closeness all the days of his life. But Abraham did not achieve this closeness suddenly, in one day. Through his good deeds he advanced gradually, day by day, to ever higher levels, until he reached the level of perfection.

Excerpt from Zohar, *Vayetzei* 48

Let us consider the phrase "And he dreamed . . ."[5] (Genesis 28:12). Why is it that God appeared to Jacob only in a dream? After all, Jacob was the paragon of the Patriarchs, and he had this vision in Eretz Yisrael, a place eminently suited for Divine revelation. The reason that Jacob's vision occurred in a dream is that, at that moment, Jacob was not married, and he was therefore an incomplete human being. Moreover, Isaac was still living at the time of his dream, and Jacob's hour of pre-eminence had not yet arrived. He therefore saw God in a dream rather than experiencing a vision in a wakeful state.

Excerpt from Zohar, *Vayetzei* 49

Later, upon [Jacob's] returning to Eretz Yisrael, accompanied by his children and his wives, it says, "God appeared to Jacob and blessed him" (Genesis 35:9) and furthermore, "God spoke to Israel in a night vision" (Genesis 46:2). Here the vision did not come to him in

a dream. He had reached a loftier level suitable for experiencing a vision in a wakeful state.

Excerpt from Zohar, *Vayeshev* 253

Consider how the Holy One, Blessed is He, causes the wheels of fortune to turn in the world, for the sole purpose of elevating the righteous. In order to bring about Joseph's rise to power, He provoked Pharaoh's anger at his servants, as it is written, ". . . the Egyptian king's wine steward and baker offended their master, the king of Egypt" (Genesis 40:1). All these events were generated as a means of elevating the righteous Joseph to power. Now reflect about this. It was a dream that caused Joseph's decline [as he was sold into slavery as a result of his brothers' jealousy, which was prompted by his dreams], and it was a dream [Pharaoh's dream] that propelled him to mastery over his brothers and dominion over the entire world.

Excerpt from Zohar, *Beshalach* 193

"And Israel saw the great power that God had unleashed against Egypt, and the people were in awe of God . . ." (Exodus 14:31). There seems to be no rational connection between the two clauses of this verse. It appears as though their "seeing the great power" was the motive for their "being in awe of God." Are we to infer from this that before this event they were not in awe of God? Rabbi Yehudah offers the following answer: The old father Jacob, who descended into exile together with his children and [in a spiritual sense] suffered with them through the exile, actually saw the revenge and the mighty deeds the Holy One, Blessed is He, performed in Egypt. That is what is meant by "And Israel saw"—it is referring literally to Israel, meaning Jacob.[6]

Excerpt from Zohar, *Vayechi* 241

Granted that Adam sinned, but the entire world? In what sense did it sin? Why was death decreed for all creation? You certainly cannot say that the whole world ate from this tree, and therefore death was imposed on it. This simply is not so. This is what happened. When Adam was created, he stood erect. All the creatures of the world saw him and stood in awe of him. They were drawn to him as servants are to a king. He said to them, "You and I, let us bow down and kneel before God, our

Maker" (Psalm 95:6). But when they saw Adam bowing down to "that place" [the "left side," the side of evil] and attaching himself to it, they all followed him. This is what brought death to the entire world.

Excerpt from Zohar, *Vayechi* 242

Adam thereby became subject to many changeable aspects: justice alternating with mercy, death alternating with life. His choice of the "left side" caused this inconstancy. That is the meaning of "the flaming sword that revolves" (Genesis 3:24)—it revolves from one extreme to the other: from good to evil, from mercy to justice, from peace to war. In a general sense, it revolves from good to evil, for it says, "But from the Tree of Knowledge of good and evil do not eat" (Genesis 2:17).

Excerpt from Zohar, *Vayechi* 244

Consider this. Concerning the World to Come it is written, "For as the days of a tree shall be the days of My people" (Isaiah 65:22). "The days of a tree" refers to "that Tree," the Tree of Life, about which it says, "He will swallow up death forever and the Lord God will wipe away tears from all faces" (Isaiah 25:8), for the Tree of Life is not subject to change or to death.

Excerpt from Zohar, *Shemot* 188

"And she kept him hidden for three months" (Exodus 2:2). What lesson can we learn from "three months"? Said Rabbi Yehudah: This is an allusion to the "third month" mentioned in the verse, "In the third month after the Israelites left Egypt . . ." (Exodus 19:1) (the opening verse of the story of the Giving of the Ten Commandments at Sinai). The "three months" are to be understood as follows. Moses' greatness in the knowledge of Sublime Splendor (the inner Truth of the Torah) was not recognized until that "third month," when the Torah was given through him and the Divine Presence came to rest on him in full view of all Israel. For this reason it says, "She could no longer hide him" (Exodus 2:3)—until that moment [of the Revelation on Sinai] no one knew that God had spoken to him, but at Sinai it says, "Moses spoke and God replied with a Voice" (Exodus 19:19).

Excerpt from Zohar, *Yitro* 126

What is written concerning the creation of man? [Scripture says,] "You clothed me with skin and flesh" (Job 10:11). If this is true, what, then, is man himself? If you would say that man is nothing but skin, flesh, bones, and veins, that is not so. For surely man is nothing but the soul. When [Job] speaks of skin and flesh, bones and veins, all these are only clothing. They are man's outer garments, but not man himself. When a person dies, he divests himself of the garments he wore.

Excerpt from Zohar, *Yitro* 127

The skin in which man is clothed, as well as his bones and veins, all are a reflection of the mystery of the "*Chochmah Elyonah*," the Higher Wisdom. [That is to say], the skin is a reflection of a spiritual concept; it is comparable to the "curtain" about which is written, "He stretched heaven like a curtain" (Psalm 104:2).

Excerpt from Zohar, *Yitro* 128

His bones and veins are the *merkavot*, the "chariots," the metaphysical inner core, meaning that the veins are the soul of the garment; the bones represent the life-force of the garment that surrounds their inner core, the *sod adam ha'elyon*, the mystery of spiritual Man.

Excerpt from Zohar, *Yitro* 129

The mundane world parallels the spiritual world. Man stands at the inner center. His bones and veins represent the *merkavot*; the flesh covering the bones, and the skin, in turn, covering the flesh, are analogous to the heavens that cover all. It is all a "*sod*" (mystery), the lower, mundane *sod* a reflection of the higher, spiritual *sod*. The garments upon garments are a reflection of the heavens above heavens. That is the meaning of the verse, "God created man in His image, in the image of God" (Genesis 1:27). The mystery of man below is identical with the mystery of above.

Excerpt from Zohar, *Yitro* 550

"Honor your father and your mother" (Exodus 20:12)—Honor them by showing them all forms of respect: Make them happy by performing good deeds, as it is written, "The father of the righteous will greatly rejoice" (Proverbs 23:24). That is the meaning of honoring your father and mother.

Excerpt from Zohar, *Yitro* 556

Just as a person honors God, so must he honor his father and mother, for they are in a partnership with God. [There are three partners involved in the creation of a human being: God, his father, and his mother. His parents give him his body, while God gives him his soul.]

Excerpt from Zohar, *Yitro* 557

"You will then live long" (Exodus 20:12) [literally, that your days may be lengthened]—Because there are days in the Higher World, meaning the seven *sefirot* (emanations) of *Chochmah*—Wisdom; *Gevurah*—Power of Judgment; *Tiferet*—Beauty; *Netzach*—Victory; *Hod*—Glory; *Yesod*—Foundation; *Malchut*—Kingdom. On these *sefirot* man's life in this world is dependent. . . .

Excerpt from Zohar, *Devarim*

The people of the surrounding communities assembled, each demanding that the rabbi be buried in their midst. Then, the bed upon which the body lay rose up and flew through the air, preceded by a torch of fire, until it reached the cave at Meron. Here it descended, and everyone knew that Rabbi Shimon had reached his final resting place. All this took place on the thirty-third day of the Omer, which is the eighteenth day of the month of Iyar.[7]

Excerpt from Zohar, *Shemot* 14b

Such was the [overwhelming spirit] of Rabbi Shimon ben Yochai; when he began to open his mouth to discourse on themes of the Torah, there was total silence, to the extent that not a sound was heard in all the heavens above and below. Commentary by Rabbi Moshe Chaim Luzzatto in *"Adir Bamarom"*: "The perfection of Torah is absolute; in the presence of its Truth every voice is stilled." Compare *Midrash Rabbah* 29:9, "When God gave the Torah on Mount Sinai, not one bird chirped, not one ox howled—all stood in silence."

Excerpt from Zohar, *Emor* 105b

In the days of Rabbi Shimon ben Yochai a man would say to his fellow, "Open your mouth and let your words shine forth." Commentary by Rabbi Moshe Chaim Luzzatto in *"Adir Bamarom"*: When the light of the great mystical Truth reaches this world, it is in danger of being captured by the *"sitra achra"*—"the Realm of the Other Side," the world of Evil. To prevent this from happening, the Light is not disseminated. There is, however, one channel through which this Light radiates from the atmosphere of Gan Eden to the atmosphere of this world, a channel that is safe from any peril. . . . The sages in the days of Rabbi Shimon ben Yochai were acquainted with this channel. The study of *sod*—mystical secrets—therefore, did not place them in jeopardy.

Excerpt from Zohar, *Vayikra* 28b

The Holy One, Blessed is He, decreed that the inner Light of the Torah, the very essence of its mysteries, be concealed in the mystery of *"Or–Raz."*[8] He revealed to Israel only the simple meaning of the Torah text—the *peshat*—in the mystery of *"ner mitzvah"* ("the mitzvah is a lamp"). Commentary by Rabbi Moshe Chaim Luzzatto, *"Adir Bamarom"*: *The mystery of "ner mitzvah"*—This means that the laws of the practical mitzvot contain a diminished light, as it is written, "For the commandment (mitzvah) is a lamp, and the Torah is light." The mitzvah aspect of the Torah will be revealed, but the great *or*, the inner light of the Torah, will be concealed (since *"or"* [light] equals *raz* [mystery]).

RABBI YEHUDAH HECHASID
רבי יהודה החסיד

born: Speyer, Germany, c. 1150
died: Regensburg, Germany, 1217
Ethicist, kabbalist.

Rabbi Yehudah HeChasid's father, who led a famous yeshivah in Speyer, instructed him in the kabbalistic teachings. Although he possessed vast talmudic knowledge, he emphasized piety and the mystical meaning of prayer and led a life of self-denial and fasting. His pureness of heart and fear of God are evident in his work, *Sefer Chasidim,*[1] which was highly acclaimed. It covers all aspects of Jewish life. Capturing the student's attention with parables and anecdotes taken from daily life, he imparts the most profound concepts of ethics, prayer with concentration, philosophical themes such as reward and punishment and Divine justice, and laws for day-to-day living, such as Shabbat and Festival laws. The work has remained a favorite classic. Here and there we find in *Sefer Chasidim* instructions based on Kabbalah, rather than Halachah, that have gained acceptance, such as the custom to refrain from marrying a woman with the same name as one's mother. The beautiful hymn, *"Shir HaKavod"*—Song of Glory—beginning with the words *Anim Zemirot* (Pleasant Psalms), has been attributed to Rabbi Yehudah HeChasid. It is recited at the conclusion of the morning service on Shabbat and Festivals. Because of the hymn's great holiness, the Ark is opened. A number of Rabbi Yehudah HeChasid's writings still exist in manuscript form.

שכד ספר חסידים

אחותה [ח] לפי שאמרו חכמים אחד ממאה אין זוכין להוליד בנים משתי אחיות. אבל אם לא הניחה בנים אם יקח לאה אז יוליד ממנה לפי שהראשונה אחותה לא ילדה לו. וכן אם מתה לאדם בתו וילדה לו אשתו בת אחרת אם הראשונה הניחה בן או בת או יקרא פעם שניה בשם המתה כיון שיש לה זרע ואם אין לה זרע לא יקרא השניה בשם המתה ויהיו לו בנים מן השניה [ט] כן ענין השער וצריך רחמים גדולים להפוך השער מעגינו [י]. וכן ב׳ אחים אחד נשא אשה אמר לו אחיו עסוק שיתנו לי אחות אשת אחי או בתה או אמה. או האב לקח אשה ואמר הבן עסוק שיתן לי אחותה או בתה כל הירא דבר ה׳ לא יעסוק בזה. כתיב (תהלים כ״ה י״ב) מי [זה] האיש ירא השם יורנו בדרך יבחר וכתיב (קהלת ט׳ ד׳) כי מי אשר יבחר אל כל החיים יש בטחון יחבר קרי יבחר כתיב (ב) כיון שאמרו [יא] לשלישי לא תנשא או לרביעי מר כדאית ליה ומר כדאית ליה אם עבר ונשא אשה שבעליה מתו הרי עתיד ליתן את הדין שהוא מסתכן בעצמו דכתיב (בראשית ט׳ ה׳) ואך את דמכם לנפשותיכם אדרוש והוא המית את עצמו [יב].

תעח וכן יש דברי׳ שאמרו חכמים למה בניו של אדם מתי׳ [א] לשוא הכיתי את בניכם מוסר לא לקחו אכלה חרבכם נביאכם כאריה משחית (ירמי׳ ב׳ ל׳) הרי ת״ח היודע זה ועובר עליו הרי עתיד ליתן את הדין עליו שגרם מיתה לבניו [ב], ומה שאמרו [ג] הקובר את בניו מוחלין לו עונותיו שמקיים את הדברים שבנים מתים עליהם ולא מי שעובר עליהם ואמרו [ד] תינוק בית אשה סימן, אשה לשלישי או לרביעי לא תנשא אם מתו בעליה זה אחר זה לאחר שבאו עליה [ה] ומתו בלא בנים [ו] או מיד לאחר בעילה כמו בער ואונן שלא עכבו אצל תמר [ז], ותינוק

ברית עולם

שבתי וראה דאעיקרא קשיא ליתא דבו בפרק מרבית העם שנות דור ודור נהגו זיווגים אלו ושכיחי טובא ולא היה עה״ר בזה אך עתה דלא אשתכח הרוצה לעשות זיווג בזה יש בו עה״ר ושומר נפשו ירחק מזה דאיכא עה״ר ורו״ק.

פירוש

יהי׳. (ב) צ״ל יכחר קרי וחבר כתיב כיון וכו׳ ור״ל שמרומז בזה מי שרוצה לחבר וליקח אשה ובחר אל כל החיים ולא יקח אשה שמתו בעליה.

מקור חסד

[ח] אזהרה כ״ו אות לח. ובחס״ל מכנה״ג אהע״ז סי׳ ס״ב ועליות אליהו הערה נ״א. [ט] במילי דחסידותא דאם אינו השם ההוא ממש אין קפידא, וביותר במה שרבים נוהגים ליתן שם לנקבה ע״ש זכר בשינוי קצת אח״כ אין חשש מלקרא בשם הזכר כסדרו, ואם מוסיף לו עוד שם מצטרף אין חשש, ועי׳ שו״ת בית נפתלי סי׳ סג—סד. [י] ע׳ שואל ומשיב מה״ת ח״ג סי׳ ס״ו ושו״ת בית יצחק יר״ד ח״ב סי׳ קס״ג. [יא] יבמות ס״ד ב. [יב] ע׳ בבא קמא צ״א ב.

תעח. [א] ע׳ שבת ל״ב ב ת״ר בעון נדרים כו׳ ר״י הנשיא אומר בעון ביטול תורה כו׳. [ב] ע׳ בתנא דב״א פ״י לא די לבן אדם שמתו בניו בחייו אלא שדנין אותו עליהם כו׳ ועמש״כ להלן סי׳ תשס״ז. [ג] ברכות ה׳ ע״ב. [ד] ע׳ חולין צ״ה ב. [ה] ע׳ יבמות ס״ד ב רה״א מעיין גורם ורא״א מזל גורם, מאי בינייהו, איכא בינייהו דאירסה ומית, והנה קיי״ל כר״א שמזל גורם וא״כ גם באירסה ומת אסור, ורבינו כתב אך לאחר שבא עליה הרי דפסק כמ״ד מעיין גורם ועי׳ שו״ת חוות יאיר סי׳ קצ״ז. [ו] ע׳ בס׳ נוצר חסד מהגה״צ מהרי״א מקומרנא באבות פ״ג שאם יש לה בנים מבעלה לא הוית קטלנית, ויעוין בשו״ת שואל ומשיב מה״ת ח״א ס״ס י״ד, ושם ח״ג סי׳ פ״ז ובשו״ת בית יצחק אהע״ז ח״א סי׳ מ״ד ומנחת פתים אהע״ז סי׳ ט, ובהערות שבסה״ס צור יעקב אות צ״ג (ע׳ רס״ג). [ז] ע׳ בראשית רבה פ׳ פ״ה, ויעוין

Page of *Sefer Chasidim*, by Rabbi Yehudah HeChasid. From the new annotated edition published by Mossad Harav Kook.

SELECTIONS FROM RABBI YEHUDAH HECHASID'S WRITINGS

Excerpt from *Sefer Chasidim,* par. 7

What is the basic principle of piety? A man who is drawn to living a life of piety will encounter difficulties because people will scorn and humiliate him. They will say things to hurt him, and they will remind him of past misdeeds. These scoffers should not cause him to abandon his resolve to follow the ways of chasidut (piety). He should make the change to devoutness gradually, one small step each day, ignoring all sneers and taunts. Scripture says about this man, "If you are wise, you are wise for yourself" (Proverbs 9:12). But about those who mock him it says, "Those who make a man an offender by words" (Isaiah 29:21), meaning, by speaking words of scorn against people who perform mitzvot. It is a grave sin to say to a *ba'al teshuvah* (a returnee to Torah practice), "Remember the things you used to do." Having renounced his previous way of life and having chosen the life of piety, he should disregard being made their laughingstock. He should be aware that his humiliation is a source of great merit for him; that the pure fear of God has entered his heart, purifying his heart and body of all evil; that Heaven is helping him to buttress his fear of God, as our sages say, "He who comes to cleanse himself receives Divine aid."[2] Heaven will grant him the means to attain complete repentance.

Excerpt from *Sefer Chasidim,* par. 117

A Jew who hears that people are taking him for a non-Jew must declare, "I am a Jew." We learn this from Moses. He said to God, "Since I do not merit to enter the Promised Land, let my bones be buried there, just as Joseph's bones are buried in the Land of Israel." Said the Holy One, Blessed is He, "He who acknowledges his nationality will be buried in his country. Joseph, who declared 'For I was kidnapped from the land of the Hebrews' (Genesis 40:15), is buried in the Land of Israel. But you remained silent when you heard it said about yourself, 'An Egyptian rescued us from the shepherds' (Exodus 2:19).[3] You did not say, 'I am a Hebrew.' Therefore, your bones will not enter the Land of Israel."

Excerpt from *Sefer Chasidim,* par. 677

[What about] a person who is attacked by bandits and hold-up men who are trying to rob him of his possessions? He knows that he cannot overwhelm them, but he has a chance to escape. If this man says, "Since they are taking all my possessions, my life has become worthless," and does nothing to save himself; or an avenger who is killed while pursuing a murderer who is stronger than he; or a person whose house is on fire, and he risks his life entering the blazing flames in order to save his possessions; all these are in violation of the commandment against suicide, "Only of the blood of your own lives will I demand an account" (Genesis 9:5).

Excerpt from *Sefer Chasidim,* par. 377

If a goodhearted person married a convert who is goodhearted, modest, and benevolent, then it is better to marry one of their children than to marry a Jew who does not possess these qualities, because the offspring of the convert will be tzaddikim (righteous) and good people.

Excerpt from *Sefer Chasidim,* par. 514

It is written, "If not, say so, and I will go to the right or to the left" (Genesis 24:49).[4] This verse teaches us that if someone is courting a girl who rejects his advances and does not wish to marry him and tells him so, he should not pursue the matter, but should immediately turn his attention to another prospective match.

Excerpt from *Sefer Chasidim,* par. 1062

If you see two people whispering into each other's ear, control your curiosity and don't ask them what secrets they are telling each other, lest you make liars out of them. If they would have wanted you to know, they would have told you. Since obviously they don't wish to share their confidences with you, they will tell you a lie.

Excerpts from his Will and Testament:

12. Don't visit the same grave twice on one day.
15. Don't weep excessively for a deceased person. There are three days for weeping, seven days for eulogizing, thirty days for mourning . . . beyond that God says, "Don't be more merciful than I am."
26. A person should not marry his deceased wife's sister, unless he has small children and she has pity on them.
30. Don't celebrate the weddings of two of your children on the same day.

35. You should not designate the same person as *sandek* (the one who holds the baby during circumcision) for more than one of your children.

45. Don't cut down a fruit-bearing tree.
46. Don't write in a book, "This book belongs to . . ." Just write your name, omitting "This book belongs to . . ."

RABBI MOSHE CORDOVERO—THE REMAK
רבי משה קורדובירו—רמ״ק

born: location—? date—1522
died: Safed, Israel, 1570
Kabbalist. Popularly known as the Remak, the initials of Rabbi Moshe Cordovero.

Rabbi Moshe Cordovero's birthplace is unknown, but the name Cordovero indicates that his family originated in Cordova and fled Spain during the expulsion of 1492. The Remak lived in Safed, studying under **Rabbi Yosef Karo,** the author of *Shulchan Aruch,* and receiving kabbalistic instruction from his brother-in-law, the famous kabbalist and poet, Rabbi Shelomoh Alkabetz, composer of "*Lechah Dodi.*" Rabbi Moshe Cordovero established a *bet midrash* (house of learning) for Kabbalah, and one of his students was **Rabbi Chaim Vital.** Considering the Zohar to be the fundamental book of Kabbalah, he dedicated his life to expounding its concepts. His first major work was *Pardes Rimonim.*[1] It is a classic book that explains the kabbalistic system. *Or Yakar,* his commentary on the Zohar is sixteen volumes long and exists only in manuscript form. *Elimah Rabbati*[2] is a treatise on kabbalistic problems. *Tomer Devorah*[3] is a seminal work on ethics in harmony with Kabbalah. Rabbi Moshe Cordovero was the foremost kabbalist of his era, revered for his superior knowledge as well as for his piety, his pureness of heart, and his otherworldly saintliness. **Rabbi Yitzchak Luria,** the **Ari,** was one of his great admirers, referring to him as Moreinu veRabbeinu, our Master and Teacher.

ספר
שיעור קומה
להרב הגאון החסיד והעניו אור עולם מופת הדור
הקדוש המקובל אלהי מוהר״ר משה קורדאווירו
זצלה״ה זיע״א, מצפת תובב״א.
מקום אשר עמד אדמת קודש, והאיר לעולם באור
זך ובהיר כעצם השמים לטוהר, ונותה אור זוהר,
אשר היה יותר משלש מאות שנה נגוז ולא יצא
לאור עולם עד היום הזה.
בעהמ״ח ספר הפרד״ס, אילימה רבתי, ועוד ספרים.
יצא לאור במצות ובהוצאות הרה״ח מוהר״ר דוב זאב
ב״ר יוסף ז״ל. וחתנו האברך המופלג מוהר״ר יהושע
ב״ר בנימין הלוי נ״י, גרייפער.
נדפס פה עיר הקדושה
ירושלים
שנת תשכ״ו לפ״ק

Title page of *Shiur Komah* (first published in Warsaw, 1883), a work explaining kabbalistic concepts. One of many books written by Rabbi Moshe Cordovero, the Remak. The letters following the word *miTzefat,* "of Safed," are the abbreviation of *tibane vetikonen bimeherah beyamenu,* "May it (Safed) be rebuilt speedily in our days."

SELECTIONS FROM THE REMAK'S WRITINGS

Excerpt from *Tomer Devorah,* Chap. 2

Man, in his effort to emulate his Creator in His secret aspect of *Keter* ("Crown"), must exhibit certain fundamental traits. The one all-encompassing trait is that of humility. It is rooted in the Divine emanation of *Keter,* which descends and gazes downward . . . likewise, man should not arrogantly look skyward, but,

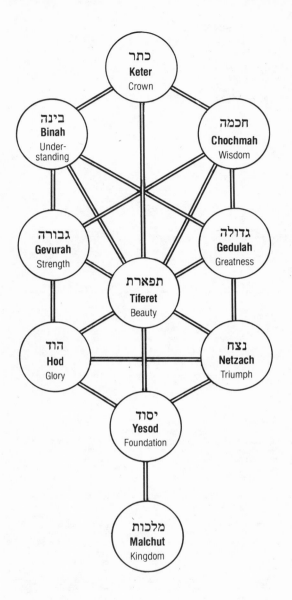

Illustration from *Pardes Rimonim*, Gate of the *Tzinorot* (Conduits), Representation of the Spiritual *Sefirot* (Emanations).

imbued with a sense of inner shame, should always keep his eyes downcast. Generally, the trait of humility becomes manifest in the way a person holds his head. A head held high is the mark of an arrogant person, whereas a poor man always lowers his head. There is no one more humble and forbearing than our God in His Divine attribute of *keter,* which is the essence of compassion. You should always keep your ears open to hear good things. False or disparaging remarks should never enter them. Emulating Divine "Hearing," you should listen only to favorable and beneficial things, but close your ears to tidings that provoke anger. Let your eyes never gaze on anything disgraceful, but keep them wide open, looking on those less fortunate with all the compassion you can muster. When you see a destitute person in distress, don't look away; be inspired to have mercy on him. Let your face always be smiling and greet everyone with a cheerful countenance. Let only good tidings and Torah words emanate from your mouth. Never say anything shameful. Never let a curse, words of anger and resentment, or idle talk emerge from your mouth.

Excerpt from *Tomer Devorah*, Chap. 4

How can you emulate the Divine quality of *Chochmah* (Wisdom)? God's wisdom permeates all Existence, as the psalmist expresses it: "How great are Your works, O God, You make them all with wisdom" (Psalms 104:24). Similarly, you should impart your wisdom to others by sharing your knowledge and insight with your fellowmen, teaching each individual according to his intelligence.

RABBI YITZCHAK LURIA ASHKENAZI—ARI HAKADOSH

רבי יצחק לוריא אשכנזי—האר״י הקדוש

born: Jerusalem, Israel, 1534
died: Safed, Israel, 1572
Reverently known as Ari HaKadosh, the holy Ari (from the initials of Ashkenazi, *Rabbi* Yitzchak, *or* Ari, *meaning Lion). Kabbalist.*

After the Ari's father's early death, his mother moved to Cairo to be with her brother, Rabbi Mordechai Francis, who raised the young boy. He studied Torah and Kabbalah under Rabbi David ben Zimra, author of the famous *Teshuvot Radbaz* (Responsa) and Rabbi Bezalel Ashkenazi, author of *Shittah Mekubetzet*, a basic text for talmudic scholars. After his marriage, the Ari lived the life of a hermit, refining his character, rising to such heights of sanctity as to be worthy of Divine revelation. In 1570, after spending twenty years in seclusion, the Ari moved to Safed, the center of kabbalistic study at that time. He wanted to study under the foremost kabbalist, **Rabbi Moshe Cordovero, the Remak,** author of *Or Yakar*, a commentary on the Zohar. The Remak died shortly after meeting the Ari, who now attracted a circle of devoted disciples. The Ari did not write down any of his teachings. These were recorded by his disciples, mainly by his foremost pupil, **Rabbi Chaim Vital**, in his work *Etz Hachaim*.[1] The Ari's thoughts, as they emerge in *Etz Hachaim,* are based on the Zohar, dealing with such esoteric concepts as *tzimtzum*—the voluntary restriction of the Divine Light; *klippot*—shells, evil "covers" of man's spiritual core, that form a barrier between man and God; and the four worlds—*Atzilut, Beriah, Yetzirah,* and *Asiyah*.[2] A number of very popular *zemirot* (songs to be sung at the Shabbat table) are attributed to the Ari: *"Azameir Bishvachin," "Asadeir Lis'udata,"* and *"Benei Heichala"* in Aramaic, and the famous *"Yom Zeh leYisrael Orah veSimchah"* (Hebrew), all interwoven with mystical allusions. These themes are far beyond the comprehension of all but a small number of truly saintly men who live in each generation. (*For excerpts, see p. 226.*)

ספר

שער רוח הקדש

דרוש א א)

יבאר בו ענין הנבואה ורוח הקדש מה ענינם, וגם יבאר ענין המדרגות שלהם. דע, כי בהיות האדם צדיק וחסיד, ועוסק בתורה, ומתפלל בכונה, ודאי הוא שאין לך דבר שאין לו ממש, כי אפילו אותו הקול היוצא, ע״י הבאת המסה אינו לבטלה, כנזכר, בזוהר פרשת שלח לך. ב) ואין הדבר ההוא הולך לבטלה ח״ו, אך בודאי הוא שממנו נבראים מלאכים, ורוחין קדישין, קיימין ועימדין כנזכר בפרשת בשלח דף נ״ס. וכמשז״ל, כל העושה מצוה אחת קנה לו פרקליט אחד וכו׳, ג) כי מדבור האדם, נוצרים מלאכים טובים או רעים, כפי דבורו. וכמו שכתב בתיקונין, כי כשהאדם עוסק בתורה, אותם הקולות וההבלים דנפקי מפומיה, נעשים מרכבה אל נשמות הצדיקים הראשונים, לרדת למטה ללמוד תורה לאדם ההוא. וכנזכר בסבא דמשפטים דף ק׳ ע״ב, ענין ההבל והדבור והקול כמו שיתבאר ענין שלשתם לקמן בע״ה.

אמנם הכל הוא כפי מעשה האדם, כי אם אותה התורה שיעסוק בה, קורא אותה לשמה, יהיה המלאך הנברא משם, קדוש הוא מאד, ועליון מאד, ונאמן בכל דבריו באמת גמור. וכן אם קורא אותה בלי שבושים וטעיות, יהיה המלאך ההוא בלי טעות, ויהיה נאמן בכל דבריו. וכן המצוה שעושה האדם, אם היא כתקנה נעשה ממנה מלאך קדוש מאד. וכמ״ש ז״ל, כל העושה מצוה אחת, קנה לו פרקליט אחד וכו׳. וכפי מה שחסר מאותה מצוה, כן יחסר אור המלאך ההוא. ואמנם ודאי הוא, שגדול הוא כח המלאך הנעשה מעסק התורה, מכח (המלאך) הנעשה ע״י אותה המצוה, ואין להאריך בפרטים אלו.

והנה ענין המלאכים המתגלים אל (בני) האדם, ומודיעים אותם עתידות, וסודות, ונקראים בספרים מגידים. כי אלו הם נבראים, מעסק האדם בתורה ובמצות. ויש אנשים שאין המגידים הנזכרים מתגלים להם כלל, ויש מי שמתגלים להם, והכל הוא כפי בחי׳ נשמותיהם, או כפי מעשיהם, ואין להאריך בזה. ויש מגידים אמיתיים לגמרי, והם הנעשים מן התורה או

הגהות ומראה מקומות

א) שער היחודים פרקים א׳ ב׳ ג׳.
ב) דף קסח: קסט.
ג) אבות פ״ד מ״ג. שער הפסוקים פרשת וירא דף נ״ד ט״ב ד״ה וז״ס.

Page of *Shaar Ruach Hakodesh,* the Ari's teachings; this page contains a discourse on celestial beings.

RABBI CHAIM VITAL
רבי חיים ויטאל

born: Safed, Israel, 1543
died: Damascus, Syria, 1620
Kabbalist.

Rabbi Chaim's father, Rabbi Yosef Calabrisi, was a celebrated *sofer* (religious scribe), noted for his exceptional piety. Rabbi Chaim studied Torah under **Rabbi Moshe Alshich,** the famous Torah commentator, and he studied Kabbalah under the prominent kabbalist **Rabbi Moshe Cordovero, the Remak.** When **Rabbi Yitzchak Luria, the Ari,** arrived in Safed in 1570, Rabbi Chaim became his closest disciple in the study of Kabbalah. The Ari selected him to record his profound mystical thoughts, and when the Ari died in 1572, during an epidemic that ravaged Safed, Rabbi Chaim Vital was considered his successor and spiritual heir. In 1576 Rabbi Chaim Vital began to lecture on Kabbalah to a large group of devoted students. He gained the reputation of being a miracle worker. By applying practical Kabbalah, he cured many afflictions and exorcised spirits in Safed and during his travels through Syria and Egypt. He compiled the Ari's kabbalistic teachings in *Etz Hachaim*[1] ("Tree of Life"), in conjunction with original writings on the importance of Kabbalah and the Ari's approach to mysticism. Among the other writings of Rabbi Chaim Vital are: *Sefer Hagilgulim,*[2] on the transmigration of souls; *Shaarei Kedushah*[3] on reward and punishment; *Likutei Hashas,*[4] a commentary on the aggadic portions of the Talmud, according to the Ari's teachings; and *Sefer HaLikutim,* an anthology of Torah thoughts. He was greatly admired by rabbis and kabbalists alike, but found a severe critic in Rabbi Yaakov Abulafia, the rabbi of Damascus (he lived in Damascus from 1594 until his death). In 1620, while preparing for his return to Safed, he fell ill and died.

Title page of *Peri Etz Chaim* by Rabbi Chaim Vital. The title page reads: "Written by the Kabbalist Rabbi Chaim Vital, as he heard it from his distinguished master, the Holy Lamp, Rabbi Yitzchak Luria Ashkenazi, which he spoke according to the true kabbalah he received from Elijah [the Prophet]."

SELECTIONS FROM RABBI CHAIM VITAL'S WRITINGS

Excerpt from *Sefer HaLikutim, Ki Tetze*

Concerning the *yefat to'ar* (captive woman) it is written, "When you wage war against your enemies, God will give you victory over them, so that you will take captives. If you see a beautiful woman among the prisoners and you desire her, you may take her as a wife" (Deuteronomy 21:10). The Gemara in *Kiddushin* 51 explains this law as a concession to man's natural desires. [If the Torah would forbid intimacy with captive women, the prohibition would probably be ignored.] Now, this rationale is difficult to understand. Should we sanction a transgression as serious as this just because a man might succumb to his natural inclination? And a serious transgression it is, for he who has sexual relations with a non-Jewish woman remains bound to her in this world and in the World to Come. The story is told of a man who was near death. The doctors told him that his only cure was to see a certain woman for whom he felt a strong desire. The rabbis told him, "It is better for you to die than to see her" (*Sanhedrin* 75). Surely, in the case of the captive woman, where his life is not threatened, he should not give in to his natural tendencies. But the underlying idea can be explained on the basis of the *Ma'amar HaSaba*.[5] We must remember that before going to battle, the officers sent home anyone who was afraid or fainthearted because of sins he committed (Deuteronomy 20:8). Hence, only men who were free of sin went to war. A perfectly righteous person such as that will not yield to his instincts to be intimate with a non-Jewish woman. . . . If a man who is a perfect tzaddik feels a powerful attraction to a non-Jewish woman, it is an indication that her soul is a captive of the *klippot*.[6] That is what is meant by the verse, "When you wage war against your enemies, God will give you victory over them." The fact that you ascribe your victory to God rather than to your superior weapons and strategies proves that you are a perfect tzaddik. Now, if you see among the captives a beautiful woman, you should realize that she is a pure and holy soul, held captive and in subjection by the *klippot*. Free this soul from her bondage by marrying her. By her conversion the soul will return to its original roots.

Excerpt from *Etz Hachaim*, Gate *Kitzur Abya*, Chap. 10

The primordial substance of which the earth is composed is called "*tohu*."[7] Since it is without form, it is unidentifiable until it acquires form, which is the soul. When substance and form are united, the result is called *bohu*. In the *bohu* state, the four basic elements of *esh* (fire), *ru'ach* (wind, air), *mayim* (water), and *afar* (dust, earth) come into being. The fusion of substance and form is *bohu*; formless substance is *tohu*.

Excerpt from *Etz Hachaim*, Gate *Olam Hayetzirah*, Chap. 2

Even if a person rises early for the purpose of studying and engrossing himself in the Torah, nevertheless his higher soul does not return to him until he prays and responds, *"Baruch HaShem hamevorach le'olam va'ed"*[8] ("Blessed is God, the blessed One, for all eternity"). At that point the soul returns to his body. Indeed, the response contains five words, corresponding to the five levels of the soul: *Nefesh, Ruach, Neshamah, Chayah,* and *Yechidah*.[9]

RABBI YEHUDAH LOEW OF PRAGUE—THE MAHARAL
רבי יהודה ליווא מפראג—מהר״ל

born: Posen, Poland, 1525
died: Prague, Bohemia, 1609
Popularly known as the Maharal, the abbreviation of Moreinu Harav Loew, *our teacher Rabbi Loew. Talmudist, kabbalist, philosopher.*

The Maharal was born to a distinguished family of rabbis that traced its ancestry to King David. In 1553 he was elected rabbi of Nikolsburg and the Province of Moravia, where he remained for the following twenty years. In 1573 he moved to Prague, where he opened a yeshivah and became mentor of many outstanding disciples. The most prominent among these is **Rabbi Lipmann Heller,** author of *Tosefot Yomtov* on the Mishnah. In 1592 the Maharal accepted the position of rabbi in Posen, returning to Prague in 1598 to serve as its chief rabbi. He was a prolific writer, and his works include: *Tiferet Yisrael*[1] on the greatness of Torah and mitzvot; *Netivot Olam,*[2] on ethics; *Be'er Hagolah,*[3] a commentary on rabbinic sayings; *Netzach Yisrael,*[4] on exile and redemption; *Or Chadash,*[5] on the Book of Esther; *Ner Mitzvah,*[6] on Chanukah; *Gevurot Hashem,*[7] on the Exodus; and many others. The Maharal's works reveal his illustrious personality as a profound thinker who penetrates the mysteries of Creation and metaphysics, clothing kabbalistic themes in a philosophic garment. His unique approach to Jewish thought influenced the ideologies of Chasidism and Mussar. A staunch leader of his community, he became the hero of many legends in which he appears as the defender of Prague Jewry against all its enemies, assisted by the Golem, a robot he made and gave life to by placing sacred writings in his mouth. The Maharal's synagogue, *Altneu Schul,* still exists today and is preserved as a shrine by the Prague municipal authorities, who in 1917 erected a statue in his honor. In the Torah-observant world the Maharal lives on in his writings, which are an enduring source of wisdom and inspiration.

ספר

גבורות ה׳

ממורינו ורבינו, גאון מעוזנו, הרב רבי יהודא
ליוואי בר רבי בצלאל זללה״ה

בעל המחבר ספר גור אריה על התורה, ס׳ תפארת
ישראל, נצח ישראל, נתיבות עולם, ובאר הגולה, אב״ד
ור״מ דק״ק פראג יע״א.

הנקרא הרב מהר״ל מפראג ז״ל.

מספר את הגבורות, אשר פעל קורא הדורות, מצאת ישראל
ממצרים לחירות, כח מעשיו ואת הקורות, אמרותיו אמרות
טהורות, מפנינים ופז יקרות, לטועמיהן עינים מאירות:

ונלוה עתה מחדש מפתח למאמרי חז״ל

שנת תשט״ו לפ״ק

יצא לאור ע״י
הרב שמעון מאשקאוויטץ

ברוקלין נ. י.

Title page of *Gevurot Hashem* by Rabbi Yehudah Loew of Prague, the Maharal. Profound philosophical and kabbalistic discourses on the miracles of the Exodus.

SELECTIONS FROM THE MAHARAL'S WRITINGS

Excerpt from *Gevurot Hashem,* Chap. 18

[Moses] looked all around, and when he saw that there was no one around, he killed the Egyptian and hid his body in the sand.

(Exodus 2:12)

The Maharal: *And hid his body in the sand*—Our sages comment on this passage: "The people of Israel are just like sand." Sand does not produce any sound when it is stirred. This stems from the smallness of its physical nature. The smaller the material substance of a body, the less audible it is. The same holds true for the Jewish people, who have a supernal, spiritual nature. Their true essence remains concealed and goes unnoticed. Silent like sand, they do not publicize the transcendental aspect of their being.

Excerpt from *Gevurot Hashem,* Chap. 46: Time, Motion, and Matter

Time and matter are two concepts that are completely interrelated. Time is essentially motion; motion is a function of matter. Thus, time, motion, and matter are an integral whole. A physical object can be defined in terms of its six surfaces: top, bottom, right, left, front, and back. There is, however, a seventh dimension—the center, which bears no relation to any of the six surfaces. It is an intangible, incorporeal entity, a point in space, having no dimensions. Time, which, as we have said, forms an integral part of physical matter, is measured by the six weekdays and the seventh day, the holy Shabbat. The six weekdays correspond to the six sides of a material object, while Shabbat represents the incorporeal center.

Excerpt from *Gevurat Hashem,* Chap. 51: Matzah, the Unleavened Bread

On the night of Passover the Children of Israel were freed from bondage in a supernatural way, a deliverance completely devoid of any material aspect. It is to commemorate this supernatural aspect that they were commanded to eat the matzah, the unleavened bread—bread in its most simple form, devoid of any extraneous ingredients. Spiritual freedom means basic simplicity, total independence from material wants. In the same vein, Scripture relates that they "left Egypt in a rush" (Deuteronomy 16:3). This indicates that their liberation was instantaneous, without passage of time. What occurred was timeless and metaphysical. This timelessness is inherent in the matzah, a bread that comes into being virtually in an instant, without undergoing the time-consuming process of leavening.[8]

Excerpt from *Tiferet Yisrael:* Why Was the Torah Not Given at the Beginning of Creation?

One may ask, "Why was not the Torah in its entirety given at the time of Creation?" After all, the Torah is the ultimate purpose of Creation. In the words of our sages, "The world was created because of the Torah." Now, since the Torah is the blueprint of Creation, it would have been proper and fitting for God to give the Torah at the outset of Creation, when He molded and formed all His creations. This question may be answered thus. The Torah was conceived specifically for the people of Israel who, at the time of Creation, had not yet come into being. Now you may ask, "Why was not the people of Israel called into being at the time of Creation and bestowed the Torah at the same moment?" This question has no justification at all. It would have been quite inappropriate for our forefathers, or even the nation of Israel itself, to have come into being at the beginning of Creation. It was Israel's destiny to be created at the end of all Creation. This concept is inherent in the very nature of Creation. Man, the crown of worldly existence, for whom all was created, was the last to be created. Among all the nations in the world you will not find one that appeared after the emergence of Israel. You see, Edom, Ishmael, even Ammon and Moab were great nations long before Israel was established as a people. This was a direct consequence of the law of Creation: that perfection comes only at the end. Now, just as Man, the most perfect of all creations, constituted the completion of Creation, so too, Israel, the most perfect nation in the world, was brought into being after all other nations. This explains why Israel was not created at the beginning of Genesis.

Excerpt from *Tiferet Yisrael,* Chap. 13

There are people who rate the sciences as superior to the Torah, because, they say, the sciences deal with subjects of primary importance, such as astronomy and the celestial forces, whereas the Torah is concerned with common, inconsequential issues. Bear in mind that the Torah, since it is perfect, comprehends the totality of all knowledge. The fact that some Torah laws appear to be insignificant and trivial should come as no surprise. The Torah is actually comparable to man. Man occupies the lowly physical world, even though he is endowed with a Divine soul that is rooted in the Heavenly Throne. Although he is flesh and blood, he radiates the image of God, the highest level of spirituality. Now you may ask, "How can corporeal, mortal man merit everlasting life?" Don't focus on the physical aspect of man. Think of the Divine spirit, the soul, that dwells in him. It is through his soul that man attains everlasting life. And so it is with the Torah. Although the mitzvot may appear to be insignificant rituals, each mitzvah comprises dimensions that reach the loftiest heights of the World to Come. In that respect, the mitzvot form a perfect analogy to man and his soul. Just as man, standing in a mundane world, harbors a soul that reaches to the World to Come, so too do Torah and mitzvot delineate actions in the physical world that are moored in the exalted heights of the spiritual world.[9]

Excerpt from *Gevurot Hashem,* Chap. 68, The Oral and the Written Law

The Torah that God gave to Israel includes both the Written and the Oral Law. The Oral Law is the commentary on the mitzvot that were given in writing. Now, you may ask, why was not everything given in written form? . . . The Oral Law could not possibly have been given in written form because it explains the details of the mitzvot. This task is infinite because there is no end to its minutiae. To write down only fragments would produce an incomplete work. Thus, the Oral Law should not be written down. A written record implies perfection and completeness. Oral transmission is by nature incomplete, as speech itself is inherently incomplete, in the sense that after you have uttered a word, it vanishes into nothingness. When you utter the next word, the previous one is gone. Conversely, the Written Torah, which is perfect and complete, should not be recited orally (by heart). That would mean reducing the Written Torah, which is perfect, to a state of imperfection.

RABBI MOSHE CHAIM LUZZATTO—
MESILLAT YESHARIM
רבי משה חיים לוצטו—מסילת ישרים

born: Padua, Italy, 1707
died: Acco, Eretz Yisrael, 1747
Ethicist, kabbalist, poet.

For his biography and excerpts, see Part IV, pp. 133–135.

Excerpt from *Choker Umekabel,* Chap. 18, The Counting of the Omer

The concept underlying the counting of the Omer is this: The wisdom of the world is contained in the fifty Gates of Wisdom. Moses attained forty-nine of these Gates, but the fiftieth Gate—that of the quintessential Wisdom—he did not attain. Analogously, there are forty-nine days of counting the Omer, and on the fiftieth day [which is the festival of Shavuot] the Torah was given. Just as there are forty-nine Gates of Wisdom and Holiness, so there are forty-nine Gates of *Tum'ah*—Defilement: "God has made the one opposite the other" (Ecclesiastes 7:14), a good and an evil inclination, the forces of impurity opposite the forces of holiness. When Israel was in Egypt, they degenerated and reached to the depth of the forty-ninth Gate of Defilement. They had to be taken out of this state. God wanted to extract Israel from these forty-nine Gates of Defilement in stages, by illuminating on each day between Passover and Shavuot the Gate of Holiness that is the antithesis of its opposite Gate of Defilement. This *tikkun* (correction, restoration) comes back to life each year in the counting of the Omer, on the forty-nine days between Passover, the day of the Exodus, and Shavuot, the day of the Giving of the Torah. Shavuot represents the illumination of the fiftieth Gate of *Binah* (Understanding) and *Kedushah* (Holiness).

ילקוט ידיעות האמת

כרך ראשון

והוא תורתו של רבינו משה חיים לוצאטו זצוקללה"ה
מה שהאיר עינינו לפרש לברר ולסדר
ידיעות של עיקר ושרש מאמתיות תורתנו הק'

הלא המה מחבוריו הנפלאים והק':

בראש וראשון א ספר דרך ה'
(כללי האמונה והעבודה)

ועליו ב מאמר העיקרים
(סדור קצר מידיעות עיקר שבאמונתנו הק')

ג מאמר על ההגדות
(ברורים בדרכי אגדות חז"ל למיניהן)

ד מאמר החכמה (בדלוג כללי חכמת האמת)

ה ולקוטים מספרו "אדיר במרום"
(ידיעות מפיצות אור גדול על ענינים שונים
מהם קשים ביותר)

הוצאת "תורה ומסורה" ניו יארק תש"ו

Title page of *Yalkut Yediot Ha'emet,* a compendium of discourses by Rabbi Moshe Chaim Luzzatto.

APPENDIX OF ADDITIONAL COMMENTATORS

The great works that have been excerpted in these pages represent only a small fraction of the rich heritage that our sages have transmitted to us. A sizable library building would be required to house their complete writings.

The following pages provide the names of a number of preeminent commentators, halachists, talmudists, and thinkers whose works have not been included for lack of space. Their writings, just as those discussed in this book, have enriched, comforted, and guided the Jewish people throughout the ages.

TORAH COMMENTATORS

R. Shmuel ben Meir—Rashbam
רבי שמואל בן מאיר—רשב"ם
born: Ramerupt, France, c. 1085
died: France, 1174

R. Chizkiyah Chizkuni
רבי חזקיה חזקוני
Provence, France, c. 1250

R. Levi ben Gershon—Ralbag
רבי לוי בן גרשון—רלב"ג
born: Bagnols, Provence, 1288
died: France, 1344
Wrote Bible commentary.

R. Yitzchak Abarbanel
רבי יצחק אברבנאל
born: Lisbon, Portugal, 1437
died: Venice, Italy, 1508

R. Chaim Yosef David Azulai—Chida
רבי חיים יוסף דוד אזולאי—חיד"א
born: Jerusalem, Israel, 1724
died: Livorno, Italy, 1806
Wrote Chomat Anach, Shem Hagedolim.

R. Yaakov Kranz—Dubna Maggid
רבי יעקב קרנץ—המגיד מדובנה
born: near Vilna, Lithuania, 1741
died: Dubna, 1804
Wrote Ohel Yaakov.

R. Yaakov Tzvi Mecklenburg
רבי יעקב צבי מקלנבורג—הכתב והקבלה
born: 1785
died: 1865
Rabbi of Koenigsburg, E. Prussia
Wrote Haketav Vehakabbalah.

R. Baruch Halevi Epstein—Torah Temimah
רבי ברוך הלוי עפשטיין—תורה תמימה
born: Bobruisk, Russia, 1860
died: 1940
Wrote Torah Temimah.

TOSAFISTS

Rabbi Yitzchak ben Meir—Rivam
רבי יצחק בן מאיר—ריב"ם
born: Ramerupt, France, c. 1090
died: France, c. 1130
Brother of **Rabbeinu Tam.**

Rabbi Yitzchak ben Asher—Riva
רבי יצחק בן אשר—ריב"א
died: Speyer, Germany, c. 1130

Rabbi Eliezer ben Natan—Ravan
רבי אליעזר בן נתן—ראב"ן
born: Mainz Germany, c. 1090
died: Germany, c. 1170

Rabbi Yitzchak of Dampierre—Ri
רבי יצחק מדנפיר—ר״י
born: Ramerupt, France, c. 1120
died: Dampierre, France, c. 1200
Nephew of **Rabbeinu Tam.**

Rabbi Yehudah HeChasid
רבי יהודה החסיד
born: Speyer, Germany, c. 1150
died: Regensburg, Germany, 1217
Kabbalist, author of *Sefer Chasidim.*

Rabbi Shimshon of Sens—Rash
רבי שמשון משאנץ—ר״ש
born: France, c. 1150
died: Eretz Yisrael, c. 1230
One of the most important tosafists. Our editions of
Tosafot were written by Rabbi Shimshon.

Rabbi Moshe of Coucy
רבי משה מקוצי
Coucy, France, early 13th century
Tosafist, author of *Sefer Mitzvot Gadol,* abbreviated
Semag (Soncino, 1489), which defines the 613 com-
mandments.

Rabbi Yechiel of Paris
רבי יחיאל מפאריש
born: Meaux, France, 1190
died: Eretz Yisrael, c. 1268

Rabbi Eliezer ben Yoel Halevi—Ravyah
רבי אליעזר בן רבי יואל הלוי—ראבי״ה
born: Mainz, Germany, c. 1140
died: Würzburg, Germany, c. 1225

Rabbi Yitzchak ben Avraham—Ritzba
רבי יצחק בן אברהם—ריצב״א
born: Dampierre, France, c. 1210

Rabbi Yitzchak of Corbeil
רבי יצחק מקוביל
died: Corbeil, France, 1280

Rabbi Eliezer of Metz
רבי אליעזר ממיץ
died: Metz, France, c. 1175
Author of *Sefer Yereim* (Vilna, 1892), a halachic
compendium, arranged according to the 613 commandments.

Rabbi Elazar Rokeach of Worms
רבי אלעזר רקח מגרמייזא
born: Mainz, Germany, c. 1160
died: Worms, Germany, c. 1238

TALMUDISTS

Rabbeinu Chananel
רבנו חננאל
born: end of 10th century
died: Kairouan, Egypt, c. 1055
Wrote commentary on the Talmud.

R. Shemuel ben Meir—Rashbam
רבי שמואל בן מאיר—רשב״ם
born: Ramerupt, France, 1085
died: France, 1174

R. Yeshayah of Trani Hazaken—Tosafot Rid
רבי ישעיה דטראני הזקן—תוספות רי״ד
born: Trani, Italy, c. 1180
died: Trani, Italy, 1260

R. Shelomoh ibn Aderet—Rashba
רבי שלמה אבן אדרת—רשב״א
born: Barcelona, Spain, 1235
died: Barcelona, Spain, 1310

R. Yomtov ibn Asevili—Ritva
רבי יום טוב אבן אשבילי—ריטב״א
died: Seville, Spain, c. 1320

R. Menachem HaMeiri—Bet Habechirah
רבי מנחם המאירי—בית הבחירה
born: Carcassonne, France, c. 1249
died: Perpignan, France, c. 1315

R. Yaakov Yehoshua Falk—Penei Yehoshua
רבי יעקב יהושע פלק—פני יהושע
born: Cracow, Poland, 1680
died: Offenbach, Germany, 1756

R. Aryeh Leib Ginzburg—Shaagat Aryeh
רבי אריה ליב גינסבורג—שאגת אריה
born: Weisun, near Minsk, Russia, 1695
died: Metz, France, 1785

R. Yitzchak Minkowski—Keren Ora
רבי יצחק מינקובסקי—קרן אורה
born: Minsk, Russia, 1788
died: Karlin, Russia, 1852

R. Yehoshua Leib Diskin—Maharil Diskin
רבי יהושע ליב דיסקין—מהרי"ל דיסקין
born: Grodno, Poland, 1816
died: Jerusalem, Israel, 1898

R. Yosef Dov Soloveitchik—Bet Halevi
רבי יוסף דוב סולובייצ'יק—בית הלוי
born: Nisviz, Poland, 1820
died: Brisk, Poland, 1892

R. Shalom Mordechai Schwadron—Hagahot
Maharsham
רבי שלום מרדכי שוודרון—הגהות מהרש"ם
born: Zlotchov, Poland, 1835
died: Berzan, Poland, 1911

R. Avraham Borenstein—Avnei Neizer, Eglei Tal
רבי אברהם ברנשטיין—אבני נזר, אגלי טל
born: Bendin, Poland, 1839
died: Sochatchev, Poland, 1910
Sochatchever Rebbe

R. Yosef Rosen—Tzofenat Pane'ach
רבי יוסף רוזן—צפנת פענח
born: Rogatchov, Russia, 1858
died: Vienna, Austria, 1936

R. Yosef Engel—Gilyonei HaShas
רבי יוסף ענגל—גיליוני הש"ס
born: Tarnow, Poland, 1859
died: Vienna, Austria, 1920

R. Baruch Ber Leibowitz—Birkat Shemuel
רבי ברוך בער ליבוביץ—ברכת שמואל
born: Slutzk, Russia, c. 1862
died: Vilna, Lithuania, 1939

R. Chaim Ozer Grodziensky—Achiezer
רבי חיים עוזר גרודזנסקי—אחיעזר
born: Ivye, Lithuania, 1863
died: Vilna, Lithuania, 1939

R. Naftali Trop
רבי נפתלי טראפ
born: Grodno, Poland, 1871
died: Radin, Lithuania, 1929

R. Elchanan Wasserman of Baranovitch
רבי אלחנן ווסרמאן
born: Birz, Russia, 1875
died: Slobodka, Lithuania, 1941—murdered by the
Nazis

R. Yitzchak Zev Soloveitchik
רבי יצחק זאב סולובייצ'יק
born: Volozhin, Lithuania, 1889
died: Jerusalem, Israel, 1960

HALACHISTS

Rabbeinu Gershon Meor Hagolah—Light of the Exile
רבנו גרשון מאור הגולה
born: Metz, France, c. 960
died: Mainz, Germany, 1040

R. Meir HaKohen of Rothenburg—Maharam Rothenburg
רבי מאיר מרוטנבורג—מהר"ם מרוטנבורג
born: Worms, Germany, 1215
died: Ansisheim, Alsace, 1293

R. David ibn Zimra—Radbaz
רבי דוד אבן זמרא—רדב"ז
born: Spain, 1480
died: Safed, Israel, 1574

R. Yoel Sirkes—Bayit Chadash (Bach)
רבי יואל סירקיש—ב"ח, בית חדש
born: Lublin, Poland, 1561
died: Cracow, Poland, 1640

R. Avraham HaLevi—Magen Avraham
רבי אברהם הלוי—מגן אברהם
born: Gumblin, Poland, 1637
died: Kalish, Poland, 1638

R. Yosef Te'omim—Pri Megadim
רבי יוסף תאומים—פרי מגדים
born: Lemberg/Lvov, Poland, 1727
died: Frankfort-on-the-Oder, Germany, 1792

R. Yonatan Eibshutz—Kreti Upleti, Yaarot Devash
רבי יהונתן אייבשיץ—כרתי ופלתי, יערות דבש
born: Cracow, Poland, 1690
died: Hamburg, Germany, 1764

Rabbi Aryeh Leib Heller—Ketzot HaChosen
רבי אריה ליב הלר—קצות החושן
born: 1745
died: 1813

COMMENTATORS ON MUSSAR

R. Naftali Amsterdam
רבי נפתלי אמסטרדאם
born: Salant, Lithuania, 1832
died: Jerusalem, Israel, 1916

R. Yitzchak Blazer of Petersburg
רבי יצחק בלזר מפעטערבורג
born: Shnipchuk, near Vilna, Lithuania, 1837
died: Jerusalem, Israel, 1907

R. Yerucham Levovitz
רבי ירוחם לואויץ
born: Luban, Russia, 1874
died: Mir, Poland, 1930
Mashgiach (spiritual guide) of the Mirrer Yeshivah.

R. Yechezkel Levenstein—Or Yechezkel
רבי יחצקאל לוונשטין—אור יחצקאל
born: Warsaw, Poland, 1884
died: B'nei Brak, Israel, 1974
Mashgiach (spiritual guide) of yeshivahs in Mir and Ponivitz (Israel).

CHASIDIC SAGES

R. Dov Ber of Mezritch—the Maggid of Mezritch
רבי דוב בר ממזריץ—המגיד ממזריץ
born: 1698?
died: 1772

R. Yaakov Yosef of Polnoya—Toledot Yaakov Yosef
רבי יעקב יוסף מפלנאה—תולדות יעקב יוסף
born: 1710
died: 1874

R. Elimelech of Lizhensk—No'am Elimelech
רבי אלימלך מליז׳נסק—נועם אלימלך
born: 1717
died: 1786

R. Yechiel Michel—the Maggid of Zlotchov
רבי יחיאל מיכל מזלוצ׳וב—המגיד מזלוצ׳וב
born:1721?
died: c. 1786

R. Aharon of Karlin
רבי אהרן מקרלין
born: 1736
died: 1772

R. Menachem Mendel of Vitebsk
רבי מנחם מנדל מויטבסק
born: 1730?
died: 1788

R. Meshullam Zishe of Hanipol, the Rebbe Reb Zishe
רבי משולם זישא מהניפולי—רבי רב זישא
born: 1718?
died: 1800

R. Yaakov Yitzchak Horowitz—the Chozeh (Seer, Visionary) of Lublin
רבי יעקב יצחק הורויץ—החוזה מלובלין
born: 1745?
died: 1815

R. Yaakov Yitzchak of Pshis'cha—the "Yid"
רבי יעקב יצחק מפשיסחא—היהודי הקדוש
died: 1814

R. Avraham Yehoshua Heshel of Apta
רבי אברהם יהושע השל מאפטא
born: 1755
died: 1825

R. Naftali of Ropshitz
רבי נפתלי מרופשיץ
born: 1760
died: 1827

R. Shalom Roke'ach of Belz
רבי שלום רקח מבלז
born: 1779
died: 1855

R. Yechezkel Halberstam of Siniawa
רבי יחזקאל הלברשטם משינובה
born: 1811
died: 1899

R. Yaakov David of Amshinov

רבי יעקב דוד מאמשינוב

born: 1814
died: 1878

R. Chanoch of Alexander

רבי חנוך מאלכסנדר

died: 1870

R. Yitzchak of Boyan

רבי יצחק מבויאן

born: 1850
died: 1917

R. Yisrael of Sadagora

רבי ישראל מסדיגורה

born: 1853
died: 1907

R. Yerachmiel Yitzchak Danziger of Alexander—
Yismach Yisrael

רבי ירחמיאל יצחק דנציגר מאלקסנדר—ישמח ישראל

born: 1853
died: 1919

R. Shimon Shalom Kalish of Amshinov

רבי שמעון שלום קליש מאמשינוב

born: 1883
died: 1954

PHILOSOPHERS

R. Shelomoh ibn Gabirol

רבי שלמה אבן גבירול—מקור חיים

born: Malaga, Spain, c. 1021
died: Valencia, Spain, c. 1058
Wrote *Mekor Chaim*.

R. Yosef ibn Tzaddik

רבי יוסף אבן צדיק—עולם קטן

born: So. Spain, c. 1075
died: Cordova, Spain, 1149
Wrote *Olam Katan*.

R. Shem Tov ibn Palquera

רבי שם טוב אבן פלקירה—המבקש

born: Palquera, Spain, c. 1225
died: Spain, c. 1295
Wrote *HaMevakesh*.

Rabbi Meir Aldabi

רבי מאיר אלדבי—שבילי אמונה

Toledo, Spain, mid–14th century
Wrote *Shevilei Emunah*.

R. Profiat Yitzchak Duran

רבי פרופייט יצחק דוראן—אל תהי כאבותיך

Spain, late 14th–early 15th century
Wrote *Al Tehi KaAvotecha*.

R. Yosef ibn Shem Tov

רבי יוסף אבן שם טוב—כבוד אלוהים

born: Castille, Spain, c. 1400
died: Spain, c. 1460
Wrote *Kevod Elokim*.

KABBALISTS

R. Avraham ben David of Posquieres—Ravad III

רבי אברהם בן דוד מפושקיירש

born: Narbonne, Provence, c. 1120
died: Posquieres, Provence, c. 1197

Rabbi Shemuel HeChassid

רבי שמואל החסיד

born: Speyer, Germany, c. 1120
died: Speyer, Germany, c. 1175

R. Yehudah ben Yakar

רבי יהודה בן יקר

born: Provence, France, c. 1150
died: Spain, 1225

R. Azriel of Gerona

רבי עזריאל מגירונה

born: Gerona, Spain, 1160
died: Gerona, Spain, 1238

R. Elazar Rokeach of Worms—Sefer HaRokeach

רבי אלעזר רקח מגרמייזא—ספר הרקח

born: Mainz, Germany, 1160
died: Worms, Germany, 1238

Rabbi Yosef Gikatilla—Shaarei Orah

רבי יוסף גיקטליא—שערי אורה

born: Castille, Spain, 1248
died: Penafiel, Spain, c. 1310

R. Menachem Recanati

רבי מנחם ריקנטי

Italy, late 13th–early 14th century

R. Shelomoh Alkabetz
רבי שלמה אלקבץ
born: Saloniki, Greece, 1505
died: Safed, Israel, 1576
Wrote *Lecha Dodi*.

R. Moshe de Leon—Sefer HaRimon
רבי משה די ליאון—ספר הרמון
born: Leon, Spain, c. 1250
died: Spain, 1305

R. Moshe Alshich
רבי משה אלשיך
born: Adrianople, Turkey, 1508
died: Damascus, Syria, 1593

R. Yehuda Loew of Prague—the Maharal
רבי יהודה ליווא מפראג—מהר״ל
born: Posen, Poland, 1525
died: Prague, Bohemia, 1609

Rabbi Yeshayah Horowitz—Sheloh
רבי ישעיה הורויץ—של״ה
born: Prague, Czechoslovakia, 1565
died: Tiberias, Israel, 1630

R. Chaim ibn Attar—Or Hachaim
רבי חיים אבן עטר—אור החיים
born: Sale, Morocco, 1696
died: Jerusalem, Israel, 1743

R. Eliyahu of Vilna—Vilna Gaon, The Gra
רבי אליהו מוילנא—הגר״א
born: Vilna, Lithuania, 1720
died: Vilna, Lithuania, 1797

NOTES

I. TORAH

Rabbi Shelomoh Yitzchaki—Rashi

1. An English translation of his Torah commentary by A. M. Silbermann has been published by Feldheim Publishing Co., Jerusalem, 1985, and a linear translation by S.S. & R. Publishing, Brooklyn, New York, 1949.

2. This is the widely misunderstood *jus talionis*, the law of retaliation. Rashi presents the talmudic interpretation.

3. He is guiltless only if he kills the burglar during the actual break-in, but not at any other time.

4. The toil and exertion are implied in the word *teileichu*—literally "walk" (in My laws), walk long distances, exert yourself in search of Torah instruction.

5. As the number of observant Jews increases, their strength grows exponentially.

6. In the aftermath of the episode of Balaam, *"Israel began to behave immorally with the Moabite girls"* (Numbers 25:1). This was done at Balaam's advice, as stated in Numbers 31:16, *"These (women) are exactly the ones who were involved with the Israelites at Balaam's instigation."*

7. *Vayevarech* generally is rendered "he blessed." Rashi gives a different translation—"he greeted."

8. Note the similarity: *mecherotehem* and *machaira*.

Rabbi Abraham ibn Ezra

1. The place of Ibn Ezra's death is uncertain. His gravesite is variously said to be in Calhorra, Northern Spain, Rome, London, and Northern Galilee, Israel.

2. First printed with the Torah text in Constantinople 1522. Printed separately in Naples, 1488. Most recent edition by Mossad Harav Kook, Israel (annotated).

3. A person is naked only *after* his clothes have been removed.

4. The difficult text, literally *if so, why am I*, is interpreted by Rashi as "if pregnancy is so painful, why did I pray to have children?"

5. The verse states that Joseph was placed in *beit haso'ar*. Other than in this chapter, this term does not occur in the Bible. (It may be called a *hapax legomenon*, the term used for a word that occurs only once in Scripture.) The first time it occurs, in the present verse, it is followed by the clause, "the place where the king's prisoners were kept." This leads Ibn Ezra to think that *beit haso'ar* may be an Egyptian term, which is then translated as "the place where the prisoners were kept." He observes that a similar case of a foreign term being translated into Hebrew is found in Esther 8:10, where the word *achashteranim*, clearly a Persian word, is followed by its Hebrew definition: *benei haramachim*, [meaning] swift steeds bred of a mare. The commentary exemplifies Ibn Ezra's terse style of writing.

6. Eminent talmudist, poet, and statesman, 993–1055.

7. Ibn Ezra often is quite blunt in dismissing opinions with which he disagrees.

8. *Ukesamim beyadam*—they had magic in their hand; they had the ability to perform magic.

9. This comment is an illustration of the brevity of Ibn Ezra's style. He indicates with one word that beauty is not an absolute concept. It is relative, depending on personal taste. "Beauty is in the eye of the beholder."

10. This verse introduces Moses' final oration to the Children of Israel on the day of his death. It merely states "Moses went" without mentioning where he went.

11. Ibn Ezra lived in the first half of the 12th century!

12. "To eat" is used metaphorically, meaning to learn, to understand.

Rabbi David Kimchi—Redak

1. First printed in 1480.

2. Naples, 1590.

3. Constantinople, 1710.

4. Noah and his sons, followed by his wife and his sons' wives.

5. In both quotations the angel is described as *"man."*

6. The Torah comprises 248 positive commandments and 365 negative commandments, totaling 613. There are 7 Noachide commandments, which are to be observed by all mankind. By adding *soreik*, i.e. 606 commandments to the 7 Noachide commandments, we arrive at the total of 613 mitzvot, given to the Jewish nation.

Rabbi Moshe ben Nachman (Nachmanides)—Ramban

1. Mossad Harav Kook published a Hebrew annotated edition in 1967. An English translation by Rabbi Dr. Charles

B. Chavel has been published by Shilo Publishing House (New York, 1973).

2. The verse indicates that it was Pharaoh himself who hardened his heart. It was only in connection with the latter five plagues that *God* made Pharaoh obstinate, as with the sixth plague of boils, where "God hardened Pharaoh's heart" (Exodus 9:12).

3. According to the Talmud, the word *totafot*, "insignia," alludes to the head tefillin.

4. Everything that happens is God's will. Thus, every breath we take is as much a miracle as the parting of the Sea of Reeds.

5. The Midrash relates that the sea was divided into twelve parts, one for each tribe.

Rabbi Bachya ben Asher—Rabbeinu Bachya

1. First published in Naples in 1492 and reprinted more than 20 times, most recently by Mossad Harav Kook, Jerusalem.

2. In the written Torah scroll there is no space inserted between *vayechi*, the first word of the portion of *Vayechi*, and *me'od*, the last word of the preceding portion, *Vayigash*. Thus, there is no indication that a new portion is beginning with *vayechi*. It is "sealed."

3. The two other exiles were the Egyptian exile, lasting 210 years and ending with the Exodus, and the Babylonian exile, which began with the destruction of the first Temple in 421 B.C.E. and ended seventy years later.

4. The *olah*, "burnt offering," was burned completely on the altar.

5. When the Israelites moved toward the land of the Amorites against God's will, the Amorites attacked them with bee-like vehemence.

Rabbi Ovadiah Seforno

1. Commentaries on Genesis and Exodus translated by R. Raphael Pelcovitz, Mesorah Publications, 1987.

2. Adam was placed in the Garden of Eden for the purpose of occupying himself with spiritual pursuits, with "receiving the flow of intelligence" emanating from God. Spiritual pursuits require a joyful and serene frame of mind, which is promoted by an aesthetically pleasing environment. It was to that end that God planted the trees that were "pleasant to look at." The reference to 2 Kings concerns the prophet Elisha, who was unable to receive prophecy until his spirits were lifted by the pleasing sounds of the minstrel's music.

3. The true essence of God is concealed from the human mind. We gain knowledge of God through the ways in which He reveals Himself: Mercy, Justice, Truth. . . . By emulating the Divine attributes, man reaches perfection, the ultimate purpose of man's creation.

4. This is a reference to "*The soul of man is the lamp of God*" (Proverbs 20:27).

5. Seforno highlights the invaluable contribution to children's education made by their elders. He cites the example of Moses and Aharon, products of the education and guidance imparted by Amram, their father, Kehat, their grandfather, and Levi, their great-grandfather.

6. *Re'em*, unicorn, alternately rendered rhinoceros, wild ox, or bison. In this commentary, Seforno offers a beautiful explanation of the metaphor.

7. Psalm 80:9.

8. Jerusalem Talmud, *Shevi'it* 6a; also *Vayikra Rabbah*, end of Chapter 17.

9. Man must make a choice. There is no middle ground, no room for compromise or concession regarding obedience to God's commandments.

Rabbi Moshe Alshich

1. After the sin of the Golden Calf, God wanted to destroy the people of Israel. Thereupon Moses uttered this prayer in their defense.

2. The verse speaks of the second tithe, which must be eaten in Jerusalem. If Jerusalem is too far, it may be redeemed for money, which must then be spent on food in Jerusalem, and the food must be consumed there.

3. We refer to God as the *Makom*, the Place of the world, to indicate that the whole universe is His place. There is no place that is devoid of His presence. Alshich's homiletical interpretation offers an illuminating psychological insight.

Rabbi Yeshayah Horowitz—The Sheloh

1. Amsterdam, 1648.

2. God had told Jacob to end his stay with Laban and "return to the land of his fathers." The Sheloh discusses the manner in which Jacob presented the impending move to his wives.

3. Rabbi Yitzchak Luria, prominent kabbalist, Eretz Yisrael, 1534–1572.

4. This refers to a region of northeast Spain.

5. Balaam's donkey, seeing God's angel obstructing his passage, moved to the side, crushing Balaam's foot against the wall. Balaam, who could not see the angel, angrily struck the donkey three times. God then gave Balaam the power to see the angel, who berated him for beating the donkey. Balaam replied, "I have sinned! I did not know that you were standing on the road before me."

Rabbi Shlomoh Efraim of Luntchitz—Kli Yakar

1. Lublin, 1602

2. In this verse Moses announces to Pharaoh the impending plague of locusts, the eighth of the ten plagues.

3. As indicated by the order in which they are listed in the verse.

4. The commentary focuses on the meaning of "new" in the context of this verse.

5. This paragraph deals with the prohibition against eating blood.

Rabbi Chaim ibn Attar—Or Hachaim

1. First printed in Venice in 1742. Printed in all editions of *Chumash Mikraot Gedolot* and printed separately and annotated by *Air Bohir* (Brooklyn, 1973).

2. What did God who is omniscient mean by this question?

3. Or Hachaim interprets Adam's nakedness as his sense of shame, failure, and inadequacy.

4. *Pirkei de Rabbi Eliezer* 14.

5. Isaiah 40:28.

6. If the text merely would have stated, *Justice you shall follow,* these men, being competent judges, would be satisfactory.

Rabbi Eliyahu of Vilna—the Vilna Gaon

1. Dubrovna, 1804.

2. Shklov, 1798.

3. Lemberg, 1839.

4. Shklov, 1803.

5. Horodno, 1806.

6. This commentary is a typical example of the Vilna Gaon's system of demonstrating by means of ingeniously found allusions the unity of the Written and the Oral Torah.

7. This is inferred from Numbers 15:40, speaking of the tzitzit, "You will thus remember and keep *all My commandments.*"

8. These headings have been written by the author.

9. If the Torah is not ground like flour, you cannot extract its essence, the halachah.

10. Until the last day of his life he is always searching for more possessions.

Rabbi Moshe Sofer (Schreiber)—the Chatam Sofer

1. Pressburg 1855, 1864.

2. Pressburg 1895, 1897. Reprinted many times.

3. Announcing His plan to create Eve, God said, *"It is not good for man to be alone; I will make a compatible helper for him"* (Genesis 2:18).

4. This paragraph delineates the laws concerning the appointing and duties of a Jewish king.

Rabbi Samson Raphael Hirsch

1. Altona, 1836, in German; English translation by Bernard Drachman, New York, 1942.

2. Published in Frankfort, 1920. English translation by Isaac Levy, Judaica Press, Gateshead, England, 1982.

3. This passage announces the second of the Ten Plagues, the invasion of Egypt by countless frogs.

4. *Lamed,* aside from being the name of the letter, also carries the meaning "to teach."

5. In this comment, Rabbi Hirsch enunciates, in capsule form, his view on the purpose and meaning of the Diaspora.

Rabbi Meir Leib ben Yechiel Michael—Malbim

1. Warsaw, 1860–1876.

2. Several volumes are available in English translation by Zvi Faier, Hillel Press, Jerusalem, 1978.

3. The creation of light is the subject of a very thorough and profound philosophical analysis in Malbim's commentary on Genesis 1.

4. This commentary represents a prime example of a prevalent feature of Malbim's exegesis. In his view, duplication of words or phrases is not done merely for the sake of literary embellishment, but each expression conveys a very specific message, as do "*rod*" and "*staff*" in the present verse.

Rabbi Avraham Shemuel Binyamin Sofer (Schreiber)—the Ktav Sofer

1. 1873–1894.

2. Pressburg, 1879. Reprinted many times, most recently in Jerusalem in 1966.

3. This comment clearly exemplifies the Ktav Sofer's fierce struggle against the reformers' attempts to invalidate the Torah.

Rabbi Naftali Tzvi Yehudah Berlin—the Netziv

1. First edition in Vilna, 1879–1880. Second edition in Jerusalem, 1938.

2. Warsaw, 1892.

3. This is a reference to Numbers 15:37 (the third segment of the Shema). The thread of *techelet* refers to one of the threads of the tzitzit (tassels) that was dyed blue. Since nowadays the special blue wool is not available, the tzitzit can be made entirely white (Menachot 38a).

4. This paragraph describes the procedure to be followed when offering the bikkurim, the first fruits. Bikkurim are brought from the seven species for which the Land of Israel is famous: wheat, barley, grapes, figs, pomegranates, olives, and dates. The laws delineating their offering can be found in the Mishnah (Tractate *Bikkurim*) and Rambam (The Laws of Bikkurim). The present comment illustrates one of the main features of the Netziv's commentary, that of demonstrating the unity of the Written Law (Torah) and the Oral Law (Talmud).

5. Compare the English idiom, "first quality."

Rabbi Meir Simchah Hakohen—Meshech Chochmah, Or Same'ach

1. Published in Riga in 1927. Most recent edition: Israel, 1978.

2. Jacob, setting out on his journey to Egypt to go and see his long lost son Joseph, has a prophetic vision in which God reassures him with the words of the present verse.

3. In the fortieth year after the Exodus, the Children of Israel did not have any water. They angrily vented their frustration on Moses and Aaron.

4. The fruits always associated with the former three species (compare Deuteronomy 8:8).

Rabbi Yaakov Kamenetzky

1. New York, 1986.

II. MISHNAH, TALMUD, AND MIDRASH

Rabbi Yehudah HaNasi—Rabbeinu HaKadosh, Rabbi

1. An excellent English translation of the Mishnah with a commentary has been published by Mesorah Publications, Brooklyn, New York. Other English translations are by Philip Blackman (Judaica Press, Gateshead, England, 1983) and by Yavneh Press (New York, 1965).

Rabbi Ovadiah Yarei of Bartenura—Rav

1. First printed in Venice in 1548/1549.

Rabbi Yomtov Lipmann Heller—Tosefot Yomtov

1. Prague, 1615–1617; Cracow, 1643.
2. Breslau, 1818.

TALMUD

1. There are numerous Hebrew editions of the complete Talmud and individual *masechtot*. An annotated English translation has been published by Soncino Press (London, 1936–1952).

Rabbi Yaakov ben Meir—Rabbeinu Tam

1. The Torah decrees in Leviticus 23:40 that on the Festival of Sukkot we take the four species, i.e., the *lulav* (a date-palm branch), an *etrog* (citron), twigs of a myrtle tree, and brook willows. The *lulav* bundle is taken in hand every day of Sukkot, except on Shabbat.

2. They were sailing to Rome in 96 C.E. on a mission to gain favors for the Jewish people from the newly crowned Emperor Nerva (Marcus Cocceius), in which they achieved some success (*History of the Jewish People*, Mesorah Publications, Brooklyn, New York, 1986).

3. The above selection contains a number of elements that can be found in a typical Gemara: (1) the initial step of finding the scriptural basis for the Oral Law mentioned in the Mishnah, (2) a discussion of the legal ramifications of the law

under consideration, in this case the principle of *matanah al menat lehachazir shemah matanah*—a gift made on condition that it be returned is a valid gift, (3) an *aggadic* lesson, in this instance, devotion to mitzvot.

4. The reading of the Megillah is a mitzvah that is dependent on a fixed time and women are normally not required to observe such precepts. The accepted practice is for women to listen to the Megillah read by a man.

5. Their secondary role is inferred from the word "also."
6. "Also" in the sense of "likewise."
7. That is, 1,200,000.
8. If he steals an ox or a sheep, he must repay five oxen for each ox and four sheep for each sheep (Exodus 21:37). For all other thefts, he pays twofold.
9. *Lo pelug* means that we don't make exceptions to a general rule, even if the reason on which the rule is predicated does not apply (literally, do not divide, do not make a distinction).

Rabbi Shemuel Eliezer Eidels—Maharsha

1. The various volumes of *Chiddushei Halachot* and *Chiddushei Aggadot* were first published in Posen in 1602, 1621, 1627, and 1631.
2. After surviving one of the abovementioned four hazardous situations, we thank God, reciting the *berachah* (blessing) of "*Hagomeil*."

Rabbi Yeshayah Horowitz—the Sheloh

1. This is an important theme in Jewish thought. When Israel is in galut (exile), the Shechinah (Divine Presence) is also in galut. In the same vein, God reassures Jacob before he leaves Eretz Yisrael to join his son Joseph in Egypt, saying, "I will go to Egypt with you" (Genesis 46:4).
2. Leviticus 26:14–43.

Rabbi Chaim Yosef Gottlieb of Stropkov—the Stropkover Rav

1. Edited by Rabbi A. M. Israel of Hunyad (Brooklyn, 1963).
2. For example, eating meat that is uncooked or matzah that is made of mildewed grain.

Rabbi Avraham Yeshayahu Karelitz—the Chazon Ish

1. *Chazon Ish*—The Vision of Ish, *Ish* being the acronym of Avraham Yeshayahu.
2. *Glory of the Generation* (B'nei Brak, Israel, 1966).

Rabbi Aharon Kotler—Reb Aharon

1. Jerusalem, 1987.
2. Reb Aharon, the great Torah leader, who—like the prophet—loved Torah students like his own children, sees in

these children the fulfillment of God's promise. Having witnessed the Holocaust, the "hiding of the Face," he rebuilt the Torah that was lost. He thereby became God's instrument in fulfilling His promise "that the Torah will not be forgotten by their descendants."

MIDRASH

1. Pinchas' mother was "of the daughters of Putiel" (Exodus 6:25). Putiel alludes to Joseph, who conquered (*pitpeit*) his passion (note the similarity between Putiel and *pitpeit*).

2. These headings are the author's.

3. The underlying thought is that, by deciding who are the partners in a marriage, God determines the nature and character of the offspring, and thereby guides the course of history. According to *Sota* 2a, marriages are determined even before birth, "Forty days before the formation of a child, a *Bat Kol* (Heavenly Voice) announces 'This person is to marry so-and-so's daughter.'"

4. I.e., He who has faith in God will be helped by Him in time of danger. According to the midrash, Moses composed this Psalm on the day he completed construction of the Tabernacle. As he entered the Divine Clouds he was enveloped in "the shadow of the Almighty" (*Midrash Rabbah*, Chap. 12, *Midrash Tanchuma, Ki Tisa*).

5. This is the number of boards from which the Tabernacle was constructed (Exodus 26:18).

6. You will merit to see the Final Redemption.

7. This title refers to **Rabbi Yehudah HaNasi**, the compiler of the Mishnah.

8. "If you come across a bird's nest . . . you must not take the mother along with her young. . . . You must first chase away the mother, and only then may you take the young" (Deuteronomy 22:6).

III. HALACHAH

Rabbi Nissim—Ran

1. Rome, 1545.

2. Constantinople, 1533.

3. Kiddush—sanctification—is a prayer recited at the beginning of Shabbat; Havdalah—distinction—is recited at the end of Shabbat.

4. On Shabbat, as on Festivals, you are forbidden to walk a distance of more than 2,000 cubits from the place where you spend the Shabbat. If you are in a city, we measure the 2,000 cubits from the outskirts of the city. A cubit (*amah*) is about 22 inches in length (21.25–23.5 inches, depending on the halachic authority).

5. This means the reading of the familiar texts of Scripture and Mishnah, as opposed to the study of Gemara, which needs greater concentration.

Rabbi Moshe ben Maimon (Maimonides)—Rambam

1. English translation, ed. Philip Birnbaum (New York, Hebrew Publishing Co., 1967). Also available, 5 volumes, trans. Rabbi Eliyahu Touger (New York/Jerusalem, Maznaim Publishing, 1987).

2. In his *Sefer HaMitzvot* (Book of Commandments), Rambam enumerates the 248 *mitzvot assei*—(positive commandments) and the 365 *mitzvot lo ta'asse*—(negative commandments, prohibitions). It was written as an introduction to his *Mishneh Torah*.

3. These are the concluding paragraphs of the entire *Mishneh Torah. Mishneh Torah* opens with "The foundation of all basic principles and the pillar of all wisdom is to realize that there is a First Being." Thus, this monumental work begins and ends with the knowledge of God.

4. Rambam carefully chose this metaphor to indicate that although physical comforts and pleasures will be available, they will be considered "as dust"—no one will attach any importance to them.

Rabbi Avraham ben David of Posquieres—Ravad III

1. One of the most important and ancient mystical works, thought to date from talmudic times or earlier. First published in Mantua, Italy in 1562. Over 100 commentaries have been written on it. *Yetzirah* means creation.

2. Underlying this difference of opinion is a greater controversy. Rambam believes (*Kings and Wars* 12:1), "There will be no difference between our age and the Messianic era except for the freedom of subjugation to foreign rule." Ravad opposes this view, arguing that the Messiah will usher in a miraculous era in which the entire world will change. Their debate is reflected in their respective conceptions of the person of the Messiah, Rambam seeing him as a political leader who will restore Israel's independence and induce them to observe the Torah, whereas Ravad views him as a superhuman miracle worker.

3. The *hadas* (myrtle twig) is one of the Four Species that make up the *lulav* bundle. The *lulav* bundle consists of one *lulav* (palm branch), three *hadassim* (twigs of the myrtle tree), and two *aravot* (willow twigs), which are tied together, and an *etrog* (citron). The Four Species are taken in hand every day of Sukkot, except on Shabbat. The *lulav* bundle is held in the right hand, the *etrog* in the left. After the blessings are recited, the Four Species are waved.

4. *Seder Hadorot*, page 162, quoting *Sefer Michlal Yofi*, explains that Ravad is referring to a revelation he had received from Eliyahu HaNavi (the Prophet Elijah). In two other instances Ravad reports experiencing similar metaphysical revelations, one in Rambam, *Beit Habechira* 6:14, where he says, "Thus it was revealed to me," the other in Rambam, *Mishkav uMoshav* 7:7, where he states, "Blessed is God, Who reveals His secret to those who fear Him" (meaning to

Ravad). In spite of such heavenly corroberation, later authorities, such as Ramban, disagreed with Ravad, in keeping with the principle of "*lo vashamayim hi*"—[The Torah] is not in heaven" (Deuteronomy 30:12). It does not require new prophetic insights. *Seder Hadorot*, by Rabbi Yechiel Heilprin (1660–1746), *rosh yeshivah* of Minsk, Russia, is one of the most authoritative Jewish histories, based entirely on traditional sources. It was first published in Karlsruhe, Germany, in 1769.

Rabbi Asher ben Yechiel—Rosh

1. Venice, 1552.
2. Pieve de Sachi, 1475.
3. The *tekiah* is a simple sound; the *shevarim* is three successive sounds; the *teruah* consists of nine short, staccato sounds. Each of the three successive *shevarim* sounds is as long as three *teruah* sounds. In the order of *tekiah-shevarim-teruah-tekiah,* the sound of each *tekiah* should be as long as the *shevarim* and the *teruah*, that is, the length of eighteen sounds. In the order of *tekiah-shevarim-tekiah*, each *tekiah* should be as long as the *shevarim*, that is, the length of nine sounds. The same holds in the order of *tekiah-teruah-tekiah*.

Rabbi Yaakov Baal Haturim—the Tur

1. *Gematria* is a system of interpretation by which words are converted into numbers. For example: Genesis 1:4—את האור (*et ha'or*, the light) has a *gematria* of 613 (add 1, 400, 5, 1, 6, and 200). The word בתורה (*batorah,* in the Torah) is also 613 in *gematria* (add 2, 400, 6, 200, and 5). The total number of laws contained in the Torah is 613. Since *et ha'or* equals *batorah,* the underlying thought of this equation is that the Divine Light of the first day of Creation radiates through the 613 mitzvot of the Torah.
2. Pieve de Sachi, 1475.
3. The Tur lived in abject poverty all his life.

Rabbi Yosef Karo—Bet Yosef, Shulchan Aruch

1. Sephardi Jews are the descendants of Jews from Mediterranean and Middle Eastern countries.
2. Ashkenazi Jews lived in France, Germany, Poland, Russia, etc.
3. Venice, 1564.
4. Venice, 1574–1576.

Rabbi David HaLevi—Taz

1. Lublin, 1646.

Rabbi Shabtai HaKohen—Shach

1. Cracow, 1652.
2. Amsterdam, 1663.
3. It is unclear whether Rema requires sticking the knife into earth for cutting cheese or also requires it for cutting the bread to be eaten with the cheese. *Taz* and *Shach* have conflicting views in this regard.

Rabbi Moshe Isserles—Rema

1. Next to the familiar square script (*merubba,* four-sided), the semi-cursive Rashi script is the most widely used letter type. Most commentaries to rabbinic works are written in Rashi script, in contrast to the main text, which appears in square script.

Rabbi Yisrael Meir HaKohen Kagan—the Chafetz Chaim

1. Vilna, 1873.
2. Vilna, 1884.
3. It was completed in 1907 and has seen numerous editions (an English translation was published by Feldheim Publishers, Spring Valley, New York and Jerusalem, 1987).
4. The mitzvah of Shabbat was given in two miraculously simultaneous commands: " 'Remember (*zachor*)' and 'keep (*shamor*)' the Shabbat day to make it holy" (Exodus 20:18, Deuteronomy 5:12).

Rabbi Yechezkel Landau—the Noda Biyehudah

1. Prague, 1776.
2. Prague, 1783.
3. Prague, 1794.
4. The reading of the *Shema* may not be delayed past the first quarter of the day. In the summer this can be quite early.
5. A minyan is a quorum of ten adult males.

Rabbi Shelomoh Ganzfried—Kitzur Shulchan Aruch

1. Since its publication in 1864, hundreds of editions have been printed, some with extensive commentaries, and millions of copies have been sold. It has been translated into all modern languages. An English translation by Hyman E. Goldin was published by the Hebrew Publishing Company (New York, 1961). A new linear, phrase-by-phrase translation has been published by Rabbi Avrohom Davis (Metsudah Publications, 1988).
2. Based on *Shulchan Aruch, Orach Chaim* 1:1.
3. I Samuel 22:10 relates that when King Saul learned from Doeg the Edomite that Achimelech the Priest had given to David food and the sword of Goliath, he ordered that all the priests and the entire city of Nov be killed.
4. Based on *Shulchan Aruch, Orach Chaim* 611:1.
5. Based on *Shulchan Aruch, Orach Chaim* 616.
6. Based on *Shulchan Aruch, Yoreh De'ah* 158.
7. From *Shulchan Aruch, Choshen Mishpat* 227.

8. From *Shulchan Aruch, Choshen Mishpat* 201, 204.

9. From *Shulchan Aruch, Even Ha'ezer*, 5 and *Choshen Mishpat* 272.

10. From *Shulchan Aruch, Yoreh De'ah* 335.

Rabbi Moshe Feinstein—Reb Moshe

1. New York, 1959; B'nei Brak, Israel, 1981.

2. B'nei Brak, Israel, 1988.

3. Brooklyn, New York, Mesorah Publications, 1986.

IV. MUSSAR

Rabbi Moshe Chaim Luzzatto—Mesillat Yesharim

1. Amsterdam, 1740. The book gained great popularity and has seen many editions. It is available in English translation by Shraga Silverstein, Feldheim Publishers, Jerusalem/New York, 1974.

2. The opening paragraphs of *Mesillat Yesharim*, Chap. 1.

3. This fitting parable teaches the principle of *emunat chachamim*—faith in our sages. We should heed their advice, for they have "reached the tower." By assimilating Torah into their thinking process they have gained control over their *yetzer* (inclination).

4. An unopened palm branch, one of the "Four Species" the Torah commands us to take on Sukkot (Leviticus 23:40). A stolen *lulav* is invalid (*Sukkah* 29b).

Rabbi Chaim of Volozhin—Reb Chaim Volozhiner

1. Vilna, 1824.

2. This commentary is based on the profound mystical kabbalistic teachings of the Zohar on *Parashat Yitro*.

3. The Talmud relates in *Gittin* 6b that Elijah the Prophet reports that God was engaged in the study of the chapter, "The concubine in Gibeah" (Judges 19) at the very same time that Rabbi Evyatar and Rabbi Yonatan were discussing this subject here on earth. God even quoted their respective opinions on the matter. This is evidence that God joins us in our earthly Torah studies.

4. It should be noted that Reb Chaim Volozhiner was a man of legendary humility.

Rabbi Yisrael Lipkin of Salant—Reb Yisrael Salanter

1. Vilna, 1900.

2. Chanoch was the seventh generation after Adam. This interpretation is typical of Rabbi Yisrael Salanter's approach. Man achieves "mystical union" and attaches himself to God by emulating God's attributes, lavishing goodness and kindness on others, treating them with honesty and fairness.

3. This statement against Reform and Haskalah exemplifies his struggle to stem the tide of these movements.

4. Mussar fulminates against the evils of *leshon hara* (talebearing, slander, and gossip). **Rabbi Yisrael Meir HaKohen** wrote an entire book, entitled *Chafetz Chaim*, on the subject.

5. Mussar regards humility in thought and deed as one of the most praiseworthy traits one should strive for. *Mesillat Yesharim*, the inspired classic work on Mussar by Rabbi Moshe Chaim Luzzatto, devotes Chapters 23 and 24 to an analysis of this trait.

6. The message of Mussar must bridge the gap of comprehension of Torah on an intellectual level to complete emotional absorption of Torah in the depth of the soul.

7. Rabbi Yitzchak Blazer was the foremost student of Rabbi Yisrael Salanter and is mentioned as the publisher of all of Rabbi Salanter's writings.

8. These paragraphs provide a concise insight into the meaning of Mussar.

Rabbi Simchah Zissel of Kelm—the *Alter* of Kelm

1. New York, 1957.

2. This commentary is typical of Rabbi Simchah Zissel's approach to Mussar ethics. He sees the *sechel* (intellect) as the foundation of Mussar. The intellect is the dominant force in man's spiritual life by means of which he comes to understand the value of Mussar.

3. When the Israelites conquered Jericho, Achan, in violation of God's decree, secretly took some of its spoils. Thereupon Israel was beaten in their attempt to take the city of Ai. When Joshua, deeply distressed, asked God the reason for the defeat, God replied, "Israel has sinned" (Joshua 7:11). Note that God did not identify Achan as the sinner. (According to *Sanhedrin* 11a, Joshua asked, "Who is the sinner?" God answered, "Do you take Me for an informer? Cast lots." Achan was then identified by means of lots.)

4. This chapter relates how Jacob, following his departure from Laban, prepared to meet his brother Esau. The commentary demonstrates the Mussar approach of probing deeply into the motivations that prompt our actions.

5. Rabbi Yisrael Salanter, Rabbi Simchah Zissel's mentor, and founder of the Mussar movement, lists *seder*, orderliness, as one of the thirteen character traits one should strive to attain. Rabbi Simchah Zissel made order and punctuality the cardinal points of his philosophy of Mussar.

6. Kosher slaughter. The *shechitah* knife must be extremely sharp-edged. The slightest nick in the edge renders the slaughtered animal nonkosher.

Rabbi Yosef Yozel Hurwitz of Novardok—the *Alter* of Novardok

1. *Yalkut* (lit. *anthology*) is a thirteenth-century midrashic work.

Rabbi Nosson Tzvi Finkel of Slobodka—the *Alter* of Slobodka

1. Jerusalem, 1959.

2. This comment incorporates one of the central ideas of Mussar: that we must never attempt to gain spiritual perfection at the expense of our adherence to the rules of ethics.

Rabbi Eliyahu Lapian

1. Jerusalem, 1972–1975.

2. By committing a sin a person loses his resistance to that sin. He will tend to repeat it, thereby further weakening his sense of guilt, until in the end the forbidden act does not appear sinful to him any longer.

3. This commentary provides a striking example of the primary importance Mussar attaches to gaining control of natural impulse and passion. Mussar teaches methods and techniques of *kevishat hamiddot*—conquering bad traits and inclinations.

Rabbi Eliyahu Eliezer Dessler

1. Israel, 1955. An English translation of the first 100 pages is available under the title, "Strive for Truth" (New York, 1978).

2. Metaphorically, it may be said that this primordial light was stored away and hidden in the Torah, where with dedication and sincere effort we can rediscover it.

3. *Bereishit Rabbah* 9:7.

4. *Yetzer,* or *yetzer hara*—evil inclination.

5. Figuratively, "eating" denotes learning, understanding—wisdom is food for the soul. Compare, "Eat this scroll" (Ezekiel 3:1).

Rabbi Chaim Leib Shmulevitz

1. Israel, 1980.

2. Southfield, Michigan, Targum Press, 1988.

3. *Yalkut* is a thirteenth-century midrashic work.

4. There is today in Israel a growing number of *kibbutzim* that observe *shevi'it,* the Sabbatical Year.

5. Only continuous, uninterrupted study will lead to greatness.

6. In the realm of the spirit, the whole is infinitely more than the sum of its parts.

V. CHASIDISM

Rabbi Israel ben Eliezer—the Baal Shem Tov, Besht

1. Published in 1780.

2. The essence of man is his thoughts. This is a guiding principle in chasidic thought, eloquently explained by Rabbi Moshe of Kobryn, "Be careful not to think negative thoughts,

for whatever you are thinking, that is your reality. Your negative thoughts will plunge you into adversity; so be sure to think only good thoughts" (*Darkei Tzedek,* p. 10).

3. The world depends on three things: on Torah study, on the service of God, and on kind deeds (*Mishnah Avot* 1:2). Chasidism tries to instill Jewish self-esteem and combats feelings of Jewish inferiority spawned by suffering, abject poverty, and life-long persecution.

4. Also called *Amidah.*

5. Isaac and Jacob did not routinely emulate Abraham's approach to serving God, but they searched for God, found Him, and cleared their own individual path to serving Him. Since Chasidism stresses the importance of intense and joyful prayer—a new approach to serving God—this is a recurring theme in chasidic literature.

6. *Hitlahavut*—religious fervor—one of the pillars of Chasidism, is the theme of this commentary. We ask God to rejuvenate our spirit, to keep our *hitlahavut*—ecstasy—for Torah and mitzvot alive, so that they will not become mere routine observances.

7. The prayer emanating from the broken heart of a *baal teshuvah* finds all heavenly gates wide open, something not even the Baal Shem Tov's prayer can achieve.

8. By curbing our natural instincts we turn them into instruments for good. Any attempt at eradicating them will utterly fail. For example, a natural instinct toward gluttony can be curbed by following the dietary laws of the Torah and eating in moderation, which will result in promoting spiritual and physical health. Eradicating this instinct by fasting and ascetic self-deprivation leads to a lifelong inner conflict and continuous disappointments.

Rabbi Levi Yitzchak of Berditchev—the Berditchever

1. This comment aptly illustrates the central role of the tzaddik in Chasidism. The tzaddik is the channel for God's blessings to the Jewish people.

2. Genesis 41:45. According to Targum and Rashi, the name means "revealer of secrets."

3. This commentary mirrors the Berditchever's philosophy. He was the great defender of the Jewish people, seeing sublime qualities in the simplest of Jews, engaging in disputes with the Almighty Himself, pleading the cause of his people.

4. A moving example of the Berditchever making a plea to God on behalf of the Jewish people.

Rabbi Shneur Zalman of Liadi—the Baal HaTanya

1. Slavita, 1796. English translation by Rabbi Nisen Mangel, Kehot Publication Society, Brooklyn, New York, 1965.

2. Stettin, 1864.

3. "So does the heart of man to man"—i.e., the love of one person for another awakens a loving response toward

himself in the heart of his friend. How much more so will reflection on the manifestation of God's love toward us inspire love for Him.

Rabbi Simchah Bunam of Pshis'cha— Rebbe Reb Bunam

1. Breslau, 1859. The book has been reprinted numerous times, most recently in Israel.

2. This chapter relates the story of Joseph's temptation by his master's wife. The present verse is Joseph's refusal of her advances.

3. To a Jew, the ends do *not* justify the means.

4. Thunder is the emotional agitation stirred by fervent prayer. The most desirable prayer is that which emanates from the heart, without any outward manifestation of inner feelings. Sincerity in prayer is one of the cornerstones of Chasidism, a theme emphasized in the writings of all chasidic rabbis.

5. These headings are the author's.

6. Rebbe Reb Bunam stressed the importance of self-analysis. We must examine and search our soul for the motives that prompt our behavior. Was the hermit motivated by piety or by the desire to gain recognition for his piety?

Rabbi Nachman of Bratzlav

1. These quotes from Rabbi Nachman of Bratzlav appear on a large sign on the wall of the study hall of the Brooklyn branch of the Bratzlav Yeshivah at 851 47th Street. They comprise the fundamentals of Bratzlav Chasidut: indomitable faith in God, ecstatic joy, and fortitude in the face of adversity.

2. Lithuanian yeshivot are modeled after the yeshivah of Volozhin, founded by Rabbi Chaim Volozhiner, who lived from 1749 to 1821. In these yeshivot the emphasis is on a clear and penetrating analysis of the talmudic text and its commentaries. The rigorous curriculum demands total concentration and diligent application. After World War II, many of these yeshivot were transplanted to America and Israel. In America, the foremost of these yeshivot is Beth Midrash Govo'ah in Lakewood, New Jersey, founded by Rabbi Aharon Kotler. Before World War II he led the yeshivah of Kletzk, Poland.

Rabbi Yitzchak Kalish of Vorki—the Vorker Rebbe

1. Hagar and her son Ishmael had been sent away by Abraham. She was roaming in the desert, her water supply exhausted, when God's angel appeared to her.

2. This comment epitomizes the Vorker Rebbe's philosophy, following Kotzk and Pshis'cha, which demands utter inward sincerity toward God, without ulterior motives and external display of emotion.

3. Just like Jacob, the Rebbe's mind dwells on heavenly concerns, even when he is asleep.

4. In this comment, the Vorker Rebbe stresses one of the main themes of Vorker chasidut: the value of inner piety that is hidden from the outside world.

5. The outstanding characteristic of the Vorker Rebbe was his boundless *"ahavat Yisrael,"* his love of the Jewish people. This commentary reflects this great love.

6. This comment reflects the Vorker Rebbe's keen insight into human nature and his boundless love for the Jewish people.

7. Zimri had committed an immoral act with a Midianite woman. Pinchas drove a spear through them, killing them, thereby calming God's anger, and the plague that had struck Israel was arrested. The Vorker Rebbe points out in this comment that a true zealot, like Pinchas, is motivated by genuine love for his people.

8. These headings are the author's.

Rabbi Menachem Mendel of Kotzk— the Kotzker Rebbe

1. Most recent edition, Israel, 1971.

2. This commentary reflects the great importance chasidic thought attaches to prayer that comes from the heart.

3. The word *sivlot* (forced labor) stems from the root *saval* (to tolerate, suffer, endure), from which is derived the term *savlanut* (forbearance, patience). Clearly, this commentary raised the spirits of the downtrodden Jews of Eastern Europe and instilled in them a sense of pride and self-confidence. It is as topical today as it was then.

4. Chasidut teaches that *deveikut,* attachment to God, is the highest level of perfection man can attain. He can reach it only through complete self-nullification and humility.

5. The present chapter relates that before going into battle, the priest exempted from military service anyone who had built a new house, planted a vineyard, or betrothed a woman. In conclusion, the abovementioned verse exempts anyone "who is afraid or fainthearted." With his comment, the Kotzker Rebbe focuses on the chasidic principle of the importance of disregarding the negative aspects of sin, but rather to concentrate on doing good in a spirit of joyful optimism.

6. These headings are the author's.

Rabbi Yisrael of Rizhin—the Rizhiner

1. Warsaw, 1884.

2. Warsaw, 1906.

3. Jerusalem, 1921.

4. New York, 1951.

5. These words were spoken at the time of *Mattan Torah,* the Giving of the Torah at Sinai.

6. The word *korban* (offering) is related to the verb *karav* (to approach, to come near). A *korban* brings man closer to God, and through a *korban,* Creation is brought closer to its fulfillment.

7. In this homiletic exposition the Rizhiner points out that

you should "learn Torah" in order to fulfill the mitzvot, but you should not study it as an object of historical or linguistic research, or for the purpose of comparative religion, archaeology, or other science.

8. With this comment, the Rizhiner presents a concise characterization of a tzaddik, a chasidic Rebbe. The Rizhiner's "court" was known for its affluence and opulence, yet the Rebbe never derived any personal benefit or enjoyment from his wealth.

9. This verse, from Balaam's blessings, serves to convey the thought that a spark of Jewishness, a Divine spark, is latent in the heart of even the most alienated Jew, a spark that can ignite at any moment.

Rabbi Yitzchak Meir Alter of Ger— Chiddushei Harym

1. Warsaw, 1886. Novellae on the Codes dealing with the laws of judges, witnesses, and lending.
2. Warsaw, 1878. Novellae and original interpretations.
3. Josefov, 1867. Responsa on four parts of *Shulchan Aruch* (Code of Jewish Law).
4. Jerusalem, 1950.
5. The glorious tradition of Gerrer Chasidut and scholarship continues to grow and is flourishing today in Israel and the United States.
6. This paragraph in the Torah describes the effects of the ninth plague in Egypt, darkness.
7. In this verse Moses replies to Pharaoh's offer to let the people go, provided they leave their sheep and cattle behind. The Gerrer Rebbe metaphorically expounds that God is the ultimate judge of the sincerity of our prayers.
8. When God's honor is under attack, neutrality is no virtue. We must fight back.
9. This chapter delineates the dietary laws. The present verse lists species of unclean birds that may not be eaten, among which is the stork.
10. *Chasidah* and *chesed* are etymologically related.
11. There are seventy primary nations in the world, speaking seventy basic languages.

Rabbi Shlomoh HaKohen Rabinowitz of Radomsk—Tiferet Shlomoh

1. Radomsk, 1869.
2. Abraham pleaded with God to spare Sodom and her sister cities. God, unable to find even ten righteous men among their population, left Abraham, rejecting his appeal.
3. After revealing himself, Joseph addresses these words to his brothers. The commentary highlights one of the key objectives of chasidic teaching: to serve God with a joyful spirit.
4. A fundamental chasidic concept is not to burden oneself with self-reproach and guilt feelings, brooding over past transgressions. One should go forward doing good and drive away all negative thoughts.

5. These cities were designated as cities of refuge for someone who accidentally committed a murder. See Exodus 21:13, Numbers 35:10–34, Deuteronomy 19:1–13.
6. This verse introduces Moses' final oration to the Children of Israel on the day he died.

Rabbi Chaim Halberstam of Sanz— the Divrei Chaim

1. Lemberg, 1875.

Rabbi Yehudah Aryeh Leib Alter of Ger— Sefat Emet

1. New York, 1953.
2. The highest level of closeness to God can be attained only through *mesirat nefesh,* self-sacrifice.
3. Throughout rabbinic literature, Joseph is referred to as *Yosef hatzaddik,* Joseph the righteous one.
4. This mitzvah, instituting the month of Nissan as the first month of the Jewish year, ushers in the chapter of the Exodus. It is the first mitzvah given to the nation of Israel. Appropriately, the Gerrer Rebbe sees in it a symbol of Israel's enduring historical mission.
5. In the abovementioned passage, Pharaoh relates his dream to Joseph. On a deeper level of understanding, the Gerrer Rebbe finds in it an allusion to a fundamental kabbalistic idea.

Rabbi Yoel Teitelbaum of Satmar—the Satmar Rav

1. Today Satmar chasidim number in the tens of thousands, with numerous yeshivahs, synagogues, and communal institutions in all parts of the world. An elegant new residential community was erected in Monroe, New York, to house the growing number of Satmar chasidic families, and there is a burgeoning Satmar community in Eretz Yisrael. The Satmar Rav's tomb in Monroe is visited by thousands of devout chasidim annually.

VI. PHILOSOPHY

Rabbi Saadyah Gaon

1. Amsterdam, 1653.
2. *Iggeret Teiman,* in *Iggarot HaRambam,* Rabinowitz ed., p. 156.
3. Throughout the painful years of the 2,000-year Exile, this chapter in Daniel has served as the basis for calculations of the advent of the messianic age.

Rabbi Bachyah ibn Pakudah—Chovot Halevavot

1. First printed in Naples in 1490. In 1611 it was translated from the Arabic by Rabbi Yehudah ibn Tibbon. It has

been translated into all major Western languages. The English translation was done by Moses Hyamson (Jerusalem, 1962–1978).

2. All natural elements have different properties, yet the bodies that are composed of these elements have many similarities; man and beast are both endowed with a life force, with limbs and organs and other corresponding features; both share many characteristics with plants, etc.

3. Each "Creator" would create beings that are unlike any other in order to demonstrate his uniqueness as a creator. Since all creations have common characteristics, it follows that one Creator must have created them all.

Rabbi Yehudah Halevi

1. Fano, 1506.

2. English translation by Hartwig Hirschfeld, New York: Pardes, 1946, and by Rabbi Avrohom Davis, New York, 1979.

3. This is a central idea in Rabbi Yehudah Halevi's philosophy. The Jewish people is the very heart of humanity, the servant of God, whose suffering atones for all the sins of the world.

4. Rabbi Yehudah Halevi, being a Levite and a brilliant poet, was eminently qualified to comment on the merits of music.

5. Christianity and Islam are seen as instrumental in weaning the nations of the world from paganism toward monotheism, paving the way for the coming of the Messiah, when the entire world will come to recognize the One true God, and the people of Israel as the bearer of His message.

Rabbi Moshe ben Maimon (Maimonides)—Rambam

1. Translated into Hebrew by Yehudah al-Charizi and others. Most recently translated into Hebrew from the Arabic by Rabbi Yosef Kafich (Jerusalem, 1964). First printed in Naples in 1492.

2. For selections from *Mishneh Torah* see section on Halachah, pages 101–103.

3. The word *yad* (hand) in Hebrew is written the same as the number 14, an allusion to the fourteen volumes of his work.

4. English translation to *Moreh Nevuchim* is *The Guide of the Perplexed*, trans. by Shlomoh Pines (Chicago: University of Chicago Press, 1963). Other English translations of works by the Rambam are: The Commandments, *Sefer Hamitzvot*, trans. by Charles B. Chavel (London: Soncino Press, 1967); The Commentary to *Mishnah Aboth*, trans. by Arthur David (New York: Bloch, 1968); Eight Chapters (*Shemonah Perakim*), ed. by Joseph I. Gorfinkle (New York: Columbia University Press, 1912); *Mishneh Torah*, ed. by Philip Birnbaum (New York: Hebrew Publishing Co., 1967); *Mishneh Torah* 5 vols. trans. by Rabbi Eliyahu Touger (New York/Jerusalem: Maznaim Publishing, 1987).

5. In this chapter the Rambam outlines his view of the "golden mean" as the ideal course to follow in life. The way of Torah can be found in moderation. He repudiates extremism in any form: asceticism or withdrawal from society, as well as extravagance.

6. Moses was announcing a miracle from God to the rebellious Korach and his followers, a miracle that would prove Moses' mission to be divinely ordained. In the miracle that followed, Korach and his men were swallowed up by the earth.

7. The word *mikreh* ("accident") in this context is to be understood in philosophical terms, meaning any feature, element, or accompaniment of an object not essential to the conception of it.

8. God's revelation at Sinai, at the Giving of the Torah.

Rabbi Yonah of Gerona—Rabbeinu Yonah

1. Berlin, 1848. Printed in the Vilna edition of the Talmud.

2. Cracow, 1612.

3. *Shaarei Teshuvah* has been published many times. English translation by Shraga Silverstein (Jerusalem/New York: Feldheim, 1967).

4. The mitzvah of tzitzit (fringes, tassels) is mentioned in Numbers 15:37–41. It is the third paragraph of the *Shema*.

5. Rabbi Yochanan ben Zakkai to his disciples.

Rabbi Yosef Albo—the Baal Ha'ikkarim

1. Soncino, 1485.

2. Rabbi Yosef Albo's remarks are directed at Christian doctrine. He effectively refutes its theology.

VII. KABBALAH

Rabbi Shimon ben Yochai

1. From *Adir Bamarom*. *Adir Bamarom*, by Rabbi Moshe Chaim Luzzatto, is a commentary on the *Idra Rabba* (Great Assembly) segment of the Zohar, in the portion of *Naso*. It deals with profoundly esoteric matters. Selections of *Adir Bamarom* have been included in *Yalkut Yediot Ha'emet*, an anthology of the writings of Rabbi Moshe Chaim Luzzatto (New York, 1946).

2. Rabbi Ashlag lived from 1886 to 1958. His work is entitled *"HaSulam"* ("The Ladder") and consists of 21 volumes (Jerusalem: Ashlag, 1945–1958).

3. The verse continues, ". . . they will be in your palace, in your bedroom . . . even in your ovens. . . ." The frogs thus jumped into the flaming ovens in fulfillment of God's will.

4. *Sefirot* means spheres or stages through which the Light of the Creator is emanated to man.

5. The verse relates Jacob's dream of the ladder that was

standing on the ground, reaching up toward heaven. He had this vision in Bethel, before leaving Eretz Yisrael on his way to Charan.

6. In Genesis 32:29, we are told that Jacob's name was changed to Israel (*Yisrael*).

7. The Torah decrees, in Leviticus 23:15, that, beginning with the second day of Passover—the day of the Omer offering—we are to count forty-nine days, and that on the fiftieth day, we celebrate Shavuot. This count is called *sefirat ha'Omer*, the counting of the Omer. After reciting the appropriate *berachah* (blessing), the Omer is counted nightly. To this very day, on the thirty-third day of the Omer, called *Lag ba'Omer*, tens of thousands of people travel to Meron to offer prayers at the tomb of Rabbi Shimon ben Yochai.

8. "*Or–Raz*" translates as "Light–Mystery." The numerical value of the Hebrew letters of "*or*" (light)—*alef, vav, resh*—comes to 207 and equals the numerical value of *raz* (mystery)—*resh, zayin*—which also amounts to 207, alluding to the concealment of the inner Light of the Torah.

Rabbi Yehudah HeChasid

1. Bologna, 1538.
2. *Shabbat* 104a.
3. Jethro's (Re'uel) daughters say this when replying to their father's question, "How did you get to come home so early today?" (Exodus 2:18). According to *Devarim Rabbah* 2:8, Moses was standing outside, overhearing how they described him as "an Egyptian."
4. Eliezer asking Laban's and Bethuel's consent for Rebecca to become Isaac's wife.

Rabbi Moshe Cordovero—the Remak

1. Saloniki, 1552; Cracow, 1592.
2. Brody, 1889.
3. Venice, 1589.

Rabbi Yitzchak Luria Ashkenazi—Ari HaKadosh

1. A popular biography of the Ari is "*The Arizal*," by Nechemia Piontac (Brooklyn: Mesorah Publications, 1988).
2. The world of Emanation, the world of Creation, the world of Formation, and the world of Action, respectively. These are the stages of existence, from the purely spiritual *Olam haAtzilut* to the material *Olam haAsiyah*. In *Kabbalah* they are referred to as *Abya*, the acronym of their initials: Atzilut, Beriah, Yetzirah, Asiyah.

Rabbi Chaim Vital

1. Published many times, most recently in Jerusalem in 1910.
2. Frankfort-on-the-Main, 1684.
3. Constantinople, 1734.
4. Livorno, 1784.
5. *Ma'amar HaSaba* is a discourse in the Zohar on the portion of *Mishpatim*. It expounds on mystical themes, such as *gilgul* (reincarnation). This is the belief that souls are reborn in different bodies to atone for sins they committed in previous lives. Through metaphorical interpretation these concepts are derived from Torah verses.
6. A mystical term meaning "forces of evil."
7. This is a reference to Genesis 1:2, "The earth was *tohu* and *bohu*," commonly translated as "without form and empty."
8. This is the response to the *chazzan's* recitation of "*Barechu et HaShem Hamevorach*" in the morning prayer.
9. The soul rises from its lowest level, *Nefesh*, through a series of stages, *Ruach, Neshamah, Chayah*, to the highest level, *Yechidah. Yechidah* (lit. oneness) represents total union with the Light of God. This level is unattainable until the coming of *Mashiach* (Messiah).

Rabbi Yehudah Loew of Prague—the Maharal

1. Prague, 1593.
2. Prague, 1596.
3. Prague, 1598.
4. Prague, 1599.
5. Prague, 1600.
6. Second part of *Or Chadash* (Prague, 1600).
7. Prague, 1589.
8. Matzah, being free of the dictates of the material and of time, is the true symbol of liberty.
9. This commentary exemplifies the Maharal's approach of presenting kabbalistic thoughts in philosophical terms.

INDEX OF BIBLICAL VERSES

INDEX OF SAGES AND COMMENTATORS